The Limits of British Influence

The Limits of British Influence

South Asia and the Anglo-American Relationship, 1947–56

Anita Inder Singh

Pinter Publishers
London

St. Martin's Press
New York

Pinter Publishers Ltd
25 Floral Street, Covent Garden, London WC2E 9DS, United Kingdom
and **St. Martin's Press**
175 Fifth Avenue, New York, NY 10010

First published in 1993

British Library Cataloguing in Publication Data
A CIP catalogue record for this book is available from the British Library

ISBN 1 85567 160 3 (Pinter)

ISBN 0-312-09955-X (St. Martin's)

Library of Congress Cataloging-in-Publication Data
Inder Singh, Anita.
    The limits of British influence: South Asia and the Anglo–
American relationship, 1947–56/Anita Inder Singh.
        p.   cm.
    Includes bibliographical references and index.
    ISBN 1 85567 160 3. – ISBN 0 312 09955-X (St. Martin's Press)
    1. Great Britain—Foreign relations—United States.   .2. Great
Britain—Foreign relations—South Asia.   3. United States—Foreign
relations—Great Britain.   4. United States—Foreign relations—
South Asia.   5. South Asia—Foreign relations—Great Britain.
6. South Asia—Politics and government.   7. South Asia—Foreign
relations—United States.   I. Title.
E183.8.G7I53   1993
327.41054–dc20   93–12372
                                                                                        CIP

Typeset by Florencetype Ltd, Kewstoke, Avon
Printed and bound in Great Britain by Biddles Ltd., Guildford and King's Lynn

Contents

Preface

Historiographical lacunae as well as contemporary concerns lend timeliness to this work. It is the first historical account of South Asia and the Anglo–American relationship, and it covers the period from the British decolonisation in the Indian subcontinent in August 1947 to the Suez crisis in 1956. Two themes – decolonisation in South Asia and the cold war – provide the backdrop for this study. Since the eighteenth century India had occupied a special place in Britain's imperial constellation; it was the grandest symbol of her world power. In 1947 the British relinquished their hold over an area they had ruled for almost 200 years, and the transfer of power to India and Pakistan had a lasting impact on Britain's international position.

Britain's dealings with the newly independent India and Pakistan also had a bearing on her ties with her closest ally, the United States, after 1945. The British conceived their post-war relationship with the United States in the context of the cold war. The Anglo–American relationship was the pivot of British foreign policy and through that link, British governments hoped to preserve Britain's status as a great power. One of the arguments of this book is that the British did not have an illusion of power between 1947–56, for they realised that they were not the equal of the superpowers after 1945 (though Britain was, arguably, still a great power), and that they did not possess the wherewithal to safeguard all their world-wide interests. But they thought that with what they saw as their superior wisdom, character, and international expertise, they could remain a leading international influence. This study of the place of South Asia in the Anglo–American relationship will explore whether this British aim was realistic and to what extent it was achieved.

Probably because South Asia was not a major theatre of the cold war, studies of the Anglo–American relationship and the cold war have neglected the region. However, an adequate understanding of the post-war alliance between two world powers requires an analysis of their policies in all areas of the world. What were British and American aims in a region to which neither perceived a Soviet military threat? How did they look upon each other on the subcontinent? What were their attitudes to the foreign policies of India and Pakistan? Why did the US penetrate South Asia, and did it bolster or undermine Britain's influence in the area?

Diplomatic archives in Britain and the United States have provided ample evidence to sustain a study of the position of South Asia in the regional and global contexts of the Anglo–American relationship. In general, this book will highlight perceptions and outcomes of foreign policy and will not discuss domestic influences on foreign policy or the domestic consequences of foreign policy. Where relevant to its main themes, the book will detail the formulation of policy in London and Washington. On other occasions, only the gist of the official debates will be brought out, partly because the nuances and variations of policy or perception have been elaborated elsewhere, partly because it is not necessary to amplify them from the perspective of this book.

Today, the cold war has ended, but the full story of international diplomacy during the first cold war has not yet been told. One reason is that the archival sources which would facilitate it have only recently become available in Britain and the United States. The story that has been narrated so far has also been fashioned by the world view of those who have written it. Until recently the historiography of the cold war was dominated by American scholars who concentrated on bipolarism and on the effects of American policies on the rest of the world. Their most frequent assumption was that influence flowed in one direction – from stronger to weaker powers. This assumption has aroused much criticism from European and some American historians, who have rightly brought out the initiatives taken by European countries in shaping the cold war.[1]

In 1945, Britain was still a world power, pitted against global communism, defending her interests wherever threatened and seeking to sustain the preservation of her international status as a means to prevent other countries from coming under communist domination. Britain was also a principal in the cold war and had outlined a containment policy in Europe and Asia before the Americans sketched theirs. In Asia, with which a large part of this book is concerned, the nature of British and American concerns differed. For Britain the Asian cold war began in June 1948, with the outbreak of the communist insurrection in Malaya, but the US only joined forces against Asian communism after the establishment of the communist regime in China on 1 October 1949.[2] And the British conceived a key role for India in containment before the Chinese communists consolidated their power. In South Asia and the Middle East, too, Britain had been the dominant Western power for more than a century.

If Indian independence had far-reaching consequences for Britain's global position, Indian nonalignment challenged the idea of a world divided into two power blocs and was disliked by both superpowers. As the cold war recedes into historical memory, much is being said about the emergence of multiple centres of power. But even at the height of the cold war, the superpowers were not omnipotent. The independent foreign policies of newly emergent states pointed to a diffusion of power in the international system. While no independent country could ignore the US and Soviet Union after 1945, great powers did not always set the international political agenda. The foreign policies of weaker states like India and Pakistan could run counter to the interests of world powers; as we shall see, Pakistan's alliance with the US in 1954 harmed Britain's position in South Asia and the Middle East; Indian nonalignment frustrated both the US and Britain. Influence was not always a one-way street: weaker countries were not always helpless pawns in the hands of great powers, especially when two great powers, allies of unequal strength, were competing for influence in South Asia.

The two Western allies did not, then, represent a monolithic mass; nor did newly independent states. Unlike India, Pakistan showed her acceptance of bipolarism by taking the initiative to establish military ties with the West soon after her creation in August 1947 and entering the American alliance system in 1954. India and Pakistan serve as useful case studies of the regional and international complications that can result from the interaction of disparate interests of newly independent states and great powers. The political fragmentation of the globe that they represented and the challenge they posed to Western security interests was in evidence after 1947, and it is surprising that these phenomena have hitherto received so little scholarly attention.

This is not a study of Britain's "decline",[3] although the extent to which it brings out the limits of British influence, and consequently contributes to an understanding of how the United States replaced Britain as the dominant global power, might render it of interest to "declinologists". "Limits of influence" do not, in my view, point to "decline". It is true that American power expanded at a time when Britain found it difficult to hold on to what she already had; the United States called the tune with Pakistan in 1954 and enhanced its standing in Pakistan at Britain's expense. Yet for all its expanding reach, the US did not have much influence over India, and it is arguable that Indo–US relations were sour precisely because the US could neither coax nor pressure India into giving up nonalignment. And if Britain's inability to influence the US on occasion or to safeguard her interests in Asia or the Middle East suggest that she lacked the power to back up her diplomacy, it is also worth remembering that American military and economic expansion did not imply an all-powerful United States. So a secondary – and unintended – outcome of this book is its contribution to the ongoing debate on America's "rise" and Britain's "decline" – if only by calling those concepts into question.

To explain some of the terms used in this book: before August 1947, 'India' refers to British India; 'South Asia' refers to India and Pakistan from 15 August 1947, when the British transferred power to two successor states on the subcontinent. 'West' and 'Western' refer to Britain and the United States. 'Nonalignment' emphasises India's determination to stay out of military alliances with any country of the Western or communist bloc and to avoid being tied down to a particular line of action because of membership of a cold war bloc or of the Commonwealth. It also signifies Indian attempts to maintain friendly relations with all countries whether belonging to military blocs or not. On the whole, I have used the names of countries as they appear most frequently in the archival records of that time – for example, Ceylon, and Cambodia and Formosa rather than Sri Lanka, Kampuchea and Taiwan. Except when quoting, I have used 'Iran' in the text for the sake of consistency, although British officials often referred to 'Persia'. After the establishment of the communist regime on the mainland on 1 October 1949, 'China' refers to the People's Republic of China. Except when quoting, I have used British spelling.

This book is based largely on archives and private papers at the Public Record Office, Kew; the India Office Library and Records, London; the Bodleian Library, Oxford; Churchill College, Cambridge; the National Archives, Washington DC; the Harry S. Truman Library, Independence; the Dwight D. Eisenhower Library, Abilene; and the Nehru Memorial Museum and Library in New Delhi.

The Faculty of Social Sciences, University of Oxford, sponsored a series of lectures in the Hilary Term of 1988 which helped me to plan this book. Thanks to an invitation from the Centre for Indian Studies, St Antony's College, Oxford, to spend the academic year 1987–8 as a Guest Fellow, I started writing it. The Governing Body of St Antony's College elected me as a Senior Associate Member in 1991, thus presenting me with the opportunity to complete the book in a friendly and stimulating environment. I am grateful to the Harry S. Truman Foundation for awarding me a grant which enabled me to carry out research in the United States in the summer of 1988.

Several colleagues gave me the opportunity to try out my ideas at seminars and conferences. They include Dr Anne Deighton, Professor Ravinder Kumar, Professor Ian Nish, Professor Tapan Raychaudhuri, Professor Adam Roberts and Dr Anthony Seldon.

Dr Peter Catterall, Professor Alex Danchev, Dr Rosemary Foot, Professor John Gaddis and Dr Avi Shlaim have all read parts of the manuscript and have offered much constructive criticism.

Dr David Reynolds and Professor Ralph Smith have given excellent advice on several occasions. Professor Donald Cameron Watt has shared his unrivalled insights into the subject. Dr Christopher Coker has read the whole manuscript and has offered generous support. The responsibility for any errors of style or judgement is mine.

Good editors, archivists and librarians are a boon to the historian. Editorial advice from Pat Kirkpatrick proved invaluable. Mr Erwin Mueller and Mr Herb Pankratz showed me how to make the most of the rich intellectual resources of the Harry S. Truman and Dwight D. Eisenhower Libraries respectively. Rosamund Campbell runs a friendly and efficient library at St Antony's College.

Most of all, I wish to thank my husband, Anders Åslund, whose *joie de vivre* always makes him good company, a welcome distraction from writing and a reminder that the best is yet to be.

ANITA INDER SINGH
January 1993

Abbreviations

AWF	Ann Whitman File, Eisenhower papers.
ANZUS	Australia, New Zealand and the United States (the ANZUS pact nations).
BNA	Office of British Commonwealth and Northern European Affairs, Department of State.
CAB	Cabinet papers.
CAF	Central African Federation.
C-in-C	Commander-in-Chief.
CCAC	Cabinet Commonwealth Affairs Committee.
CCOSC	Cabinet Chiefs of Staff Committee.
CDC	Cabinet Defence Committee.
CENTO	Central Treaty Organisation.
CIA	Central Intelligence Agency.
CIBC	Cabinet India and Burma Committee.
CIGS	Chief of Imperial General Staff.
CINCELM	Commander-in-Chief, US Naval Forces, Eastern Atlantic and Mediterranean.
COCCR	Cabinet Official Committee on Commonwealth Relations.
COS	Chiefs of Staff.
COSC	Chiefs of Staff Committee.
CRO	Commonwealth Relations Office.
DDE	Dwight David Eisenhower
Deptel	Department of State telegram.
DO	Dominions Office.
DS	Department of State.
Dulte	Telegrams from Secretary of State Dulles while away from Washington.
EEC	English Electric Company.
EL	Dwight D. Eisenhower Library, Abilene, Kansas.
EPU	European Payments Union.
ERP	European Recovery Programme.
FO	Foreign Office.
FR	*Foreign Relations of the United States*

HMG	His/Her Majesty's Government.
IBCM	India and Burma Committee Meeting.
JCS	Joint Chiefs of Staff.
MAAG	Military Assistance Advisory Group.
MAP	Military Assistance Programme.
MDA	Mutual Defence Assistance.
MDAP	Mutual Defence Assistance Programme.
MEC	Middle East Command.
MEDO	Middle East Defence Organisation.
MFN	Most Favoured Nation.
MSA	Mutual Security Agency.
MSP	Mutual Security Programme.
NAI	National Archives of India.
NATO	North Atlantic Treaty Organisation.
NEA	Bureau of Near Eastern, South Asian and African Affairs, Department of State.
NNC	Neutral Nations Commission.
NNRC	Neutral Nations Repatriation Commission.
NSC	National Security Council.
PREM	Prime Minister's Office.
PRO	Public Record Office, London.
PM	Prime Minister.
POW	Prisoner of War.
PPS	Policy Planning Staff.
PSF	President's Secretary's File, Truman papers.
PUSC	Permanent Under-Secretary's Committee.
RAF	Royal Air Force.
SACME	Supreme Allied Commander in the Middle East.
SANACC	State–Army–Navy–Air Force Coordinating Committee.
SCUA	Suez Canal Users' Association.
Secto	Telegrams from US Secretary of State at international conferences.
SEATO	Southeast Asia Treaty Organisation.
SOA	Office of South Asian Affairs, Department of State.
SS	Secretary of State.
SSCR	Secretary of State for Commonwealth Relations.
SW	S. Gopal (ed.), *Selected Works of Jawaharlal Nehru* Second Series.
T	Treasury.
Tedul	Telegrams to Secretary of State Dulles while he was away from Washington.
tel.	telegram.
TL	Harry S. Truman Library, Independence, Missouri.

TOP	N. Mansergh and P. Moon (eds), *The Transfer of Power*
UK	United Kingdom.
UK-Ankara	United Kingdom Ambassador in Ankara.
UK-Colombo	United Kingdom High Commissioner in Colombo.
UK-Karachi	United Kingdom High Commissioner in Karachi.
UK-New Delhi	United Kingdom High Commissioner in New Delhi.
UN	United Nations.
UNCURK	United Nations Commission for the Unification and Rehabilitation of Korea.
US, USA	United States of America.
US-Colombo	United States embassy in Colombo.
US-Karachi	United States embassy in Karachi.
US-London	United States embassy in London.
US-New Delhi	United States embassy in New Delhi.
USSR	Union of Soviet Socialist Republics.
WO	War Office.

Introduction

The story goes that, sometime in the nineteenth century, a successful candidate for the Foreign Office examination was asked what he thought were the three most important things in life. He replied, 'God, love, and Anglo–American relations'.[1] His placing of *realpolitik* on a par with the spiritual and the romantic would have struck a chord with British policy makers after 1945. In the age of the cold war, British officials felt that Britain's survival as a great power – indeed her national survival – was dependent on her tie with the United States.

For many Britons, the Anglo–American relationship itself had spiritual and fraternal overtones: a bond manifesting the destiny of two peoples united by culture, language and liberal democracy, and the necessity of joining forces against Soviet military expansion after 1945 as they had against Nazi Germany during the Second World War. Articulating these British hopes at Fulton, Missouri in March 1946, Winston Churchill called for a 'fraternal association of the English-speaking peoples. This means a special relationship between the British Commonwealth and Empire and the United States'. What was really so special about the relationship? Was the notion of specialness just a myth fostered to cushion the British from the shock of decline after 1945? The relationship has stimulated much intellectual debate.[2] But there is no doubt that the Anglo–American relationship was the pivot of British foreign policy after 1945, and through it Britain hoped to preserve her global pre-eminence.

In 1945 Britain was a great power with world-wide interests, military bases and forces; along with the United States and the Soviet Union she received the surrender of Germany and Japan and was one of the three peacemaking powers at Potsdam. At the end of the war she was the strongest power in West Europe and the second power in the Western world, but she lacked the wherewithal to retain that status in the long term. Militarily, neither Britain nor any other European country could single-handedly halt the expansionist Soviet military behemoth in East Europe; this fact alone brought home to Britain that she was not the equal of the US and the USSR. Traditionally Britain's military power had rested on her supremacy at sea, but the development of the atomic bomb changed the strategic landscape and unhinged the long-held basis of British defence planning. In the spring of 1949 Foreign Office officials conceded that '[t]he attraction exerted by pound sterling and the Royal Navy is now less strong than that of the dollar and the atom bomb'.[3] The United States was the only country to emerge richer rather than poorer from the war, and in 1945 it possessed two-thirds of the world's total gold reserves, the world's largest navy and a monopoly of the atom bomb. And Britain's potential to wage a conventional war was surpassed by that of the superpowers: the British Empire–Commonwealth, which had raised 12 million men during the Second World War, would be no match for the Soviet Union, which could easily mobilise more than 30 million.[4] Economically, Britain emerged exhausted from the war. Her debts had soared from £476 million in August 1939 to £3,355 million in June 1945, and she was in the unenviable position of being the world's largest debtor nation. For the first time in her history she lacked the industrial and economic resources to support her diplomacy.

The British knew that their hope of national survival and of remaining a great power depended on the Americans sharing their interest in a strong Britain. This interest the Americans had, if only because they were aware that their country was not omnipotent. In March 1946 the American Chiefs of Staff viewed the maintenance of the British empire as a major goal of US foreign policy and warned that 'the defeat or disintegration of the British Empire would eliminate from Eurasia the last bulwark of resistance between the United States and Soviet expansion'. Militarily, America's present position as a world power was 'of necessity closely interwoven with that of Great Britain.'[5] American officials deemed the economic recovery of Britain and the continued stability of the Commonwealth, through which they gained access to a world-wide network of bases and economic resources, as indispensable to the implementation of their own foreign policy. The prevalence of British influence beyond the formal empire and British leadership of the Commonwealth served US security interests. To the Americans the vehemence of Soviet propaganda against Anglo–American unity only testified to its strength as a major deterrent against Soviet aggression.[6] The Anglo–American relationship, then, was one of mutual advantage and interdependence. Although the British and the Americans knew that the greater dependence was Britain's, neither of them regarded Britain as a docile subordinate.

British expectations of the relationship were shaped by the aims of their foreign policy and by their perception of their world role. After the Yalta Conference, Churchill had ruefully described Britain as a small lion standing between a huge Russian bear and a great American elephant.[7] But Churchill, like many British officials, was also determined that Britain and the Commonwealth–Empire should attain equality with the superpowers. As Foreign Secretary in the Labour government from 1945–51, Ernest Bevin shared this aim. Aware of her weakness, Britain was on guard against being displaced by the United States. There was no escaping dependence on the US; yet London hoped that Britain's Empire–

Commonwealth would eventually make it possible for her to emerge as leader of an independent Third Force.[8] Whether heading a Third Force, or whether leaning on the US, the British made the case that a powerful Britain was indispensable to world stability. Underlining Britain's role as the defender of the ethical and spiritual values of Western civilisation and unwilling to bow before America's financial might, Bevin declared in January 1948 that economic progress was insufficient in itself to halt the Soviet threat. 'Political and, indeed, spiritual forces must be mobilised in our defence.' American largesse was necessary to create a Western Union in Europe, 'but the countries of Western Europe which despise the spiritual values of America will look to us for political and moral guidance and for assistance in building up a counter attraction to . . . communism'. Britain, claimed Bevin, had the material resources in the Colonial Empire; 'if we develop them, and by giving a spiritual lead now we should be able to carry out our task in a way which will show clearly that we are not subservient to the United States of America or to the Soviet Union'.[9]

By the beginning of 1949, a host of domestic and international crises — including the end of Lend-Lease, pressures for early demobilisation, the balance of payments deficit, the sterling crisis, the Berlin blockade, the communist coup in Czechoslovakia and the outbreak of the communist insurgency in Malaya – had ruled out the likelihood of Britain leading a Third Force comprising Europe and the Commonwealth–Empire, and in March 1950 Bevin acknowledged that 'the day when we, as Great Britain, can declare a policy independently of our allies, has gone'.[10] Yet it is doubtful that he, or other British officials, were reconciled to this idea. To them, the maintenance of British power remained an end in itself, and the cold war justified it. As Gladwyn Jebb, then leading Britain's delegation to the UN, admitted in February 1950, 'the phrase "cold war" so far as we are concerned, really involves the whole question of the maintenance of the United Kingdom's position in the world, and can therefore in the long run be equated with our general foreign policy'.[11] Economic weakness necessitated scaling down military involvements, but disengagement from existing imperial ones was ruled out because it would reduce Britain to second-rank status. This thinking revealed the extent to which the British self-image was inspired by their formal and informal empire. Britain's dire financial straits augured difficulties in her sustaining imperium, but all was not lost. American munificence would both uphold Britain's global standing and meet the economic and defence needs of Britain, the Commonwealth and Europe – and the Americans could be coaxed into taking their cue from Britain. By virtue of what they perceived as their unrivalled flair for diplomacy, their political sagacity, their moral and intellectual calibre,[12] British policy-makers assumed their ability to enlist the United States in support of a role which Britain could no longer manage on her own. Yet the apparent official confidence in Britain's international *savoir-faire* was accompanied by some uncertainty as to whether they would actually be able to accomplish this. As Anthony Eden, the Conservative Foreign Secretary, advised the cabinet in June 1952, Britain should persuade the US to take on the 'real burdens', while retaining 'as much political control – and hence prestige and world influence – *as we can*'.[13] In other words, the British knew they were not the primary global power, but they hoped to remain a leading influence with American help.

The British did not act in a vacuum, and, from the perspective of this book, the fulfilment of their hopes of remaining a major influence depended on the interplay of American, Indian and Pakistani diplomacy within a changing international environment. The United States was the country Britain sought to influence first and foremost, and its ability to do so depended on numerous factors such as historical traditions and contacts with India and Pakistan, the Middle East and Asia; how Britain and the US related these areas to one another, the economic and military means available to carry out their policies – and the American perception of their own world role as well as that of the British.

Like the British, the Americans saw their own country's role stemming from its uniqueness. American internationalism perceived US interests to be at stake in any international circumstances. America's strength was not the consequence of an empire but flowed from her innate virtues, her pragmatism and democracy, which would serve as an example to all men. The Truman Doctrine of March 1947 exemplified the moralistic, Messianic sense of mission in American foreign policy. 'If we falter in our leadership, we may endanger the peace of the world – and we shall surely endanger the welfare of our own nation.'[14] The United States was the self-styled keeper of the world's conscience; the future of the world depended on America's willingness to act for the universal good. The courses which the US chose to pursue would have a bearing on Britain's hopes of remaining the principal influence.

Influencing the United States was only one part of the story. Decolonisation in South Asia, and the emergence of India and Pakistan as independent actors on the world stage after August 1947, showed that great powers were not omnipotent. The political fragmentation of the globe coincided and interacted with the rise of the superpowers, and bipolarism did not imply a watertight division of the world. This reality was not lost on the British. They knew that the United States as well as local actors and circumstances could affect the outcome of British policy as much as anything that they themselves did. South Asia was the stage on which the British played out their first post-war act of decolonisation. India was the jewel in the Crown, and it seems odd that the British relinquished it at a time when they hoped the Empire–Commonwealth would help them to remain the equal of the superpowers, especially when there was no significant American pressure on them to wind up the Indian empire;[15] when, in fact, the political and military imperatives of the cold war renewed British *and* American interest in the strategic advantages of South

Asia to Britain and, by logical implication, to the West. The main question posed in Chapter One is whether decolonisation and partition reflected the fulfilment of a long-term commitment to Indian independence, or whether they were prompted by the rising pressures of Indian nationalism or Britain's post-war weakness. The answers are important, for whether decolonisation represented the fruition or failure of British policy would determine the extent of influence Britain would have over the newly independent states of India and Pakistan.

Unconditional independence and partition were fraught with unprecedented consequences for the British. India and Pakistan were the first dominions to go to war with each other, and Pakistan's inability to secure as much British help as she wanted propelled her into the American military orbit in 1953–4. Indian nonalignment deprived Britain of her biggest and most valuable strategic prize; why London broke with historical precedent to admit a republican India into the Commonwealth is relevant to our understanding of British efforts to remain the primary international influence. The timing was also significant. The British took the decision in March 1949, around the same time that they conceived India's central part in diplomatic containment in Asia and also ruled out Europe and the Commonwealth becoming a Third Force. Thus, even as they acknowledged their dependence on the US in Europe and Asia, they intended the New Commonwealth to preserve the façade of undented British power.

Against this background of rivalry between India and Pakistan and Britain's diminishing influence in the subcontinent, how much leverage would Britain have with the US? Chapters Two, Three and Five will discuss the emergence of Anglo–American differences over India's role in Asia. Chapter Two will show how history and geography moulded British and American priorities and perceptions during the cold war and initially created a similarity of outlook between London and Washington on the British role in South Asia. This accord did not last long: changing circumstances gave rise to unprecedented disagreements between Britain and the United States.

In contrast to Britain's overall dependence on the economic and military sinews of American power, it appears somewhat curious that India, one of the world's poorest countries, was simultaneously seen as her great diplomatic and strategic asset in Asia. The British image of India was defined by the part India had played as the hub of important sea-routes between Europe, Africa and the Far East; India had been the base from which the British maintained their control of the Indian Ocean in peacetime and extended their trade and influence in Arabia, the Persian Gulf, Southeast Asia, and the Far East. During the Second World War it had served as the base for the South East Asia Command, as well as for British and Commonwealth armies fighting in the Middle East. Indian independence deprived Britain of her foremost strategic reserve, but Britain remained, nevertheless, the dominant power in the Indian Ocean and controlled the key points of communication along a maritime route passing through the Middle East, the Persian Gulf, to Malaya, Singapore and Hong Kong. India lay in the centre of this route, and the British could not ignore her when framing a policy for the area as a whole.

British officials viewed India's role in the Asian cold war in the context of Britain's post-war military and economic weakness, her desire to remain an Asian and global power despite that weakness, her imperial stake in Malaya and Hong Kong, her hope of retaining independent India in the Commonwealth, her wish to preserve the Commonwealth as an independent political, military and economic entity – in short, as a reflection of her international power and prestige. Inextricably linked to these hopes, especially after Indian independence in 1947, was the realisation that Britain could not increase her military involvement in Asia. Diplomacy, then, would be the main instrument of her influence. This occasioned little concern among British officials, who did not perceive a Soviet military threat to Asia.

However, communism could appear attractive in an area rife with poverty and social inequalities; Malaya, Indonesia and Indochina proved the point. Not surprisingly, when the economic problems of Asia were discussed by the British, it was through the prism of the cold war and as an argument for preserving British influence in Asia. It followed that economic development was the need of the hour, and Britain could convince Asians of her interest in their welfare by encouraging regional economic collaboration. Recognition of, and accommodation with, Asian nationalisms were intrinsic to the policy of diplomatic containment; local nationalisms were to be courted so that they could be turned to the British advantage. The success of this policy would hinge on the extent to which British diplomacy could work its way through the disparate interests of Britain's friends – India, Pakistan, and most of all, the US. For the United States would be underwriting Britain's position in Asia.

Nonalignment ruled out any formal military links between Britain and India and was emblematic of their fundamentally different aims in Asia. Studded with paradoxes, the bond between imperial Britain and newly independent India was warm and friendly. India favoured an Asia free from great-power interventions, while Britain considered Western influence, especially her own, as Asia's indispensable insurance against communism. Yet the British allowed a republican India in the Commonwealth with a view to keeping up the façade of their status as an Asian and world power and using India to persuade other Asian countries of Britain's sympathetic concern for their progress. The governments of both countries were committed to democracy and agreed that communism had to be contained, and both believed that military means were not necessarily the answer in Asia. Perhaps this was partly because neither possessed the wherewithal to engage in military containment. But both also acknowledged the uses of diplomacy as an instrument of containment. For example, following the triumph of the communists in the Chinese civil war in October 1949, both India and Britain thought that recognition of the communist Chinese regime could make containment viable, whether against internal subversion or external expansion.

China was the catalyst of friction between the United States, Britain and India in the Asian arena. Anti-communism, American interest in a strong Britain and British dependence on the US – none of these factors could bring about agreement between the British and Americans on the means of containment in Asia, and India came to symbolise the division between them. Geography and history provided part of the answer. During the nineteenth century, the United States had positioned itself in Asia through its acquisition of Hawaii, Alaska and the Philippines and the opening of trading links with China and Japan. After 1941, the US acquired a strategic frontier in the Western Pacific, running from Alaska through the Aleutian Islands and Japan to the Philippines. Between 1945–8, the US conception of national security included a strategic sphere of influence within the Western hemisphere, and the domination of the Atlantic and Pacific Oceans, with far-flung bases and alliances to project American power globally. Seen through the Atlantic–Pacific prism, India and the Indian Ocean simply did not appear important to the United States. This was to lead to differences with Britain, whose Asian strategy centred round India. For Indian nonalignment was anti-thetical to an American policy underlining military containment by the end of 1949. Barely six months later, by June 1950, the Americans were perceiving Formosa as critical to their defensive perimeter strategy of containing China and the USSR against its Asian rim, so it is hardly surprising that they ruled out making India the keystone of containment in Asia.

China became the greatest bone of contention between the US, Britain and India. Chapters Three and Five will illustrate how British and American differences over India came to mark the cleavage between a US which stressed military containment,[16] and a Britain, which, not wishing to increase military engagements in Asia, emphasised the diplomatic containment of China. British attempts to rein the US in during the Korean war because of Asian – meaning Indian – opinion, did not cut much ice with the Americans. The main differences concerned the limiting or expanding of the conflict; for the Americans, limiting the conflict was not an end in itself, as it was for the Indians and British. The British feared that the war on the Yalu would provoke one on the Elbe, and that they would be drawn into a military conflict in Asia in the name of alliance unity. This they neither wanted nor could afford. The Indians, for their part, were apprehensive that a major war with China could easily escalate into a world war. By the beginning of 1951, the coincidence of Indo–British outlooks made the Americans perceive India as a baneful influence on the UK, and induced them to reconsider their dependence on Britain and the Commonwealth in Asia.

To Britain and India, the idea of diplomatic containment did not appear wholly unrealistic. Neither was a principal in the Korean or Indochina wars, but by 1954, Indo–British diplomatic exchanges helped to terminate what were, until then, the two greatest military conflicts in post-war Asia. In November 1952, they contributed to a compromise between China and the West on repatriating prisoners of war, paving the way for the signing of the Korean armistice in July 1953. Making use of Indian ideas behind the scenes in the summer of 1954, the British played a leading role at the Geneva conference which ended the war in Indochina.[17] Significantly, a shared belief in diplomatic containment prevailed in spite of divergent long-term aims. The Indians did not want communism to expand, but they did not wish to see the continuance or preservation of Western power in Asia, while the British deemed Western influence, especially their own, essential to contain communism.

Indo–British contacts during the Korean war and the Geneva conference aroused American suspicions of Indian influence over Britain. Distrust of nonalignment prompted the Americans to bar India from the Korean political conference in 1953, while the British tried to include India. The Geneva accord on Indochina was a British attempt to contain China by replacing the French empire by independent, neutral states on her borders and by obtaining assistance from neutral Asian countries to guarantee the peace, but it was disliked by the US as a compromise with communism. By 1954 the Americans were toying with the idea of some form of Western military intervention in Indochina as the only way to rescue it from communism, and they were prepared to go ahead without the British if necessary.[18] British diplomacy contributed to the end of the first Indochina war, but Britain could not pay any price to enforce the Geneva settlement. The Americans possessed the economic and military means to ignore and override something they disliked and eventually to expand their military influence. Gradually but surely, the Americans blurred the distinction between US power as a means of containment and as an end in itself.

The tension and interaction between means and ends were also illustrated by Anglo–American differences over Pakistan's role in Middle East defence. More than that, as Chapter Four will show, these differences developed into an Anglo–American tug-of-war for influence in Pakistan and the Middle East. The loss of India in 1947 redoubled British determination to retain primacy in the region which centred on their possession of the Suez base. This aim was endorsed by the Americans. Until 1950–1, the US was content to support British hegemony in the Middle East. Like Britain, the US did not regard Pakistan as a strategic asset in the Middle East and rebuffed her overtures for military aid and association with the West in the area. But a stormy Anglo–Egyptian relationship, and an upsurge of nationalism in many Middle East countries, challenged Western security interests, and the Americans came to look upon British imperialism as a liability to the West. Gradually, the US grew sceptical of the British idea of a Middle East defence organisation (MEDO) with Egypt as its linchpin. Worried that such an organisation would never take off, the Americans sought alternatives to a strategy which hinged on Egypt. Between 1951–3, this necessity gradually transformed their image of Pakistan from a strategic non-starter into a worthy ally for them. The British demurred. Influenced by their traditional vision of the whole subcontinent as a strategic entity and as a source of their power in the Middle East, the British did not wish to annoy India, especially when they were, in addition, suspicious of Pakistan's Islamic underpinnings and contemptuous of her inability to sort out her domestic imbroglios. Unpersuaded that Pakistan alone could make any substantial contribution, they spurned her offers to participate in Middle East defence. Still the dominant Western influence in the Middle East and Pakistan, the British restrained the US from recruiting Pakistan as a partner in the Middle East until 1953.

Following a visit by Secretary of State John Foster Dulles to the Middle East and Pakistan in May 1953, the Americans judged MEDO to be redundant, and were impervious to British advice to keep MEDO as a going concern. The Americans then devised a strategy to link Pakistan and Turkey in a Northern Tier arrangement and to give military aid to Pakistan within this framework. Military assistance to Pakistan resulted from a confluence of US global interests and Pakistan's desire to strengthen herself against India. It marked the beginning of the end of British military influence in Pakistan and, within seven years of decolonisation, established the US as the dominant power in South Asia – an area which the British had ruled for almost 200 years. Whether Pakistan's enlistment as an American ally strengthened the West in the Middle East is doubtful, but it undermined the British position both there and in Pakistan.

The Americans buttressed Britain's ascendancy in the Middle East as long as they felt it served their security interests; when they perceived it as disadvantageous to America's interests, they distanced themselves from the British and resorted to means which weakened them. Whittling down the British does not seem to have been the American intention, but it was the outcome of their policy and of the tentative new measures they evolved to protect the Western position in the Middle East.

American policy during the Suez crisis was only the culmination of that trend. Chapter Six will bring out the limits of British influence over the US, India and Pakistan, and it will highlight how the Suez crisis put paid to the British illusion that they could retain their ascendancy in the Middle East and sustain their international role with American backing.[19] In both Asia and the Middle East, India and Pakistan demonstrated that the shared British and American aims of containing communism and upholding Western influence did not lead to agreement on means; while differing

Indian and British objectives frequently produced agreement on tactics, to such an extent that the US came to believe that British strategies would harm American interests. Moving away from the British in the Middle East and Asia, the US formulated means which ultimately defeated British ends. The story that follows is one in which ends and means became inextricably interwoven; the means conceived by Britain and the United States were the fruit of varied reasoning, history and perceptions. Above all, their respective resources determined the means each wished to use; and the means, in turn, created new ends.

1. Decolonisation in South Asia and its aftermath, 1947–9

I THE END OF EMPIRE: THE DEBATE

> . . . there is perhaps no country in the world potentially more important to us, except the United States, than India with its vast population, immense trading possibilities and key position in Asia.[1]

In the 1990s the strength of Britain's ties with the USA and Western Europe is unquestionable, while British links with India have continually weakened since her independence. Lord Addison's advice to the Labour government in November 1947 thus rings strangely, reflecting the unfamiliar vision of another age, long past; and it is difficult to believe that the British wound up their Indian empire less than fifty years ago. Addison's counsel, given barely three months after the transfer of power to India and Pakistan, reminds the reader of the significance to the British of the subcontinent, as the heartland of their empire. It would be unrealistic to assume that their 200-year-old stake in South Asia ceased at the moment of independence, and Addison's advice is only one of many illustrations of a substantial British interest in post-imperial India. It does raise the question why, if India was so important, did the British decolonise at all?

There are no easy answers to this question, especially as policy-makers in London considered Britain's empire as an essential component of her standing in the world; indeed of her national identity. Moreover, the British withdrew from the subcontinent at a time when they thought their empire would help them to remain an independent great power and to hold their own against both superpowers. They also considered its preservation essential to strengthen the anti-communist front in the cold war. Decolonisation, then, appears contrary to the professed British desire to retain their global stature. How was this apparent contradiction reconciled by the transfer of power to India and Pakistan on 15 August 1947? The nature of decolonisation determined the extent of British influence over the newly independent India and Pakistan and subsequently bore upon their aspiration to preserve the substance of *Pax Britannica*. It also had an impact on the ways in which they could use the Anglo–American relationship as the pivot of their foreign policy after 1945. Evidence of American influence on the British to decolonise in August 1947 is conspicuously absent.[2] Nevertheless, it can be asked to what extent Britain's relationships with India and Pakistan influenced her dealings with the United States and impinged upon the chances of her winning American support for her interests. These are among the main questions posed in this book.

Until now, two quite contradictory themes have dominated traditional British perceptions of empire and decolonisation. On the one hand, most British policy-makers linked their country's global status to the empire; and in 1945, the Conservative party considered the empire to be Britain's 'supreme achievement'. The Conservative and Labour parties both shared the vision of Britain as a world power and of the empire as an integral part of that power, so that the British could hardly talk about their international status without taking their Empire–Commonwealth for granted. Attlee, like Churchill, had no intention of presiding over the dissolution of the British empire.[3] Other Labour politicians echoed this sentiment. In 1944, Emmanuel Shinwell declared: 'we have no intention, any of us, of throwing the British Commonwealth of Nations overboard in order to satisfy a section of the American Press, or indeed anyone else.' As Foreign Secretary, Ernest Bevin was in complete agreement: 'I know that if the British Empire fell, the greatest collection of free nations would go into the limbo of the past, and it would be a disaster.' Indeed, the election manifestos of the Labour and Conservative parties in 1945 stressed a world role for Britain and the preservation of empire.[4]

Historians have suggested a variety of factors to explain the post-war dismantling of empire. These include Britain's economic travails and the European cold war which focused Britain's attention on Europe. Whatever the merit of these views from hindsight, they leave unanswered why Conservative and Labour politicians, officials from the Foreign, Dominions, Colonial and Commonwealth Relations Offices and the Chiefs of Staff all desired the preservation of the empire, and why Britain's post-war economic weakness only seems to have reinforced their determination to maintain it.[5]

From a somewhat different perspective, Indian independence has often been extolled as the greatest achievement of the Attlee government.[6] This is puzzling, to say the least, since the possession of empire *and* its relinquishment cannot have been lauded as achievements at the same time. Moreover, after August 1947 Britain still possessed the rest of her empire and had every intention of holding on to it, formally if possible and informally if there was no other alternative: in fact she was determined to compensate for the loss of India by preserving her ascendancy in the Middle East.[7] This hardly suggests that decolonisation in South Asia was either a welcome accident or a carefully planned prelude to winding up the rest of the empire.

So the contradiction between decolonising while proclaiming Britain's intention to hold fast to empire has to be disentangled. At one level, the subject of decolonisation in South Asia would require a detailed history of the Raj, the Indian national movement and the partition of India[8] which are beyond the scope of this book. Whether the Raj or Indian nationalism were Good Things or Bad Things will not be debated; in this work both are accepted as *faits accomplis* which confronted each other at cross purposes. This chapter will inquire into the motives behind decolonisation and whether the British attained their goals.[9]

To answer these questions one has to pose another. Why did the British decolonise and partition the Indian subcontinent in August 1947 – and not earlier or later? It is worth remembering that the Indian National Congress was founded in 1885 but did not demand full independence until 1920 and the complete severance of all links with the Crown until 1930. So there was nothing 'inevitable' about the call for independence or about a favourable British response to it. It used to be argued that the seeds of decolonisa-tion lay in the introduction of representative government under the Government of India Acts of 1919 and 1935, but recent research[10] shows that these measures were intended to strengthen not end the Raj. They did not transfer any substantial powers to Indians. Their aim was simul-taneously to take the sting out of nationalism by winning over moderate nationalists, uphold the Raj with their support–and to defeat the Congress. The provincial elections of 1936–7 brought home to the British that this strategy was not succeeding; that the Congress was one of the chief parties in the negotiations for transfer of power in 1946–7 represented the failure of British efforts to checkmate the Congress.[11]

If Indian independence was not a long-term British goal, then what induced the British to end their Indian empire in August 1947? After all, some Muslim Leaguers wanted the Raj to last another ten years. And Muhammad Ali Jinnah, leader of the All-India Muslim League, asserted in April 1946 that: 'The British government was asking the Indian people to take self-government and the Indians were unable to do so.'[12] Congress–League differences had afforded the British a pretext to prolong empire; why then did they quit when these differences were exacerbated? On 20 February 1947 the Labour government announced that the British would pull out of India by 30 June 1948. But on 3 June 1947, Lord Mountbatten, the Viceroy, stated publicly that the British would transfer power to the new dominions of India and Pakistan on 15 August 1947. This suggests rapidly changing decisions, which are not adequately explained by the traditional British claim that the Labour government were committed to Indian independence. The Labour party and government were not bound by ideological unity on empire any more than on other issues. Even if such unity had prevailed, Clement Attlee, as Prime Minister, knew that the party in power did not represent 'an ideological abstraction but . . . the people of this country'. His government's views on India or the rest of the empire were related to their perception of Britain's place and role in the post-war international order, and their aims were moulded by the experience of Labour ministers in the War Cabinet, as members of a national coalition, not of a party in office or in opposition, and they devoted their energies to the British national interest.[13] It is also unlikely that the Conservative Party, which proudly proclaimed itself as the party of the empire, and with Winston Churchill at its helm, would have allowed the Labour government to dissolve the empire on ideological grounds. In fact it is the Conservative acquiescence in the relinquishment of what they regarded as Britain's 'supreme achievement' which appears rather remarkable.

The Conservative and Labour parties actually had quite similar ideas about what should be offered to India after the war. While recognising the need for political advance in India, the election manifestos of both parties in 1945 stressed a world role for Britain and the maintenance of her empire. In June 1945, the Conservatives offered India a renewal of the Cripps proposals of 1942, and 'complete freedom under an agreed constitution of her own devising'. The Conservative election manifesto of 1945 favoured dominion status for India and greater consultation between Britain and India. The Labour manifesto also renewed the Cripps offer and proposed the advancement of India to responsible self-government. ' "Planned progress" of our colonial dependencies' was envisaged.[14] Both parties were advocating political liberalisation in India but not full independence; nor were they setting any date for it.

II THE OFFER OF INDEPENDENCE

Historians will long debate the complex circumstances that led to Indian independence and, with their passion for origins, will seek to identify the cause of all causes. Would the British have granted independence if Britain had not been weakened by war? Alternatively, would a British government confronting a plethora of domestic predicaments have quit empire *in the absence* of widespread political turbulence in India? If the cold war impressed upon British officials the necessity of preserving their Empire–Commonwealth as a manifestation of their power, and if Britain's domestic problems did not quench the desire for empire, some historians emphasise that the reason why independence was offered cannot be understood without reference to popular pressures in India itself.[15] A wave of political unrest, part of a chain of disturbances since 1942, swept India in the winter of 1945–6. It was not the first test of British strength in India. In 1920 and 1930 they had suppressed widespread disaffection presumably because they wished, and were able, to do so. In 1945–6, political turmoil was on an unprecedentedly large scale and the British feared that they would not be able to stamp it out. The chances are that the unexpected conjunction of political tumult in India and Britain's economic woes[16] created a crisis of bewildering fluidity and eroded the authority and legitimacy of the Raj. Failure to squash any challenge to the Raj would have ramifications far beyond India, especially at a time when Britain's position in Greece and in the Middle East was shaky, and any exposure of weakness in India would dent the façade of her "great power".

The problem of confronting the growing political storm was compounded by the deteriorating administrative machine in India. The trials of the Indian National Army in November 1945 brought into the open the nationalist sympathies of Indian administrators and military men. The crumbling of the imperial edifice has been attributed to the progressive Indianisation of the Indian Civil Service since 1919.[17] But it was not until January 1946 that the Home Establishments' records showed Indians holding 50.68 per cent of the posts and marginally outnumbering the British in the Indian Civil Service; in the Indian Police Service, Europeans held 60.41 percent of the posts. The impact of Indianisation on the imperial destiny presented itself not in numbers but in the doubtful commitment of Indians to empire. A totally Indianised service, composed of loyalists, would not have sapped the foundations of the Raj. Since the Quit India movement of 1942, the British had continually acknowledged that they could not rely on Indian officials in the event of mass unrest.[18]

For an empire which, as Lord Linlithgow admitted, was acquired and preserved by the sword,[19] the crunch came with the recognition of nationalist sentiment among the Indian armed forces. With his knowledge of the men he commanded, Field-Marshal Sir Claude Auchinleck, the Commander-in-Chief of the Indian army, informed his superiors in New Delhi and London early in 1946 that 'any Indian officer worth his salt is a Nationalist'.[20] More British troops offered the only prospect of shoring up a creaking administrative apparatus, and in January 1946, the cabinet debated a suggestion by Auchinleck to strengthen the British garrison in India. But Auchinleck had anticipated Indian opposition to such a move and sought to counter it with the deception tactic that the British forces were in India for a short spell of training before leaving for Indonesia.[21] Two developments ruled out such a course of action. First, on 4 February 1946, the British Chiefs of Staff reported that British troops could not be moved from the Middle or Far East without disrupting seriously the British position in those areas. At home, demobilisation was proceeding apace, and the shortage of manpower was 'forcing' the Defence Committee to make reductions with the result that 'we are now left with an irreducible minimum in all areas where our commitments continue'.[22]

Then there was conclusive evidence of the weakening foundations of the Raj. In January and February 1946 mutinies in the Royal Indian Air Force and Navy respectively revealed the split in the military base of empire. The mutinies took the British by surprise. Both were eventually suppressed, but racial sentiment in the armed forces was now intense, and the loyalty of

Indian military personnel could not be taken for granted. On 22 February the Chiefs reiterated that additional British troops could not be despatched to India.

With political unrest showing no signs of abating, and with little prospect of quelling it, the Labour government now had to think of constitutional expedients to avert violence. This was the background to the Cabinet Mission which arrived in New Delhi on 24 March 1946. Its aim, as described by Attlee, was to set up machinery to frame a constitutional structure in which Indians would have 'full control of their own destiny and the formation of a new interim government'. Soon after their arrival in New Delhi, the Mission summed up the tenuous British hold over India and acknowledged that they could not face the situation in India 'with the same confidence as in the past' as they were unsure whether the forces behind law and order would do their duty. 'They felt this lack of confidence for the first time.'[23] It was against this background that they would negotiate the terms of a transfer of power with the Congress and Muslim League.

III IMPERIAL DEFENCE AND INDIAN INDEPENDENCE

Although prompted by administrative and political exigencies, the offer of independence in March 1946 was not made without regard for Britain's position as a great power. The cabinet wished to reconcile independence with preservation of the content of *Pax Britannica*. The concern with defence emanated from the top: Attlee held the defence portfolio until December 1946. The participation of an independent India in imperial defence was central to any official discussion of the possible terms of an independence settlement, and the reason lay in the strategic significance of India to Britain, a significance that was renewed and enhanced with the onset of the cold war.[24] Discussion of this factor is relevant at this stage, partly from the perspective of decolonisation and partly because it was to have a bearing on the British conception of India's role in the Asian cold war.[25]

India made Britain a Far Eastern power and spurred Britain's involvement in the Middle East and the Mediterranean. India was the backbone of British military power east of Suez. During the nineteenth century the British used Indian troops in the Crimea, China and New Zealand. Over one million Indian soldiers served overseas in the First World War, and India's entire contribution to the war was paid for by the British–Indian government. Some 2.5 million Indian soldiers fought for the Allies in 1939–45, and Lord Wavell regarded them an indispensable factor in Britain's victory over the Axis. India's manpower contribution in the Second World War roughly equalled that of all the Commonwealth countries put together and was surpassed only by that of Britain, which raised five million men. Domestic political considerations precluded the maintenance of wartime levels of conscription after 1945, but this did not occasion much alarm in London because the British expected to have access to Indian manpower after the war. At another level, India was a training ground for British officers, 60,000 of whom were trained in India before 1939 and their expenses fielded by the government of India. On account of her economic potential, India became a major supply base for the allies in the Second World War.

India also appears to have been something of a financial reservoir for imperial defence. In 1934–5, India, Australia and South Africa spent £36.95, 5.5 and 1.2 million respectively on defence. In 1937–8, the figures were £38.48, 10 and 1.8 million respectively. Britain spent more than any of them – £197 million in 1937–8. But Britain's defence expenditure represented 23.2 per cent of her total expenditure while India's defence budget comprised 40.8 per cent of her total expenditure.

With India buoying up the sword arm of empire, it was natural that British policy-makers should want a post-imperial relationship which would safeguard Britain's strategic interests. Sir Stafford Cripps's offer of March 1942 promised elections to a constituent assembly after the war and the right to secede from empire. It is well known that the war cabinet did not intend Cripps's offer to lead to any concrete political advance, and in accordance with their expectations and those of the Viceroy, Lord Linlithgow,[26] it failed to resolve the deadlock between the British, Congress and Muslim League. So it seems curious that the cabinet took the precaution of including in this political window-dressing a condition that any recommendation by the Indian constituent assembly for independence would be accepted by the British government subject to the signing of a treaty to safeguard Britain's military and financial interests.[27] There was no debate in the war cabinet about the need to include this provision; India's engagement in imperial defence simply seems to have been taken for granted. The assumption flowed in some measure from the inter-war controversy between the government of India and the British government as to whether India's defence responsibilities should be limited to her own territory or seen against the wider network of imperial security. By 1939 the British had decided that India should be drafted into imperial defence. The decision was taken, ironically enough, just when active Indian nationalist pressure on the British to quit India was becoming irresistible.[28] The Cripps Mission failed because of Winston Churchill's refusal to allow any political liberalisation, which to him was a stepping stone to the liquidation of empire.[29] But Churchill's anachronistic imperialism was not an isolated phenomenon. In January 1943, Linlithgow advised Leo Amery, then Secretary of State for India, that the answer to the question of India's post-war status should be 'highly conservative'.[30] Exactly what Amery hoped to accomplish by renewing the Cripps proposals in 1943 is not clear, but it was certainly not the termination of the Raj. Next to winning the war, he wrote to Churchill in April 1943, Britain's supreme goal must be to keep India within the empire. The loss of India would weaken the British position in the Middle East and the Indian Ocean. Somewhat exaggerating the importance of the Raj, Amery conjured up visions of a third world war caused by the Indian empire in dissolution. It would be in the British interest to have a stable and united India as a partner in the Commonwealth.[31]

Amery's vision was shared by Bevin, then Minister of Labour in the War Cabinet. In June 1943. Bevin wished to develop 'India including Burma up to the Persian Gulf', as an organic defence area in partnership with the British Commonwealth. The sterling balances would finance industrialisation in India in order to maintain a defensive and highly mechanized force, which the British would support with sea and air power.[32] The concern was echoed by Attlee, as Dominions Secretary in the War Cabinet.[33]

Little constitutional progress was made during the war, so the accession of the Labour government to power in August 1945, with its expressed desire to settle the Indian problem, raised expectations of political advance in India. The nature of the agreement sought by the Labour government depended partly on the situation in which Britain found herself at the end of the war. Britain's straitened circumstances did not prompt the Labour government to initiate any radical departures in defence or imperial strategy. The cold war added a new urgency to a traditional British interest and enhanced rather than diminished their desire to keep India within the imperial security system. This British aim was endorsed by the Americans,[34] who thought that British military bases on the subcontinent could be used to launch a possible attack on the Soviet Union. Both from the British and American viewpoints, the international situation appeared to demand and justify the pursuit of Britain's imperial interests.

Not surprisingly, then, the Labour government did not intend to make an unconditional transfer of power. Theoretically the British conducted the negotiations for the transfer of power on the basis that India would be free to secede from the Commonwealth, but Attlee and his colleagues preferred a united India within the Commonwealth. With a political rationale akin to that of Amery, the Labour government's directive to the Cabinet Mission made clear that it would accept the Indian constituent assembly's recommendation for independence only if 'satisfactory arrangements' were made for the defence of the Indian Ocean area. The cabinet's determination to secure a military agreement was reported by General Mosley Mayne, the Military Secretary to Lord Pethick-Lawrence, Secretary of State for India, to Auchinleck in the first week of March 1946.

At a meeting at Chequers last week-end of the new 'Big Three' – Pethick-Lawrence, Alexander and Cripps! – to discuss with the Prime Minister a mass of questions connected with the Ministerial Mission to India, it was decided that 'as a condition precedent to implementing a new constitution, satisfactory arrangements must be made for the defence of the "South East Asia Area".' *There was no soldier present at that meeting. . . .* What it amounts to is that the Prime Minister has it in mind to make it a condition, precedent to the grant of Dominion Status or independence to India, that India should undertake to provide defence forces sufficient for her own local defence and in addition assist, in Commonwealth or United Nations interests, in the defence of the "South-East Asia Area".

When asked for his opinion. Mayne said that Indian politicians could not 'at this stage' be expected to agree to this condition, but he 'was told, nevertheless, to devil into the question'. The decision to include the defence proviso in the Cabinet Mission's offer to the Indian parties on 16 May 1946 was made in anticipation of Congress opposition to it. There was unanimity in the cabinet over an Anglo–Indian military treaty and Cripps favoured telling the Congress of British intentions if necessary. It is noteworthy that independent Labour opinion shared the official conception of British defence interests and cherished hopes of a common system of military and financial relations between an independent India and Britain.[35]

In July 1946, Wavell and the British Chiefs affirmed that the principal advantage of India to Britain was strategic. One of India's main assets was 'an almost inexhaustible supply of manpower'; she could produce 'as many soldiers as the Commonwealth can maintain'. At a time when Britain was experiencing difficulties in raising sufficient forces to fulfil her world-wide obligations, the release of some 50,000 men from India, if it were to become independent, would be a welcome addition to the British armed forces in Europe. However, relief to British manpower commitments was seen as the 'only advantage' which would accrue to Britain if India became independent, implying that Britain might have much to lose from decolonisation. India's rich natural resources would make her a valuable military base, and her industrial potential was capable of expansion to meet the extra load placed upon it in war. In the age of atomic warfare, there was also 'increased necessity for space, which would allow of proper dispersion of base installations', and India could fit the bill. Deposits of thorium around Travancore would become 'of increasing importance' to the British, who regarded the atomic bomb as the key to post-war global power. India was 'the only suitable base' from which the British could sustain military operations on a large scale in the Far East. If India left the Commonwealth, the British position in the North Indian Ocean would be weakened, and oil supplies from the Persian Gulf could not be guaranteed. Wavell, the Chiefs and the cabinet concurred that without a friendly transfer of power and a military pact with India, the British stood to lose very heavily by abandoning India. Significantly, one of the main reasons why the cabinet rejected Wavell's proposals for an unconditional British withdrawal from India by the spring of 1948 was that India's co-operation was vital for the maintainance of Britain's strategic position in the Middle and Far East.[36] In other words, quitting India without securing military links could lead to the disintegration of British power and the abandonment of many a grand design of imperial strategy.

All these plans ignored the grain of Jawaharlal Nehru's many public statements between 1945–7 that India would not allow foreign bases on her soil, join any power bloc or accept anything less than an unconditional transfer of power.[37] Military and foreign policy aspects of an Anglo–Indian treaty and of India's affiliation to the Commonwealth received top priority in official memos and discussions as the negotiations for the transfer of power went on,[38] although they were never mentioned to Indian leaders. In 1946, British power and influence were running out, and wishful thinking formed the basis of their future strategic plans in India.

IV IMPERIAL DEFENCE AND THE CASE AGAINST PAKISTAN

The concern with imperial defence determined British attitudes to the Muslim League's demand for a state of Pakistan. Administrative weakness and political unrest were not the only trends in India in 1946. Also discernible was the trend towards Pakistan, which was crystallising with the Muslim League's success in winning 76 per cent of the total Muslim vote in the elections of 1945–6. The League's triumph owed something to the Congress failure to win popular Muslim support, the British policy of divide and rule, and above all to Jinnah's unique blend of organisational skill, obduracy and dialectical brilliance in negotiation. Divide and rule had been the imperial maxim as long as the Raj seemed to bask in eternal sunshine; as mounting political disorder necessitated a transfer of power, the case for Pakistan did not win British support. And the British dislike of Pakistan in 1946–7 was later to have a bearing on their attitudes to Pakistan's role in Middle East defence and their differences with the Americans on that score.[39]

The British judged that an independent Pakistan would not be militarily and economically viable.[40] Pakistan would not be able to sustain its defence expenditure, which would amount to four times its central revenues. The western and eastern halves of Pakistan would be exposed to Soviet and Chinese aggression respectively. Even with powerful allies Pakistan could not be defended without Indian help in providing alternative bases of communication. It might have enough manpower for defence, but the cost of training new army technicians would be long-drawn-out and expensive. As it did not have any industrial areas, all arms would have to be imported to the value of 35–50 per cent of the budget. For the India Office, defence was the 'crux' of the issue of partition. The military men agreed: defence was the 'key pin' of the problem; it alone made the case for Pakistan 'fall to the ground'. Policy-makers in London and New Delhi did not overlook the advantages of the Pakistan alternative, especially if India refused to remain in the Commonwealth, but the political logicality of a withdrawal into Pakistan did not appeal to the Chiefs. Pakistan would be in two halves, and the forces needed for its defence would be as great as those needed for that of India. Pakistan would have insufficient resources for defence, the cost of which would fall on Britain. A British alliance with Pakistan might push the Congress towards the USSR. The British would also have to contend with non-Muslim minorities in Pakistan who might act as a fifth column. Pakistan appeared impracticable, so officials seem to have discarded it mentally. This helps to explain why drafts of independence treaties did not contemplate the Pakistan option. To the British, it was imperative that negotiations for a transfer of power to an undivided India should succeed, for it was the only basis on which they could keep India within their global defence network. It is as if the British prejudged political issues in India and held fast to the alternative they preferred. Therefore they did not work out any contingent strategy should the second, undesired possibility become reality.

The rejection of Pakistan also contained within it an intrinsic assumption that defence arrangements with an independent, undivided India would materialise. It was probably a case of the wish giving birth to the thought. A united India would be of the greatest strategic advantage to the British, if only because the army would not be divided. They wanted to have access to India's industrial and manpower potential and to use her territory for operational and administrative bases. Partition would destroy the homogeneity of the Indian army and would be a solution of last resort if the only option was complete failure and chaos. If it had to be adopted, every effort would be made to secure agreement on some sort of central defence council which would include not only Pakistan, Hindustan and the princely states but also Burma and Ceylon. Scuttle was humiliating, partition undesirable, a united India necessary to safeguard British interests. Under the circumstances, the only acceptable option was that negotiations for the transfer of power to *one* India must succeed. It is curious that at a time when British policy-makers worried about their lack of power to enforce a settlement, their strategical designs were at cross purposes with those of the Congress and the League, which had won huge popular mandates in the all India elections of 1945–6 and whose political objectives were poles apart. What settlement could emerge out of an imbroglio in which all three parties to the negotiations had opposing political goals?

V   INDEPENDENCE AND PARTITION: WHAT DID THE BRITISH ACHIEVE?

It was not long before the negotiations came unstuck, as the Congress and League fell out over the terms of the Cabinet Mission Plan of 16 May 1946. The political division between them spilled over into a series of communal conflagrations and held out the spectre of a sweeping anti-British wave, as both parties blamed the British. It was doubtful whether loyalist services alone could have suppressed decisively the growing political and social unrest. Indeed it was in the administrative inability to crush such disturbances, which were often accompanied by violence, that the British confronted their most intractable administrative problem. The unreliability of the services had led Wavell to advise the war cabinet to widen *political liberalisation* between 1943–5 but not to wind up the Raj.[41] The deepening political and communal instability added a new dimension to the crumbling administrative and military foundations of the Raj. More than 20,000 people lost their lives in the communal storm which raged through Bengal and Bihar between August and October 1946. The unprecedented scale and savagery of the communal carnage undercut the British capacity to keep order and led Wavell to contend on 7 September, and again on 23 and 30 October 1946, that on administrative grounds, the British could not govern India for more than eighteen months; they should therefore resolve to terminate the Raj by March 1948.[42]

Wavell's advice was not destined to please the cabinet. The effect of withdrawal on Britain's international prestige weighed most with the Labour government in rejecting his counsel. To leave India before the Congress and League had agreed on a constitution would be construed by the world as an act of weakness and would seriously undermine Britain's international position, and Britain's problems in Palestine and Egypt made it essential to avoid any policy which smacked of scuttle. Parliamentary opinion also mattered; it would be difficult to defend a policy of hasty retreat in parliament. As Pethick-Lawrence confided to Wavell on 28 September 1946, 'there would be great difficulty in securing such authority without a constitutional settlement unless a situation existed which justified such a step on grounds of undeniable necessity.' Withdrawal as an act of cold blood and not under irresistible pressure would signify defeat, 'the most complete condemnation of our own policy and an admission of our own futility',[43] for which the blame would descend on the Labour government. The cabinet concurred with Wavell that the administration was shaky and that the British would not be able to crush a mass revolt. But they wanted to pursue negotiations until failure became a certainty.[44] In effect, they were reluctant to tell Parliament that the British might transfer power in the near future because they expected a breakdown and could do nothing about it.

By the first half of December 1946 the chances of a political agreement on the basis of the Cabinet Mission Plan seemed remote, as the Muslim League refused to enter the constituent assembly for a united India. Partition appeared on the horizon; as the India and Burma Committee realised, 'the pressure of events' was leading to 'some form of Pakistan'.[45] Rummaging around for an alternative, the Labour cabinet now considered the withdrawal statement they had rejected two months earlier. This is signficant, for it goes against the conventional wisdom that Mountbatten's hastily devised plan to transfer power in August 1947 precipitated partition: rather the evidence is that the imminence of partition was the

immediate cause of the British decision to issue a withdrawal announcement. It was then that the cabinet considered treading the path of no
return, and of declaring the British intention to wind up the Raj. A
withdrawal announcement still savoured of defeat, but it would be 'a
powerful weapon to secure that we did in fact depart from India with
dignity, and would give the best chance of leaving behind us an ordered
and responsible Government. In our present weak position, could we
afford to discard such a weapon? The consequences of our being driven to
leave India through weakness would be far worse.'[46] The statement should
be worded carefully: it should not hint at a political climbdown but should
proclaim an imperial *tour de force*. On 31 December 1946 the political
alternative that had hitherto been construed as a defeat was recast as a
political and moral triumph:

The general feeling of the Cabinet was that withdrawal from India need not appear
to be forced upon us by our weakness nor to be the first step in the dissolution of
the Empire. On the contrary this action *must be shown to be* the logical conclusion,
which we welcomed, of a policy followed by successive Governments for many
years.[47]

The League's final refusal to enter the constituent assembly on 31
January 1947 meant that a British declaration of intent could not be
delayed, and on 20 February 1947, the Labour government announced
their decision to end the Raj by 30 June 1948. Contrary to the intentions of
the cabinet in March 1946, the British would pull out of India although no
constitution had been drawn up; no provision for the rights of minorities or
resolution of financial and military matters had been made. The statement
of 20 February 1947 acknowledged that there was no clear prospect that a
constitution accepted by all parties would emerge. But it attempted to gloss
over the political impasse with the specious assertion that the time had
come to transfer power to Indians in fulfilment of the long-term plans of
the British, and 'nothing should be said which would suggest that *we are
not in a position to prevent Indian parties from seizing power themselves*'.
Attlee confided to Lord Mountbatten, whom the cabinet had appointed to
succeed Wavell as Viceroy in March 1947, that the historical and rhetorical
part of the statement was intended to keep the opposition quiet.[48]
   In the Commons debate on 5 March 1947, Cripps rhetorically posed the
question whether, in the absence of agreement between Indians, 'could we
have been in any way certain that we should have been able to discharge
our responsibilities after that . . . date?' Yet, as Henry Raikes, the
Conservative MP from Liverpool discerned, Cripps had said that one
alternative was to fix a terminal date, the other was to carry on for some
years. It was impracticable to carry on. In effect, alleged Raikes, Cripps
had not put up any alternative; 'he merely said bluntly that there is no
possible alternative other than to run out of India, irrespective of to whom

we hand over, in the course of the next 16 months'.[49] This was confirmed
by Wavell.

We should . . . thus avoid being responsible for, and probably involved in, any
widespread breakdown of law and order which may result from the communal
situation or from labour troubles induced by revolutionary preaching or economic
conditions. The worst danger for us is an anti-European movement which might
result in the killing of some of our nationals, and of our having to carry out an
ignominious forced withdrawal; instead of leaving in our own time and
voluntarily.[50]

Attempting to portray the imminent end of the Raj as the consummation of
Britain's imperial mission, the statement of 20 February 1947 was in reality
a device to extricate the British from responsibility for the disintegration of
the administration and from a situation which might endanger their position to the point of compelling them into a virtual retreat from India.

The statement precipitated a communal blood-bath in the Punjab in
March 1947. Foreseeing an outbreak of civil war, Sir Evan Jenkins, the
Governor of the Punjab, warned that any administration would be replaced by chaos in June 1948. '[A]ll the King's horses and all the King's
men' could not prevent the old administrative machine from falling to
pieces.[51] Soon after his arrival in India on 22 March 1947, Mountbatten felt
that the only hope of stemming the violence and administrative bedlam lay
in early independence and partition, and he advised the Labour government to hand over power to the governments of two dominions by 15
August 1947, as the last date by which the British could avoid responsibility
for a complete administrative breakdown.[52]

An early transfer of power also held out the prospect that a Congress-
governed India would remain in the Commonwealth. Once they knew that
the British offer of independence stood firm, Congress leaders agreed with
Mountbatten that India should not break with the Commonwealth out of
bitterness and that she should remain in the Commonwealth at least until
June 1948. As a gesture of goodwill, Congress leaders invited Mountbatten
to serve as the first governor-general of independent India. The invitation
cheered British officials, who thought that India's participation in the
Commonwealth presented the best chances of securing military links with
her.

The British had, however, to contend with the Muslim League. Until
May 1947, when it had appeared that a free India would leave the
Commonwealth and become a republic, the Muslim League had voiced
enthusiasm for Pakistani membership of the Commonwealth and a British
governor-general of Pakistan. With the Congress and League both wishing
to have a British governor-general, the stage seemed set for Mountbatten
to function as a common governor-general of India *and* Pakistan and to use
such a position to create joint defence ties between the two dominions.

Here Jinnah smelt a rat. He knew that Mountbatten would try to bring the two dominions together. This would naturally serve the interests of Congress leaders, who had very friendly personal ties with Mountbatten. Intent on obtaining a divorce from India, Jinnah made clear to Mountbatten on 4 July 1947 his intention to assume the governor-generalship of Pakistan himself. The British were dismayed. Mountbatten himself had never wanted to become governor-general of only one dominion, but Attlee favoured his acceptance of the Congress invitation because it was 'a great boost for Britain, and for the Commonwealth . . . If Mountbatten *had* left India, it would have looked like a victory for that twister, Jinnah'![53]

That Jinnah got his way marked the end of any chances of the two dominions coming closer together; the League's insistence on the division of the British Indian army[54] dismembered Britain's foremost strategic asset east of Suez, and the partition riots set the seal on an interminable Indo–Pakistani acrimony. As partition and the transfer of power had been dictated by political and administrative exigency, 'contrary to expectations', no provision for formal treaties with the new dominions had been made, and there was nothing to provide the British with a card of re-entry enabling them to retain contacts for future military agreements. Commonwealth defence was in jeopardy.[55] Thus the British achieved none of their aims with an unconditional transfer of power and partition of India in August 1947. The political and strategical exigencies of the cold war had dictated the retention of India within the imperial defence nexus; the political imperatives of Indian and Pakistani nationalisms thwarted the attainment of that aim. If the British had not been able to achieve their objectives even while they still held the reins of power – albeit a fast-ebbing power – would they be able to do so after India and Pakistan became independent?

VI BRITAIN WITHOUT THE SWORD-ARM OF EMPIRE

Circumstances alter situations; the independence and partition of India reflected and changed the facts of British power. The British were quite clear about the strategic requirements they wanted India and Pakistan to fulfil: as Commonwealth members, they should 'accept the obligation' to defend neighbouring territories, 'including the possibility that this might entail the employment of some of their forces outside their own territory'. The inference was that 'the two Dominions would have to maintain in peacetime defence organisations larger than they would need for their own purposes, and that we should next consider what inducements, material, financial, or political, we could offer in order to persuade them to do what we want'.[56]

British hopes of winning Indian collaboration in Commonwealth defence were not dimmed by Nehru's declarations, before and after independence, that India would not join any power bloc but would remain nonaligned. Since its entry into the interim government in 1946, the Congress had demanded the return of Indian troops serving under British command in the Middle and Far East. The Congress call highlighted the extent to which the British relied upon the Indian armed forces, which accounted for their eagerness to have an independent India participate in Commonwealth defence. After independence, the Indian government wanted all Indian troops to return home by early 1948, so that the Indian army could be reorganised. The British conceded that the justness of the Indian claim would make it difficult for them to give a negative response, but they were understandably concerned about the adverse effects of Indian troop withdrawals on Commonwealth defence arrangements. India had some 30,000 troops overseas under British command, and the gravest complications would arise in Malaya and Burma, where the Indian units comprised the bulk of the administrative forces. In mid-1947, there were 12,000 Indian administrative troops in Malaya and Burma. If they were removed, Burma would need at least 2,000 British administrative troops until her own units took over; Malaya would require some 3,000 until June 1948 if a 'serious administrative situation' was to be avoided. The British would not be able to find replacements for Burma; they could do so in Malaya only with the 'greatest of difficulty'. Military spokesmen warned the cabinet that the loss of Indian manpower would be 'extremely serious to the defence of the Commonwealth'. In addition, the weak post-war British economy would entail the withdrawal of 21,000 British troops from overseas by March 1948. By that time, 'with the exception of very small forces maintaining links on our lines of communication our garrisons in the Far East will be virtually confined to Malaya and Hong Kong', and the British would find it 'extremely difficult' to achieve their military objectives.[57] With India, which could supply almost as many soldiers as the Commonwealth could maintain at her own expense, the Labour government naturally desired an early defence agreement.

In Britain itself, the constraints imposed by demobilisation and a struggling economy meant that the British could not replace Indian troops to shore up their position in the Far and Middle East. For the last two hundred years, wrote Bevin to Montgomery, then CIGS, on 18 October 1947, the British had had a mobile force which could be called into play when needed, not necessarily for offensive purposes but primarily to give the foreign secretary 'a very necessary psychological argument' in defending and asserting British interests abroad. Britain's African empire could provide manpower, but it would be difficult to move African troops from the colonies where they were trained, and to use them in sudden emergencies elsewhere. The armies of Middle Eastern allies, even if trained and equipped by the British, could not be moved from their homelands 'merely in order to help us out of a difficulty'. The post-war British army was 'nothing more than a glorified militia for home defence'.

When this revolutionary change in the whole character of the British army was realised by foreign governments, it was 'bound to have a profound effect – of disillusionment among our allies and friends and of glee among our enemies'. Coming after the withdrawal of British troops from Japan, Burma, India, Iraq and Palestine, Egypt, Greece and Italy, 'it will be interpreted as the abdication of Great Britain as a world power'.[58]

Bevin was not contemplating mobilisation for war. What he had in mind was the need to have in peacetime a mobile force at home which could be used to reinforce at any moment the meagre number of British troops which would be 'protecting our interests and fulfilling our commitments abroad'. He was thinking of ' "local emergencies" and "incidents" which may call for quick action on our part if we are to restore our position and assert our authority before the general situation has got out of hand'. The loss of the Indian army and demobilisation together would make it difficult for the British to make a show of force: the ability to assert their presence internationally had been a symbol of their "great power"; and they would, understandably, have liked to continue to have this capability. In October 1949, the Cabinet Defence Committee admitted:

The effect on Army organisation of the granting of self-government to India and Pakistan is often overlooked. For here was a highly trained expandable reserve on which we could count in time of emergency or war. While the cost of this Army to the United Kingdom in peace was relatively small, it was a definite factor in our potential military strength.[59]

The Indian army had been an essential element in British power, one which proved irreplaceable. Talk about armies in the age of the bomb was neither facile nor an imperial hangover; as the Americans were to discover in Korea and Vietnam, land warfare was not obsolete. After Indian independence, Britain's armed forces were the largest possessed by any country apart from those of the superpowers, and her navy was positioned world-wide. But with the domestic choice in favour of butter over guns, she would be constrained in the *use* of her military strength.

VII NEW DOMINIONS AT WAR

Whether Britain would be able to achieve her military aims on the subcontinent after decolonisation would depend to a considerable extent on the foreign policies of India and Pakistan. For independence implied, above all, sovereignty in foreign policy. The presence of a British governor-general in India, under whose supervision partition arrangements would be made between India and Pakistan, and the fact that British troops continued to serve in the armies of both countries pointed to an extended British stake in the subcontinent. British interests would be best served by a stable, democratic and friendly India, with whom they could establish close political, diplomatic, military and economic links. However, it will be evident from the following account that the path to such a relationship was not smooth. The British had to choose their tactics, modify and redefine their goals as necessitated by changing developments on the subcontinent.

The post-partition acrimony between India and Pakistan proved the first major diplomatic headache for the British, a Gordian knot that was to circumscribe the extent of their influence in South Asia. Hostility between the two dominions stemmed from the political divide between the Congress and Muslim League before decolonisation, and the bitterness did not end when their leaderships assumed office in India and Pakistan respectively. Communal violence accompanied the transfer of power on an unprecedented scale; thousands of refugees crossed the new international borders of India and Pakistan, and a disintegrated administration, inherited from the British, broke down completely in both countries. Pakistan symbolised the antithesis of the secular, united India that the Congress had sought to achieve; while Pakistani leaders knew that as a political minority, they might never have won their nation-state without British support.

After partition, the old differences between the League and Congress were transposed into hostility between India and Pakistan. Statements by Indian leaders against partition, probably motivated by their sorrow at the division of India, signified to Pakistan India's determination to destroy her, and security against Indian aggression was the *raison d'être* underlying Pakistan's diplomatic and military initiatives after partition. In October 1947, Jinnah appealed for Commonwealth intervention to clear up the manifold problems resulting from the partition riots. His request embarrassed officials in London. Reluctant to act as umpire in an Indo–Pakistani scrimmage, the Labour cabinet observed that Jinnah had not defined the kind of intervention desired; the nearest definition was his suggestion of 23 September that a team of Commonwealth representatives visit India and Pakistan for joint discussions. In any case, India would not be amenable to any foreign intervention. Investigations would only rake up the past bitterness between India and Britain; solutions were unlikely to emerge and links between the new dominions and the Commonwealth might be strained. Clearly the Labour government did not want to intervene, and the Pakistani request was dismissed on the grounds that Pakistan, as the weaker country, was trying to gain sympathy and publicity. The matter would be left 'to peter out in its present untidy state', and Jinnah would be told that the British would not do anything that India found unpalatable.[60] It was one of the earliest indications that a desire to keep in India's good books would shape British policy towards Pakistan. To Pakistan, the British attitude was 'a cold douche' to her hopes of 'fraternal assistance', and revealed the 'falsity of the allegedly "family" relationship existing within the Commonwealth'. The deference to India, in the name of constitutional etiquette, lost the British much goodwill in Pakistan.[61] The truth of the matter was that the British were discomfited by Indo–Pakistani animosity, and their inability to cut the Gordian knot threatened to spoil their relations with both the new dominions. It was also an unpleasant reminder of their loss of power on the subcontinent, and their attempts to stay aloof from the Indo–Pakistani imbroglio signified a cautious attempt to come to terms with it.

The outbreak of Indo–Pakistani hostilities over Kashmir in October 1947 spelt another embarrassment for the British, for it was the first occasion that two dominions had gone to war with each other. London knew that Pakistan had connived in an invasion by tribesmen from the North-West Frontier Province – a fact which led India to expect British support against Pakistan. But British officials were divided. Some thought that Kashmir, with a Muslim majority population, should go to Pakistan; others wanted to curb a potentially aggressive Hindu India.[62] Their vacillation greatly dismayed Pakistan, whose leaders had sought dominion status and proclaimed their loyalty to king and Commonwealth even before partition. Pakistan was now rewarded by British patter about the indefinable strength of the Commonwealth, which could be likened to 'the Mystic Marriage of St. Catherine when she had been hoping for the more solid satisfactions of a double bed'.[63]

Kashmir earned the dubious honour of being the first interstate conflict to be discussed by the UN Security Council, where Philip Noel-Baker, as Secretary of State for Commonwealth Relations, committed the British very heavily to the Pakistani position. This greatly annoyed Attlee, who thought Noel-Baker had left the British with no room for manoeuvre. India, with which the Labour government hoped for military ties, was angered at Britain's failure to condemn aggression and contemplated quitting the Commonwealth.[64] In New Delhi, Mountbatten was alarmed. Caught in the Indo–Pakistani cross-fire, he counselled Attlee that a just settlement of the Kashmir conflict would swing India round to the Anglo–American side. The Chiefs also advised that the British stance in the Security Council should not lose sight of the necessity of military links with India.[65]

However, there was no single interpretation of British interests in London. Bevin, for one, sang his own tune. With an eye to British interests in the Middle East, he contended that the alienation of Pakistan would tarnish Britain's image in the region.[66] It is difficult to take this seriously, if only because there is little evidence in British archival records that the Kashmir dispute – or South Asian affairs – aroused any interest among Middle East countries at this time. Bevin's unease probably sprang from some fanciful notion of a monolithic "Islam" laying siege to British interests and not from any well-informed analysis of the extent of Pakistan's influence in the Middle East. In fact, as Chapter 4 will show, one of the reasons why British officials resisted US attempts to draft Pakistan in Middle East defence between 1951–3 was precisely because they felt

Pakistan had little clout in the region. But divisions between pro-India and pro-Pakistan elements existed in the CRO and even in the cabinet, and, not wanting to come down on one side or the other, the British annoyed both dominions. Alienating India could drive her out of the Commonwealth; supporting India could destroy Pakistan, which had been created by an act of the British Parliament.[67] Disagreements within the cabinet made for a vacillating, poorly co-ordinated British policy on Kashmir. Their equivocal attitude reflected their fast-ebbing influence in South Asia.

Neither the partition riots nor the Indo–Pakistani dispute over Kashmir dimmed British hopes of securing military co-operation with India or of Indian membership of the Commonwealth. Foreign Office memos about the advantages to Britain of India's presence in the Commonwealth did not emanate from purblind optimists, but the broad consensus in London was that Indian membership would serve British interests in the long term. Behind the anticipation of military partnership with India lay the frustrating reality that her future in the Commonwealth was uncertain. Until and unless India decided to stay in the Commonwealth, the British could not hold defence talks with her. The uncertainty about India's adherence to the Commonwealth meant that the British had to keep her at some distance while simultaneously looking for ways that would bring about the desired Anglo–Indian military links. For example, following the decision of the constituent assembly in January 1947 that India would be a sovereign independent republic, the Labour cabinet had decided in March 1947 to bar Indian officers from attending British service colleges so that they did not gain access to top-secret military information. Nevertheless the British hoped to influence Indian defence policy. India's overtures to the UK for military aid were regarded by the Chiefs as a suitable opportunity to do this, and they advised the cabinet that 'the sooner the proposed defence discussions with India were held the better'. Another opportunity to pull strings arose with a request by India, also in late 1947, for the services of British officers in India's armed forces where her own were not available to fill senior posts.[68]

The issue of service conditions of British officers in India illustrates the cabinet's eagerness to encourage India to remain in the Commonwealth, and also to dissuade her from turning to other foreign powers – that is, outside the Commonwealth. Needing British officers far more than India, Pakistan had agreed to a British proviso that they would remain under British jurisdiction. India, however, rejected the condition that an Indian C-in-C would not be able to try British soldiers under his command as 'wholly incompatible' with dominion status. The Cabinet Defence Committee decided in November 1947 that acceptance of the British stipulation would indeed establish 'a colour bar incompatible with Dominion Status'. It would also embarrass the Indian government, and A.V. Alexander, now Minister of Defence, advised that as the retention of India within the Commonwealth was 'a matter of major strategic importance to us we should not lightly weaken the position of the present Indian administration'. Extra-territorial rights for British officers might also result in recurrent friction which might, eventually, 'have an important influence on India's ultimate decision to stay in the Commonwealth'. The British would inform Pakistan of the agreement with India and express readiness to offer Pakistan the same terms. The Indian request for British officers would after all provide the British with the opportunity to coordinate India's armed forces with those of other Commonwealth countries and to achieve the standardisation of Commonwealth forces.[69] For the moment, however, the reality was the uncertainty about the continuing participation of India and Pakistan in the Commonwealth, so they were excluded from immediate defence plans while the British awaited the decision of their governments.

VIII THE BRITISH REBUFF PAKISTAN

Despite partition, the British seem to have visualised the subcontinent as a single political and strategic entity. The strategical use they had made of South Asia before the transfer of power, and the fact that they did not radically revise their defence planning soon after decolonisation, probably reinforced this image. Discussing the reorganisation of their regional commands after Indian independence, the Chiefs envisaged India and Pakistan as a link and a base for protecting British interests in the Middle and Far East.[70]

It is significant that the British image of an undivided subcontinent and their desire that India remain in the Commonwealth led to their cool response to a Pakistani overture for a military alliance. In September 1948, Major-General W.J. Cawthorn, the British deputy C-in-C of the Pakistani army, forwarded a secret message from Liaqat Ali Khan, the Prime Minister of Pakistan, to Attlee. Liaqat professed Pakistan's fear of communism as a danger to her own stability and her eagerness to start talks on military co-operation with the British. Liaqat said he would sound out his cabinet only if he was sure of a favourable response from the British government. Liaqat's missive raised a new problem for the British: how could they keep the available bird in the hand without losing the one in the bush which they regarded as the more valuable prize? The exchanges between the Prime Minister's office, the CRO, the FO and the Chiefs over the next few months reflected the British dilemma and also their preference. Philip Noel-Baker, then Secretary of State for Commonwealth Relations, informed Cawthorn of the difficulty of making such an arrangement unless India was prepared to do the same, and of the further difficulties which would 'inevitably arise' before the Kashmir dispute was settled. At the same time, the prospect of military co-operation with a willing Pakistan was not unattractive, and Attlee agreed with the Chiefs that staff conversations could be started 'provided we kept India informed'.[71]

But the idea of defence talks with Pakistan did not get very far, for the Chiefs saw no immediate benefit resulting from defence parleys with Pakistan. A Pakistani government might, in theory, place West Pakistani airfields at the disposal of the West, but would they really be an asset? In peacetime the West would never have enough forces to defend such bases. Here the Chiefs' unspoken thought was that the British would not fritter away their meagre resources to create and defend a new stake in Pakistan. And the construction of Western bases might precipitate a Soviet attack on Pakistan in the early stages of a war to forestall the Allies from using them. The inference was that Pakistan would be more of a liability than an asset. American help was necessary to buoy up the British position in the Middle East, but any deployment of US forces in Pakistan could only be at the expense of their effort in the oil-rich Middle East, to which the British gave priority over South Asia. More significantly, Pakistan was excluded from the British conception of the Middle East: *Egypt* was the nucleus of the British position in the area. Political developments in Southeast Asia since June 1948 also rendered the British reluctant to pay the price for a not-very-reliable Pakistani contribution to Middle East defence. In the context of the Malayan insurgency, British officials outlined, between February and August 1949, their Asian cold-war strategy and assigned to India a key role in it.[72] Given that the Chiefs thought that nonaligned India should be assisted and encouraged to take the lead in Asia against communism even if she left the Commonwealth, it was evident that the British would not alienate India for the sake of problematical benefits of any military links with Pakistan. Unilateral discussions with Pakistan might give India the impression that the British were ' "ganging up" ' against her; while defence talks with India could not be held unless she decided to remain in the Commonwealth. Pakistan should be told 'frankly' that the British would not hold defence discussions with her until October–November 1949 when the 'future of India' became apparent. Attlee agreed with the Chiefs on the need to be 'more indefinite' about the date in case the forthcoming Commonwealth Prime Ministers' meeting in April 1949 made it necessary to open discussions with India on a treaty basis.[73] This implied that the British did not wish to provoke India into quitting the Commonwealth by holding defence parleys with Pakistan.

India's decision to remain in the Commonwealth kept alive the interest of some British policy-makers in defence co-operation with her and Pakistan, despite the prevalence of their hostility over Kashmir. 'It was greatly to our strategic advantage', noted A.V. Alexander, 'that these two large countries, with their extensive resources in manpower and material, had decided to remain within the British Commonwealth.' Overruling initial objections by the Chiefs, the cabinet decided, in June 1949, to lift the ban on Indian and Pakistani officers attending British service colleges.[74]

Yet how could defence collaboration with both India and Pakistan be achieved? India showed little interest in military discussions. Pakistan sought alignment with the UK, but in the summer of 1949, she complicated matters by demanding a guarantee against aggression ' "from *any* quarter" '.[75] The story of the British response to the new condition imposed by Pakistan is significant, for it reflects the British attitude to India and their general position in the subcontinent and the manner in which they related these considerations to their international position. On 24 June 1949, L.B. Grafftey-Smith, High Commissioner in Pakistan, reported that Liaqat Ali Khan had assured him that he wanted the Commonwealth connection for Pakistan. But Liaqat felt 'even more strongly' about the territorial integrity of Pakistan. Liaqat confirmed the High Commissioner's impression that fear of India's aggressive intentions 'is an obsession in Pakistan'. Liaqat was confident of full Commonwealth support if the Soviets invaded Pakistan. ' "What I fear is that Great Britain and the world would look on with folded arms if India attacked us." '[76]

The possible consequences of a military guarantee to Pakistan were irreconciliable with the British desire to retain Commonwealth unity as a source of their international status. War between India and Pakistan would be an unprecedented event as the Commonwealth was based on mutual co-operation and consultation between members on defence and other matters. Any military guarantee to Pakistan might drive India out of the Commonwealth, and 'would certainly' make her very hostile to the British. This reason was not considered 'suitable for communication' to the Pakistani government. The British could not escape the dilemma by offering guarantees to both India and Pakistan, for they would then be placed in the 'impossible position' of helping India against a Pakistani attack and Pakistan against an Indian attack. The Commonwealth might give a guarantee against the aggressor, but it might well be impossible to determine who the aggressor was. Assuming that the UN identified the aggressor – the British were loth to have the Commonwealth or themselves entrusted with this thankless task – and the Commonwealth took action against the aggressor, then for practical purposes the latter would leave the Commonwealth. The British generally assumed that India, as the stronger power, would commit aggression, though the Chiefs did not rule out the possibility of fanaticism producing the 'most improbable and illogical situations, and this was particularly so in a Moslem country which might try to initate a "Jehad" '. It is interesting that in most despatches the discussion usually centred round what policy towards Pakistan would push India out of the Commonwealth; Pakistan was seldom the subject of a similar debate. This was largely because Pakistan, as the weaker state, would be more dependent on the Commonwealth for support; and her threats of finding 'other friends' were regarded by the Foreign Office as 'of academic interest . . . since they merely tend to show irritation over Kashmir, and not any genuine pro-Russian feeling'.[77] A strong, anti-communist India outside the Commonwealth would be a better security prospect for the British than a weak Pakistan which would have to be propped up at every level by a financially exhausted Britain. So the British studiously avoided the question of guarantees against India. The British rationale at once mirrored the limits of their influence in South Asia, their parallel perceptions of Pakistan's minimal prestige in the Middle East and of India's high standing in Asia.

It is somewhat curious that the British blamed the Indo–Pakistani conflict for the absence of defence parleys and considered a resolution of the Kashmir dispute a 'major objective in Commonwealth defence policy'.[78] There was an element of wishful thinking in this idea, for what certainty was there of defence ties with India or Pakistan or both if the Kashmir conflict was settled? Would Nehru's government have aligned with the West if the conflict had never existed? And, as British officials themselves noted four years later, Pakistan might also have been nonaligned in the absence of animosity over Kashmir. From the more general Commonwealth aspect, too, the British were unrealistic, for there was no Commonwealth defence policy. In hoping for formal military ties with India, the British were anticipating something that no other Commonwealth country had given them. On the other hand they could not impose anything on India any more than they had on other dominions. Like them, India could join the Commonwealth and pursue an independent foreign and defence policy. The British acknowledged this, but the frequent draft treaties until the end of 1949 suggest a certain inability to grasp the Indian nettle.

Pakistan's hostility towards India did offer the British an opening to maintain a military foothold on the subcontinent which they rejected. Even if India had quit the Commonwealth in that event, it is unlikely that she would have walked into the Soviet camp, given Soviet hostility towards India at this time. It is likely that the military opportunity proffered by Pakistan was not exploited because the British had not made any major revision in their strategic planning since the partition of India, and so they clung to their traditional image of the Indian subcontinent as the key to their strategy in the Middle and Far East. Decolonisation in itself did not cause the loss of *all* British military influence in South Asia; the British failed to take advantage of the opportunity presented by Pakistan's search for security against India. The reason was that they adjudged India to be the more valuable strategical and political prize and went to great lengths to woo her. Pakistan simply did not command an influence in the Middle East analogous to that of India in Asia. The ways in which this perception of India induced the British to keep an Indian republic in the Commonwealth, as a source and mirror of their global influence, will be discussed in the next section.

IX MAKING THE NEW COMMONWEALTH

Partition was a strategic embarrassment; India, Pakistan and Britain knew that their aims diverged; India threatened to walk out of the Commonwealth on Kashmir. Why, then, were the British so eager to keep India in the Commonwealth? Especially when there were signs of considerable official and public antipathy to Britain on issues as varied as imperialism, power politics, racial discrimination, British commercial interests, and when minor Indian officials and the press often put 'an evil construction on British activities and policies'? Admittedly, many Indian officials did voice an interest in links – formal or informal – with the Commonwealth.[79] The problem was how to reconcile India's desire for independence, in substance and symbolically, with her membership of the Commonwealth which reflected Britain's status as a great imperial power.

The way out of this dilemma lay in the post-1947 British conception of the Commonwealth and of its place in their foreign policy as a whole. Britain may have balanced herself, in Churchill's famous phrase, among three concentric circles – Europe, America and the Commonwealth. But Churchill's rhetorical stance camouflaged the fact that all the circles were not of the same size and were therefore not of uniform priority to Britain. For there was no question that the US, not the Commonwealth, was the bulwark of British security, and when a conflict of interest arose between the two, the British knew that they would plump for the United States. Even while they held their Indian empire, they co-operated more closely in defence matters with the US than with the Commonwealth. There was no continuity of military or political discussion with the Commonwealth; such discussions were remote and intermittent and played no part in the formulation of British policy. Commonwealth military liaison had 'no work of major importance to do';[80] it merely disseminated information.

Nothing illustrates the second-rank status of the Commonwealth better than the exchange of military information between Britain and Commonwealth countries. Britain could pass on American military information to them only after obtaining official American approval of each item. The British Chiefs of Staff found such formalities 'entirely unsatisfactory', since they 'seriously jeopardised' defence arrangements with the old dominions. But self-interest dictated that Britain would distance herself from the old Commonwealth: in the words of a British official – ' "We tell them three-fourths of what we know" '.[81] This meant that the Commonwealth relationship – even if it involved only the old dominions – could never be one among equals, whatever the strength of British rhetoric on the Commonwealth might be. The British would always be the first among not-so-equals. And the Commonwealth could not be the bastion of British security.

If the Anglo–American relationship mirrored Britain's dependence on the US, the Commonwealth reflected her desire to achieve, eventually, equality with the superpowers. The Commonwealth symbolised Britain's global stature, all the more important when her economic predicaments were shaking the foundations of her power. The façade of an undented Commonwealth provided the British with a mental and emotional pillar of unshakeable strength, an aura of unflappability, in a world in which their ability to shape events was dwindling. The Commonwealth was deeply ingrained in the British self-image, perhaps all the more so because it had seldom been defined. This was partly by accident, partly by design. Lord Roseberry is first said to have used the term in 1884, while assuring an Australian audience that the 'fact of your being a nation need not imply any separation from the Empire . . . There is no need for any nation, however great, leaving the Empire, because the Empire is a commonwealth of nations.' British socialists apparently liked the idea of a Commonwealth of communities flying the British flag. That ideologue of the Commonwealth, Lionel Curtis, considered the word 'empire' a misnomer for self-governing nations within the Empire and conceived of a commonwealth of nations. To some, the Commonwealth was synonymous with empire; to others they were coterminous but implied a distinction between colonies and self-governing dominions within the empire. The two did not contradict each other as it was assumed that colonies would eventually achieve self-government. Indeed, as Patrick Gordon Walker, Secretary of State for Commonwealth Relations in the Labour government was to claim, 'There could have been no Commonwealth had there not been a British Empire.'[82]

After 1945, the British had no doubt that the Commonwealth must serve as an independent and strong unit among the world's front-rank powers. The Commonwealth was the wellspring of Britain's power, a manifestation of her global status and an instrument of her foreign policy. Believing that 'Britain's greatness lies in the Commonwealth',[83] Attlee was one of its most enthusiastic protagonists. The Commonwealth gained strength through the united front it presented to the world. In October 1947, the Chiefs described Commonwealth unity as essential to give Britain a chance of survival and victory in war; without the Commonwealth Britain would lose much of her 'effective influence and flexibility of power'. The British desired Indian participation in a system of Commonwealth defence which would be flexible enough to cope with the varying outlooks of its member states, while allowing for a war to be directed from a location other than the UK. The problem was that Commonwealth defence had never been organised formally. The main links between the UK and old dominions from the defence aspect were first, the common allegiance of all Commonwealth members to the Crown; second, their shared belief that any threat to one member would affect the security of the rest of the Commonwealth; and third, kinship, security, commercial and other ties which had been strengthened in two world wars.[84]

Commonwealth relations were not defined by treaty obligations or formal agreements. In practice much would depend on the extent to which Commonwealth governments agreed on the need for a common defence policy. This would require similar political objectives, though in the case of the Commonwealth any difference would 'probably to a great extent be offset by our common allegiance and other ties'. The British also wanted India and other Commonwealth countries to accept only British *matériel* and training for their armed forces. The British desire to standardise equipment and organisation indicated more than the wish to lead, or to retain links with, Commonwealth countries, for, after 1945, they sought the same arrangements with France and the Benelux countries. The dependence of Britain's allies on her for military technology would contribute to building up her primacy among them. The British were in fact disturbed at the prospect of the dominions turning to the US for weaponry. As for India, before independence, Mountbatten had consoled the Labour cabinet that Nehru's opposition to military bases for foreign powers on the subcontinent did not include Britain: the foreign power Nehru 'undoubtedly had in mind was the United States'. After the transfer of power, he reportedly warned Nehru against "dollar imperialism", and the British were apprehensive of Indian approaches to the US for military aid.[85] Against this background Britain wished to build up the Commonwealth as an independent unit among the world's chief powers: with both Western Europe and the Commonwealth behind her, she hoped to become the equal of the superpowers.

Military considerations were not the only factors behind the British interest in keeping India in the Commonwealth. India's membership was seen as highly favourable to Britain's international prestige at a time when the Communist threat intensified in Europe and Asia. Britain's security was tied up with that of West Europe, but most West European countries were then taking the first steps to economic recovery and were too weak to defend themselves against Soviet aggression. The actions of the Soviets enhanced rather than dispelled West European fears: in June 1948 they blockaded Berlin. Earlier, in February, the communists had seized power in Czechoslovakia. In Asia, the outbreak of the communist insurgency in Malaya in June 1948, the ongoing civil war in China in which the communists were gaining the upper hand, the communist challenge to the French empire in Indochina all imbued the traditional British interest in keeping India in the Commonwealth with a new sense of urgency.

The Indians too were concerned at the upswing in communist fortunes. Only a fortnight before the communist take-over, India had named Czechoslovakia as her nominee on the Security Council commission in her dispute with Pakistan. Nehru believed that the communists had used the wrong means to attain power in Czechoslovakia, therefore nothing good could come out of their coup. In January 1949 he told Strang in New Delhi that the results of communism in the USSR 'must in the long run be evil because the means are evil'. India had additional reasons to be disquieted by Soviet behaviour. In Moscow, Indian diplomats were irked and frustrated by the Soviet vilification of India as a campfollower of the West. Between March and October 1948, a series of communist insurrections in Burma, Malaya, the Philippines and Indonesia alarmed the Indians, for the Soviets were also inciting the Communist Party of India to open rebellion. Detecting a Soviet hand in the Telengana uprising in the summer of 1948, Nehru's government crushed it ruthlessly. India's disillusion and annoyance with Britain over Kashmir lingered on, but the Commonwealth offered her an alternative to political isolation at a time when Indo–US relations seemed fated to a state of perennial gestation, and the Soviet Union exhibited relentless hostility. Soviet antipathy to India tipped the scales in favour of Commonwealth membership, and Nehru admitted that he was to some extent acting under 'a certain pressure of circumstances'.[86] But if India and Britain perceived communist threats to their security, it did not mean that India would align herself with Britain or water down her insistence on remaining in the Commonwealth as a republic.

The British were pleased at the resolution passed at the Jaipur session of the Congress in December 1948 which hinted that a republican India would like to maintain all links with the Commonwealth. In January–February 1949, the Treasury, the Board of Trade, the Foreign, Commonwealth Relations and Colonial offices debated the issues involved in having an Indian republic in the Commonwealth: apparently they had by early 1949 come round to the idea that India would not pay allegiance to the Crown. Apart from political and diplomatic factors, economic considerations for and against keeping a republican India in the Commonwealth were also discussed by British officials.

In London, the debates over economic issues took into account Britain's post-war dilemmas and her hopes of sorting them out. Britain's economic dependence on the US reinforced the Labour government's desire to rely on British colonies and the Commonwealth for raw materials and markets. The Labour government regarded colonial development as one solution to the dollar problem. In October 1948 Bevin was optimistic that if Britain pushed on African development, 'we could have [the] US dependent on us, and eating out of our hand, in four or five years. Two great mountains of manganese are in Sierra Leone, etc. [The] US is very barren of essential minerals and in Africa we have them all'.[87] For his part, Cripps thought the British should aim to keep as wide an area as possible of multilateralism based in sterling.

Britain was a debtor at the end of the war, and in August 1946 she owed her largest debt – £1,160 million – to India. This was reduced to £960 million in July 1948 by offsets for military stores left behind and provisions for the payment of pensions of the Raj. In 1947 £35 million were released. Following the collapse of sterling in August 1947, India and Britain negotiated sterling and dollar releases periodically. In January 1948 they agreed that India would get £18 million for six months, of which £10 million would be in dollars. This was because it was felt that the imposition of 'excessive economy' in spending dollars could provoke India into leaving the sterling area. In July 1948 a three-year agreement stipulated that India would receive £40 million over the next two years. But by the end of 1948, Britain's gold and dollar trading deficit rose sharply because of heavy drawings by India and 'seasonal factors'.[88]

India was dissatisfied with Britain's slow repayment of sterling balances.[89] Nevertheless, the Treasury discounted the chances of an indignant Indian walk-out from the sterling area. India's hard-currency deficit was being met in part through the central reserves of the sterling area. Her post-independence food shortage and her need to import consumer goods to counter inflation had created a substantial deficit on her current account which would probably continue. This deficit could only be met through further releases from India's blocked sterling balances, and India was likely to conclude that she would have a better chance of getting generous releases if she remained in the sterling area. Moreover, her recent request to the British government for advice on financial matters indicated her desire to retain close financial ties with the UK. India had in fact a major interest in maintaining the value of sterling markets, since it was in the form of goods purchased for sterling that she would ultimately spend her sterling balances.

The arguments of the Board of Trade and the CRO in favour of keeping India in the Commonwealth should be seen against the background of Britain's post-war export deficit. The Labour government emphasised exports to redress Britain's balance of payments and to close the dollar gap. The colonies and the Commonwealth were to be the springboard of Britain's post-war economic recovery. In September 1947, Bevin dismissed the idea of a European Customs Union on the grounds that Europe handled only 25 per cent of British trade, and he suggested its replacement by a customs union of the Commonwealth and 'certainly of the Empire'.

With Britain giving priority to exports, her chief gain from Indian participation in the Commonwealth revolved round the continuance of imperial preference, which would be difficult, even impossible to maintain if India left the Commonwealth. The British desire to preserve imperial preference went against the American demand that they abolish it. Imperial preferences had been undeniably of great assistance to the British during the slump of the thirties, and were 'still given considerable value'. Preferences bound by the Indo–British Trade Agreement of 1939 covered some 30 per cent of British exports to India or six per cent of British world exports in 1947. These preferences were important to Britain since they fell mostly on items facing competition from the US and Japan. If India left the Commonwealth, Britain would have to treat her as a foreign country and her citizens as aliens. The 'most serious of the practical consequences' would be that other foreign countries whose commercial treaties with Britain included a most-favoured-nation (MFN) clause would be able to claim 'that we should extend to them and their nationals any special benefits or privileges which we accorded to India or her citizens'. Such claims would be 'politically very hard to meet', as they would come mainly from the Brussels Treaty powers, with whom Britain was in the course of establishing 'very close relations'. It would be 'quite impracticable' to avoid the claims of Britain's own allies by terminating all MFN treaties. Such an action would be 'most harmful' to British subjects in those countries, and perhaps to her political relations with them, and British trade and shipping interests would also become vulnerable.

But why should the British wish to give special treatment to Indian nationals and goods if India left the Commonwealth? The Board of Trade and CRO noted that treating Indians in the UK as aliens would affect their rights of entry, residence and activity. These rights were 'at present the only interest . . . which India has in the United Kingdom to balance the United Kingdom's much greater interests in India'. India could retaliate if the activities of Indians in the UK were curtailed, and the upshot would be discrimination against British commercial banking, insurance, trade and shipping interests in India. Their capital value was anything between £150 to £600 million and the invisible earnings of this capital accounted for £20 million a year in covering the British balance of payments with India. Under a MFN treaty they would be liable to higher taxation as foreign firms, whereas at present they were treated as national firms. Consequently there would be severe effects on British companies, especially in relation to taxation, which could substantially reduce their invisible earnings. There was no certainty that British economic privileges would continue if India remained in the Commonwealth, but if she did, Britain could 'always claim – on that basis – to be accorded rather better treatment than any foreign third country. There would be no hope of this if we, too, became foreigners in India'. Anticipated Indian restrictions on foreign investments compounded British fears, and they expended some effort in trying to convince the Indian government that the British were not foreigners. On 13 August 1948 Sir Terence Shone, then High Commissioner in New Delhi, told Nehru that

. . . India being a Commonwealth country the nationals of other Commonwealth countries should be given more favoured treatment than nationals of other countries. Indeed he said that they did not like being referred to as foreign interests and would prefer to be called non-Indian interests in India because of their long association with India. Normally the most favoured nation treatment which might apply to . . . the USA or *any other like country* should have no bearing on Commonwealth countries which still stood somewhat apart because of the Commonwealth nexus and should therefore be given somewhat better treatment.[90]

The preferential treatment enjoyed by India in the UK covered some 50–60 per cent of her total exports to Britain.[91] As a primary producer,

India would be affected only marginally by the removal of preferences. She would be able to find other markets for her goods, and it was unlikely that any country would significantly want to restrict her exports. Preferences enjoyed by the British in India were not given to other dominions at that time. They covered manufactured goods such as motor vehicles, cycles, chemical preparations, electrical apparatus and cotton piece-goods. Their value was difficult to assess since 'we are afforded a measure of defence' against foreign competition by quantitative import restrictions on goods from hard-currency countries and the Indian demand for consumer goods. In the long run their value would be 'considerable' especially with the re-emergence of Germany, Japan and other European countries as competitors. If British goods were accorded MFN treatment, this would mean that British cotton piece-goods would face a high protective tariff of 60 per cent and would compete on equal terms with Japanese cotton goods, while local production would be protected by the 60 per cent *ad valorem* duty. The British would also have to compete on equal terms with foreign suppliers of several products, worth £12 million in 1938, £27 million in 1947 or 30 per cent of their total 1947 exports to India.

Also, as India's development plans bore fruit, she would produce more goods herself and her market for imports would decline. Even if India stayed in the Commonwealth, Britain could lose imperial preferences, but she could then strive to retain them as long as possible and extract maximum negotiating advantage from their withdrawal which she could not do, 'if we lose our *right* to have preferences at all'. Consequently, British exports to India would ultimately drop to 'a mere trickle of high-quality specialities, and any hope of recovering our pre-war position in the market, itself a mere shadow of our former state, will be irretrievably lost'.

On the whole, then, British trading interests would be worst affected if India left the Commonwealth. As long as she remained a member, existing safeguards for preferences could be expressed in general terms in commercial treaties, so that it would be possible for India to give Commonwealth countries all kinds of preferences without the risk of challenge by foreign countries. Her leaving the Commonwealth would render necessary the enshrining of any such favours in formal treaty clauses. In this shape they would become much more open to challenge by foreign countries on MFN grounds in the International Court of Justice and correspondingly harder to obtain from India. Indeed the chances of obtaining even informal unilateral assurances from India would be poor. A hostile India might not accord British goods MFN treatment, while being free to grant American companies and goods more favourable treatment than to Commonwealth countries. The Commonwealth connection would not necessarily dissuade India from applying discriminatory measures against British goods and companies, if she regarded these as being in her national interest. But India's retention in the Commonwealth offered 'the best hope' of maintaining friendly economic relations and obtaining 'fair treatment' for other

Commonwealth nationals in India. All in all, Britain's economic interests entailed keeping a republican India in the Commonwealth.

Summing up the political and diplomatic considerations, the Foreign Office noted that Nehru's emphasis on nonalignment and the abolition of colonialism suggested that he was interested in achieving leadership of an Asia from which all Western influence had been excluded and that this took precedence over the struggle against communism or any conception of Commonwealth solidarity.[92] This was not an accurate interpretation of Nehru's views. Nehru wished to see a continuance of Western influences and culture in Asia, but he wanted an end to colonial domination and the withdrawal of Western military forces which were its symbol. Nehru was aware that it was not only Western intervention which was unwelcome to Asians; intervention by India would equally be regarded as "foreign intervention".[93] Either the Foreign Office genuinely misunderstood Nehru, or they tended to equate a tangible military presence with "Western influence". The Foreign Office rightly noted that India's adherence to the UN and her economic dependence on the Commonwealth – 45 per cent of her total trade was with the Commonwealth and 28 per cent with the UK – implied that it would not be in her interest to break completely with the Commonwealth. The presence of a republican India might be construed by the world as a sign of of Britain's post-war weakness and of her desperation to hang on to the Commonwealth at any cost. But this would be outweighed by the advantage of a republican India which wanted to join rather than secede from the Commonwealth. The size and power of the Commonwealth would be preserved in the eyes of the world, 'and particularly of potential aggressors', and such a settlement would be 'a further tribute to the Anglo-Saxon genius for compromise'.[94]

Continuing consultation and collaboration with India would afford the best opportunity to influence her foreign policy. Britain's imperial concerns could also benefit. The Colonial Office thought that India's presence in the Commonwealth would encourage moderate nationalists in the colonies who were less likely than their more extremist counterparts to demand a complete severance of ties with the Commonwealth.[95] India in the Commonwealth might even help to preserve the rest of the empire. 'There may be some advantage', mused Sir Gilbert Laithwaite, then at the CRO, 'given the great negro population of the Colonial Empire, in avoiding any suggestion that the Commonwealth is a White Man's Club'.[96]

India's secession from the Commonwealth would also have world-wide repercussions. The USSR had voted for the admission to the UN of Burma, which had left the Commonwealth while vetoing the application of Ceylon, which remained a member, and India's departure from the Commonwealth might be exploited to the full. India might come under Soviet influence and show 'greater intransigence' in world affairs.[97]

For the Chiefs it mattered little whether or not India remained in the Commonwealth – what was of import was a friendly India. On 14 February

1949, they suggested that India should be given assistance, even if she left the Commonwealth, to encourage her to take the lead against communism. By the beginning of April 1949, the Chiefs had concluded that India was unlikely to agree to any treaty which demanded 'mutual defence plans' with Britain 'for a region of common interest'. They left it to the cabinet to decide whether defence co-operation should grow out of 'the existing friendly relationship' with India.[98]

The cabinet favoured taking the risk. With British forces locked in battle with communist guerrillas in Malaya since the summer of 1948, they found the threat of communist encroachment in Southeast Asia 'very real'. With India in the Commonwealth, the British would maintain 'a solid front against communist domination in the East'. On 27 April 1949, Attlee recommended to the King that a republican India be allowed to stay in the Commonwealth, and on 27 April 1949, the Commonwealth Prime Ministers' conference in London endorsed his decision.[99] The sun had set on the British empire; would it ever rise on the New Commonwealth?

X BRITAIN'S PRIORITIES: COMMONWEALTH OR ANGLO–AMERICAN RELATIONSHIP?

Decolonisation in South Asia in August 1947 was not the result of a long-term British plan; it was carried out at a time when Britain hoped to remain the leading world power and had every intention of keeping India within her global defence network and preserving the substance of *Pax Britannica*. Unconditional independence for India and the creation of Pakistan were the unintended outcome of a decolonisation which resulted from British weakness in the final trial of strength with the Congress and the Muslim League. They marked the end of British hopes of using the subcontinent as a strategic base and dismantled the imperial security system. Anticipating opposition from the Congress to any talk of military ties, the British never discussed them with Indian leaders before the transfer of power. They pinned their faith on staff conversations with India after independence, but Indian nonalignment determined that these would never materialise.

This did not mean that India cut off all military and economic links with Britain. Indian independence opened the door to amicable Indo–British relations; to friendship between Labour and Congress leaders, Nehru and the Mountbattens. Nehru also cultivated warm personal ties with Churchill, who had once thought that Nehru had good reason to be Britain's 'bitterest enemy'; and with Eden, who in 1945 had seen little prospect of a political settlement in India as long as Gandhi was alive.[100]

Independence opened a new and cordial Indo–British dialogue on bilateral and international issues. Indeed, it is remarkable that Indo–British diplomatic exchanges were more frequent and much closer than diplomatic contacts between Britain and Pakistan, which sought alignment with the West soon after partition and eventually enrolled in Western military pacts.

However, the path to warm post-independence relations between India and Britain was not strewn with roses, and inevitably the roses had their thorns. Soon after his arrival in New Delhi as High Commissioner, Sir Terence Shone was astonished at 'the unbridled taunts, criticisms, innuendos and misrepresentations levelled against the United Kingdom'.[101] At another level, Harrow and Cambridge left their social and intellectual imprint on Nehru, but they never made a loyalist collaborator of him. In fact, Nehru and Gandhi spent a total of nine and eleven years respectively in prison for their anti-Raj activities. Nor could any personal friendliness disguise the fact that nonalignment was in the first instance a move away from *Britain* which frustrated British hopes of retaining the substance of their "great power" after decolonisation. The new amicability did not soften the determination of Nehru's government that India should become a republic, and India only agreed to stay in the Commonwealth on that condition. Britain remained the main source of arms and economic aid to Pakistan until 1954, and to India until the mid-sixties, but this was qualified by the fact that India and Pakistan did not identify with British interests, and after independence and partition, they were the masters of their own foreign policies. As Shone concluded with sad realism: 'The old trainer has gone; the old rider has been unseated, or has abandoned the saddle – whichever way one looks at it. The filly must be free to run under her own colours and with trainers and riders of her own choosing.'[102]

In 1949, the British broke with precedent and welcomed a republican India into the Commonwealth. That decision was taken in the knowledge that the New Commonwealth would reflect the shadow rather than the substance of their "great power". What it still preserved was the façade of their power; in the changed political, military and economic circumstances created by the cold war it was a political device aimed at avoiding any impression that the Commonwealth and British power were disintegrating. But it would never be the pivot of Britain's foreign policy and the cornerstone of her security. As the Chiefs summed up, 'The Anglo–American association, which is governed by no treaty and no Statue [sic] of Westminister, is far more effective and far more powerful than the association of U.K. [sic] and the rest of the Commonwealth.'[103] At the same time, the Empire–Commonwealth still made up the weft and warp of the British self-image as a global power, the unconscious habit of thinking like a great power, even as the Anglo–American relationship signified the recognition that Britain was no longer an independent world power. Reconciling necessity and tradition or habit would be like putting together the pieces of a jigsaw puzzle. Would Britain, with her influence diluted by domestic and external constraints, complete the picture by balancing herself among her relationships with an American ally self-righteously determined to save the noncommunist world; an India equally self-righteously convinced that she could save herself, and a Pakistan wanting the West to save her not from communism but from India? Britain would have to take into account two newly born states at loggerheads with each other; and they would have a bearing on her relationship with the United States in the Asian cold war and in the Middle East.

2. Britain, the US and South Asia, 1947–9: priorities, perceptions and the cold war

I BRITAIN RENEWS HER STAKE IN ASIA

India is the key to the whole problem of South-East Asian regional co-operation. [Permanent Under Secretary's Committee Final Report, 20 August 1949]

. . . it would be unwise for us to regard south [sic] Asia, more particularly India, as the sole bulwark against the extension of communist control in Asia. [NSC 48/1, 23 December 1949]

The one point on which the British and Americans concurred was that there was no Soviet military threat to South Asia. The subcontinent was therefore not a major theatre of the cold war. But Britain and the USA were world powers, and their global interests delineated their images of India and Pakistan. This did not necessarily imply complete accord or a common policy in the area. Geography, history, strategic interests and their individual self-images all went into the making of their dissimilar mental pictures of India and Pakistan.

How did the British see India in the cold war in which the USSR was Britain's archenemy? Britain's security priorities were Europe, which was exposed to Soviet aggression, and the Middle East, where her dominant post-war position was challenged by regional nationalisms, especially in Egypt and Iran. A Soviet threat to India and Pakistan receives the odd mention in official documents: for example, in June 1948 the Chiefs of Staff regarded the USSR as 'the only potential threat' to India and Pakistan, and that too in a discussion on keeping India in the Commonwealth, in which they enumerated the 'Military Advantages to India and Pakistan of Remaining in the Commonwealth'.[1] But they did not expect a world war within the next five years, so it would appear that they reckoned a Soviet assault on the subcontinent to be a distant scenario. From their general lack of emphasis on South Asia, one can deduce that they did not antici-pate the cold war spreading there. The old idea of "defending" the North-West Frontier did arise, but it was no longer a British responsibility.

Pakistan had inherited that burden from them, but she could not carry it without India's assistance. And as the British did not foresee an early abatement of Indo–Pakistani tension, the inference was that the North-West Frontier would remain undefended against the Soviets. However, this does not seem to have occasioned any great alarm among British officials, probably because a Soviet threat to that area was not visible. Had one really existed, it is most unlikely that it would have received only cursory references in post-1947 British memos: after all, a Soviet presence – or even mere designs – on the North-West Frontier would have imperilled the British position in the Middle East. Decolonisation in South Asia may have absolved the British from responsibility for the defence of the Frontier; what is somewhat more remarkable is that the Russian menace – real or imagined – which had afforded a pretext for existence of the Raj for almost a century, finds scant mention in official records after the British pulled out of the subcontinent. It was a telling example of how the perception of a threat can be conjured up or waved away by the presence or withdrawal of a great power from a particular position and by changed political circumstances.

If India was not a major arena of the cold war, what strategic role did the British envisage for her? Many British officials, including Attlee, Cripps, Mountbatten and the Chiefs of Staff, thought that India's presence in the Commonwealth and defence links with her would facilitate Britain's survival as a front-rank international power. They criticised Indian neutralism as fence-sitting and escapism and berated the rivalry between India and Pakistan and their inability to think in 'global' terms.[2] This implied that India and Pakistan should identify with Britain's global interests and their armed forces should participate in imperial defence. But what was glossed over in the strictures of Indian neutralism was the coincidence of outlook between the Indians and British that there was no Soviet military threat to South Asia. The British did not ask themselves why India should identify with their causes, especially if these included the maintenance of the empire as a symbol of *Britain's* international prestige and power. Also overlooked was the cold-shouldering of Pakistan's gratuitous applications for membership of a Middle East defence association, and it was anticipated that Pakistan, like India, would remain neutral in a world war.[3] The British did not question India's democratic credentials. However, while Indian officials assured American policy-makers of New Delhi's support in a world war, they do not appear to have given similar assurances to the British. At no time after Indian independence did British officials assume, or seem reasonably confident of, Indian backing for the West in a war, although many of them hoped for military ties with India.[4]

Keeping India in the Commonwealth was aimed at preserving the façade, if not the substance, of *Pax Britannica*, and its importance was enhanced by the cold war in Asia. For Britain, the Asian cold war began with the outbreak of the communist insurgency and the declaration of the emergency in June 1948 in Malaya. Officials including William Strang, Permanent Under-Secretary in the Foreign Office, Esler Dening, Assistant Under-Secretary and Malcolm Macdonald, Commissioner-General in Southeast Asia articulated an Asian cold war policy between February and August 1949.[5] Their basic premiss was that an independent Third Force led by Britain and the Commonwealth was not feasible and that Britain would be dependent on the US in Europe and Asia. They conceived Britain's role in the Asian cold war in the context of Britain's post-war economic frailty and her inability to increase military engagements overseas. Britain sought to remain an Asian and global power despite her manifold travails and to preserve her imperial niche in Malaya, Hong Kong and Borneo. Diplomacy, then, would of necessity be the main instrument of her influence. This was no misfortune, since British officials did not perceive a Soviet military threat to Asia.

However, the outbreak of communist-inspired insurrections in Burma, Indonesia and the Philippines in 1948–9 persuaded the British that the Soviets still aimed at world hegemony and roused their fears that the Stalinist technique could succeed without an actual invasion. The post-partition bitterness and poor economic conditions in India and Pakistan jeopardised their political stability and made them a fertile breeding ground for communism. In Southeast Asia, the prospect of communist successes was not fanciful. The British were engaged in combat with communist guerrillas in Malaya; communist-tinged nationalisms appeared to be gaining the upper hand in Indochina and Indonesia, and, in the Chinese civil war, a communist triumph appeared likely.

How could Asian communism be contained? The answer to this question lay in the British perception of their own role in the Asian cold war.[6] In Malaya they were challenged by communist subversion, but Southeast Asia came third on the list of their strategic priorities, after Europe and the Middle East. Britain's interests in Europe and the Middle East were already overstretching her limited economic resources, ruling out an extension of her military involvement in Southeast Asia. This did not, however, diminish Britain's desire or claim to be an Asian power. Officials started from the premiss that while Britain could not dominate Southeast Asia, she was, among the Western powers, in the best position to contain regional communism. Britain was an Asian power because of her links, through the Commonwealth, with India, Pakistan and Ceylon; her ties in the Western Union with the French and the Dutch, and her possession of Malaya, Hong Kong and Borneo. Britain's Asian credentials were thus justified in terms of her connections with both the newly independent South Asian nations *and* European colonial powers. Officials then built up Britain's claim to a 'particular position' not enjoyed by other Western powers in Asia. The Americans had the greatest volume of trade with the Far East and Southeast Asia, but their standing was not as high as that of the British, partly because they lacked historical connections with the area, partly because of the failure of their China policy, partly because of their reluctance to take the lead in Southeast Asia. The Dutch and the French had imperial stakes in the region, but because of their defeat at Nazi hands in 1940 they lacked the prestige of the British and were regarded 'merely as liberated nations' by Asians, in whose eyes they also carried the stigma of colonialism. The British glossed over the possibility that their possession of Malaya and Hong Kong might earn them a similar stigma. Perhaps this was because the Malay élites were collaborating with them against the communists. There was no question of withdrawal from Malaya and Hong Kong, which would be construed by the communists as a defeat for Britain. The British did not anticipate much pressure from other Asian countries on this score. Despite strong opposition to colonialism, Indian officials had described the Malayan communists as 'bandits' and 'terrorists' and had not criticised British military action to suppress them. While they expected a communist triumph in the Chinese civil war, the Indians did not think that Britain could be forced out of Hong Kong. London happily concluded that Britain enjoyed a position of advantage in Asia. This should be used to engender closer co-operation between East and West, otherwise there was 'a very real danger that the whole of Asia will become the servant of the Kremlin'.

If there was no Soviet military threat to South or Southeast Asia, why should Britain need to "protect" the region, and how should she do it? The improbability of Soviet agression made it unnecessary to offer Asian countries large-scale military aid. This argument suited a Britain which was unable to offer such assistance. But the will of local peoples to resist internal communism in Asian countries should be strengthened. This could best be achieved by promoting economic development in South and Southeast Asia, and by bringing Asian countries together in a regional economic association. There would be obstacles in its path. All Asian countries were very suspicious of anything that smacked of Western imperialism or dictation, and a regional association might well acquire anti-Western overtones. But if mutual interest, equality and co-operation were assured, this danger could be overcome. Britain's Asian horizons were wide: if a common front could be built up from Afghanistan to Indochina, it should be possible to contain a Russian advance southwards and to preserve communications for the West across the middle of the world.

One question does arise. Since the "common front" would not have any military teeth, and a Soviet advance was envisaged only in a remote, even unforeseeable future, why should Britain shoulder new and indefensible "responsibilities"? Officials admitted that the British were enlarging the area of their interests in Asia which they would not be able to defend in a war. One cannot help wondering whether the case for a "common front" was really another pretext to preserve and extend British influence in Asia, in spite of the economic and military constraints imposed by Britain's postwar predicaments. Withdrawal from Asia because of her domestic encumbrances would destroy Britain's Asian credentials and leave a void in the global edifice of British power. The British dilemma was how to uphold their international position despite diminshed economic and military resources. To them, the cold war justified the preservation of British power. Since officials had started from the assumption of British indispensability in Asia, the distinction between the maintenance of British power as a means of containment and as an end in itself was not clear.

It is in relation to the idea of containing communism through regional collaboration that one should see the importance given India in the Asian cold war. 'India is the key to the whole problem of South-East Asian regional co-operation.' The British vision of India's position in Southeast Asia was moulded by the memory, still fresh in the official mind, of her role as the nucleus of the Southeast Asia Command during the Second World War. Additionally, the fact that the British had not undertaken any major revision of their strategic planning after decolonisation in South Asia probably accounted for the perpetuation of their traditional strategic image of India, especially since Britain retained her control of key communication points in the Indian Ocean. In 1949, Britain's immediate Asian interests – Malaya, Borneo and Hong Kong – lay at the eastern end of a maritime route through the Middle East, the Persian Gulf, India, Burma, Malaya to Singapore and Hong Kong. The basic geopolitical point emerging from the memos of Strang, Dening and Macdonald was that India was not only situated in the very centre of this route, but more dramatically, as Strang informed the cabinet in February 1949, she was placed half-way round a periphery skirting the USSR from Oslo to Tokyo, so the British could never lose sight of her when formulating an Asian policy. It is significant that all three of them highlighted India's political standing before the cabinet decision in March 1949 to allow a republican India in the Commonwealth; and they probably overcame Bevin's reluctance to this unprecedented move.

The Commonwealth Prime Ministers decided to keep a republican India in the Commonwealth on 27 April 1949. Coming just three weeks after the formation of NATO, Indian membership of the Commonwealth had pro-Western hues. British officials nevertheless anticipated problems in securing Indian collaboration in a regional association. India would be suspicious that her participation in a Western-sponsored regional grouping would entangle her with the power blocs. She would also be hostile to British colonialism, and I.M.R. Maclennan of the CRO cautioned that 'it might not be an unmixed blessing for us if India were to take an active part in building up a South East Asian front. Pandit Nehru's ideas about Colonialism are well-known.'[7] Dening concurred that Nehru might strive to build up an anti-Western front. But if he failed to do so, 'then there will be no front, which would also be disadvantageous to Western interests, because without a united front Communism may be expected to make good headway in the region'.[8] On the other hand, India could be an asset to Britain in Southeast Asia. Decolonisation was proof of Britain's democratic intentions; it would avoid any charge of colonial domination, even while the British clung to Malaya, Hong Kong and Borneo. India's suspicions about colonialism, her fear of being 'used as a pawn in a European–Moscow chess match' could be overcome by using the Commonwealth as the starting point of regional collaboration. The Commonwealth approach would also allay Pakistani and Ceylonese fears of *India's* lead in a regional association, since Britain, Australia and New Zealand would be involved as well. On balance the British viewed their friendly ties with India as a character reference for their progressive and democratic intentions in Asia.

Moreover, India needed economic aid. Under the Commonwealth umbrella, the British could retain the initiative in Asia, while ensuring that India did not work against them in the region. British leadership of the Commonwealth would assure other Asians that regional collaboration was 'not another name for Greater India or Mahabharat'.[9] The inference was that Britain would "save" Asia from communism as well as Indian domination, and it bolstered the case for her indispensability in Asia. That Asian countries should not want to be under India's thumb was understandable and was acknowledged by Nehru; why Asians should prefer to take directions from the British was not asked. This was probably because officials presumed that British influence was essential to contain Asian communism and then searched for ways to make it attractive to Asians. They viewed India and the Commonwealth as the means to convince Asians of Britain's concern for their well-being and to forge regional economic collaboration. Such collaboration would be the chief instrument of what would essentially be diplomatic containment, while the British would guide the Commonwealth–Asian front along an anti-communist path. Echoing the advice of his officials in April 1949, Bevin urged a more active British interest in Southeast Asia, if only to prevent India from stealing a march on Britain. 'If we wait too long', he warned Attlee, 'we may find ourselves no longer able to influence the situation', since a tendency was developing on Nehru's part 'to issue invitations to conferences without asking the United Kingdom'. So he took up Macdonald's suggestion for a Commonwealth Prime Ministers' conference to address economic problems in Southeast Asia.[10] Macdonald's advice contained the seeds of the Colombo plan, which was presented to the Commonwealth Prime Ministers' conference in January 1950. The idea of economic cooperation to contain communism and to preserve Britain's leverage in Asia cut across party lines and was taken up by the Conservative administration after 1951. As Lord Reading, Minister of State for Foreign Affairs, summed up in 1954, the Colombo Plan had great political significance, 'negatively as a valuable anti-Communist influence and positively as a powerful link with the West and as such an effective counter to the "Asia for the Asians" cry'.[11] But intrinsic to the British strategy of regional economic collaboration was their appreciation of the strength of emerging nationalisms in Asia. To give only two illustrations, in August 1950 Bevin stressed that since the end of the war, 'the policy of His Majesty's Government in South and South-East Asia has been to encourage the legitimate aspirations of the peoples of the area for independence'.[12] And in October 1951, R.H. Scott, then Assistant Under-Secretary of State in the Foreign Office, reiterated that the first objective of British policy in the Far East was to establish good relations between Western and Asian powers on a basis of equality, respect and mutual interest.[13] The point was underlined frequently by British officials in their memos and to the Americans after 1949. British policy was dictated partly by their reluctance and inability to expand militarily in Asia, partly by their desire to harness Asian nationalisms to their interests and to retain pre-eminence in Asia. Once again, the case for British influence as a means of containing communism easily became a justification for the preservation of British influence in Asia as an end in itself.

II THE UNITED STATES AND SOUTH ASIA: 1947–9

Early in 1949, Strang's assertion that the British had a unique role to play in Southeast Asia was qualified by his recognition that they could not play it alone. The best course would be to combine British experience with American resources. The chances of Britain persuading the US to subsidise her position in Asia would depend in large measure on US relations with India, which was the keystone of Britain's strategy of diplomatic containment, and this in turn would hinge on the importance the US attached to South Asia. In a world in which great powers could dominate but not necessarily order the international system to their liking, much would also depend on whether India would be amenable to Western advice.

Few countries illustrate better than India the divergence between the American and British world views. The British were convinced that a close association with the Indian subcontinent would enhance their international stature and ward off Asian communism; in contrast, South Asia hardly occupied any place in the American self-image or historical imagination.[14] History partly accounted for the difference. The US had few historical links with the area. There was no American Clive to found an Indian empire; no Kipling to glorify and romanticise the "White Man's Burden"; no Mountbatten to relinquish it with grandeur. American interests in Asia centred round the Pacific; it was China which seized the American imagination as India did the British. As a result of the Pacific War, America's military frontier extended from Alaska and the Aleutian Islands to Japan, Okinawa, Korea and the Philippines.

Only the imperatives of the Second World War roused some American interest in India. Following the Japanese attacks on Pearl Harbor and Singapore in 1941, the allies sought greater Indian co-operation with the war effort, and in January 1942 Roosevelt urged the British to quicken the pace of political advance. How and why this came to be construed by many British officials as American pressure to put an end to the Raj is beyond the scope of this book, and only a few suggestions can be offered. Perhaps it was because of a long-standing American perception of the US as a champion of anti-imperial movements and the American habit of lecturing the British, time and again, on the moral evils of empire. Roosevelt has sometimes been perceived as an anti-imperial idealist who wanted the French and British to wind up their empires. But recent research[15] suggests the need to distinguish between myth, rhetoric and reality and also to recognise the prevalence of complex strains in an attitude to empire which was a mix of idealism, pragmatism, racism, Churchillian influence – and which gave priority, above all, to American security interests. It is arguable that strategic considerations were at the root of Roosevelt's exhortations to the British in 1942. Political and military concerns and the overriding importance of maintaining harmony within the Western alliance induced the Roosevelt administration to take a conciliatory attitude to colonial empires during the war. For example, in August 1942, Roosevelt had advance notice of British plans to quell the Quit India movement, and he viewed with substantial sympathy Churchill's repressive course against Indian nationalists.[16]

American and British notions of American anti-imperialism have to be considered alongside Indian dismay at US apathy to Indian nationalism. As political and social unrest surged in India after the end of the war, American prestige and popularity were at a low ebb.[17] It is not even clear whether American officials really wanted an end to the Raj or to European empires. They realised that the US was not omnipotent and needed allies in the cold war. European colonies guaranteed bases, economic resources and markets to the US, while nationalism had a potentially anti-Western tinge.[18] Moreover, an anti-imperial idealism did not necessarily imply a liking of nationalism. In January 1947, Henry Grady, then ambassador to New Delhi, decried the growing sense of Indian nationalism which often manifested itself in criticism of the UK and US. Truman's response to Grady's complaint was succinct: 'the attitude of Asia toward the United States and Great Britain is one that is to be expected and all we can do is to try to live it down.'[19] The tension between the American anti-imperialist self-image and the Indian perception of the US buttressing European colonialists was to recur. A few months after Indian independence, Grady was indignant at Nehru's tendency to tar the US with the imperialistic brush and his overlooking what Grady thought was American support for the Indian national movement.[20] Putting pressure on the British to grant a larger measure of self-government in furtherance of Western security interests was one thing; coping with nationalist criticism of the US when its colonial allies appeared to be safeguarding those interests was another. As the State Department admitted in May 1948, 'Our current involvement with these [European] powers is necessarily so great that no effective means of overcoming Indian suspicions of our motives with respect to dependent areas has yet been found.'[21] The US did not anticipate an easy time in South Asia: American diplomats in New Delhi and Karachi thought that India and Pakistan possessed only a thin veneer of Western culture. Islamic Pakistan might look westwards through the Middle East, but India was seen as being primarily oriental – and by implication anti-West – in outlook.[22]

The American anti-imperialist ideal and the concern with strategic interests cut across each other. At one level, in March 1946, the State Department contemplated sending a congratulatory message to the Labour government for announcing their intention to negotiate an independence settlement with the Congress and Muslim League. The idea did not appeal to Attlee. 'It looks like a pat on the back to us from a rich uncle who sees us turning over a new leaf', he commented acerbically.[23] On another plane, American officials thought that decolonisation weakened their European allies, and that the emergence of newly independent states put a question mark over American access to their strategic resources.

Britain was unquestionably America's chief ally. Britain's power and her value as an ally stemmed from her industrial production, the competence of her armed forces, and the world-wide extension of the Commonwealth and empire, with its numerous bases for military use and its resources of men and materials. Some US officials looked on Indian independence as a post-war retrenchment measure by a financially weak Britain, which had been unwilling or unable 'to hold off the violent demands of the Indian nationalists'.[24] The State-Army-Navy-Air Force-Co-ordinating Committee (SANACC) regarded South Asia as politically and economically uncertain after the British withdrawal. Washington assumed that the British would try to preserve the substance of their power in India and retain access to military bases in India and Pakistan. Between January 1946 and 1948, the Near Eastern and African Department (NEA) wanted the British to achieve satisfactory political settlements in South Asia so as to be able to pursue their global strategy. They also hoped that British ideas of military co-operation with India and Pakistan would succeed (although the content of that co-operation was not defined). American policy-makers realised that the British would not be able to impose their will on India and Pakistan. In a negative sense, India and Pakistan 'must be considered the military equals of British power within this area, since they can deny access to their territory and resources.'[25] The Americans hardly raised the question whether India would want such arrangements. This reflected a tacit difference about the meaning and substance of independence as seen through the eyes of American officials and Indian nationalists. To the Indians, the use of the Indian army by the British had reflected their subservient status; the decision not to have military links with Britain was a political decision, symbolising sovereignty in foreign policy. The point seems to have eluded American officials.

Concern for Western security was the overarching theme in official American debates on South Asia. After August 1947, the Americans were content to entrust the British with the task of wooing India and Pakistan to the Western bloc. The idea of India being a British domain even after independence was quite widespread among American policy-makers and was favoured to the extent of ignoring Indian sensitivities about their independent foreign policy. In response to an assertion by Girija Shankar Bajpai, Secretary General in the Ministry for External Affairs, that India was responsible for her own foreign policy, Loy Henderson, then ambassador in New Delhi, tactlessly – if truthfully – asserted that India was 'still a new state', and it would take Americans time to adjust to the 'altered world situation'.[26] The fact was that Henderson, like many other US officials, relied on the British to steer India to the West. The Americans were content that the British were safeguarding Western interests, and one does not sense much feeling of competition on the American side. The stability of the Commonwealth was 'a major objective' of US foreign policy. The Americans regarded Indian membership of the Commonwealth as a triumph of British statesmanship; it would enable the Commonwealth to dominate the Indian Ocean and to continue to support the US in the Far East. It would also keep India well-disposed towards the West. Essential US security interests were 'adequately' looked after by the British and illustrated that US influence need not be jeopardised by decolonisation if the new state and former imperialist power maintained amicable connections.[27] The emphasis was on what *Britain* had achieved; the Indian government was not given any credit for the foreign policy which had made possible the burying of past bitterness and the building up of new and friendly ties with the British. It was a view *de haut en bas* in which India was viewed as a pawn useful to the British – and to the West – in the cold-war chess game; when seen as an independent actor, she was not considered especially sympathetic to the West. As we shall note on many occasions in this book, independence of Indian thought and action, when it asserted itself against the US, came as a disagreeable shock to American officials.

How did South Asia fit into the policy of containment? Like their British counterparts, US officials realised that India and Pakistan were of their own volition cool to the USSR and that the Soviets would find it very difficult to invade the subcontinent. Local communist parties did not pose a strong challenge to their democratic governments, who were expected to remain in power for the next five years. The tradition-bound societies of India and Pakistan would be resistant to communism, while the intellectual classes of both countries were appreciative of Western culture and were turning to the US for economic and military aid. The US was the outstanding or only source of the capital goods, technical and financial assistance necessary for their economic development. The Indian and Pakistani armies were equipped with British and US *matériel*, and so long as they remained dependent on the West they were unlikely to turn against it.[28] At this stage there was no conflict of interest between the British and Americans on South Asia being in the British sphere of influence, and the US looked on Britain as a collaborator, even a surrogate, on the subcontinent.

To a global power like the United States, the "loss" of any part of the world to the Soviets would constitute a defeat in the struggle against international communism; the loss of South Asia, with its economic and military potential, its vast population and military bases, would 'gravely affect' the security of the US. Because of its geographical position, the subcontinent could dominate the Indian Ocean region and exert a strong influence on the Middle East, Central Asia and the Far East. Air bases at Karachi, Rawalpindi and Peshawar might prove important in conducting air operations against the industrial areas of the Soviet heartland or in defending Middle East oil, while the sea lanes leading to Indian and Pakistani ports were safe from attack by Soviet air or naval forces. But this description of South Asia by the SANACC in April 1949[29] referred to the *potential* importance of the region to the US and not to immediate American priorities. Exactly how "vital" was South Asia in the fight against communism?

The essential fact was that the US neither discerned any external Soviet threat to the subcontinent, nor foresaw the prospect of successful communist subversion. The Americans also regarded South Asia as British terrain. The State Department affirmed that 'it would appear to be in our interest that the British continue to have, from the global point of view, the paramount responsibility for the maintenance of international peace and security in South Asia.' For all these reasons, the Americans did not give South Asia high priority. In March 1949, the US Chiefs thought that the Soviet Union had 'more remunerative objectives' in Europe and the Middle East, and in the event of war was unlikely to expend 'any substantial military effort' in South Asia. A few months later, the SANACC placed India and Pakistan in the fourth of seven groups of countries listed in order of significance to the US.[30] The low ranking given South Asia moulded American responses to Indian and Pakistani appeals for economic and military largesse. The inference was that there was no confluence of interest at this stage between India, Pakistan and the US – the confluence was between Britain and the US on the British role in South Asia. The point is important, since it was American disapprobation of the British role in the Middle East and South Asia, and the congruence of US and Pakistani interests which were, eventually, to pave the way for American military aid to Pakistan in 1953–4.

Soon after Pakistan's creation in August 1947, some American officials noted her potential attractions to the US, but there were few pointers to an early convergence of US and Pakistani interests. Unlike India, which made nonalignment the hallmark of her foreign policy, Pakistan's fear of India motivated her pleas for military links with the US soon after partition. In October 1947 Pakistan went to the US with a long military shopping list which suggests that she was trying to get help from wherever possible. Pakistan asked for financial assistance for a five-year period to build up her armed forces. She requested $170 million to build up an army of 100,000, consisting of one armoured division, five infantry divisions, a small cavalry establishment; to replace and remodel existing arms and equipment and to pay personnel. For the Air Force, Pakistan wanted $75 million for twelve fighter squadrons, three bomber squadrons of fifty aircraft, four transport squadrons and 400 training wings of 200 aeroplanes as well as funds for ground facilities and payment of personnel. Pakistan estimated that $60 million would be needed to build up a navy of four light cruisers, sixteen destroyers and other facilities.[31]

The American response highlighted the disparate political interests and priorities of the US and Pakistan. The SANACC observed that Pakistan was thinking of the US as a primary source of military strength and that a positive US reply would involve 'virtual U.S. military responsibility for the new dominion'. No legal authority existed to grant such financial aid to Pakistan – probably because the US had not yet formulated a military policy for South Asia. The State Department also noted that the British military role in the subcontinent was unclear,[32] and the Americans showed little inclination to jostle with the British in the region. The main reason for the negative response to Pakistan's plea was the subcontinent's low ranking in the US diplomatic and strategic pecking order. For example, in February 1948, when discussing Asia, a PPS report concentrated on the Far East.

To the US Chiefs of Staff, India and Pakistan did not meet criteria which determined American military priorities such as strategic location, terrain and economic ability of a country to support a military programme against the Soviets. The troops of India and Pakistan were hardly sufficient to meet their internal security requirements. As Pakistan's relations with her neighbours, India and Afghanistan, were likely to remain strained for some time, it would be unrealistic to upgrade her in American priorities. India and Pakistan were classed as 'probable neutrals' in a war.[33] With the odds stacked against India and Pakistan becoming choice American allies, it is not surprising that in October 1948, George Marshall, then Acting Secretary of State, was unimpressed by Liaqat Ali Khan's exposition of the strategic importance of Pakistan in Middle East defence. The US, re-sponded an unobliging Marshall, was already helping Greece, Turkey and Iran, but US resources were limited so there was 'a limit to what we could do'. In April 1949, the US Chiefs of Staff speculated that Pakistan might be useful as a base for operations in the Middle East, but this appears to have been a distant scenario. For the immediate future, they concluded that it would suffice to make commercial arrangements which, in an emergency, would facilitate the development of the Karachi–Lahore area. Echoing a general British view, the US Chiefs noted that Pakistan had inherited responsibility from the British for the defence of the North-West Frontier, but the Frontier's security would require joint action by Pakistan, India and Afghanistan. The politic course would be to promote co-operation between them.[34] Like the British, American officials shrugged off Pakistan's requests for military grants and also her professed interest in Middle East defence. This is significant, since Pakistan signed a military treaty with the US and joined SEATO in 1954, the British-sponsored Baghdad Pact in 1955 and CENTO in 1958, and, in the wake of the Soviet invasion of Afghanistan, was regarded by the Reagan administration as being 'on our side'. Pakistan's recruitment in US-sponsored pacts was not a foregone conclusion, and the evidence from both British and American sources cautions against reading the present from hindsight. In 1949, the outstanding fact was that India and Pakistan did not rate very highly as potential American allies, and the Americans were happy to have the British as their surrogate in South Asia.

III . . . INDIA SHOULD GET ON THE DEMOCRATIC SIDE IMMEDIATELY

[(Ambassador Henry Grady in conversation with the State Department, 26 December 1947)]

How much could the British surrogate achieve, given the complications created in Indo–US relations by India's independent foreign policy? Pakistan's early supplications for military funding encountered American indifference as did Indian entreaties for economic largesse. India faced severe economic problems on achieving independence. In 1947, more than 85 per cent of 350 million Indians lived in rural areas which had inadequate irrigation facilities. India imported two to three million tons of food grain every year, yet grain consumption for many Indians fell below the national average. The Indians knew that the British could not fulfil their expectations of economic assistance; Britain's post-war travails, and her slowness in repaying the sterling debt she owed India probably alerted the Indians to Britain's dim promise as an aid donor. To policy-makers in New Delhi, India's economic woes underlined the paramount importance of cordial relations with the USA. Meeting Henry Grady on 9 July 1947, a few weeks before independence, Nehru made it plain that India would want American capital goods. The US, intimated Nehru, was the only country from which the quantities needed could be obtained.[35]

Grady strongly favoured US aid to India. In December 1947 he urged the State Department to recognise that economic aid was the 'most effective channel for keeping India on our side and under our influence'.[36] But

India hardly caught the attention of high US officials, and Grady does not appear to have had an opportunity to communicate his views to either Truman or Marshall.

Early in 1948, economic problems culminated in a surge of labour unrest, led by the Communist Party of India. Nehru was persuaded of Soviet connivance in the disaffection; this suspicion deepened with Soviet abuse of Indian neutralism and charges that India was a lackey of the British. 'That of course is complete nonsense', retorted an indignant Nehru 'and if a policy is based on nonsensical premises it is apt to go wrong.'[37] Soviet hostility to India did not enhance Nehru's admiration of the Soviet Union. He was certain that in the event of a world war India would line up with the West. On his instructions, in April 1948, Girija Shankar Bajpai, regarded by Grady as an official whose views on international affairs were 'practically identical' with those of the US, voiced his government's dismay over Soviet policy and stated that India could only associate with those nations sharing her ideals of freedom and democracy. Bajpai also made India's first formal request for American economic assistance. The US, he said, was 'the only country . . . in a position to aid India'.[38] But he received little encouragement from the State Department, and his remarks were neither discussed by Assistant Secretaries of State or regional bureau chiefs, nor brought to Truman's attention. One reason was the priority given by the US to West Europe. To Bajpai's lament that the US showed very little interest in India, Henderson's blunt response was that '[u]nfortunately, the United States found it necessary to concentrate its efforts and resources on resisting aggression in certain other parts of the world.' Moreover, some US officials were distrustful of the independence of Indian foreign policy. For example, Robert Lovett, Assistant Secretary of State, thought the US should not endorse India's 'overt neutrality'. Sceptical of Indian assurances of support in a world war, the State Department held that neutrality ruled out a common orientation between Indian and American foreign policies.[39]

US officials recognised that India's refusal to join up with the West stemmed partly from nationalism. But they could not quite reconcile her assurances of help in war with nonalignment. Moreover, given their global *and* bipolar outlook, it was easy for them to interpret the anti-imperialist strain in Indian foreign policy as anti-West and pro-communist. For instance, when India and the USSR voted together on colonial issues at the UN in January 1947, John Foster Dulles alleged that in India Soviet communism exercised a strong influence through the interim government. Nehru was shocked, yet painfully aware how Indian attempts to judge issues on their merits could be misunderstood amid the tensions of the cold war.[40] Indian nationalism was both anti-colonial and anti-communist, but the Americans seemed unable to appreciate any attitude that was not consistently pro-West. Meeting Nehru in Paris on 16 October 1948, George Marshall discerned Nehru's awareness of the 'interaction of Soviet policy and world Communism', but he cautioned Washington that Nehru glossed over the communist threat in Asia and overstressed the evils of colonial rule.[41]

How easily Indian strictures of the US attitude to European imperialists could be construed as "anti-American" was illustrated by Nehru's sharp reproof of America's 'tacit approval and acceptance' of the Dutch police action in Indonesia in mid-December 1948. US officials were taken aback, partly because they were then negotiating behind the scenes to bring about decolonisation in Indonesia and partly because they thought India intended to forge an anti-Western "Asiatic Association" at the Asian Conference in January 1949. In New Delhi, Henderson saw this as evidence of Nehru's 'lack of stability' and his 'animosity' toward the US. George Kennan, then heading the Policy Planning Staff, feared a possible polarisation between the Atlantic community and Asia. 'This would not be such a serious trend for us were we only an Atlantic power', he wrote to Henderson, 'but as we are [a] world power with vital interests and therefore responsibilities on all the globe we must regard recent developments in southern Asia with deep concern.'[42] The universalisation of US "responsibilities" left little room for compromise, and American officials were not mollified by Nehru's assurance that Indian criticism of American softness on colonial aggression was not motivated by hostility towards the US.

The resolutions of the New Delhi conference on Indonesia from 22–4 January 1949 bore out Nehru's attitude. They were moderate, and the most farreaching of them only called for the re-establishment of the Indonesian republic. India did not seek sanctions against the Netherlands, rail against the US or try to organise any Asian bloc. The participants reaffirmed their commitment to the UN and their support for Security Council negotiations over Indonesia.

American officials were pleased with the conference. Dean Acheson, now Secretary of State, observed that the conference had not been unfriendly to the US, and he attributed this partly to the State Department's efforts offstage to encourage the conference to remain within the UN framework and to avoid the establishment of an anti-Western bloc.[43] But it is unlikely that Nehru ever intended to form an Asian bloc or to foment animosity towards the West. In 1948, India turned down a suggestion by Thakin Nu of Burma for a regional association and, given the limited economic resources of most Asian countries, was cool to the idea of an Asian bloc.[44] Then, in February 1949, Nehru indicated his desire to visit the US later in the year to confer with the Truman administration and to educate himself about the US, and in March both governments agreed that his visit should take place in the autumn. In April, Nehru announced the appointment of his sister Vijayalakshmi Pandit as ambassador to the United States. Mrs Pandit was known for her pro-Western sympathies; the news of her appointment, coming around the same time as India's decision to remain in the Commonwealth, demonstrated India's leaning towards the West. Generally, Indian officials sought closer ties with the US, if only because it was potentially India's largest aid donor, and Nehru even wondered: 'why not align with the United States *somewhat* and build up our economic and military strength?'[45] The "somewhat" did not imply that India would don a mental straitjacket identical to that of the US, but both countries could search for common ground and play a constructive role in Asia. Common ground, however, could not easily be found, and Indian hopes were doomed to disappointment. In April 1949, a formal Indian request for aid evoked no response from the Americans. The announcement of the Point Four programme by Truman in January 1949 offered possibilities of increased economic assistance to India, but it was vaguely conceived and was largely a cosmetic measure designed to increase Truman's political stature. Moreover, it ranked as low-priority legislation, and Congress did not act on it in 1949.[46] Indian hopes of American largesse as a stimulant to greater Indo–US co-operation did not strike a chord with American officials.

The Americans were not about to upgrade India in their list of priorities, and they were also unresponsive to *British* suggestions for munificence to India. Having named India as the key to regional colloboration, but able to give her only limited economic assistance, the British tried to talk the Americans into making India the major beneficiary of US aid programmes in Asia. Sounding Acheson on the subject in Washington in April 1949, Bevin elicited the answer that American thinking about India had only been 'along vague lines'. Acheson's reply reflected the general American distrust of nonalignment: the US, he told Bevin, was 'doubtful about India'.[47] Nevertheless, knowing of Nehru's forthcoming visit to the US in October 1949, Bevin and the Foreign Office continued to press the US in favour of economic aid to India. In July 1949, Bevin told Lewis Douglas, US ambassador in London, that India had a pivotal position in Asia and might be persuaded to assume leadership of a Western-backed Asian front. Then, on 12 September, Archibald Nye, High Commissioner in New Delhi, reiterated the British viewpoint to Henderson. Since the UK would 'be unable in view of its own precarious financial position to give any substantial additional assistance' to India, it would be necessary for the US to give 'greater assistance . . . in stemming the rising tide [of] communism in Asia'. On the same day, Dening conferred with American officials in Washington, but he found them disinclined to offer large-scale economic aid to India. In general, the State Department took their cue from Acheson. Sceptical that economic development was a general panacea for Asia, Walton Butterworth, then Director of the Office of Far Eastern Affairs, stipulated that India should recognise the character of the Communist menace both to herself and to the other states of Southeast Asia.[48] Nonalignment was confirming the low priority the US assigned to India.

India's shunning of anti-communist pacts only heightened the American dislike of nonalignment. In March 1949, Bajpai saw little point in India joining forces with the West to wage an ideological war in Burma or Malaya, while she would resist any communist agression as firmly as she had fought off internal communism. However, this thinking made little impression on Henderson. Then, in late 1949, there was annoyance among US officials at India's refusal to enrol in a Pacific pact with the Philippines and Formosa.[49] In contrast, the Indians did not displease the British, who had little enthusiasm for the idea. Dening took issue with the 'distinct [American] tendency to use the Philippines as a stalking horse in South East Asia while choosing to ignore the fact that this horse is not only weak-kneed but internally unsound'. The Foreign Office dismissed the idea of a Pacific Pact sponsored by the Philippines.[50] There could not have been a better illustration of the divergent British and American worldviews, and American suspicions of nonalignment would reverberate, quite discordantly, on Britain's Asian cold-war strategy.

IV NONALIGNMENT AND THE ANGLO–AMERICAN RELATIONSHIP

Ambassadors *can* matter; it is possible that the personality of Loy Henderson did little to inspire mutual sympathy between India and the US. Married to a virulently anti-Soviet White Russian, Henderson prided himself on his staunch anti-communism. He had headed the NEA in 1947, and an official who worked under him recollected that anti-communism was the overriding theme of the day, and that there was no room for disagreement with him on assessments of Soviet tactics.[51] Perhaps this helps to explain his impatience with the Indian assertion that Chinese nationalism would emerge stronger than communism, although that opinion was shared by some officials in Washington. To Henderson the Indian stance typified 'a certain smugness in Indian government circles regarding China'.[52] Henderson's dislike of Indian "neutralism" probably arose from his conviction that communist aggrandizement was masterminded by the Soviets all over the world. Both these themes echo in his reports from New Delhi and must have influenced officials in the State Department. There was little empathy between him and Nehru: Nehru thought that Henderson lacked understanding of Indian aspirations for economic development; and Vijayalakshmi Pandit had seen her brother 'freeze up' while talking to Henderson.[53]

Henderson was outraged at Nehru's criticism of the US which he attributed to his effeminate qualities, his lack of stability – and British influence.[54] Henderson ascribed Nehru's anti-US bias to his schooldays in Britain. He was not wide of the mark, for the young Nehrus were certainly exposed to British nationals critical of the Americans, and, on one occasion Vijayalakshmi Pandit told Henderson that Nehru's British tutors had always spoken disparagingly of the Americans. Henderson himself thought that Nehru's image of Americans as 'crass', 'overgrown' people owed something to his British friends and that it was encouraged by the British who did not wish to see closer Indo–US links at the expense of Indian ties with the Empire–Commonwealth. Henderson's suspicions of British machinations to influence Nehru against the US were not entirely unfounded. Soon after independence, and probably aware of India's desire for US economic aid, Mountbatten warned Nehru about the dangers of "dollar imperialism", and Grady reported that he was receiving no co-operation from British diplomats in New Delhi. (Exactly what co-operation he expected is not clear.) The British scientist Lloyd Boyd-Orr was opposed to American technicians and scientists in India, and some British officials and businessmen took the line that the Americans were 'more dangerous' than the Russians so far as India was concerned, and 'it would be unfortunate for American influence to displace the stabilising influence of the British'. Whether the British really wanted close Indo–US relations is raised by Henderson's recollection of a conversation he had with Bevin in London on his way to take up his ambassadorship in New Delhi in 1948. Bevin intimated that Nehru had threatened to take India out of the Commonwealth if Britain's relations with the US continued to be closer than those with India. There is no record of this in British documents.

Bevin then told me that it was extremely important to the United Kingdom for India to remain in the Commonwealth and, therefore, it would like to do what it could to assuage Nehru's feelings. He wondered whether I would mind if Sir Archie . . . would refrain from showing any particular friendliness toward me and the American Embassy, and if from time to time he would be publicly critical of the United States.

Henderson replied – rightly – that he did not think it was possible for the UK and US to have friendly dealings in one country and unfriendly ones in another. If Henderson's recollection is accurate, *Bevin's* motives in sounding him out are questionable. They could not have been disinterested or calculated to improve Indo–US relations; indeed they had the effect of persuading Henderson that the Indian government 'was inclined to regard the United States with suspicion and dislike'.[55] At the same time, Bevin might have been trying to discourage any prospect of Anglo–American co-operation in India, which might diminish British influence in New Delhi, and putting the onus for that on Henderson.

For their part, British officials were nonchalant about Indian strictures of the US. In March 1948, A.C.B. Symon, then High Commissioner in New Delhi, discounted the anti-Western tones in a parliamentary speech by Nehru with the advice that the speech was intended for domestic consumption, and he counselled Grady that the West should not try to press Nehru to join their power bloc. Then, in January 1949, Strang found Henderson 'much incensed by Indian criticism of the American way of life and of

United States policy, more so, I should have thought, than he need be'. Though Henderson had given his staff strict instructions not to express or countenance anti-British sentiments, Strang thought he was 'rather restive at finding that Indian criticism is so often directed against the United States rather than against the United Kingdom'. There is hardly any evidence that British officials tried to persuade the Indians of the rightness of US policy. Archibald Nye did reprove the Indian failure 'to appreciate that they need America much more than America needs India'. Any experienced diplomat would be irritated by the Indian proclivity to lecture other people 'on the highest moral plane'. But on balance Nye blamed the Americans for their fractious relationship with the Indians. The Americans might make greater headway with the Indians 'if they were rather less direct in their approach, less quick to take offence and readier to make allowances for the growing pains of a country which is, after all, a newcomer to the international scene'.[56] As Indian criticism was levelled at the US more often than the UK, the British could happily counsel the Americans to be more patient with New Delhi.

What role did British influence play in aggravating Indo–US friction? American diplomats in New Delhi reported a keen sense of rivalry on the British side and British attempts to curb US influence. However, at this stage, British diplomats did not mention American efforts to deflate British influence – rather one discerns some smug satisfaction in their missives to London that the Americans, not the British, were the target of Indian criticism. Essentially the subcontinent was not an American concern, and the Americans classified the area as British turf. The odds were therefore against India and Pakistan coming within the ambit of American influence, although this was due more to US apathy to the region than to a lack of interest on the part of India and Pakistan. As we have seen, Pakistan's entreaties for military funding elicited no response from the US between 1947–9; and Indian approaches for American economic aid were usually turned aside by American officials on grounds ranging from the demand for American engineers being greater than the supply to the American insistence that India allow more private enterprise and rely less on official aid.[57] To the Indians, this showed insensitivity to their viewpoint. Mutual criticism sparked off mutual resentment and indignation, and Indo–US antagonism soon acquired its own momentum. It did not emanate from British machinations, however diabolical. The disparate goals of India and the US largely accounted for their mutual antipathy, which in the long run ran counter to the British interest.

Yet India and the US could not ignore each other. With the communist spectre hovering over China and Southeast Asia in 1948–9, Acheson perceived Nehru as 'a world figure of great influence and . . . we looked to him to assume the leadership in the rehabilitation of Asia . . . in this role the entire world now had a claim upon him as one of its great statesmen'. Nehru, recollected Acheson in his memoirs, 'was so important to India and

India's survival so important to all of us, that if he did not exist – as Voltaire said of God – he would have to be invented. Nevertheless, he was one of the most difficult men with whom I have ever had to deal.' On the eve of Nehru's first official visit to the US, American attitudes to him vacillated between those policy-makers who were simply distrustful of nonalignment and those who saw him as a staunch pro-Western influence in Asia. In September 1949, Philip Jessup, ambassador-at-large, regarded India, and particularly Nehru, as 'the most solid element with which the United States can associate itself' to check communism in Asia. Louis Johnson, then Secretary of Defence, acclaimed Nehru as 'one of the best and potentially one of the strongest friends of the United States in the whole of Asia'. But a more matter-of-fact Under Secretary of State James Webb thought the Americans should not count on India's alignment with the US; in any case, Nehru's was a goodwill visit, and US policy goals for India were still vague at best. Echoing this view, Joseph Mathews, Director of the Office of South Asian affairs had 'no great expectation of Nehru's visit . . . there is little hope that Nehru will dramatically announce that he has seen the light'.[58]

Nehru was not inclined to see the *American* light. His visit to the US in October 1949 drove deeper the sources of mistrust between the US and India. At a meeting with Acheson, Jessup and George McGhee on 13 October, Indian officials made no contribution to a discussion on US responsibilities as a major power. Generally, both sides spoke at cross purposes. Acheson was convinced that 'Nehru and I were not destined to have a pleasant personal relationship', and complained that Nehru had lectured him like a public meeting. The highlight of the "lecture" related to disagreements on dealing with communism in different parts of the world. In China, Nehru predicted that nationalism would emerge stronger than communism, while communist victories in 'neighboring countries' could give a fillip to Indian communists. India had little faith in the USSR and did not discern many opportunities of co-operation with her. Nehru thought the US should avoid dealing with the Soviets with their chosen weapons of name-calling, deprecation and verbal belligerency, since the Soviets were 'very hard to beat in the use of these weapons'; instead 'a sort of "mental jiu jitsu" would be more productive'. Nehru did not subscribe to Acheson's view that communist participation in a nationalist coalition would neces-sarily result in their liquidating their opponents and capturing control; this may have happened in East Europe, but in India, Burma and Indonesia the communist strategy of operating first under cover of the left wing of the local nationalist movement and then securing control of it had misfired. He was hopeful that the communists would similarly come to grief in Indochina.[59]

Nehru believed that Asian nationalism proffered the best answer to communist subversion, and he emphasised the import of anti-colonialism in Asia to Truman. This left Truman cold, and he responded with a discourse on lessons from American history. 'We found that the solution of the colonial problem was not the end . . . It had taken a great civil war to teach us that we must live peacefully together and it had taken involvement in two world wars to bring home to us that we could not be independent of peoples beyond our shores.'[60] There was no mistaking Truman's dislike of Indian nonalignment, and the intellectually discerning Nehru could not have missed Truman's meaning. The flaunting of wealth and material prosperity shocked Nehru's sensitivity: at a lunch in New York he was informed that twenty billion dollars were collected round that table. Nehru was also unimpressed by the social conversation at the White House: at the state banquet in his honour Truman and the Chief Justice were, for the most part, engrossed in a *tête-à-tête* over the merits of Missouri Bourbon and Maryland whisky. Nehru summed up Truman as a mediocre man who was unfit to carry out his international responsibilities, while Truman 'didn't seem to think that man liked white folks'. The visit was a fiasco. India needed American aid, but Nehru did not wish to appear suppliant. He was indignant at what he saw as American imperiousness: they had expected 'more than gratitude and goodwill and that more I could not supply them'. Nor did the visit excite American interest in, or sympathy for India. Only a week after Nehru's departure from Washington, the State Department turned down a proposal by Henderson for a $500 million aid programme for India.[61]

Notwithstanding the communist triumph in the Chinese civil war by October 1949, the intertwining of personal friction and political disorientation were confirming India's low ranking on American priorities. The emergence of communist China was to set the seal on that low priority, which put a question mark over the fulfilment of Britain's Asian cold war strategy.

V INDIA, THE WEST AND THE RECOGNITION OF COMMUNIST CHINA

China was the most pressing Asian concern of the US in in 1948–9. For the United States, the rout of the Kuomintang and the establishment of the People's Republic of China on 1 October 1949 represented a grievous political defeat and marked the start of the Asian cold war.[62] The British, on the other hand, were more detached. While communist control of the mainland was not to their liking, British prestige was not at stake since Britain had not been directly involved in the civil war. The communist triumph highlighted the Anglo–American gulf over containment in Asia. The British were minded to recognise the communist regime, which was a *fait accompli*. Diplomatic ties also offered the best chances of safeguarding their future trading interests in China, and Labour and Conservative politicians were at one that recognition was not intended to confer a compliment on the communists but to secure a convenience.[63] India's determination to recognise the communist government is also said to have influenced Britain's decision, partly because London was receptive to Indian ideas on China and partly in the interests of Commonwealth unity.[64] These views have left some questions unanswered. The British were in contact with both the Americans and Indians during the Chinese civil war; why were they more susceptible to Indian rather than American advice, especially as the US was the pivot of the Anglo–American relationship as well as the ultimate bulwark of Western security in Asia?

A summary of British, American and Indian attitudes during the Chinese civil war will help to assess the extent of Indian influence on the British decision to establish diplomatic ties with communist China. By the end of 1948, Nehru was inclined to believe that the communists would emerge victorious in China. He did not welcome this prospect, for the success of the communists would give impetus to the spread of communist ideas and would endanger Southeast Asia. The views of the British Chiefs on the strategic threat Chinese communism could pose to Southeast Asia coincided with those of Nehru in March 1949. But Nehru held that Chinese nationalism would ultimately prove stronger than communism.[65] This thinking was shared by some US officials including Kennan and Acheson, who even contemplated the possibility of driving a wedge between the Soviets and Chinese communists.[66] In fact, in March 1949, it was Bevin who was unconvinced that the Chinese communists would deviate from policies followed by communists elsewhere.[67] On recognition of the communist regime, there was more than one opinion in London and Washington, and Indian attitudes were not necessarily closer to those of the "British" than of the "Americans".

Yet perceptions of the communists as orthodox communists or nationalists did not alone make policy; policy was determined by political necessity and official assessments of the nature of the relationships Britain, the US or India wished to have with China. Britain's interest in accommodating China arose from the desire to promote her trading interests in a potentially large Chinese market and from the calculation that it would be easier to hold on to Hong Kong with Chinese acquiescence. These became the dominant strains in British thinking. For India, good relations with China, which was the largest independent country in Asia *and* her neighbour, seemed a matter of common sense. By the summer of 1949, both India and Britain awaited some signal of interest in recognition by their governments.

The Americans vacillated. Officials debated the pluses and minuses of recognition, but it is important to see which arguments in the debate ultimately defined the policy and determined the American stance in discussions with the Indians and British. If the Americans were seeking accommodation with the communists and ruminating over the possibility of exploiting any Sino–Soviet differences, why did so much of the friction in

Indo–US relations stem from American annoyance at the Indian "softness" on Chinese communism? Why were the British aware that their recognition of the communist regime would displease the Americans? It is because the case against recognition eventually won the day in Washington, and it is this case that the Americans defended and propagated in exchanges with the British and Indians. In late September 1949 Acheson issued a White Paper calling for the overthrow of the communists. At the end of October, a draft of NSC 48/1 posited that continued challenges to the communists were in the interests of the US, while accommodation would 'greatly weaken our position in Asia'. The possibility of "Titoism" and of a Sino–Soviet split were recognised. But 'it would be folly . . . to base United States policy on the faint hope or distant prospect of "Titoism" in China, and thus to deny to the United States the moral strength of opposing communism because of its basic evil.' If American officials blew hot and cold between coming to terms with the enemy or engaging in a war of attrition, they ultimately justified their political choice on the high moral ground. Meanwhile a State Department brief on Nehru's visit advised Truman that countries like China, 'which have fallen under Communist domination . . . almost inevitably become colonial appendages of the new Russian empire'.[68] In his talks with Nehru in Washington in early October, Acheson was sceptical of Nehru's forecast that Chinese nationalism would eventually triumph over communism and would lessen the communist government's subservience to Moscow, and the Indians knew that their recognition of the communists would mar their none-too-promising relations with the United States.[69]

Given the American stance, British and Indian recognition of the communist government could not be the routine recognition of an established fact;[70] and India and Britain had to contend with its cold war dimensions. On 1 October 1949 the communist regime invited recognition by foreign governments. The USSR did so on 2 October; Bulgaria and Romania on 3 October and Hungary and Poland on 4 October. The American refusal to follow suit created a vexatious problem for the British and Indians. Nehru felt that the establishment of a stable government in China could not be ignored. How it should be acknowledged 'is a matter of careful thought'. In the circumstances, recognition by a non-communist country could easily be construed as pro-communist. British recognition in the teeth of US opposition could further convey the impression of Western disunity. The problem was how to recognise the Peking government while not appearing sympathetic to the communists or revealing fissures in the Western alliance.

Concurrent recognition by non-communist countries offered the best way out of the dilemma, but the British could not count on a consensus either with their European allies or the Commonwealth.[71] With their imperial stakes in East Asia, the Netherlands and France were closely concerned with the problem, but Australia, New Zealand and Canada were hesitant to recognise the new régime. India and Britain were the only Commonwealth countries with strong interests in recognising China, and Bevin was keen that they should do so. On 27 October 1949 he informed the cabinet that if the British recognised China 'it would be important to ensure that the Indian Government took action at the same time'. Alive to the differences among Commonwealth countries, Nehru was prepared to defer recognition briefly. On 12 November he told Bevin that India did not wish to act too hastily, but she would not delay a decision for too long. Since 1948, the Indian government had been influenced by the reports of K.M. Panikkar, the Indian ambassador in Peking. Panikkar was not a political radical: having served various Indian princes, his own political experience had been, according to Nehru, of a 'reactionary kind'. An Indian government memorandum of 21 November 1949 contended that there was no substantial opposition to the communists. Recognition would not imply approval of the communists or of their policies, only the recognition of a 'political and historical fact'. Bevin told Nehru that 'it would be desirable, if recognition were to be granted to the Chinese Communist government, for a timetable to be worked out and for all to act together if possible.' An orderly and proper decision might even persuade the US, and at the Commonwealth High Commissioners' meeting in London on 15 November he suggested recognition early in the New Year. But there was little sign of a realisation of Bevin's hopes of a concerted Commonwealth approach. Canada was reluctant to walk out of step with the US; the Australians wanted assurances that the communist regime would carry out its international obligations; New Zealand and Australia wished to postpone a decision until after their elections on 30 November and 10 December respectively. Domestic communism was an important issue in both countries, and it would be difficult to reconcile opposition to it with recognition of China.

British officials hoped to dissuade the Indians from recognition before the Colombo conference on 9 January 1950, while 'stimulating' a decision by other Commonwealth countries.[72] But the Indian government memorandum of 21 November warned that a delay in recognition might embitter the communists and enable them to rouse popular sentiment against foreigners; economically it might hamper trade and commerce. These arguments were taken up by the Foreign Office and formed the substance of instructions to Sir Oliver Franks, then British ambassador in Washington. Meanwhile, Bevin told Krishna Menon, then high commissioner in London, that there was no disagreement between the British and Indian governments in principle; it was 'therefore a matter of timing', and he did not commit himself to any date. India wanted to accord recognition after the UN General Assembly session on 25 December 1949; Britain wished to defer a decision until after the Colombo conference in January 1950.

On 1 December Bajpai told Frank Roberts, then Deputy High

Commissioner in New Delhi, that London had not replied to the Indian suggestion that the communist government be recognised between 15 and 25 December 1949.[73] The Indians wanted an early decision, especially as "China" was supposed to be chairing the UN Security Council in January 1950. Bajpai solicited British views on the date of recognition and their ideas for dealing with the question of Chinese representation in the Security Council. Roberts notified Bajpai that the British would take a decision in mid-December. But the Indians would not postpone recognition until the Commonwealth Prime Ministers' conference at Colombo in January 1950, and they insisted on according recognition by the end of 1949. With this knowledge, Bevin decided on 15 December 1949 that the British would recognise China on 2 January 1950, a week before the Colombo conference. This decision showed an Indian influence on the timing of recognition. On 19 December Nehru formally intimated to Attlee that India would recognise communist China on 30 December 1949. Nehru regarded the problem as primarily Asian, implying that he did not wish an Indian decision to appear dependent on a British or Commonwealth one.[74] The situation in Indochina led the British to postpone recognition until 6 January 1950[75] which hinted at additional influences on the timing of their decision. Indian arguments were taken up by the British where their outlooks were similar; but in general, Indian influence concerned the timing more than the principle of recognition, and it was not the only influence even on the timing. In any case, British receptivity to Indian ideas stemmed not from any apprehension about Commonwealth unity, to which the Indians did not pose a threat and in which they also had an interest, but from the British desire to go ahead without offending the Americans and without giving the communists a handle to interpret recognition as a sign of dissension within the Anglo–American relationship.

This logic did not go down well with the Americans, with whom the Indians and British were simply out of tune. NSC 48/1 of 29 December 1949 kept open the alternative of recognition, but counselled restraining other countries from early recognition because US interests in China would be adversely affected if it stayed out.[76] India and Britain had their own reasons to recognise China. Once they had done so, China became the greatest bone of contention between Britain and the United States on the one hand and between India and the US on the other. The coincidence of British and Indian interests in recognising the Peking regime led the State Department to allege that British susceptibility to Indian opinion was a complication in the Anglo–American relationship.[77] This oversimplified or even ignored the many complex reasons for which the British wished to have diplomatic ties with communist China.

India also came to symbolise the differences between American and British strategy in the Asian cold war, especially during the Korean and Indochina conflicts from 1950–3 and 1954–6 respectively.[78] Stressing military containment in Asia, NSC 48/1 defined the Ryukus, Japan and the

Philippines as America's first line of defence, and it categorically ruled out making nonaligned India the sole bulwark against Asian communism.[79]

Could a meeting ground be found between the British strategy of wooing Asian nationalisms through regional economic collaboration, fostered by the Commonwealth and with nonaligned India playing a significant role, and an American strategy emphasising military containment? The Commonwealth conference in Colombo in January 1950 provided a pessimistic clue. The choice of Colombo as the site of the conference itself marked the differing British and American world views. Most Americans did not know about Colombo, 'except maybe for Lipton tea bags which had a map of Ceylon'.[80] The British sought US funding for the Colombo plan but did not wish to appear eager suppliants. Making a show of importance, they kept the Americans at a distance and were tight-lipped about the conference on the plea that it was 'a family problem'.[81]

But such a show could only go so far. American bounty was necessary for the successful implementation of the Colombo plan – and it fell far short of British expectations. So the British idea of extending their influence through regional collaboration, subsidised by the United States, hung in the air. Good Indo–US relations were also intrinsic to the success of Britain's cold war strategy; the sparring between India and the US, and the American indifference to South Asia did not augur well for that. If, by the beginning of 1950, Anglo–American differences over India marked their divergent strategies in the Asian cold war, the Korean conflict was to exacerbate them further.

3. Diplomatic or military containment? India, the Korean conflict and the Anglo-American relationship, 1950–3

In answer to the Secretary's presentation, Ambassador Franks said that the British felt that we were basing our position on a moral position but since our power had collapsed they felt we would have to change our moral position. [Memorandum of conversation in Acheson's office on 5 December 1950]

. . . their [Chinese] military force . . . gives them to a large extent the leadership in Asia. They [British] had hoped that this leadership would go to India which had absorbed so much of the West. [Attlee in conversation with American officials on 5 December 1950]

In view of India's ambitions for political hegemony, its advocacy of a doctrine of appeasement, and its tendencies toward abandoning support of the principle of collective security, the United States should not at this time encourage the formation of a South Asian regional bloc, since such an organization might come under India's domination. [Recommendation made by South Asian Regional Conference of US diplomatic and consular officers at Nuwara Eliya, Ceylon, 26 February – 2 March 1951]

I THE SETTING

By the beginning of 1950, it was evident that the British would not find it easy to balance their Asian cold war policy on the tightrope of Indo–US friction. Nonalignment was not to the liking of either superpower, and India could barely murmur appreciation of one of them without incurring the wrath of the other. Indian membership of the Commonwealth had pro-Western connotations, but American officials sometimes wondered whether the Commonwealth was really bringing India closer to the West, or whether it was Britain that was being influenced by India to the detriment of Western unity and interests in Asia. Loy Henderson, for example, thought that 'Indian leaders, particularly Nehru, have been cajoled and treated as spoiled children [for] so long by other members of the Commonwealth'. However, Nehru could not be ignored: 'vain and immature as he [Nehru] is . . . he has tremendous influence in Asia', and there was nothing for it but to put up with him and to work patiently to increase his leanings towards the West.[1] But a recognition of India's or Nehru's influence did not mean that Indo–US differences were destined to be cleared up early.

To Nehru, the main architect of India's foreign policy, it seemed that neither superpower understood nonalignment. To him, it symbolised India's independence, which meant independence above all in the conduct of foreign policy. Nonalignment was thus an expression of Indian nationalism. This linked up with the fundamental premiss of India's Asian policy – that nationalism was the outstanding political force in South and Southeast Asia. The Soviet Union could capitalise on nationalist sentiment against the West, but once colonies became free they would shed the belief that they and the Soviets were natural allies. India's basic sympathies lay with the West, which was her main source of trade and aid at a time when the Soviet Union offered her little except hostility, but India could neither openly advocate alignment with a West that partly identified its power with colonialism nor do anything that would cause nationalists in Asian countries to label her as an accomplice of the West. The Indian emphasis on national sovereignty meant that the nonalignment of Asian countries would be a move away from the West, but it would also disentangle nationalism from communism.

In February 1950 Nehru reiterated to Loy Henderson that India could never line up with the Soviet Union in a war. India might like to remain neutral. But the moralist in Nehru was never far from the surface: such a policy 'might be regarded as unworthy of a great Nation. . . . in spite of the efforts of India to remain neutral in the event of a World War, he was convinced that eventually it [India] would be drawn into it and that it [India] would not side with the Communists.'[2]

This consideration applied to the outbreak of a world war; whether India would combine with the West in a more limited Asian conflict would hinge upon the Indian perception of Western policy. India's pro-Western slant did not imply any alignment with the West in peacetime or an Indian desire for a Western military presence in Asia, for India wanted Asia to be free of political and military pressures from any great power. In this sense her objectives were at variance with those of Britain and the US, who, in their individual ways, saw their presence in Asia as indispensable if Asia was to be saved from communism. These contradictory aims would irritate relations between India, the US and Britain; and especially between India and the US, since the US, not Britain, was to emerge as the expanding power in Asia. And, in so far as India was the centrepiece of Britain's Asian cold war strategy, India would spark off friction between Britain and the US as well.

The Korean war proved the first major testing ground for Indian nonalignment and of its viability, advantages and disadvantages for the West, especially for the US, which made the largest single military contribution to the UN effort in the war. Underlining India's concern over the conflict, Benegal Rau, her permanent representative at the UN, described the Far East as 'the very near East to India'.[3] India therefore kept a close watch on developments during the war. Her emergence as the main diplomatic conduit between China and the West kept her in contact with Britain and the US, and their reactions to Indian policy had a significant impact on Anglo–American relations. Indian diplomacy did not always go down well with the Americans, and Indo–US differences induced the Americans to reappraise their reliance on the British in South Asia, and more generally, in the Asian cold war. For her part, Britain was often hard put to reconcile and balance the differences between the two countries vital to the success of her Asian cold war policy. Archival sources show that the contacts between India, Britain and the US were most intense on four occasions. During the first phase of the war, from its onset in June 1950 until October 1950, Indian and Western attitudes to China were linked with the question of limiting or expanding the conflict. The British were always interested in the Indian viewpoint, but they were more influenced by the US than by India. They proved more receptive to Indian ideas during the second phase of the war, from November 1950, when China intervened, until January 1951. Then, in the autumn of 1952 there was much controversy over the repatriation of prisoners of war to facilitate the signing of the Korean armistice. Finally, the summer of 1953 saw the emergence of Anglo–American differences over India's participation in the Korean Political Conference. The main themes of this chapter will highlight the diplomatic exchanges between India, Britain and the US over these issues.

II THE KOREAN WAR: THE FIRST PHASE, JUNE–OCTOBER 1950

The Korean war began on 25 June 1950 when North Korean troops crossed the 38th parallel, which had served as the boundary between North and South Korea since 1945.[4] Britain and the US had been signatories to the Cairo declaration of 1943 and the Potsdam and Moscow declarations of 1945 which established the independence of Korea. India's involvement in Korea dated from September 1947, when she was elected permanent chairman of the UN Temporary Commission on Korea to facilitate, through elections, the establishment of a national government of Korea. All three countries were therefore concerned with the regional and international implications of the crisis created by the North Korean invasion.

Soon after news of the North Korean aggression, the UN Security Council passed on 25 June a resolution condemning North Korea and calling for an early cessation of hostilities. There was no doubt about identifying the aggressor, and India and Britain voted in favour of the resolution.

The next day, on 26 June, Truman pledged the US to military inter-vention against any further communist expansion in Asia. He ordered the stationing of the US Seventh Fleet between Formosa and the Chinese mainland, apparently to prevent attacks by either party on the other. This would "neutralise" Formosa while military operations were under way in Korea. Truman also declared that Formosa's future status must be deter-mined at the same time as a final settlement on Japan or by the United Nations. In addition, the US would extend military aid to the French in Indochina and to the Philippines government against the communist Huk rebels. His declaration stirred up the worst fears of the Peking govern-ment, which saw the US taking sides in the Chinese civil war and perceived American hostility to its very existence. In one day the US thus became involved in Korea, the Chinese civil war, the struggle between Vietnamese nationalism and French imperialism and the communist insurrection in the Philippines.

Truman's declaration aroused British anxieties, for it threatened to escalate hostilities. Alliance unity could dragoon the British into a more extended military involvement in Asia. This they wished to avoid. They feared that any widening of the Korean conflict could trigger off a Soviet assault on West Europe. Moreover, they sought to conserve their strength for the defence of Malaya and Hong Kong, and considered it imprudent to provoke China, which laid claim to Formosa under the Cairo declaration of 1943. While they did not want a communist victory in Indochina, they had no intention of expending their military resources to shore up the French.[5]

India's initial instinct was to keep out of the conflict, as she was attracted to neither the communist regime of Kim Il Sung in North Korea nor the corrupt authoritarianism of Syngman Rhee in South Korea. The Indian government were alarmed by Truman's declaration of 26 June. Since the Indians did not wish to appear supporters of French colonialism, they were embarrassed by Truman's equating of Korea with Indochina. India did not go along with the US on Formosa, which she thought should be returned to China under the Cairo declaration of 1943. Seeking good relations with China, India had no desire to antagonise her or to appear her enemy. Moreover, India could not overlook the interests of her neighbour Burma, which shared a border with China. The Indians were also apprehensive about an expansion of hostilities in Korea. Their anxieties were enhanced by the resolution introduced by the US in the Security Council on 27 June which called for military assistance to South Korea to repel the North Korean attack. American style also pricked Indian sensitivities. The Indians knew that there was no alternative to an American commander of UN forces, and that this would be General Douglas MacArthur in his capacity as commander of US troops in the Far East, but they were disquieted that he would not be reporting to the Security Council direct but through the US government. Mindful of the need for Asian backing for a UN cause, the British advised the Americans to take care to present the campaign against North Korea as a UN rather than a US effort 'from the propaganda viewpoint'. But the Americans rode roughshod over Indian sensitivities. They solicited Indian support for a resolution on which they had not consulted India; even the text of the resolution was transmitted to the Indian government through British channels. Loy Henderson attributed the omission to slow communications between Washington and Delhi, but the American tendency to consult with the UK and not India poured cold water on any spontaneous Indian desire to rally round the US. The Indian government eventually voted for the American resolution as it did not want to weaken the UN as major force for world peace. At the same time it reiterated its adherence to the principle of nonalignment.[6] This underscored its refusal to accept any American effort to connect the Korean issue with Formosa and Indochina. India's initial reluctance, and her eventual support for the resolution unveiled the complex and conflicting interests and moralities of international politics.

Archibald Nye, the British High Commissioner in New Delhi, was critical of India's hesitant attitude, but in London, officials including Bevin, Strang, Pierson Dixon and Dening shared Indian reservations about US policy. Dening worried that the US action on Formosa was 'of doubtful propriety' and could lead to embroilment with China. If Chinese aggression ignited a military conflagration in Indochina, the British would have to declare their readiness to fulfil their obligations under the UN charter, but the West might not find many Asian allies for a war against China. India would never side with the US in the absence of Chinese aggression. The British must therefore try to dissuade the US from coming to blows or near blows with China and enlarging the area of dispute. The Americans were 'on a good wicket as regards Korea', but they would run into very considerable dangers if they tried to get an alignment on other Asian questions.[7] There was a coincidence of Indian and British outlooks against entanglement with China, and British officials cited Indian opinion to strengthen their case against an escalation of hostilities which could bring on war with China.

India wanted to exploit every opportunity to drive a wedge between China and the USSR, and she discounted the Western assertion that the war was orchestrated by the Kremlin. Reiterating her plea for Chinese participation in the UN, India argued that UN membership for China and the return of the Soviet Union to the Security Council would put moral pressure on the two communist powers to use their influence to limit the Korean conflict. In January 1950, the Soviets had walked out of the Security Council ostensibly to protest against the representation of China on the Council by the Kuomintang in Formosa rather than by the Peking government.

The Indian stance riled the Americans, who contended that a place in the Security Council would be tantamount to rewarding an expansionist China with a UN seat. Moreover, the communist powers would probably indulge in delaying tactics in the Security Council to thwart the UN military effort. The American refusal to have any dealings with the communists set them at odds with the Indians. Nehru was inclined to believe that China and the USSR would not be obstructive if they returned to the UN, since world opinion would hold them reponsible if they defeated progress towards a settlement in the Security Council.[8] American officials did question the extent of the Soviet commitment to China and they weighed the chances of engineering a split between the two communist powers, but the dominant tendency in American thinking was to relegate this to some remote future.[9] The wider problem for both India and Britain was American hostility towards China as the instrument of an intractable, monolithic world communism.

Condemning the North Korean aggression was only one aspect of British and Indian diplomacy; they also explored the possibilities of a negotiated solution to the Korean conflict. In the first week of July 1950, the British approached the Soviets to use their clout with North Korea to end the war. The Americans were ambivalent. Some officials saw advantages in this course, but Lewis Douglas, US ambassador in London, voiced his apprehension to Attlee that the Soviets might demand a seat for China in the UN as a price for pulling wires with North Korea. Chinese representation in the Security Council might then result in 'a real estate swap of South Korea for Formosa'. Attlee assured him that the questions of South Korea and Chinese membership of the Security Council were 'wholly separate'.[10] But the British and Americans were not on the same wavelength. In a message to Acheson on 7 July, Bevin mulled over the chances that the Soviets might couple a willingness to put pressure on North Korea to withdraw with a demand for China's representation in the UN and recognition of her claim to Formosa. The British overture to the Soviets coincided with a personal initiative by S. Radhakrishnan, the Indian ambassador in Moscow, who took the view that if the US acquiesced in China's membership of the UN, the Peking government would support a cease-fire and the return of North Korean troops to the 38th parallel. Sceptical that the Soviets would agree to the withdrawal of North Korean forces, Radhakrishnan predicted that China's admission into the UN would defuse her tensions with the West and simultaneously open the door to the exploitation of Sino–Soviet divergences on the Korean question.[11]

Radhakrishnan's proposal found few takers. American officials were displeased at the British and Indian approaches and suspected co-ordination between them. British memos show that they were wrong, for the Indians and British had acted independently. But Acheson thought of 'getting the British and Indians straightened out', so that *both* would not attempt to mediate – here Acheson was more averse to Indian than to British advances to the Soviets. He drafted a reply to Bevin's message, and Truman wanted Henderson to receive the same material and to use it in the 'best possible way to get these ideas into Nehru's mind'. So, in his letter to

Bevin on 10 July, Acheson fulminated that the Kremlin was behind the North Korean aggression and should not be allowed to gain from it. Nor would the US countenance China's entry into the UN as long as the question of communist aggression remained unresolved. He warned Bevin that Anglo–American differences in the Far East might have serious consequences for their relationship.[12]

The vigour of Acheson's response took Bevin by surprise, and he now tried to stand his ground by maintaining the distinction between British support for the US on Korea and British hesitation over US policy on Formosa. This was done not by spelling out British reservations about American policy on Formosa but by asserting that Britain had to consult other Commonwealth countries and that 'great care must be taken' not to weaken her relations with the Commonwealth, especially India, which was an 'important influence in the Orient'. Once again the British used their "Indian pretext" to distance themselves from the Americans. This had been anticipated by Lewis Douglas, who countered by asking Bevin to join the US in persuading India that the American line was the only one which could restore security in Asia. According to the State Department record, Bevin appeared 'impressed' and promised an answer to Douglas's suggestion. Presumably he did not reply, for on 15 July 1950 Douglas proposed that the US government might explain its position on Formosa to the Indian government. Strang responded that the British 'were taking opportunities to explain to foreign representatives who made enquiries on the subject what we understood to be the American case for their action in regard to Formosa'.[13] Was there a whiff of hesitation over American policy in Strang's reply? Or was he unenthusiastic about a direct American communication to the Indians, preferring the British to act as a bridge between India and the US?

Standing aloof from the Americans was one thing; ultimately the British could not ignore them. Although Britain had long favoured China's membership of the UN, Attlee turned down a similar suggestion by Nehru on 11 July 1950. Deeply disappointed at Attlee's negative response, Nehru appealed to him again on 14 July. He also sent messages to Stalin and Acheson. Krishna Menon, the Indian High Commissioner in London, had suggested the message to Stalin, and Bajpai had thought it advisable to balance it with one to Acheson. India's missives called on the American and Soviet governments to exert their influence to stop the conflict and reiterated her hope that the presence of China and the USSR in the Security Council would facilitate a negotiated solution.[14]

The Indian intervention placed the British in an 'extremely awkward' position. Nehru did not wish to cut across the British proposals to the Soviets, but his overture went further than theirs. Nehru thought that China should be admitted into the Security Council unconditionally. India had endorsed China's admission into the UN since 1949 and did not consider it a bargain with the Soviet Union. The issue of China's representation in the UN should not get obfuscated by the outbreak of the Korean war. 'I find it difficult to believe', wrote Nehru to Attlee, 'that the North Korean invasion was staged in order to compel the United States of America and the United Kingdom to admit the New China into the Security Council and other organs of the United Nations.'[15]

Nehru was correct, but there was now a real danger of a collision between the US and India on seating China in the UN. Anxious that Asian and Western countries speak with one voice – for any division would only be exploited by the Soviets – Bevin worked to fend off a possible clash between India and the US. The Americans were unlikely to give way on their point of principle, and the British would have to fall in with them, but they could be advised to avoid arousing Indian sentiment against them. At the same time the Soviets could be told firmly that there would be no bargaining over Chinese representation and that the Soviets should prevail upon the North Korean government to end hostilties in Korea. The question of Chinese representation could then be discussed on its merits.[16]

The Soviets, meanwhile, seemed bent on creating trouble for its own sake. Replying affirmatively to Nehru's letter of 14 July 1950, Stalin said he shared Nehru's view about 'the expediency of a peaceful settlement of the Korean question through the Security Council', and he regarded the participation of the five great powers, including China, as 'indispensible' [sic]. Nehru was not disappointed with Stalin's response for it suggested that Stalin was amenable to reason. Bevin, however, demurred. To him, Stalin's answer showed a hardening of the Soviet attitude in that they were trying to make it a condition that the five great powers, including China, should meet *before* any action could be taken to settle the Korean question. Stalin had said nothing about the North Korean aggression. On Bevin's advice, Attlee wrote to Nehru that while the North Korean invasion was not staged to compel the UK and US to admit China into the Security Council, Stalin was now making China a *condition* for the settlement of the Korean affair, without disclosing any intention of resolving the conflict. Attlee conceded that there were 'very cogent arguments' in favour of Nehru's opinions on Chinese representation in the UN. But the US was bearing the main burden on behalf of the UN and could not be ignored. As the US had not yet recognised the Peking government, it would be very difficult for American public opinion to swallow a reversal of American policy towards China. Attlee did not expect the US to react favourably to Stalin's message, and he would feel 'very considerable difficulty if I were asked to try to influence them in that direction'. Acheson was shown the draft reply to Nehru and was satisfied with it.[17] Clearly the British could not go against their American ally; nor did the Soviets give them any incentive to do so.

Soviet mischief-making finally put paid to the Indian and British proposals. Much to the annoyance of the Indian and British governments the Soviets published their correspondence with the British and Indians on 18

July 1950. The inaccuracies in the Soviet version obliged Attlee to correct them publicly.[18] Having aroused the indignation of the British and Indians, the Soviets sprang another surprise on them by returning to the Security Council on 1 August, although China had not been admitted, and proceeded to behave obstructively. The Indians were taken unawares, while the British and Americans were content that the indiscretion of the Soviets had sealed the fate of Indian proposals they themselves had disliked and a collision between the West and India averted.

Yet the avoidance of a clash between India and the West on this occasion did not connote Indian or Asian support for Western policy in Korea. In a letter to Attlee on 21 July 1950, Nehru informed him of Asian distrust of the West. This was corroborated by discussions among British, Pakistani and Ceylonese officials. In Pakistan there was some glee at American reverses – as the reverses of a powerful nation – in Korea, and the Pakistani and Ceylonese High Commissioners in London warned that Soviet propaganda could have a strong effect in the face of American setbacks. Ever sensitive to the Asian viewpoint, Bevin wanted the substance of the envoys' opinions to be passed on to the State Department.[19]

The Indians were particularly discomfited with what they saw as the American tendency to ignore Asians and to negate any suggestion of an overture to the Chinese and Soviets; even pro-Western Indian officials were beginning to blame the West for the diplomatic stalemate over Korea. Nehru was also worried at the absence of any constructive initiative on Korea. What would follow even if troops were withdrawn from Korea? War was meant to achieve a certain objective not merely to defeat the enemy but something more positive. Asians could not share the Western attitude to communism. In Europe the communist threat was obvious, while Asians had experienced Western imperialism, so that the USSR did not appear as a direct menace to the nationalist sentiments or economic aspirations of the bulk of the people.[20]

Strang thought Nehru's letter 'both moderate and sensible, and that there is a good deal in what he says'. The Foreign Office concurred that constructive ideas should be sketched out. A common line on the future of Korea should be secured with members of the Security Council and in particular with the US and India. Broad objectives and also the machinery by which they would be carried out could then be announced at the UN.[21]

Despite their frequent acquiescence in American ideas, the British shared Indian concern over American policy. A paper presented to the cabinet by Bevin on 30 August 1950 revealed British unease about the lack of direction in US policy in the Far East, especially towards China. It also underlined Anglo–American strategic and tactical differences by emphasising the wisdom of recognising the strength of, and working with, Asian nationalisms, and lamenting the disregard of Asian, especially Indian, opinion by the US.[22]

Meanwhile, the Indians were apprehensive that the political impasse might last indefinitely. On 14 August Bajpai reasoned with Henderson that the UN should not hold talks under pressure, but if UN forces were tied down for many months, would it be advantageous for the 'cause of peace' for the Security Council to refuse to have any talks with North Korea unless it agreed to withdraw? If North Korean troops remained on the ground for six to eight months, while forces were being mobilised to oust them, North Korea could eliminate during that time all persons or groups with the potential ability to oppose them.[23] The Indian government then bruited proposals for an 'advisory committee' including Security Council and UN members, which would draw up plans to stop the fighting and to ascertain the future of Korea in accordance with the wishes of the Korean people. The Americans, however, remained impervious to Indian advice, and the State Department turned down the Indian proposals for an advisory committee, without offering any alternative American peace plans.

Why did the Indians so frequently fail to make a greater impression on the Americans? Poor communications between Indian and American officials were part of the answer, and the Indians were probably not in tune with the nuances of the continual debates in Washington about how much the war should be expanded or limited. The problem was compounded by the public posturing of some American officials, especially MacArthur, and by the tendency of many American policy-makers, in their discussions with the Indians, seemingly to equate negotiation and compromise with weakness and surrender. Not surprisingly, the Americans often appeared intransigent to the Indians, while they inveighed against India's pandering to China and her inclination to mind everybody's affairs. Deliberation about when, where and how to limit or widen the conflict, or to drive a wedge between China and the USSR, did take place in Washington, but the key to US policy in Korea lay in American willingness to escalate the war. Limiting the war was never a matter of principle for the US,[24] as it was for India and Britain. This probably explains American prickliness and resentment at the continual Indian advice to avoid expanding the conflict and to come to terms with China as a means of doing so. Like the Indians, some US officials, including Acheson, contemplated playing upon any Sino-Soviet divisions. But the Americans and Indians remained out of key on accommodating China, probably because the emphasis each gave to it varied greatly; and their differences over stepping up the conflict accentuated the discord between them. To the Americans, Indian homilies about compromise and negotiation smacked of pusillanimity at best and represented an Indian policy that was downright harmful to American interests at worst. India and the US were clearly working at cross-purposes, and their mutual disharmony would reverberate on Britain. The British would find it difficult to reconcile the differences between their American bulwark, whose disposition to escalate the conflict was not in Britain's interest, and a friendly but uncommitted India with whom they found common ground in limiting hostilities in Korea; the Indians because they did not want a war between China and the West; the British because they did not want alliance unity to drag them into new military commitments. The British were in a quandary, as India and the US advanced two incompatible viewpoints, both of which contributed to the fulfilment of Britain's many-layered objectives in Asia.

By mid-September 1950, Indo–US relations had touched a new low, and this worried the British. Good Indo–US relations were intrinsic to the working of British strategy in Asia. Meeting American officials in London on 18 September R.H. Scott told George McGhee that 'it was . . . of the utmost importance to realize the importance to us [British] of Indian support whatever the future held in the way of war or peace for us in Asia.' McGhee regretted that India and the US found themselves on opposite sides of the fence over China and deplored continuing Indo–US differences in Asia as 'a running sore'. But the US recognised India's importance in Asia and was trying to improve consultations with her. The British strongly encouraged this. However, the essence of the Indo–US rift could be discerned in McGhee's contrapuntal opinion 'that in the best of possible worlds the Asians would be left to decide their own fate but . . . under present conditions the Asians must first realize the threat that international Communism represents before cooperation can be fully effective.'[25] The inference was that co-operation between Asians and Americans could only be effective if Asians conformed to the American worldview. Such imperiousness held out little scope for greater Indo–US collaboration in Asia, especially as an independent foreign policy was an article of faith with India.

American intransigence over China also grated on the Indians. At the end of September 1950, the bombing of Manchuria by UN forces roused Chinese ire. The Chinese wanted to air their grievances in the UN, but the Americans would not consent to this. Nehru took exception to the US attitude. 'Here was a complaint being considered by the Security Council and it was proper that the complainant should attend.' This time the UK and India voted for a resolution which would have allowed China to be heard in the UN, but the Americans then took the line that it was not clear who represented China and vetoed the resolution. Nehru contended that the Americans, in their dislike of communist China, were acting in a manner which could not be justified,[26] but the Americans would not budge.

The US refusal to placate China had its rationale; at this juncture the Americans thought the winds of war were blowing in their favour. China had protested at the bombing of Manchuria, but UN forces had inflicted some reverses on North Korean troops, and by mid-September the Chinese were sending out feelers about their peaceful intentions. The State Department smugly deduced that the predatory Chinese had realised the futility of their policy; they could be brought to heel; and American toughness had been vindicated. On 15 September UN paratroopers made a successful landing at Inchon, and, flushed with this latest triumph, American officials debated whether or not UN troops should cross the 38th parallel. This roused some consternation among their friends. British opinion was divided on the issue, while India hoped that the fighting would cease when UN forces reached the parallel and firmly opposed their crossing it.

The prospect of UN troops entering North Korea excited the sharpest reactions from China, who saw the West threatening her own territory. On 21 September Chou En-lai conveyed a warning to the West through K.M. Panikkar that since the UN had no obligation to China, China had no obligation to the UN. Fearful that the conflict might expand, Bajpai cautioned the British and Americans of the 'real danger' of Chinese intervention if UN forces crossed the 38th parallel. Even as Nehru pleaded restraint with Chou En-lai, he urged Bevin, 'in all sincerity and friendship', that Peking was not making empty threats. Bevin shrugged off Nehru's entreaty, saying that the Chinese government was 'too statesmanlike' not to appreciate the consequences of an attack on UN troops in Korean territory. Chinese statements, claimed Bevin, were probably aimed at splintering the UN front and at minimising the results of recent North Korean defeats. Bevin invited India to join Britain in sponsoring a draft resolution calling for the restoration of peace and holding elections under UN auspices to clear the way to the establishment of a unified, independent and democratic government of all Korea. The Indians, however, kept their distance from the West. Convinced that the Chinese were not bluffing, the Indians refused Bevin's invitation.[27]

The easy drive of UN troops to the 38th parallel on 29 and 30 September raised the question whether they would cross into North Korea. Nehru reiterated that this could touch off a war with China. Perhaps because of the success of the Inchon landings, some British officials were sanguine about a UN victory. With the balance of UN opinion in favour of action, the British derided Panikkar as unreliable and volatile, even as they deplored his influence on Nehru. Britain would go ahead with the resolution even if India opposed it.[28]

In the meantime, the Americans sought to ease Indian concern. Acheson authorised Bevin to send Nehru a message saying that the US regretted the bombing of Chinese territory in Manchuria and was willing to look into Chinese allegations. This could be done informally (where and how Acheson did not say) not necessarily through UN machinery. But the Americans would only go so far. Scoffing at the 'mere vaporings of a panicky Panikar' [sic], Acheson made it plain to Bevin that allowing the Chinese to present their case would not mean any delay in military action: the Americans were all set for it. Bevin was not allowed to pass on this information to Nehru.[29]

Anxious to defuse tension, the Indians now floated a new proposal. They agreed that under the Security Council resolution of 27 June, UN forces had the right to enter North Korea for military purposes, but in the interests of peace it would be preferable for the UN to give North Korea the opportunity to lay down arms and to co-operate with the UN. Not for the first time, Indian advice was lost upon the Americans: Acheson now contended that Chinese threats were aimed at forestalling Indian support for the British resolution. The gulf between India and the West was widening. India refused to join the UN commission (UNCURK) established under the resolution on the grounds that she would have more influence on China if she were not a member.[30]

Chou repeated a warning to Panikkar on 3 October, but the case for expanding the conflict had already swept the board in Washington. By 4 October, UN forces were already north of the 38th parallel along the east coast of Korea. The British had wanted to be consulted before the parallel was crossed and to attempt to restrain China by allowing her to be heard in the UN, but Acheson contended that it was 'too late now' to bring in China. The Americans were set to go full steam ahead. Indian reports had warned of the risk of Chinese intervention, but this risk had always existed and 'a greater risk would be incurred by showing hesitation and timidity . . . we should not be unduly frightened at what was probably a Chinese Communist bluff.'[31]

The British-sponsored resolution was passed by the General Assembly on 7 October, but it did not clarify *how* its objective of 'a unified, independent and democratic government' was to be achieved. The resolution tacitly implied the crossing of the 38th parallel. It was left to MacArthur to shear off its ambiguities, and to announce, on 9 October, that unless the North Koreans surrendered at once, he would take 'such military action as may be necessary to enforce the decrees of the United Nations'. Korea could not be 'unified' unless UN forces crossed the 38th parallel. Whether this was really the intention of the British in sponsoring the resolution is open to question, but on 9 October Bevin again discounted Nehru's warnings of Chinese intervention.

China clearly deemed the crossing of the 38th parallel by UN forces to be unacceptable[32] and had been building up her forces in North Korea. By 24 November, some 300,000 Chinese troops had swung into action and inflicted crushing reverses on UN forces. To MacArthur, who had ridiculed Chinese threats to intervene, the truth had come home. 'All hope of localization of the Korean conflict . . . can now be completely abandoned. The Chinese military forces are committed in North Korea in great and ever increasing strength . . . We face an entirely new war.'[33]

III INDIA, THE WEST AND THE KOREAN WAR: NOVEMBER 1950–JANUARY 1951

In Washington the political pendulum swung from near panic to loud threats to use the atomic bomb in Korea. The American need to save face intensified their aversion to Nehru's advice that the US should not provoke China. Confronted with the fact that Indian information about Chinese intervention had proved correct, Truman reportedly fumed that 'Nehru has sold us down the Hudson. His attitude has been responsible for our losing the war in Korea.'[34] For America's allies a new situation had arisen. The conflict could not be allowed to widen, and as the spectre of world war loomed on the horizon, they stepped up diplomatic efforts. It seemed logical now to turn to India, for Nehru's calls for moderation appeared a rational necessity. Lester Pearson appealed to Nehru to mediate in Korea. 'You have consistently urged the necessity of seeking peaceful solutions through mediation and conciliation', he wrote to Nehru on 30 November. 'For these reasons your voice would have more chance of being heard above the frightening clamour than that of anyone else in the world today.' Pearson entreated him to make a public call for a cease-fire, which would facilitate a cessation of the Chinese intervention and create an atmosphere for negotiations in which Peking might participate. But Nehru was alive to the limits of Indian influence, and he was reluctant to issue any appeal unless it was clear that the US and China would be willing to accept his proposals.[35]

None the less, the Indian government left no diplomatic stone unturned and sounded Peking, London and Washington with their suggestions to end the war in Korea. The Indians were also active in the UN. On 1 December 1950 Benegal Rau, the Indian envoy at the UN, met Wu Hsiu-chuan, leader of a Chinese delegation to the UN, and handed him a written proposal for a cease-fire and the establishment of a demilitarised zone. Bajpai presented the same formula to Henderson on 5 December. The demilitarised zone would be around areas in which China had 'particularly strong strategic and economic interests'. This implied Manchuria, which was vital to China because it was her only industrially developed area. The crucial consideration underlying the Indian proposals was that in the past invasions of China had come via Manchuria and Korea. The Chinese could not forget, that during the Second World War, the Japanese had first taken possession of Formosa, then Korea, then Manchuria and had finally attacked China itself. The Peking government therefore attached the greatest importance to Formosa and to the Cairo declaration of 1943 which had been reaffirmed by Truman in January 1950.[36] On 3 December Rau forwarded Wu another proposal for a Great Power Conference, to be held only after a cease-fire. China would be represented at the conference. The agenda of the conference was not defined, but it would be confined to Far Eastern affairs. 'The immediate problem was to stop the fighting and gain time to think.'[37]

The Chinese appeared interested in a cease-fire, and on 4 December they announced their terms. These included the withdrawal of the US Seventh Fleet from the Straits of Formosa and an end to American aid to Chiang Kai-Shek.[38] British and Indian officials wanted to make full use of any Chinese inclination towards negotiations. On the eve of Attlee's departure to Washington, Nehru wrote him that China would not enter into any talks on the assumption of her having committed aggression. China would only participate on the basis of equality, and since she was not a UN member, she had no obligations to the UN. The strength of the UN was limited: effectually, it was what the UK and US could put in the field, and in view of the situation in Europe, it would not frighten China.[39]

The Indian idea of a cease-fire to gain time for negotiations caught Attlee's interest. Attlee and Nehru were now thinking along the same lines, but their logic infuriated the Americans. In Washington, the Truman–Attlee confabulations from 4 to 6 December revealed considerable divergence between the British and American interpretations of Chinese actions and intentions. Attlee's insistence that negotiations with China were necessary because the West could not win a war against her raised American hackles. The Americans bristled at the British insinuation that 'our position was so weak that we had to proceed on the assumption that we were licked in Korea'. Dean Rusk claimed the US had lost prestige but not power; it was actually more powerful now than at the outset of the war. Attlee had said there was no choice but to negotiate with China, but the obdurate Chinese would demand Formosa and a UN seat as the price of negotiations. The US would have no truck with Chinese aggression; and George Kennan summed up the prevailing mood – 'we owe China nothing but a lesson'.[40]

In this uncompromising atmosphere, Attlee also tried to impress on the Americans the need for Asian support for Western initiatives in Korea. India would not join forces with the West in a war against China, so such a war would look like an act of Western imperialism against Asians. At the same time, Attlee commended India as a pro-Western force in Asia. The Chinese, he observed, had the military resources to assume the leadership of Asia, while the British 'had hoped that this leadership would go to India which had absorbed so much of the West'. Attlee pleaded in vain: Acheson was firmly against paying any price for Asian opinion.[41] Once again, Britain's "Indian pretext" had left the Americans cold.

The Indian government continued their peacemaking efforts, and on 8 December 1950 they instructed Panikkar to pass on Nehru's proposals to Chou En-lai. Nehru suggested that Formosa should be considered *after* a settlement on Korea had been achieved, since it would affect the whole strategic and defensive position of the US in the Pacific. A copy of the instructions to Panikkar was given to the British High Commission and transmitted by them to London. Bevin praised Nehru's instructions to Panikkar as 'both helpful and constructive and generally in line with our thinking. Indeed, I do not believe we could have expected the Indians to go further. I particularly appreciate their realistic attitude towards Formosa.'[42] Early Chinese reactions to the Indian proposal raised hopes for peace in Korea. Meeting Rau on 9 December Wu told him that the Chinese wanted to see an end to the fighting ' "which had been forced on them".' This encouraged India to consider tabling a resolution before the General Assembly which would provide for a cease-fire and the creation of a demilitarised zone between the cease-fire line and the Yalu from which all Chinese troops would withdraw.[43]

The British favoured the proposal, but they came up against the American demand for a unilateral Chinese withdrawal. The US also wanted to press on with a Six-Power resolution branding China as an aggressor *before* the Chinese had an opportunity to show whether or not they intended to abide by the terms of the resolution. Such a hardline posture would lead nowhere; the Foreign Office considered it extreme and instructed Gladwyn Jebb and Oliver Franks to moderate the American stand. Bevin was against a resolution condemning China; it should leave an opening for discussions *after* a cease-fire had been agreed upon. The demilitarised zone should be marked out in negotiations, and the UN should implement any agreement arrived at. Rau and Jebb should translate this concept into a draft Asian resolution – here Bevin was keen to maintain the appearance of *Asian* pressure on China and North Korea for a settlement. To maintain the semblance of Asian and Western solidarity on Korea the British would support the resolution. To create and demonstrate this solidarity, the Six-Power Resolution should be kept in abeyance.[44]

Bevin's thoughts harmonised with Rau's. On 12 December Rau introduced a resolution proposing that a committee of three persons consult the belligerent parties to determine the basis for a cease-fire. Kenneth Younger, visiting the UN General Assembly, voiced Britain's support for the resolution, which he said was 'simple and limited and left on one side questions of praise or blame'. After some hesitation the US finally voted for it, since the first step would only be a cease-fire.[45]

But the Indian proposals were destined for rough sailing and they ran into trouble – this time from the Chinese, who looked askance at attempts to separate Formosa from Korea as tending to favour the US and constituting a threat to their security. But they did not reject the Indian proposals outright, and Chou urgently inquired of Panikkar whether the US would accept the Indian proposals. Bevin was impressed by this information, for it hinted that China was interested in the proposals, and he thought it important to have something which would not be construed as a rebuff by either Washington or Peking. He remained opposed to naming China as aggressor; otherwise the British might find themselves 'compelled to assent' to US attacks on Chinese territory which could lead to an extension of hostilities.[46] So the Americans had to be restrained.

Could the strength of Commonwealth opinion achieve this? As early as October 1950, even as the British had scoffed at Chinese threats of intervention if UN forces crossed the 38th parallel, they had pondered over the idea of getting Commonwealth support for their attempts to rein the Americans in. They had also envisaged a key role for Nehru in a Commonwealth conference. Without him a conference would serve little purpose, so he was the first Commonwealth Prime Minister to be sounded on the desirability of a Prime Ministers' meeting. The *débâcle* suffered by UN troops in November 1950 rekindled British interest in a Commonwealth conference, and on 1 January 1951 Oliver Franks mooted the idea that the British might stand a better chance of swaying the Americans if the Commonwealth could agree about Korea. It would strengthen the 'diplomatic power and influence of Britain as the heart and focus' of the Commonwealth. Attlee liked the idea: the Commonwealth could voice its desire to bring China into the comity of nations. British officials showed a resentful but patronising determination not to go along unquestioningly with the Americans. As Attlee told the Commonwealth Prime Ministers' conference on 4 January 1951, the British had to rely on the Americans but the reverse was also true: 'The United States had as great need of us as we of them . . . the United States needed both moral and physical support, especially from the Commonwealth countries.' Supporting the US 'did not necessarily mean that we should always conform to their views'. The problem was how to deflect the Americans from unwise courses without making a breach in the alliance.[47]

At the same time, Bevin tried to win Nehru's support for a Commonwealth line on Korea. The outlook was promising, for he and Nehru were at one that China should not be labelled an aggressor. The Commonwealth, Bevin averred, constituted the only group of Western and Asian countries and agreement could influence the Americans. Emphasising what he thought was the maturity of British diplomacy Bevin regretted that the Truman administration was 'only too apt to take unreflecting plunges. We had made it our business to try to restrain them.'[48] There could not have been a more telling commentary on the need to guide the Americans down a safer road as well as on the uncertainty whether the British would be able to accomplish this, notwithstanding their confidence in their diplomatic know-how.

There was considerable coincidence of outlook between the Indians and British at this stage. Nehru – and the British Chiefs of Staff – concurred that the West would not be able to win a war against China. Both Bevin and Nehru wanted the US and China to participate in a conference on the Far East; both thought that strident name-calling would drive China into a Soviet bear-hug, both tended to believe that the Chinese wish to know American reactions to the Indian proposals signalled a desire to negotiate. The time was ripe for a fresh approach: Bevin suggested that the UN express disapproval of the Chinese intervention in Korea and ask them to withdraw, but China should not be denounced as an aggressor. A UN resolution could reaffirm the Cairo and Potsdam declarations and call for a cease-fire, Chinese representation in the UN and a settlement on Formosa. Bevin's ideas were close to those of Nehru, who also proposed the establishment of Formosa as a demilitarised zone. But Nehru went further than other Commonwealth prime ministers in advocating that the Commonwealth should go ahead with its peace proposals without the US if necessary. Other prime ministers agreed with Nehru on UN membership for China and recognition of her claims to Formosa, but they were not prepared to oppose the Americans in the UN.[49]

The British could not break ranks with the Americans, but they were worried about joining the US in castigating China as an aggressor. Failure to do so would prejudice the American commitment to Europe, while the US might be more amenable to persuasion against drastic action after the condemnation had been made. The cabinet vacillated; finally, on 29 January 1951 Gaitskell and Attlee took the lead in supporting an American resolution condemning China. They did so after the US had agreed that China would be given a chance to prove her intentions to the Good Offices Committee set up by the resolution.[50] However, this is only a partial explanation for the British decision to keep ranks with the US. A minute by Pierson Dixon of 29 January 1951 clarified the rationale both behind the cabinet's initial reluctance to back the Americans and its subsequent tergiversation. The Americans, observed Dixon, did not feel a great compulsion to carry the British with them in the Far East, and the threat of disagreement 'is . . . not as potent as we might suppose . . . . If we cannot effectively change American Far Eastern policy, then we must . . . resign ourselves to a rôle of counsellor and moderator . . . It is difficult for us, after several centuries of leading others, to resign ourselves to the position of allowing another & greater Power to lead us.'[51] London was in a quandary: officials knew that the Americans could dispense with their British surrogate in Asia, while the American bulwark remained indispensable to the UK. In the circumstances the British had little option but to vote for the American resolution.

Nehru was disappointed at this British decision, even though he knew that London had come under considerable pressure from Washington.[52] Once again, India distanced herself from the West. This had quite adverse effects on her relationship with the US, for it would colour American perceptions of the British role in South Asia and the Asian cold war, and eventually, of the usefulness of Britain to the United States in Asia.

IV INDIA AND THE UNITED STATES: NON-COMMUNIST ADVERSARIES?

Korea and China were emblematic of the prickliness of Indo–US relations. Indian attitudes to the US on bilateral and international concerns were also complex. Nehru thought the US produced mixed reactions in Asia: at one level there prevailed a desire for friendly relations which flowed from a need for US assistance; simultaneously there was mistrust of US policy alongside a growing fear of China as a great power. Chinese aggression must be resisted, but peaceful solutions must be sought and no unnecessary provocations given.[53]

India had few admirers in official Washington; most American policy-makers lambasted what they perceived as her weak-kneed neutralism as well as the damage she had inflicted on American interests in Asia. This contrasted with official British views that Indian diplomacy during the Korean war had been favourable to the West.[54] The problem for the Americans was that, even in their critical eyes, India – and Nehru – epitomised the success of democracy in Asia, and, as such, could not be ignored. Indian strictures of US policy in Korea had reached a new high with the UN bombing of Manchuria and the American refusal to negotiate with China in October–November 1950. But the Americans had remained impervious to Indian advice to calm rather than inflame passions. Instead, they had tabled a "Uniting for Peace" resolution in the General Assembly which authorised the right of the Assembly to enjoin collective security measures, including the use of force, in Korea. India abstained from voting for the resolution, which to Nehru seemed like converting the UN 'into a larger edition of the Atlantic Pact'.[55]

American officials were mystified, and on 3 November 1950 George McGhee, Assistant Secretary of State for Asian Affairs, summed up their indignation, irritation and frustration with Nehru.[56] That nonalignment might be at cross-purposes with an American preference for alignment was not acknowledged; instead, Indo–US differences were laid at the door of Nehru's psyche. Blaming 'Nehru's own prejudiced attitude toward the United States' as the major obstacle to the improvement of Indo–US relations, McGhee excoriated Nehru as an 'hypersensitive egoist . . . quick to take offense at our slights, real or imagined; and reluctant to appear subject to our influence'. Nehru was a 'frustrated revolutionary' whose plans for socialist transformation had been thwarted by Gandhi's denunciation of violence and by Britain's graceful withdrawal from the subcontinent. Consequently, Nehru was 'full of spleen', jealous of American wealth and power, yet ready to denounce them whenever possible.

McGhee also departed from the frequent official line that the success of Indian democracy owed much to Nehru. The Indian Prime Minister was not really a democrat; he was 'an aristocrat in circumstances which require that he profess democracy'. His high-caste Kashmiri Brahman background was reinforced by his education 'in the aristocratic tradition of the English public school and university thirty-odd years ago'. Now McGhee had a dig at the British as well: 'It is significant that his closest British friends are found among the nobility and the intelligentsia. Occasional overtones of disdain creep into Nehru's dealings with the British Labor Government and, politics apart, it would be reasonable to assume that he would find a closer kinship with a Churchill than an Attlee.' Nehru's aristocratic outlook accounted for his differences with the democratic United States: he was 'fundamentally unable to have full confidence in any government based on the franchise of a self-reliant people'. The inference was that anyone disagreeing with the US was not democratic; McGhee arrogated to the US the monopoly of that particular and supreme virtue. He completely disregarded the fact that Nehru had to take account of *Indian* public opinion, which frequently had been critical of his government's policy on Korea as being pro-West, and the difficulties that Nehru faced in reconciling domestic opinion with the American allegation that he was unfriendly, if not hostile, to the West.[57]

McGhee had simply decided that Nehru was in the wrong, and the US was above reproach. However, there was no room for defeatism on India and Nehru. 'India', counselled McGhee, 'is too important to us and Nehru too important to India for us to take the easy road of concluding that we cannot work with [him]'. The Americans must 'redouble' their efforts to work with Nehru and to strengthen ties with India. How would they work with Nehru? Would they succeed?

The military potential of India and Pakistan acquired a new significance for the US in the context of the Korean war. In September 1950 McGhee made known to British officials in London his idea that India and Pakistan 'might collaborate on some territorial guarantee of the non-Communist countries of South and Southeast Asia'. India could protect Nepal and Burma and, in general, act as a stabilising force in the area. R.H. Scott reminded him that Indo–Pakistani enmity would render such a course impracticable, but McGhee hoped that as the nefariousness of communist designs became more transparent, India and Pakistan would eventually combine with the West. McGhee's ideas were reiterated in NSC 98/1 of 25 January 1951 which recommended that the US should try to secure such military rights as it determined to be 'essential' in South Asia and to marshal the strategic, economic and manpower resources of the region on the side of the US. If India entered the communist orbit, 'all of Asia will have been lost'. Economic development of India and her orientation to the West entailed a vigorous American policy.[58]

What did this mean in practice? Shortly after the outbreak of the Korean war, McGhee recommended aid worth $200–300 million to South Asia and the Near East. But this sum was only a fraction compared to the billions of dollars poured into Europe under the Marshall Plan. Nevertheless, the contingencies created by the Korean war amplified American fears of communist machinations in Asia and induced them to review their aid policy. They were now more responsive to British exhortations for economic generosity to India, and the first substantial expenditures for South Asia were outlined after McGhee met British officials in London in September 1950. The US would finance the Colombo Plan, but how much? The Colombo Plan allotted $700–900 million to the subcontinent, of which the South Asian governments would provide $350 million and the UK $200 million of the total outlay. NSC 68/3 suggested that the US contribute about $154 million to the area or about half the Colombo Plan deficit. But in May 1951, the Truman administration proposed only $78 million for the region, of which $65 million were appropriated to India. This was "peanuts" against the overall requirement for foreign assistance, which was $8.5 billion in 1951. The administration's priorities were clear when it asked Congress for $7 billion for West Europe, of which $5.5 billion was earmarked for military aid. Congress now came into the picture. Congress authorised a total foreign-aid expenditure of $7.3 billion, of which India would net only $54 million. Congressional reductions in aid programmes lent an air of inevitability to cuts in aid for India, if only because India was 'as remote as Antarctica' to many Congressmen. In 1952, the aid allotted to India under the Point Four programme fell to $45 million – less than 20 per cent of what Chester Bowles, who replaced Henderson as ambassador in New Delhi in October 1952, had recommended. In late 1952, the Americans disbursed $500 million to fight communism in Indochina. This sum amounted to double the estimate of India's needs for the fiscal year 1953 and underscored the American penchant for military containment. American officials at the highest levels were not minded to press Congress for greater largesse to India. Commenting on proposals by Bowles for a special appropriation to India, Acheson and Averell Harriman, Director for Mutual Security, counselled Truman that 'our decision must rest on a determination as to how vital to United States' objectives in India immediate action on his [Bowles'] additional program is. In the absence of a critical emergency, it is extremely difficult to see how separate legislation could be justified.'[59] Nonalignment had established India's low place on American security and aid priorities, and neither the Indians nor the British would be able to change that.

The onset of a severe drought in India in the summer of 1950 prompted an urgent appeal by the Indian government for American food aid in November. At the instigation of McGhee, the State Department and Truman moved quickly to give India wheat, and they gained some support in the Senate. But the vagaries of American administrative procedure had to be contended with, and the departments of the Treasury and the Budget were reluctant to endorse the aid proposal for fiscal reasons. Some officials were dismissive of India's entreaty: 'I am not quite clear that [Nehru] is "on the side of the Angels"', asserted William Foster, Administrator of the Economic Co-operation Association. 'With our resources strained to the utmost, aid should be given in fullest measure to those who are demonstrably on our side and willing to fight for it.'[60] And since India would not fight for the US, she simply did not merit large-scale assistance.

On 16 December 1950 Mrs Vijayalakshmi Pandit, India's ambassador in Washington, forwarded India's first official request for food aid to the US government. This presented the State Department with an opportunity to hint that India might have to pay a price for her opposition to many aspects of US policy in Korea. On 29 December, Acheson assured Mrs Pandit that the administration was very sympathetic to India's case. He went on to link India's need for food with US foreign-policy interests. India's attitudes on two issues would be of special significance in dealing with Congress. First, if the Kashmir dispute could be settled, 'the people on the Hill would be favorably impressed'. Turning to Korea, Acheson warned the Indian ambassador that 'members of Congress would ask whether India understands the depth of the danger we now face'. A defensive Mrs Pandit responded that India would continue to resist communism but would remain nonaligned. Acheson said no more, but McGhee carried on the discussion by telling her that 'the question of an all-out alignment did not necessarily arise'. He then raised the 'general question' of collective security in South and Southeast Asia, pointing out that 'if the Chinese Communists did turn out to be aggressive there was no apparent defense for Southeast Asia except on the basis of collective security including India and Pakistan.' Mrs Pandit reiterated her government's opposition to power blocs, but added that 'some sort of grouping was desirable and should be possible'. McGhee queried her about the nature of such a grouping, and whether it would involve 'mutual defense arrangements'. Parrying that 'it could probably not as a first step', but it 'might come later', Mrs Pandit asked McGhee where arms would come from in the event of such a pact. It was now McGhee's turn to be evasive, while leaving no doubt about American preferences. The US might supply 'small amounts of arms', but 'our case was made more difficult' by the neutralization of the military forces as a result of the dispute between India and Pakistan. Here McGhee was assuming, in the manner of many British officials, that an end to the wrangling between India and Pakistan would draw those countries into Western alliances. The US, said McGhee, would await the outcome of the forthcoming Commonwealth conference where the subject of collective security would be discussed. As for food aid, what was needed 'was a feeling of confidence in India's underlying objectives in the present world situation'. McGhee pointedly added that 'in time of world crisis there was a tendency of people with common objectives to assess their interdependence and to draw together.'[61]

Acheson and McGhee had clearly linked food aid with a reorientation of Indian policy on Kashmir and regional defence. But Nehru would not change his policies at their behest, and their attempt to intimidate his government provoked him into stinging criticism of US policy in Asia. At the same time he reiterated India's affinity to Western democracies. US officials remained sceptical: McGhee advised Acheson that Nehru's actions 'invalidate any assurances which may be conveyed in his personal message'.[62] The common practice of democracy could not ease the friction between Indian nonalignment and the US emphasis on alignment.

American annoyance with India was not confined to the White House and State Department; India also had to run the Congressional gauntlet. Opinion against her on Capitol Hill compounded the difficulties of passing a food aid bill and presaged a downturn in Indo–US relations. Invoking humanitarian considerations and appealing to American generosity, the Truman adminstration placed the bill before Congress on 12 February 1951. Nehru's strictures of US policy in Korea had not endeared him to many senators: the Democratic Senator Tom Connally summed up the Congressional mood with his accusation that Nehru was 'out giving us hell'. But the strongest attack on the bill centred round the terms on which the assistance would be given. A group within the Foreign Affairs committee called for a loan repayable with strategic materials. India already exported manganese and beryl to the US, but in 1946 the Indian government had banned the export of monazite sands because it wished to retain this thorium-producing material for Indian use. Some Congressmen suggested that the US use the proposed wheat loan to break India's embargo on the sale of her monazite sands, and the provisions of a bill introduced in the House of Representatives on 24 April 1951 explicitly demanded repayment in strategic materials. This only stiffened Indian attitudes, as it was a fundamental of New Delhi's policy that material used to produce atomic weapons should not be supplied by India to foreign countries. There was no mistaking Nehru's bitterness at the US. 'We would be unworthy of the high responsibilities with which we have been charged if we bartered away in the slightest degree our country's self-respect or freedom of action, even for something which we need so badly.'[63] The food bill eventually became law on 15 June 1951, but not before much rancour had built up between the US and India. Nonalignment sparked off Indo–US acrimony; the American tendency to wash soiled linen in public encrusted that acrimony in India and in the US.

V THE AMERICANS REASSESS THE BRITISH ROLE IN SOUTH ASIA

NSC 98/1 of January 1951 had recommended the establishment of a South Asian regional association, but this did not imply that the Americans were coming closer to British ideas of Asian regional collaboration. US policy-makers were in fact concerned at the emergence of a neutral bloc in the subcontinent under Indian leadership. In March 1951 the prospect imbued McGhee with 'a sense of urgency', and he told a gathering of US ambassadors to South Asia in Nuwara Eliya in Ceylon that the time had come to make a 'serious examination of where we stand in South Asia'. Attempts to improve consultations with India had had only limited success, and seemingly insuperable obstacles kept India and the US far apart.[64] Henderson opined that Nehru had a 'definite' though nebulous objective to convert India into a great power, which 'would not take second place to any white peoples'. Nehru was trying to achieve this by emphasising international rather than national problems, to unite 'the colored peoples of the world, particularly those of Asia, and to use the combined strength . . . from this great colored bloc . . . first to enhance the international power and prestige of India and second to be able to deal with the Western World on equal terms'. Apparently the prospect was not to Henderson's liking. This was not because India was sympathetic to the USSR, but because she was often at odds with the US. India, he went on, wanted more from the West than from the USSR 'not as a favor but as a right'. India's expectations of the USSR were different: 'It wants nothing from the Soviet bloc except occasional cooperation for the obtaining of mutually desirable immediate ends and non-interference in the colored world.' What disturbed Henderson was the trend of Indian diplomacy during the Korean war. India had 'become somewhat more energetic in its efforts to weaken the influence of the United States' over the Commonwealth, West Europe, the Middle East and Southeast Asia. (This implied – wrongly – some remarkable successes for Indian diplomacy.) India's recent diplomacy had been 'harmful' to the US, and the US should impress on 'other' friendly countries that Indian policies were mistaken.[65] Thus Henderson did not perceive Indian nonalignment as pro-communist but as a challenge to American interests in Asia. His views were also in contrast to those of British officials, who continued to see Indian diplomacy as beneficial to the West in Asia.

Neither the shortfall of US aid for the Colombo Plan nor the huffiness that characterised Indo–US relations served British interests. On the one hand, US officials still rated the Commonwealth as a plus for the West in South Asia and solicited British help in allaying Indian misgivings about US policy in Asia. The British, however, stalled: in New Delhi, Frank Roberts thought it 'undesirable that we should officially, that is, in our talks at the Ministry of External Affairs, defend or explain American policy'. But the British could discreetly present American policy in a good light to remove Indian misconceptions.[66]

By the beginning of 1951, some American officials were beginning to doubt the efficacy of Commonwealth membership in keeping India and Pakistan favourably disposed towards the West, for India and Pakistan did not unquestioningly accept British leadership. American hopes of fortifying the anti-communist front were dashed, not for the first time, in January 1951, when Commonwealth premiers failed to break the deadlock over Kashmir and to assemble a collective security grouping.

American officials were now beginning to distrust Britain's very aims on the subcontinent. McGhee alleged that Britain herself was most concerned about garnering Commonwealth support for her policy towards China – insinuating that it was somehow not quite right for her to do so. In the autumn of 1950 Henderson was disquieted that British diplomats in New Delhi fawned on Nehru, in spite of his hostility to the US, in much the same manner as Nehru flattered Chou En-lai. British officials in New Delhi appeared more inclined to take the lead in running the US down than in confining themselves to listening to Indian criticism of American policy. In January 1951 he warned that the US could not trust the British to represent the Anglo–American partnership in South Asia. To the State Department, Henderson's letter made 'unpleasant reading' and confirmed that the British were not completely frank with the US and did not necessarily favour any enhancement of American influence in the area.[67] To that extent, the British were not "with" the US. Somewhat regretfully, McGhee discerned disharmony between British and American aims in the region. With three Commonwealth members in South Asia, the UK was 'devoting every effort to restoring and consolidating the British position'. There was, according to McGhee, 'a striking contrast' between British and American goals. 'The primary objective of the United Kingdom, to which other objectives are subordinate, is to obtain permanent adherence of India to the Commonwealth.' United States policy, on the other hand, was 'concentrated upon the orientation of India, in particular, and Southern Asia in general, toward the West and away from the Soviet Union'.[68] The inference was that British efforts to maintain their influence in South Asia, and the existence of that influence, were not sufficient or conducive to steering India towards the West, even as McGhee sought co-ordination between British and American policies in the area.

The recommendations of the conference were revealing. It took up Henderson's suggestion to treat India with patience and firmness, but if her policies undermined the maintenance of peace through collective security, the US should challenge them vigorously through the media.[69] There was no getting away from the fact that India and the US often had different ideas about what was good for peace, and they did not always consider each other's policies to be conducive to that end. The Americans knew that India was not in the communist camp, but their rift with her was deep enough for them to decide on refuting publicly Indian policies which militated against their interests. India and the United States were not adversaries in the cold war, but they remained parties to a cold peace.

British officials were more sanguine about India, although they knew she would not take part in defence discussions, let alone join Western combat forces in Asia. For example, in March 1951, the CRO were keen on the idea of a Commonwealth Division in Korea and asked Commonwealth countries to send more troops. India would not oblige them: Bajpai merely replied that India did not object to an Indian Field Ambulance Unit, in service in Korea since July 1950, being grouped with a Commonwealth Division. Bajpai – no doubt intentionally, according to Nye – avoided any mention of an additional contribution from India, and Nye thought it would be 'embarrassing, as well as serving no useful purpose', to raise the question of attaching Indian officers and other ranks to a Commonwealth Division.[70] Nevertheless, the British did not write off India as anti-West. Perhaps it was partly because Pakistan, which professed a great interest in supporting Western-sponsored plans for Middle East defence, made no contribution to the Commonwealth Division.[71]

More important was the British feeling that India, in spite of nonalignment, was a force beneficial to Western interests in Asia. Two illustrations sum up the difference between the British and American outlooks on India. In September 1951 H.H. Phillips thought the US was 'too inclined' to assume that because Nehru was not 'actively co-operating with the West he is working against it'. Discounting the apparent US belief that Nehru was ready to ignore the menace of communism in order to preserve "neutralism" between the communists and the West, Phillips had 'no doubt' that Nehru was firmly opposed to communism. His espousal of "neutralism" flowed from his desire to see Asia for the Asians and was not a political ploy to 'balance and counterbalance . . . East and West. I cannot recall any case where Nehru has taken positive steps to obstruct Western policy in South-East Asia: cf. the lack of criticism by him of our actions in Malaya and Indo-China.'[72] Phillips's comments may have reflected a certain British complacency that Nehru had not censured British intervention against the Malayan communists. Since the Indians and British both recognised China's place in the Asian balance of power and favoured greater contact with her, it is possible that Phillips was glossing over Indian criticism of the US – which had provoked *American* officials into controverting that criticism as being damaging to the US. The only fault that Phillips could find with Nehru was 'that he just does nothing, and fails to use the great influence which he certainly has over the rest of South-East Asia.'[73]

From New Delhi, Frank Roberts wondered whether the American view of India was not 'far too black and white?'

If they could be brought to think of Indians in terms of varying shades of grey instead of as villains one moment and saints the next [had the Americans ever thought the latter?], I am sure it would be an improvement. It might also help with the tendency which we have noted here, and from which you have doubtless suffered in Washington, towards an urge to *do* something about India – intervene in the Kashmir dispute, get her on our side in the cold war, etc. – rather than let events take their course and influence them unobtrusively from the side-lines.[74]

Perhaps such detachment did not come easily to the Americans because of the magnitude of their involvement in Korea. Dissatisfaction with

British diplomacy on the subcontinent and the Middle East had begun to prompt a larger US military profile in Pakistan.[75] Anglo–American differences over India mirrored the wider gulf that separated Britain and the US over China – and ultimately over the best means of preserving Western influence in Asia. Six months after the outbreak of the Korean conflict, the Americans were beginning to question the value of their British collaborator in the Asian cold war. This questioning, which had its source in the American worldview and strategical perceptions, was to put the US and Britain on a collision course in the negotiations over prisoners of war in 1952.

VI INDIA, THE WEST AND THE REPATRIATION OF PRISONERS OF WAR

Despite India's disappointment at British support for the UN resolution censuring China as aggressor, the Indo–British dialogue on Korea continued, as India remained the primary diplomatic channel between the West and China. The advent of a Conservative government to power in October 1951 did not alter the friendly diplomatic exchanges between India and Britain. By the early summer of 1952, Indian mediation had helped the belligerents in the Korean war to reach substantial agreement at the negotiations for an armistice at Panmunjom, but differences on repatriating prisoners of war remained a sticking point. Under the Geneva Convention of 1949, POWs were to be returned to the country for which they had fought, but, early in 1952, the UN command (without consulting Britain) declared its opposition to non-voluntary repatriation. Truman considered it morally wrong to send back anti-communist Chinese or North Korean POWs who were likely to face death or torture when they returned home. Nothing could have been better calculated to unleash a diplomatic storm. China could not yield to terms which would allow her POWs to renounce their allegiance to Peking and march straight into Taipei's welcoming embrace. British officials were sympathetic to the American line, but held that the case for contravening the Geneva convention was weak. Legality, morality and the Anglo–American relationship all had to be weighed, and it was Churchill who finally resolved the dilemma with the decision that the Americans must be supported.[76]

This was the background to India's search for a solution which would be acceptable to the West and China. During the first week of May 1952, after meeting Chou En-lai in Peking, Mrs Pandit told Nehru that she was certain that the Chinese desired peace in Korea, but they alleged that the · Americans wanted to expand the war in the hope of splitting China from the USSR. The existing deadlock in the negotiations was caused by the US insistence that 70,000 out of 132,000 North Korean and Chinese POWs would be repatriated to the communist side. Given the propaganda implications of such terms, it was hardly surprising that the Chinese and North Korean governments reacted vitriolically, but it was not their last word. Chou En-lai suggested that a compromise might be reached at 100,000. Nehru thought that the US had made a tactical mistake in announcing the number of POWs who wished to go home, as this made it difficult for the communists to keep up appearances. It would have been wiser for the Americans to say that they had no idea how many POWs would return and then to concentrate on getting the communists to agree to some system of screening which would protect all interests.[77]

On 12 May 1952 Nehru cabled Mrs Pandit that the Chinese position was wholly unsound: that it was wrong to condemn arbitrarily some prisoners to one side and the rest to the other. There was no logic in fixing an arbitrary number, for it was not the actual number of prisoners returned that was important, but the method by which the choices were made. Nehru proposed that all prisoners be placed under neutral control and every means used to ensure that a completely friendly decision was taken in each case.[78] Eager to resolve the stalemate, New Delhi now sounded London. British embarrassment with the poor administration of the prisoner-of-war camps run by the US, and the erroneous figures the Americans had on occasion provided about the number of POWs, foretold that the Conservative government would give a sympathetic hearing to the Indians. On 21 May Krishna Menon told Eden in London that Chou seemed interested in an armistice but wanted a facesaving formula, and Menon invited Eden to 'rough out' a possible form of words without committing the British government. Knowing that India would mediate, Eden suggested that India tell China that the conclusion of an armistice would open the door to discussions on Formosa and other matters. With a view to influencing the Americans, Eden wanted the issues of Formosa and Korea to be kept separate. He emphasised this by adding that he would not offer China 'any bribes' for the conclusion of an armistice. Eden followed up his conversation with Menon the next day by forwarding to the Americans a formula based on the principle of non-forcible repatriation of POWs and the internment by an independent body of POWs not wishing to return home.[79]

On 15 June 1952, Panikkar reported that the Chinese were willing to consider two alternative proposals – the return of 20,000 Chinese and 90,000 Koreans or 100,000 communist POWs provided that included 20,0000 Chinese. The Chinese preferred the second option, under which the UN command would accept in principle that all prisoners could return home after the armistice; those who elected otherwise could be interviewed by a committee of 'neutral states agreed upon' and representatives from the Red Cross.[80]

The Chinese seemed prepared to compromise, and their reply caught the attention of the British. It could be a genuine "feeler" and should be probed cautiously but promptly. The State Department concurred that the proposal offered a way out of the impasse, and if the communists desired an armistice this might be a reasonable basis for achieving it. British and American officials agreed that the Indians might approach the Chinese and ask them what machinery they would consider appropriate to make the required clarification.[81]

But an agreement was not destined to come easily, for the Chinese made a surprise retraction from any suggestion of compromise in early July. Their reasons could not be fathomed: perhaps they were goaded by the American bombing of North Korea during the last week of June. The complexity of American attitudes and intentions also made it difficult to envisage any settlement, as the Pentagon was in a feisty mood and determined to 'fight it out'. Acheson appeared less belligerent: on 8 October, he threw the ball into the communist court and asked them to accept a UN proposal or to introduce a constructive proposal of their own. Meanwhile, the communists had mounted a series of counter-attacks on UN forces and an endless war, rather than an armistice, loomed large. Nehru was disappointed with both the Americans and Chinese; there seemed little to choose between them. Yet both sides appeared interested in a settlement; efforts for peace must, then, continue. The British were also dismayed at the failure to ease the diplomatic stalemate and feared that alliance unity might entrap them in an unwinnable war against China. To them, a settlement appeared imperative. But they were unsure what to do, since it was the US which was preponderant in the negotiations and had taken the initiative at concerting Western tactics and in stating the principles for a settlement of the POW question. The main obstacle to the conclusion of a final agreement centred round the wording of Article 51, which dealt with the repatriation of prisoners – 'whether prisoners of war who had indicated that they would forcibly resist repatriation should be compelled to return to their homelands'.[82]

Against this background Krishna Menon discussed an Indian proposal to break the deadlock with Selwyn Lloyd, now leading the British delegation to the UN. Krishna Menon will figure so often in this book as India's representative at international parleys that it is worthwhile to introduce him at this point. Secretary to the India League in London from 1929–47, he had close personal ties with many Labour politicians and had played a cardinal role in the Indian decision to remain in the Commonwealth. After independence he served as High Commissioner in London, where he earned a reputation for legalistic, long-winded statements and a razor-sharp intellect. Menon's proximity to Nehru probably aroused the pique of other Indian officials, including Bajpai, Pillai and Mrs Pandit, who lost no time in planting the blame for Indian policies unpopular with the West on his diabolical influence over Nehru. Menon's boast that he only communicated with the Prime Minister could not have endeared him to Indian diplomats. British officials put up with him when they thought his prolixity could be of use to them; some even took to him: Selwyn Lloyd recollected that he had always got along well with Menon. If the British attitude to Menon was ambivalent, most American policy-makers hated him – if only because of his seemingly acidulous contempt for everything American. One American official reviled him as 'A devil incarnate . . . a poisonous fellow . . . actively inimical to Americans'; another marvelled at his 'peculiar success in persuading almost everyone he encounters that he is really as obnoxious as he appears to them to be.' In a more charitable vein, a third admired his 'courage and nerve' and confessed, 'I rather enjoy tussling with him. He's never boring.' If his American critics are to be believed, Menon took a particular pleasure in insulting them. When Loy Henderson paid a courtesy call on him in London in the autumn of 1948, Menon reportedly started the conversation with the words: ' "Well, this is interesting; you are the first American Ambassador who has ever darkened my threshold." ' To the Americans, he became the most visible and voluble symbol of Indo–US acrimony, but he was not its cause. The roots of that bitterness lay in a wider conflict of Indian and American interests. Menon's opinions of his many detractors must await the opening of his personal papers. For the moment, it is sufficient to note that he was sent as a special envoy to the UN in October 1952 because it was the most convenient way for Nehru to get him out of New Delhi.[83]

At that time the Assembly had before it two resolutions, a Polish one demanding the return of all prisoners in accordance with the Geneva convention, and a Twenty-One Power resolution, sponsored by the US on 24 October, which insisted on voluntary repatriation of POWs. The Indian proposal attempted to reconcile both these viewpoints. It suggested that POWs could be removed from military control and handed over to a Repatriation Commission, comprising Switzerland, Sweden, Poland and Czechoslovakia, under whose supervision they might be held for an indefinite period until an amicable means was found to send them home. During the summer India had kept Canada and Britain posted about her exchanges with China. The Indian proposal went down well with Lester Pearson, serving as president of the UN General Assembly, and Selwyn Lloyd. What really aroused their interest was the apparent keenness of the Peking government to settle the controversy over repatriation and the chance of playing China off against the Soviet Union. But Pearson and Lloyd had to battle with Acheson, who 'strongly opposed' the Indian proposal, alleging that its vagueness rendered it 'very dangerous' and unlikely to succeed.[84] Disagreeing, the British took the view the West should abandon the Twenty-One Power resolution in favour of the Indian one. An Asian diplomatic initiative might win the non-Western majority in the UN over more easily than the Western-sponsored Twenty-One Power proposal. Any possibility of talks with China should also be explored.[85] Proposals from the one Asian country which was both the main diplomatic conduit between the West and China and a member of the Commonwealth could also enhance Britain's role and stature in negotiations in which they had hitherto played a dissatisfied second fiddle to what they had sometimes considered to be an inflexible and unconstructive American policy.

The strains in American policy mirrored the complexities of American politics. The Pentagon, for one, appeared truculent. Then, with Senator Joseph McCarthy conjuring up visions of communists in every nook and cranny of American government on the eve of presidential elections, the incumbent Democrats could not embark on a course which might furnish the Republicans, whose candidate was General Eisenhower, with any electoral advantage. Both these considerations shaped Acheson's strong opposition to the Indian proposals.

In the diplomatic arena, however, Acheson was isolated, and he may have underestimated the resolve of his allies to use the Indian proposals as an instrument for peace. Eden arrived in New York on 8 November 1952, soon after Eisenhower's victory in the elections. This did not make things any easier for Eden, who now had to discuss the Indian proposals with the outgoing Democratic government as well as the incoming Republican administration, which did not yet have a policy. According to Eden, the shock of electoral defeat seemed to have induced in Acheson 'a mild persecution complex' and a determination to have his way.[86] Eden was uneasy at the deference shown by both Acheson and Truman to the Pentagon, who were hostile to the Indian proposals. American opposition stemmed partly from their dislike of the suggestion that the POWs would be offered repatriation or indefinite detention and partly from the representation on the Repatriation Commission of communists, who would probably indulge in delaying tactics.

The British and Canadians hoped India would insert the principle of non-forcible repatriation; this would bestow an advantage on the West in the public eye even if the Chinese turned the resolution down. Menon understood American concerns and was flexible about the form and wording of the resolution, but he thought that any proposal should be based on the following three points. First, the resolution should avoid language which would force the communists to admit openly the existence of unwilling repatriates; second, POWs should be able to move from the custody of the detaining powers to the Repatriation Commission before they went home or to some 'other disposition'. Finally, the Repatriation Commission should comprise an equal number of countries supported by each side because a commission which did not include any communist countries would be unacceptable to China. An umpire should be chosen prior to the armistice.[87] Menon placed the resolution before the General Assembly on 10 November 1952.

On the same day, Andrei Vyshinsky, the Soviet envoy at the UN, declared his government's insistence on non-voluntary repatriation. The Americans wanted to stand firm on the Twenty-One Power resolution, but the British thought the best rejoinder to the Soviets would be to back the Indian proposal, since it combined the original Indian principle of a

Repatriation Commission with the Western insistence on non-forcible repatriation, and it seemed to offer a genuine, if remote, possibility of ending the Korean war. Such a resolution might strike a chord with Asian countries, so it was 'essential . . . to avoid snubbing the Indian initiative and thus in effect kicking India back to the top of the fence just when she showed signs of descending on our side of it'.[88] British support for India angered Acheson, who was trying to hold the British 'steadily on course with us'. On 13 November he excoriated Selwyn Lloyd who, he alleged, had sometimes spoken of the armistice as the primary objective and sometimes of 'getting the Asians on our side' regardless of an armistice.

The fundamental problem was who was deceiving whom. Was it Menon who was deceiving Lloyd or Lloyd who was deceiving Menon. [sic.] Menon's desire was to obtain an armistice by having us desert our principles . . . Menon by himself was not dangerous but Menon with Lloyd was dangerous. . . . Menon was being kept alive by Lloyd and Pearson with their brains and skill. He could not carry on as he was alone.[89]

Acheson's wrath was clearly directed at the British. He threatened that the American public would judge European attitudes as an acid test of support to the US, and he waved the possible collapse of collective security as a Sword of Damocles if America's allies came out on India's side.

On the war-path against the Indian resolution and Britain's espousal of it, Acheson now alleged that the Indians had produced a draft resolution with Soviet encouragement and had 'gotten some of our allies to go along'. America's major allies had been told that 'this nonsense had to end'. Eden mistakenly saw the Pentagon at Acheson's elbow; the State Department record reveals that Acheson actually invited more arguments against the Indian proposal *from* the Pentagon. 'He thought that the Military should be brought into this, because the points involved the very ones on which the Military had very strong views. The Secretary had argued the Military's point of view, but he needed the help of the soldiers in getting this across.'[90] Perhaps Acheson hoped that the military might swing Eisenhower against the Indian resolution; but the British took no chances.

The British were interested in Indian information that Chou had conceded to Panikkar that "secret agents" might not want to return to China, and since 'they were under orders of Chiang Kai-shek they could go back to him'. This was the first occasion that Peking had acknowledged that some Chinese POWs might not wish to return, and the Indians considered this a significant indication that China was groping for some way to continue talks. British interest was reinforced by the Indian report that while China would not accept the principle of non-forcible repatriation, 'the mechanics governing repatriation were subject to arrangement', and that China wanted an armistice.[91]

With Peking showing signs of flexibility, the British wanted other countries to transfer their support from the Twenty-One Power resolution to the Indian resolution. This only induced the Americans to pick more holes in the Indian proposals, which they tried to stave off by demanding constant clarification of particular phrases in the draft. The Indians, however, sensed a propitious moment. Dismissing all American objections to their resolution as typographical errors, they saved the situation by conceding the point on non-forcible repatriation.[92] They thus swung thirteen of the twenty-one powers behind them.

Eden now tried to enlist Eisenhower's support for the Indian proposals. Earlier, Truman had also tried to win Eisenhower over by telling him that the neutrals were trying to circumvent the principle of non-forcible repatriation.[93] Eisenhower had not seen the resolution, so he was not so much against its terms as against what he had been told they meant. His misgivings were eased by the insertion of the principle of non-forcible repatriation, and he agreed with Eden on the importance of Asian support for the West. Fortified by Eisenhower's positive stance, Eden braced himself to confront Acheson again. News that the Russians disliked the Indian resolution stiffened Eden's resolve to hold his ground with Acheson. The US, growled Acheson, would not countenance an arrangement which gave POWs the option of repatriation or 'continuing to rot' in a detention camp. For Acheson, the 'basic problem' was America's allies who wanted to accept the Indian proposal. He 'laid it on the line with Eden' and asked 'whether he was with us or against us.' Eden assured him that he was with the Americans, but 'he stressed the importance of not changing Menon's resolution so much that Menon might be unable to vote for it himself'. Acheson claimed that he had told Eden that 'he [Eden] might have to choose between our vote or the Indian vote, and he said that in that case he wanted ours'. On 20 November, Acheson conceded that the General Assembly resolution would have to be based on the Indian draft, but the Americans would get their amendments across. However, the accounts of Evelyn Shuckburgh, Eden's Private Secretary, and Warren Austin, leading the American delegation to the UN, tell a different story. Shuckburgh recorded in his diary on 20 November 1952 that 'Acheson's position virtually collapsed.' Two days later, Acheson told his staff that the Americans would have to 'fight their way out', and the Americans vowed to 'kill the Indian resolution' by demanding amendments. Also on 22 November, a report from Warren Austin makes clear that Acheson's stratagem would not succeed, for Eden was 'prepared to accept the present Menon draft rather than to risk loss of Indian support'.[94] Meanwhile, he would do his best to persuade Menon to accommodate the American viewpoint.

Nevertheless, the endorsement of the Indian resolution by their allies stuck in the American throat. Told by an irate Austin that the Americans had expected the British to go along with them, Lloyd counterposed how the British could give way 'if they believed as they did that a principle of great importance was on their side, namely, Indian support'.[95] Acheson observed bitterly: 'It would seem to me normally that those carrying the great burden of responsibility would be expected to have the principal voice in determining what should be done.' Instead, there was a tendency now to accept the leadership of India, 'which had contributed nothing to the undertaking and would assume no responsibility for the result of its actions'.[96]

While Acheson sulked, it was, paradoxically, the Soviets who finally helped the Indian resolution to obtain US support. On 23 November 1952 Vyshinsky denounced the resolution as the handiwork of Western powers. This feeling may have been prompted by the fact that Menon had spent more time in confabulations with the British and other Western representatives at the UN than with the Soviet delegation.[97] Taken aback by the Soviet broadside, but seeing in it the chance of disarming the Americans, a statesmanlike Menon redrafted the paragraphs to which the Americans had objections, and the resolution was passed by an overwhelming majority in the General Assembly on 3 December 1952.

The resolution embodied Menon's basic principle that the emphasis on non-forcible repatriation should not be worded in such a way as to admit the existence of reluctant repatriates. Paragraph 3 of the final resolution stipulated that force would not be used against POWs 'to prevent or effect their return to their homelands'.[98] The final resolution was achieved by Menon's skill at making a diplomatic compromise favourable to the West acceptable to China, and it paved the way for the signing of the Korean armistice in July 1953.

American support of the Indian resolution came after a difficult course for which Eden put the blame on what he described as their 'inept' strategy and tactics and their 'irrational dislike of any Indian proposal, even when amended . . . to meet their views'. To him, US acceptance represented a diplomatic success for the British. A concerted Commonwealth effort had given an effective lead to the General Assembly.[99] Acheson's doubtful flair for alienating America's allies, Britain's determination to end the Korean conflict, the opportunity provided by constructive Indian proposals, Eden's ability to persuade Eisenhower of their merits and the readiness of the Indians to amend them to meet American demands all played their part in America's grudging, eleventh-hour acceptance of the Indian resolution.

Soviet opposition to the Indian resolution finally clinched the issue. The US could hardly have been seen siding with the Soviets against their own allies. Yet, the eventual US vote for India did not herald greater cordiality between them, render the US more amenable to British advice to lend a friendly ear to helpful Asian countries or augment British leverage over the Americans in Korea. This was made plain during the controversy over India's participation in the conference to settle the future of Korea.

VII KEEPING INDIA OUT OF THE KOREAN POLITICAL CONFERENCE, 1953

On 19 February 1952, the parties negotiating the armistice at Panmunjom agreed that a political conference to settle the future of Korea should be convened within three months of the signing of an armistice. Well aware of India's significance and value as an intermediary with China, and having kept in close touch with India throughout the Korean crisis because of her strategic position in Asia and as a Commonwealth member, the British had informed the Americans only two days later, on 21 February 1952, of their desire to include India in any political conference on Korea. Other Commonwealth countries concurred: Canada voiced the same thought to the Americans in March 1952. The British brought up the question again with the State Department on 2 April 1952. The Americans, however, balked: U.A. Johnson, Deputy Assistant Secretary for Far Eastern Affairs, replied that the US continued to oppose India's participation on the grounds that participation in the conference 'on the UN side should be on the basis of active support of the UN military operations in Korea'. Another Anglo–American skirmish over India seemed in the offing. On 8 June, just a month before the signing of the armistice, the Americans reiterated their point, while on 20 June, Makins met Dulles to make sure that India was included in the UN delegation to the conference, and on 28 July 1953 Salisbury advised the British cabinet that the conference should include non-belligerent countries such as India. And in New York, Jebb assumed that Britain would continue to lobby for Indian participation in the Korean conference.[100]

Having railed against Indian diplomacy as detrimental to US interests during the Korean war, and Nehru as a bad influence who led the British astray into appeasing communists, American officials did not want India in the Korean political conference. But they would have to answer the British request. South Korea now provided the US with a pretext to bar India from the conference. On 5 August 1953 Syngman Rhee told Dulles in Seoul that he would not countenance India's participation because she was 'pro-communist, pro-Russian and anti-American'. Dulles attempted a feeble defence of India, saying that she was really opposed to communism but that she differed with the US on the means of containment. He added that India had contributed a field ambulance unit to the UN cause. But an implacable Rhee was in no mood to hear any tributes to India and rejoined that India should be told to take her medical unit out of Korea.[101]

Rhee's anti-Indian bias was not unpleasing to Dulles, who anticipated strong pressure within the UN to include India. But such pressure could be overcome: participation could be limited to those countries actually fighting in Korea. Back in Washington, he encountered no opposition from other American officials to the idea; and Henry Cabot Lodge, now leading the American delegation to the UN, suggested that this point could be formalised in a General Assembly resolution. On 13 August Dulles instructed the American delegation at the UN that he did not want a "roundtable" conference with neutrals; and that restricting participation to countries which had fought was in accordance with Article 60 of the armistice.[102]

The situation could not have been more awkward for the British. Only the day before, Salisbury had assured Krishna Menon that Britain would support India's presence in the UN delegation. To American officials the British made the case that India could be included as chairman of the Neutral Nations Repatriation Commission and as a neutral. Dulles at once countered that one could not find out which side India was on, and she called herself a neutral.[103] Australia and New Zealand now stood up for Britain, arguing that Rhee could not be allowed to veto the selection of participants, and they tabled a resolution in the UN for India's participation. But the Americans would not yield; Dulles warned Salisbury that they could not do any more to influence Rhee in India's favour.[104] The British were left with little leeway. They disliked Rhee, but they had no influence over him and would hardly want to be saddled with the responsibility for his refusal to attend the conference. Nor would they want to quarrel with the Americans on an issue not of primary importance to them. Backing down, Salisbury agreed that 'it was silly for us to split over this question but they had committed themselves to India'. He would do what he could to have India withdraw.[105]

The Americans left nothing to chance. On 14 August 1953, Cabot Lodge told Menon in New York that 'it would be a great embarrassment to us in our relations with Korea for India to be a member of the Conference because of the well-known attitude of the President of Korea', and on 26 August in New Delhi, George Allen urged Nehru to withdraw India's candidature for the UN delegation to the Korean conference.[106] This knowledge of US opposition foreclosed any options, and the Indians stood down. Dulles and Lodge perceived India's involuntary exit from the conference as a victory over America's allies: Dulles exulted that 'the fact that we have stopped "yessing" everyone is good'.[107] The truth was that South Korea and Britain had offered the US incompatible suggestions; and the Americans clearly said "no" to the British. Apparently Dulles did not regard listening to Rhee as "yessing" him, since the US shared his antipathy to India's participation. At the same time Dulles was not oblivious of the value of Indian mediation with China and toyed with the idea of her attending the conference as an intermediary. But there was no mistaking the intrinsic American opposition to India's participation in the Korean conference and, coupled with rumours of US military aid to Pakistan, it contributed to a plummeting of Indo–US relations at the end of 1953.[108] Aware that the US had browbeaten its Western allies, Indian officials were certainly not enamoured of American behaviour. As Nehru put it: 'Some countries who had openly stated that they would vote for us had to back out. Not only that, but American Ambassadors brought this pressure on countries in their respective capitals. It really has been an extraordinary experience to see how a great Power behaves.'[109]

India's exclusion from the Korean political conference could be construed as evidence of the hold Syngman Rhee had over the Americans. This was implied in a message Churchill sent to Nehru on 29 August 1953: 'I thought you were very wise to help the United States out of their difficulty with Syngman Rhee . . . You must be gratified by the general recognition of the wisdom and dignity of India's withdrawal.'[110] India's pull-out also averted much embarrassment for the British, who would not have been able to bridge the Indo–US gap on this occasion.

The whole episode also highlighted the American dislike of nonalignment, which was patently confirmed, around the same time, by American intentions of giving military assistance to Pakistan. There was no mistaking the limits of British and Indian influence in Asia, for it was not the UK and India which had played a major role in the Korean war. The massive American contribution to the UN effort in Korea, and the fact that they alone had some leverage over the South Korean government ensured that they would have the decisive say on India's exclusion from the Korean political conference. The Korean conflict expanded the American military presence in Asia and established the US as the dominant Asian power; it was the first step towards greater US military involvement in Asia, which reached its peak – and its nemesis – with the Vietnam war.

In contrast, Britain could just about preserve her hold over Malaya and Hong Kong, and she could not take on any new military commitments. American officials knew that their country was not all-powerful, but they were able to pay the price of their involvement – though whether they achieved the results they desired is another question.

Indian nonalignment demonstrated its value as a conduit between the West and China, but it clashed with an American policy based on alliances, and most American officials distrusted India. The British did not always see eye to eye with the Indians but made the most of the occasions when both could work together because of a concurrence of outlook. The British did not find it difficult to maintain a friendly dialogue with the Indians. This may appear surprising, since in 1953 Britain still possessed her African and Caribbean colonies, Hong Kong and Malaya, and British officials deprecated what they discerned as the unreasoning emotions underlying Indian anti-colonialism. Commonwealth ties, or a concern for Commonwealth unity, can account only in part for good Indo–British relations. The Indians were dismayed when the British did not or were unable to go along with them, for example, during the first phase of the Korean war and over the Korean political conference. Indian attitudes to the Commonwealth were not affected, if only because Indian officials knew that the British were under pressure from the Americans and that the compulsions of alliance unity made it impossible for Britain to disregard the US. But American officials – and some historians – may have got the impression that British opposition to many American ideas owed much to Commonwealth influence, since the British talked of the need for Commonwealth support – especially when they disagreed with the Americans. In any case, by 1953, the strength of the Commonwealth relationship had been diluted by factors as varied as Britain's exclusion from ANZUS in 1951, Indo–Pakistani altercations over Kashmir, India's republican status and demands in Pakistan for an Islamic head of state or even withdrawal from the Commonwealth.

A more satisfactory explanation for good Indo–British relations may lie in the fact that negotiation and compromise were to be the main instruments of Britain's policy in Asia; she did not, therefore, come into conflict with India's emphasis on diplomacy, even if their essential long-term aims differed. The British knew that an Indian military contribution could have strengthened them: they were frequently frustrated at India's failure to think in "global terms". But the phrase "global terms" did not imply *bipolar* terms to the British as it did to the Americans. The British did, after all, see themselves as an independent great power, intellectually and morally superior to the Americans, and with much more to offer Europe and Asia than the US. Affable Indo–British contacts, in contrast to cantankerous Indo–US exchanges, illustrated that British influence could be potentially more attractive to Asians than American influence, in spite of – or because of? – Britain's military weakness, which precluded British military expansion in Asia.[111]

The idea of Indian influence on Britain during the Korean war does need some qualification. It depends first on what one means by influence. If maintaining a dialogue, and modifying and refining ideas after discussion constitutes "influence", then the British and Indians did influence each other. But at that level, the British and Americans were even more susceptible to each other's influence, and the question would arise why the Americans alleged that the British were swayed by India, while disregarding the many occasions during the Korean conflict when the British did *America's* bidding. Part of the answer lies in the frequent British urging of the Americans to pay heed to Indian opinion. The British usually resorted to this advice when they disagreed with the Americans which generally coincided with agreement with the Indians on the need to restrain the US in a particular context.

On the whole, though, Britain's "Indian pretext" was all but lost upon the Americans. The allusions to India's political sagacity tended to increase American wariness of a British policy that appeared to be influenced by India. For example, on 25 April 1951, the State Department cavilled that the British made 'every effort' to strengthen India's association with the Commonwealth, and they did this 'by placating Mr. Nehru, or supporting him when possible, on many of his attitudes which are considered by the U.S. as damaging to the position of the free world'.[112] As such, any

assessment of British policy would have to take into account their susceptibility to Indian opinion. It is difficult to see what the British really
achieved by frequently citing the Indian viewpoint. Given the acrimony
that became the hallmark of bilateral Indo–US relations, the references to
India may well have accentuated American dislike of India, as the squab-
bling over the repatriation of POWs and India's exclusion from the Korean
political conference showed. Contrary to British intentions, their use of the
"Indian pretext", at best, did not influence the Americans; at worst, it
may, unwittingly, have impeded their endeavours to bridge the gulf between India and the US to *Britain's* advantage. It was not only on the
Asian cold war that the US questioned British policy towards South Asia;
as the next chapter will show, differences over the best way to safeguard
Western defence interests in the Middle East induced the Americans to
embark on a policy towards Pakistan which was wholly disadvantageous to
the British.

4. Britain and the US jostle over Pakistan – and Middle East defence, 1950–4

They [Pakistan and Turkey] had gone forward almost spontaneously after the first hint from the United States and this seemed to him [Dulles] an encouraging sign for the defence of the area [Middle East] as a whole. [Dulles, cited in Berlin (Eden) to Foreign Office, tel. 223, 18 February 1954]

[The] attempt to link their [US] offer of military aid to Pakistan with the initiation of some kind of military collaboration between Pakistan and Turkey, which might develop into some system of collective defence in the Middle East. . . . would probably be positively harmful . . .' [C (54)4, 5 January 1954]

He [Zafrullah Khan] said that he and his country [Pakistan] adhered to what he considered to be the European principle reflected in the story of the lady who wished to have her portrait done by a prominent artist in Europe and who specified in advance that the artist's rendition must do her full justice. The artist in Sir Zafrullah's story replied, 'Madam, what you need is not justice but mercy.' [State Department memo of conversation between Zafrullah and Stassen, 22 June 1954]

I THE BACKGROUND

On 25 February 1954, the US government announced its decision to give military aid to Pakistan. A few weeks later, on 2 April, Pakistan and Turkey signed a treaty of mutual cooperation, and on 19 May 1954 Pakistan and the US signed a Mutual Defence Assistance Agreement. Taken together, these events marked Anglo–American differences over Middle East defence and symbolised, within seven years of decolonisation, America's replacement of Britain as the dominant economic and military power in South Asia, a region with which the Americans had few historical ties, which they had regarded as essentially British terrain after 1947, and to which they had, until 1949, accorded low priority. Evidently something must have happened between 1950–4 to enhance American interest in Pakistan. Ideas about Britain's "decline" or of a "transfer of responsibility" from the UK to the US after 1945 do little to explain how or why this happened; they bypass the essential question why the Americans decided to penetrate an area which they had hitherto regarded as a British concern, and they tell us nothing about British feelings at being supplanted by the US in Pakistan. They certainly give no inkling that the Americans decided to give military assistance to Pakistan within the framework of a US-sponsored plan to link Turkey and Pakistan in the "Northern Tier", an arrangement which, as the Cabinet paper quoted above makes clear, displeased the British. And the Pakistani plea for mercy sounds a discordant note with the American optimism about defending the Middle East.

Until now, scholarship on the US–Pakistani relationship has highlighted its consequences in South Asia only. The idea of a strong British influence – especially that of Olaf Caroe – on US policy was first mooted by Selig Harrison. It was effectively refuted by M.S. Venkataramani and H.C. Arya who pointed out that the Americans had used Pakistani territory as a base to rush assistance to the USSR and to undertake operations in the Persian Gulf during the Second World War, and they did not need British guidance on the strategic advantages of Pakistan.[1] In any case, even if Caroe *had* influenced the Americans, his views certainly did not amount to "British" policy. But the idea of a Western conspiracy to weaken India by arming Pakistan has been popular in some Indian circles. Perhaps this is because the British publicly endorsed American military aid to Pakistan, and their public stance has been taken at face value. However, such views ignore Nehru's realisation in 1953–4 of British unease over the enhancement of American influence in the Middle East at their expense.[2]

The onus for the intellectual lacunae in earlier work on US–Pakistani relations could to some extent be placed on the unavailability of archival material on Anglo–American divergences over Pakistan's role in Middle East defence and also on a rather rosy picture of Western allies fighting communism shoulder to shoulder. What is less easy to explain is why recent work on post-1945 British policy in the Middle East, based on British archival sources, makes no reference to Anglo–American differences over Pakistan's participation in Middle East defence.[3] Perhaps this is because scholars have not questioned the intellectual and conceptual biases of the policy-makers whose confidential minutes they have read. The most likely explanation for the omission of Pakistan in discussions of Anglo–American strategy based on official British records is that Britain's Middle East strategy centred round Egypt, and British sources on the Middle East focus on those countries which fitted into the traditional British concept of "Middle East". For the British the Middle East comprised Israel and Palestine, Egypt, Iraq, Jordan and Iran and did not include Pakistan. Material on Pakistan, as on India, is listed under the Southeast Asian and Far Eastern departments of the Foreign Office. And as South Asia was not a major theatre of the cold war, historians basing their research on British archives may unwittingly have ignored its place in the global strategy of Britain and the United States.

In contrast, material on Pakistan in American archives can be found under several categories of documents – South Asia, the Near and Middle East, Middle East Defence, Mutual Security and presidential papers. Yet research on the Middle East, grounded on American archives, also makes little reference to Pakistan. It is only very recently that scholars such as Venkataramani and Robert McMahon,[4] relying largely on American records, have placed US–Pakistani relations in the context of American global strategy. But they do not spell out the consequences of US–Pakistani military ties on the British position in South Asia and the Middle East. Nor do they explain why the Americans departed from their customary practice of following the British lead in South Asia or elaborate on Anglo–American disagreements over the Middle East. On the other hand, Ayesha Jalal sees Anglo–American rivalry, rather than the Cold war, as having a decisive bearing on the strategic connections forged between the US, the Middle East and Pakistan, but she assumes from hindsight 'the tottering edifice' of the British empire and makes an unsubstantiated link between US–Pakistani ties and the Baghdad Pact, while the memoirs of Eden, Macmillan, as well as recent research based on official British documents, reveal British disappointment at America's abstinence from the Pact.[5]

All this is not to deny the significance of earlier work on US–Pakistani relations, especially that drawing mainly on archival sources. But it represents a mere nibbling at the veritable intellectual feast that has been laid out by the recent opening of British and American archives, a feast that will take some considerable time to be digested fully. This chapter will first outline British and American interests in the Middle East and then highlight the extent to which the British and Americans influenced, or failed to influence, each other on Pakistan's participation in Middle East defence. At another level, it will be shown that the independent state of Pakistan was not a passive actor in the process by which the Americans gained influence on the subcontinent at the British expense and that the congruence of American and Pakistani interests that occurred in 1953–4 owed something to Pakistani dissatisfaction with the British as well as to Anglo–American differences over Pakistan's role in Middle East defence. Pakistan's search for security against India, Anglo–American discord, the convergence of US–Pakistani interests and the British failure to uphold their dominance all ran parallel to, and cut across one other, and this chapter will identify and analyse the often confused and contradictory currents and cross-currents which culminated in the unprecedented installation of America in Britain's place in South Asia.

Britain and the United States were both world powers, and the significance they attached or did not attach to Pakistan's part in Middle East defence was ultimately determined by their conception of their global interests. A comparison of the British and American records reveals several disagreements between the US and the UK over Western strategy in the Middle East, of which US–Pakistani military ties were one manifestation. In the long run, Anglo–American differences adversely impinged upon British hopes of preserving their hegemony in the Middle East with *American* support after 1945.

What were the British and American stakes in the Middle East? During the late-nineteenth century, Britain's desire to safeguard her Indian empire against the Russians motivated her entry into the Middle East,[6] including Cyprus, Egypt and the Sudan. Britain's acquisition of a stake in the Suez Canal in 1875 signalled her ascendancy in the Middle East. The breakup of the Ottoman empire in 1919 and the creation of the mandates of Iraq, Jordan and Palestine confirmed the British as the paramount power in the region between the two world wars. The Anglo–Egyptian treaty of 1936, under the terms of which the British could station 10,000 troops on Egyptian soil, became the grand symbol of British supremacy in the Middle East. But the treaty stoked the fires of Egyptian nationalism, and, after the Second World War, in Egypt, as in India, Britain's overlordship was an emblem of imperial grandeur to the British and of humiliating domination to the Egyptians. The twain would never meet. The irreconcilability of Egyptian and British interests was to lead, by 1951, to the failure of Britain's efforts to muster regional support for a Middle East Defence Organisation (MEDO) which would uphold her paramountcy and eventually to the Suez crisis of 1956. That irreconcilability became the catalyst of Anglo–American disagreement over the best way of protecting Western interests in the Middle East; one outcome of that discord was the American entry into Pakistan in 1954.

India was both the *raison d'être* and the anchor of Britain's position in the Middle East, but her independence in 1947 only prompted the British to renew their stake in the area. There was no coyness about the reason – it was simply the British wish to remain a great power. Attlee did question the value of hanging on to 'deficit lands', but he was overridden by Bevin and the Chiefs, who stressed that Britain would forfeit her international status if she gave up her position in the Middle East. Seen through the cold-war prism this fear was understandable. The Middle East was the shield to Africa; the Suez Canal was the gateway linking the West to Asia; and – most important from cold-war considerations – military bases in the area would enable the West to launch an attack on the Soviet Union. Even as the end of the Raj logically suggested disengagement from the Middle East, so the vast reserves of oil renewed the strategic importance of the region.

The dilemma was how a Britain enervated by war could maintain her paramountcy. Bevin found an answer in partnership as a replacement for domination. This echoed the Commonwealth concept of a voluntary association of self-governing peoples which had been attractive to India and Pakistan after 1947. In the Middle East, however, the chances of partnership did not look very bright. The idea ran into trouble with Egypt, where nationalists demanded not partnership but evacuation of the 200,000 British soldiers on Egyptian soil, the dismantling of bases and the closing of clubs and barracks. In Egypt, as in India, the notion of partnership to retain *British* primacy was flawed. A significant difference between the South Asian-Commonwealth and Anglo-Egyptian "partnerships" was that in the subcontinent the Commonwealth followed the ending of British ascendancy, while in Egypt the British wished to use that concept to sustain their hegemony.

Whether or not the British sensed the flaw is unclear; what was certain was their resolve to preserve their niche in the Middle East. Unable to do so single-handedly, they hoped to bolster their standing with American support. Would the Americans be amenable to their schemes? Since the twenties oil had lured American economic interests to the Middle East, but the region assumed strategic importance for the US only during the Second World War. With the coming of the cold war the Middle East had to be "saved" from a predatory global communism, and the US expected Britain to safeguard Western security interests and backed her position on the Suez Base. This expectation signalled America's endorsement of British imperialism if it appeared to protect and advance American interests. Going against the grain of America's professed anti-colonialism, it could not be reconciled with the nascent nationalisms in the Middle East which the Americans, as much as the British, considered a danger to Western security interests. Thus far the British and Americans could work conjointly in the region. However, their definitions, images and expectations of the Middle East as a strategic region diverged. Unlike the British, the Americans regarded the Middle East as an adjunct of West European defence and not as the mainstay of their power. Also, the Americans viewed the Eastern Mediterranean as the right flank of the defence of Europe, and Turkey – a Mediterranean power supporting the sea routes to Southwest and Southeast Europe – as the natural keystone of any system of Middle East defence. Turkey and Greece were the immediate concerns of the Truman doctrine of March 1947. Moreover, the Americans did not wish to become too closely involved with the British and were content to leave the area to them. On the whole, American interest in the region was indecisive and reluctant, and between 6 August 1948 and 29 November 1950 the NSC did not produce a single paper dealing with the Middle East as a strategic entity.[7]

II BRITISH AND AMERICAN CONCEPTIONS OF PAKISTAN'S ROLE IN MIDDLE EAST DEFENCE

It was against this background that the British and Americans were to debate Pakistan's role in Middle East defence. Between 1947–50 some American officials had drawn attention to the benefits to be gained from

Pakistani participation, but their advice had not been translated into policy, if only because the Truman administration did not know what direction the US should take in the Middle East. The communist triumph in China in October 1949 heightened interest in Pakistan, all the more so because Nehru's visit to the US in the same month did not augur closer Indo–US relations, while Pakistan, commended by some American policy-makers as 'more Western than Eastern-minded'[8] and desirous of joining hands with the West in the Middle East, was a welcome contrast to nonaligned India and her shrill moral and political critiques of the US. The Americans had yet to give serious thought to Pakistani participation in Middle East defence, but they were beginning to question their own perception of Pakistan as a strategic adjunct of India. Noting the value of bases in Pakistan, a State Department policy paper of 3 April 1950 considered it 'desirable critically to review our concept that Pakistan's destiny is or should be bound with India'. Indo–Pakistani solidarity was an elusive mirage; on the other hand a strong Muslim bloc under Pakistani leadership and friendly to the US might create a balance of power more favourable to the West in South Asia. This reflected American disapproba-tion of nonalignment. The international communist menace meant that US interests would be best served by Indo–Pakistani co-operation, not rivalry. But a communist or Soviet threat to the subcontinent was more of a bugbear: in March 1949, the US Chiefs affirmed that South Asia was inaccessible from the north, and that more lucrative prizes existed for the Soviets in Europe, the Middle and Far East.[9] So the Americans were unlikely to respond with alacrity to Pakistani overtures on any kind of Middle East defence arrangement.

The Korean war induced a high-level review of the efficacy of American strategy against what was seen as Soviet-inspired communist expansion, and it prompted a reassessment of the traditional American reliance on the British in South Asia and the Middle East. With nationalisms in Egypt and Iran raising the flag of revolt against Western domination, and with the British locked in a never-ending battle with them, a shift in US policy was in the offing. During his talks with British officials in London on 18 September 1950, McGhee told them in no uncertain terms:

We [the US] had no confidence in the effectiveness of Egypt's influence and, looking elsewhere for leadership, we were bound to think of Pakistan, which was the most progressive and capable of the Moslem countries and was in a good position to point out the inconsistency of backward economic and social conditions with Moslem principles.[10]

Three months later, on 27 December 1950, McGhee suggested to Acheson a more positive US role in the Middle East and a higher American profile in the region while supporting the British. In January 1951 the NEA department recognised the British as being primarily responsible for defending Western interests in the area but saw them as a declining political influence, unable to shore up their position 'even with probable Commonwealth support.'[11]

McGhee wanted a Middle East defence arrangement without too much American involvement. This meant that the Americans must have local allies, but there was little sign of any. While harping on Britain's dwindling influence, McGhee tacitly confessed that the Americans did not have much standing in the area. Only two countries offered the US an opening to the Middle East – Turkey, which was already a member of NATO – and Pakistan, which had repeatedly avowed her anti-communist fervour and proclaimed her keenness to defend the region.

The assassination of General Razmara Ali, the pro-Western Iranian Prime Minister, in March 1951, and the nationalisation of the Anglo–Iranian oil company in April 1951 highlighted the nationalist challenge to Western interests in Iran, but the US refused to endorse a military riposte to defend the British stake there. However, the Americans soon found themselves confronting the same dilemma as the British in the Middle East. The imperialism of the big stick was a thing of the past, but Western interests had to be safeguarded, so partnership would have to replace domination. The idea was analogous to Bevin's ideas of partnership; the difference was that the Americans saw themselves seeking the partners and the British as reactionary imperialists who would remain permanently estranged from nationalists in the region. Mentally, then, the Americans were beginning to distance their own role and concerns in the Middle East from those of the British.

An independent American search for new ideas for protecting Western interests in the Middle East was on.[12] But how could any partnership be created, especially when there was a shortage of willing partners, of nations in the non-Communist Middle East who did not perceive a communist threat to *their* interests, and who therefore had no wish to be "saved" for the "free world"?

American strategic perceptions served up an answer. An outer ring from Turkey to Iran would be the most desirable line of defence, and the participation of Pakistan in the defence of Iran should be explored. Meeting the British Chiefs of Staff in Malta on 12 and 13 March 1951, the US Chiefs emphasised the importance of a Pakistani role in policing the Iraq-Iran sector. The British Chiefs had long favoured a Pakistani contribution to the defence of the Persian Gulf and agreed in principle with their American counterparts, but they stressed the need for a settlement of the Kashmir dispute. This was justified, as Liaqat Ali Khan had made it clear at the Commonwealth Prime Ministers' meeting in January 1951 that a British guarantee on Kashmir must precede Pakistan's recruitment in Middle East defence. At this juncture, neither the British nor American Chiefs were thinking of a contribution by Pakistan alone; they still thought that a military link-up between Pakistan *and* India would be necessary to create a viable security structure.[13] To that extent, the American Chiefs were still influenced by the traditional British conceptions of South Asia and the Middle East.

But the State Department had other ideas. If Kashmir was the obstacle to Pakistan's association with Middle East defence, the State Department wanted the obstacle to be removed, and if it could not be removed, it must be circumvented. NSC 98/1 of 25 January 1951 had proposed that the US obtain military rights in South Asia, and on 26 February the Nuwara Eliya conference of American envoys in South Asia, presided over by McGhee, had advocated that:

> The United States military authorities should consider on an urgent basis the desirability of the United States entering into an early understanding with Pakistan, which would provide for equipping and building up Pakistan's military forces and insure the availability of Pakistani ground forces on the western flank at the outset of war.[14]

Pakistan should be drafted into a Middle East pact and the British consulted if it materialised. Dissatisfied with the advice of the American and British Chiefs, McGhee urged the US Chiefs to give a more positive response to the idea of Pakistan's recruitment in Middle East defence. He also tried to rope the British in. Talking to British officials in London on 3 April 1951, McGhee maintained that Pakistan could be persuaded to take part in a regional alignment if the Kashmir conflict could be resolved. Echoing the NSC decision of January 1951, he ruled out a bilateral defence pact between Pakistan and the US. Pakistan might join a Middle East grouping, in which the US would not participate directly, but to which it would supply military equipment and training facilities. Unlike most countries in the region, who had yet to develop their military potential, Pakistan had an efficient army and air force, so, argued McGhee, it was 'vital' to involve her in Middle East defence.[15] Even as McGhee was determined, *faute de mieux*, to make do with whatever was available, he implicitly acknowledged the minimal American influence in the Middle East.

The Foreign Office favoured Pakistan's participation in Middle East defence in principle; and R.H. Scott agreed with McGhee that it was 'well worth trying.' But the confidential exchanges among British officials revealed their reservations about such a course. For one thing, the British were hemmed in by the Commonwealth. S.J.L Olver could not envisage the British paying the likely Pakistani price of a guarantee against India, especially as Pakistan, being 'fully aware of her strong bargaining position', was 'likely to stand out for the full price of a direct assurance against Indian aggression'. And the British could not play the honest broker and give guarantees to both India and Pakistan. From the Eastern department, L.A.C. Fry was 'entirely in favour' of trying to engage Pakistan in the Middle East. Pakistan, he suggested, might help to shield Iran against a Soviet attack; and it might be easier to sell to Pakistan the idea of defending an area nearer home since its strategic advantages to her were so much clearer. It might also be greeted cordially by the Iranians, as a pact with Pakistan would not be so open an alignment with the West. This possibility had hitherto frightened, even antagonised, Iran. R.J. Bowker agreed, and pointed out that on 15 December 1950, the British Chiefs had averred that Pakistani co-operation was 'vital' for the security of the Gulf. Searching frantically for a way to protect their stake in Iranian oil, the British tentatively conceived the idea of an Iranian–Pakistani compact to defend the Gulf. But the British could not get away from their traditional idea of an *Indian* role in Middle East defence and were unable to summon up much enthusiasm for the idea of a contribution by Pakistan *alone*. R.H. Scott ruled out any British advances to the coquettish Pakistanis: 'Unless Pakistan realises that this is in her interests she will never effectively participate.' The Americans did not seem to be right in suggesting that quite 'a low degree of security' would be acceptable to Pakistan as a prerequisite for her contribution to Middle East defence. Moreover, Pakistan would fear incurring the hostility of the USSR and exposing her cities to Soviet bombing, and her own public opinion would have to be assured that she was not joining up with Anglo–American imperialists. In any case, it was not quite clear what sort of goods Pakistan would deliver, so there was no point in alienating India as well. British lack of enthusiasm about Pakistan was summed up in their desire for 'early decisions on the possibility of employing African troops to fill the present gap in Middle East defence'.[16]

Nevertheless, the British could not make light of American wishes. American support was crucial in buoying up Britain's position in the Middle East, and their interest should not be allowed to wane. The Americans counted: and they had raised the question of Pakistani participation more than once in discussions on a Supreme Allied Commander in the Middle East (SACME). But the British and Americans were thinking on different levels. For the British the cardinal point was not really Pakistan's role in Middle East defence. The retention of their influence hinged on a rapport with Egypt, which was the kingpin of their ascendancy in the Middle East. In the summer of 1951, however, Anglo–Egyptian relations were in the doldrums, as Egypt rejected British proposals for a phased withdrawal of British troops to be completed by 1956. The Anglo-Egyptian impasse made the Americans jittery. If Britain could not persuade Egypt to become an ally, the West must find an alternative, and this necessity prompted the thought that Pakistan could, and must, serve as that alternative.

McGhee had already convinced himself of the necessity of enlisting Pakistan in the Middle East. On 2 May 1951 he told the US Chiefs: 'With Pakistan, the Middle East could be defended; without Pakistan, I don't see any way to defend the Middle East.'[17] The idea was taken up by the PPS, who recommended in a working paper on 23 May that the Arabs, Israel,

Iran and Pakistan should be invited to support a Middle East Command. American officials now discovered new reasons to recruit Pakistan in Middle East defence. A State Department policy paper of 1 July foresaw Pakistan searching outside South Asia for assistance against communist attacks, since she was unlikely to receive any help from her neighbours. This is an amazing statement, since the State Department's earlier records show that American policy-makers had discerned that Pakistan's anti-communist professions were really a pretext to secure military assistance against India. Such an assertion is explicable on the grounds that the State Department first conceived the idea of enrolling Pakistan in Middle East defence and then tried to find reasons to justify it. The State Department now took the optimistic view that Pakistan had the military manpower to block Soviet aggression through Iran, and she might also offer bases to the West in the Indian Ocean area. Pakistan's Islamic character rendered her anti-communist and therefore pro-West. The Islamic "excesses" of reactionary mullahs were not denied, but far from lessening the allure of Pakistan, they only enhanced the importance of giving succour to the pro-Western Pakistani government, which was itself imperilled by the mullahs. Pakistan's identity was now seen as distinct from that of India.[18] America's security imperatives were metamorphosing Pakistan from a poor, strategically unattractive prospect into an estimable partner in the Middle East.

The Americans still had no intention of making formal commitments to any Middle East ally, but they were prepared, along with the British and French, to help plan the defence of the area. For the moment, they would leave it to Britain to take the lead with Pakistan because she was a member of the Commonwealth,[19] and they would act in concert with the British.

How would the British respond to the idea? On 13 June 1951 the CRO had noted that previous approaches to Pakistan had always come to grief over her importunate demands for guarantees against India. The British were not disposed to oblige Pakistan. But Pakistan could be useful in the Middle East, especially in bolstering up Iran, and it might be worth taking 'considerable risks' if the Middle East could be made secure. The British could only benefit from a greater American interest in the Middle East, and the US should not be discouraged by a British snub to Pakistan.[20]

The British were not altogether immune to the military temptations dangled before them by Pakistan. On 30 August 1951, Zafrullah Khan assured Patrick Gordon-Walker that it was 'absolutely necessary' in Pakistan's interests that the Middle East should be held. The Pakistani bird seemingly in hand, Gordon-Walker cooed that 'we would at any time be prepared to discuss with Pakistan the strategy in the Middle East and the possibility of Pakistan [sic] Divisions going there should it come to war. In these circumstances we would be prepared to discuss the question of equipment.' Zafrullah then claimed that he was speaking personally and did not know the views of his government. Evidently the Pakistani bird could fly away – but it wanted to stay. Pakistani resources in manpower were so great, confided Zafrullah, that with equipment they could raise one, two or three divisions that could be used abroad without in any way weakening their essential forces against India.[21] Was a Pakistani military prize within reach? On 10 September, Attlee echoed McGhee's wishful thinking that a settlement of the Kashmir dispute might clear the decks for Pakistan's participation in Middle East defence.[22] But the British Chiefs of Staff, more down to earth, dashed these fantasies and emphasised that Pakistan should be told that she would not be allotted any equipment unless she promised to furnish troops for the Middle East. The British would also have to find out whether Zafrullah had his government's backing.[23] This, and the unsnarling of the Kashmir tangle, concerned the British for the moment.

The question of Pakistan's participation in Middle East defence could not be put into cold storage. In the autumn of 1951, MEDO ran aground on the choppy waters of Egyptian nationalism. A recrudescence of nationalist unrest shook Cairo in September, and Egypt unilaterally abrogated the 1936 treaty. On 16 October 1951, Egypt formally rejected the invitation to join MEDO. Turkey had signed up on 20 September, but without its Egyptian nucleus, MEDO proved a non-starter. Egypt's rebuff ended Western hopes of a Middle East Command in the Suez Canal zone.

The British were at a loss what to do. But Egypt's rejection rekindled American interest in Pakistan's enrolment in Middle East Defence. Sensing the chance of a more positive American response Pakistan played the courtier. On 8 October 1951, Donald Kennedy, now Director of South Asian affairs in the State Department, informed the British embassy in Washington that General Ayub Khan, the Commander-in-Chief of the Pakistani army, had voiced Pakistan's desire to participate in Middle East defence, 'but that in their [Pakistani] view it was essential that the Middle East Commander should be an American.' The State Department felt that a door had been opened by Ayub Khan's unsolicited remark, and, while keeping quiet about the nationality of the commander of MEDO, would follow it up to see if the Pakistani government were also interested. Evidently Ayub had struck the right note, for a flattered Kennedy, perhaps desirous of reciprocating the honours, wanted Pakistan to come in as a founder member of MEDO. Pakistan, gushed Kennedy, might even be useful in persuading Egypt and Arab states to join it.[24]

The British were not amused. In Washington, British diplomats maintained the stiff upper lip and appeared obliging but cautious – 'we were sure you [the FO] would be extremely keen to obtain Pakistan's association with . . . Middle East defence in whatever way it might be possible. The only difficulty might be that the active participation of Pakistan in the Command might reawaken Indian suspicions.' But in London, officials bristled, for they wanted a British SACME, in recognition of British primacy in the Middle East. General Sir Nevil Brownjohn surmised that Pakistan's short-term motive was 'undoubtedly to obtain equipment for her own domestic defence needs', while R.H. Scott's astringent comment was that Pakistan's insistence on an American commander was 'probably dictated solely by their seeing in this arrangement a brighter prospect of supplies of American arms.' Pierson Dixon deprecated the American tendency to put the cart before the horse in pressing for the inclusion of Pakistan as a founder member of a Middle East command organisation. Pakistan's enrolment would 'far from help resolve the Egyptian problem'; on the other hand she should be welcomed to participate 'in due course'. The priority should be to obtain a Pakistani commitment of troops for the Middle East. Pakistan should be put in her place and informed of the arrangement that since the commander of NATO was American, the MEDO commander would be British.[25] Even as they kept the Americans firmly on British rails, pique, displeasure and mistrust of Pakistan were uppermost in British minds.

The British could not bring themselves to respond affirmatively to the State Department's proposal for an immediate overture to Pakistan by the US, UK, France and Turkey. The Foreign Office stalled: it would, they replied, be difficult for Pakistan to join in the face of Egypt's opposition to MEDO. The American suggestion that Britain, the primary power in the Middle East, should act in concert with the lowly French and Turks threw British officials into high dudgeon. The Americans, shrieked the Foreign Office, had gone 'so far – without consulting us – as to propose making enquiries in that sense in Paris and Ankara – an action we deprecated'.[26] This absurd outburst reflected British indignation and resentment that the US had even contemplated consulting France and Turkey, for the Americans could hardly have consulted the British about what they might propose to them!

The advent of the Conservatives to power in October 1951 did not dispel British misgivings about Pakistan. Hastings Ismay, the new Secretary of State for Commonwealth Relations, and Anthony Eden, now Foreign Secretary, were against any Western approach to Pakistan. But the British would find it difficult to flout American wishes: Eden confided to Churchill that the Americans were 'pressing us hard' on Pakistan. 'The Americans take the view that we are inclined to sacrifice the advantages to be obtained from a Pakistani contribution to the defence of the Middle East for fear of antagonising India.' British officials debated the merits of yielding to the US, so as not to annoy the Americans or dampen their interest in the Middle East, but they eventually decided to stand their ground because of likely Indian and Egyptian opposition and the improbability of a Pakistani contribution.[27] Since Washington had not thought up any alternative plan to override London's dithering over Pakistan, the British viewpoint prevailed on the Americans at the close of 1951.

In January 1952, a spate of anti-British demonstrations rocked Cairo. To the Americans, the Middle East Command was a mere will-o'-the-wisp in the light of the frenzied nationalism and concomitant instability that now reigned in Egypt. The British were also rummaging around for alternatives, and on 22 January they proposed a new Middle East Defence Organisation (MEDO) which would be a 'planning, coordinating and liaising organisation only', based in Cyprus and linked to NATO.

The American response was two-pronged: a MEDO was necessary, but they were increasingly impatient at Britain's inability to find allies in the Middle East and to cement the fractured relations between India and Pakistan.[28] Their search for options renewed their interest in a grouping between Turkey and Pakistan. Pakistan was quick to seize the chance to play upon America's fears and uncertain hopes. Pakistan's own hunt for security against India also prompted her to court Turkey. To entice the Turks and the Americans, Zafrullah Khan, in February 1952, impressed on Adnan Menderes, the Turkish Prime Minister, and George McGhee, now US ambassador in Ankara, that:

the Middle East is like a train, with Turkey the engine, the remaining States the cars and Pakistan the caboose bringing up the rear, seeing that none of the cars are [sic] lost. Turkey in front looking toward the West can ignore the intervening States if she chooses, but Pakistan cannot.[29]

Ever haunted by the Soviet bugaboo, McGhee swallowed Zafrullah's alarmist portrayal of poor-little-Pakistan's plight. But the Turks, who had abolished the Khilafat in 1920, gave the cold shoulder to Pakistani talk of a pan-Islamic alliance, for they rightly discerned that Pakistan's principal motive was to fortify herself against India. Wanting the early inauguration of a Turco–Pakistani club, McGhee dissuaded Pakistan from harping on the Islamic string.[30] In general, American officials persuaded themselves that Pakistan sincerely wished to combine with the West in the Middle East and that she did crave a positive Western response to her overtures in spite of their non-committal character.[31]

British and US differences remained. On 6 May 1952 a Foreign Office draft on MEDO advocated the recruitment of Egypt and Iraq but not Pakistan. But the British Chiefs foresaw an awkward situation if the US pressed for the inclusion of Pakistan and the British resisted it, for that would become known to Pakistan and would have 'an unfortunate effect on our relations with them'.[32] Foreign Office reservations about Pakistan were accentuated by news of Zafrullah's failure to organise a conference of "Muslim" nations in the Middle East. The British had no enthusiasm for such an assembly, which would probably play to the anti-Western, anti-imperialist gallery.[33]

III THE NEGATIVE BRITISH IMAGE OF PAKISTAN

Why was the British image of Pakistan so negative? After all, Pakistan had been created by an act of Westminister in fulfilment of Britain's mission to do justice to loyal minorities in India. That, at any rate, had been the official, rhetorical explanation. In fact, Pakistan had torn apart the web of political unity fashioned by the British in India, demolished the British Indian army and unhinged British strategic designs. However, the *mélange* of British dilly-dallying and disinterest in Pakistan was not merely a matter of strategic vision or historical imagination. They were continually exasperated that any response to a Pakistani advance on Middle East security inevitably foundered on the rock of the Pakistani obsession that 'the chances of their having to fight a war of independence [against India] are always just around the corner', and their importunate badgering for military guarantees against India. Pakistan's concatenation of domestic imbroglios also delineated a bleak scenario of her future. Pakistan's dominion status was at best a mixed asset to the British, at worst a political and economic liability. Since her birth in August 1947, Pakistan had lurched from one political and financial crisis to another. The constituent assembly had failed to frame a constitution, so that Pakistan, Lord Swinton informed the cabinet in May 1953, 'cannot properly be regarded as a Parliamentary democracy on the British model'.[34] The call of democracy was vital in British – and American – answers to global communism; Pakistan's as yet unformed character, manifesting very sharp growing pains, offered precious little to the British, and they had scant patience with her coquetry, especially in the light of her manifold strategic disadvantages.

The "Islamic" factor in Pakistan's foreign policy did not alleviate British discomfiture. A state which derived legitimacy from religion could not dispense with mullahs, who served as an invaluable vehicle of popular mobilisation in favour of governments perched precariously on an ever-surging wave of economic misfortunes. The feud with India had its origins in the partition of 1947; Pakistan's domestic volatility spurred her leaders to fan the flames of Indo–Pakistani enmity as a convenient means to unite a people divided by region and class. Unable to get a grip on Pakistan's many travails, Pakistani governments clutched at the British and Indians as handy scapegoats. Pakistani officials grumbled that dominion status had not brought Pakistan better treatment than India. Pakistan, they contended with some justification, had gained nothing from dominion status; she was excluded from the defence meetings at Commonwealth Prime Ministers' conferences; she was 'Queen's territory', but the Commonwealth would not guarantee her territorial integrity against an Indian attack. Since 1950, there had been repeated demands in the Pakistani constituent assembly for an "Islamic" head of state, and by 1953, a sovereign independent "Islamic" republic of Pakistan was on the cards. If the British wished to stem the drift towards republicanism, the Commonwealth must deliver Pakistan guarantees against Indian aggression.[35]

Wincing at the prospect of a bizarre combination of the Queen and Islam, the British adamantly refused to comply with such a stipulation. Republicanism, they consoled themselves, need not have serious repercussions on British foreign policy, but it could tarnish the British image, especially in the Middle East, 'where for their own reasons a number of vocal elements will try to magnify this alleged rift in the Commonwealth'.[36] A change of government in April 1953, with Mohamad Ali as the new Prime Minister, held interest for the British only in so far as their wish to know what the new government's stance towards the Commonwealth would be. Pleased that mullah elements had been eliminated and that Pakistan would remain in the Commonwealth, Churchill was complacent. 'I have a feeling', he crowed to Swinton, 'that it may well be that the new Pakistan administration will feel pretty lonely if they descend to the Indian level by passing out of the circle of The Crown. I am so glad you are keeping this point in their minds.'[37] The British ambivalence on Pakistani republicanism revealed on the one hand their determination not to butter up to Pakistan and on the other how much an undented Commonwealth façade meant to them in terms of their international stature and influence. The extent and impact of Anglo–Commonwealth prestige in the Middle East cannot be gauged from the sources consulted; but it is worth remembering that, Commonwealth intact, the British were challenged by nationalisms in the Middle East. The chances are that the British confused (or did not draw the line between) their own grandiose perceptions of their world status and their actual ability to shape events in the Middle East.

Not only were the British sceptical about Pakistan's clout in the Middle East; more importantly, they feared that any Pakistani influence, with its Islamic underpinnings, would militate against the West. They were decidedly uncomfortable with the Islamic motif in Pakistan's foreign policy; and in May 1953, Swinton speculated that she would remain in the Commonwealth not because the Commonwealth had any political or electoral attractions – 'indeed the contrary' – but because she did not want an embittered and precipitate divorce from the Commonwealth to yield any diplomatic bounty to India. Nor was Pakistan necessarily a diplomatic asset to the British. Apart from Kashmir, on most international matters she took the same line as India. After all, both were conscious of their joint past of subjection to an external power; both stood on an anti-colonial platform in the UN; both disliked NATO and regional groupings because they whittled down the authority of the UN and because the colonial powers figured prominently in them. Pakistan had espoused the Indonesian nationalist cause in the UN and self-government in Africa; she had championed Libya's claim to independence. There was also much public enthusiasm for the anti-colonial stance in Pakistan. All told, Pakistan's promises to combine with the West in the Middle East flew in the face of reality. In general, she was 'likely to waver' between the West and the Soviet Union and would identify with Arab and anti-colonial causes, and public opinion was likely 'to give violent and irrational support for Islamic considerations.' The British did not believe that the West could count on Pakistan on any Middle Eastern issue unless Western policies were acceptable to 'the Arab

world'. Senior Pakistani military officers were strongly pro-Common-
wealth, but in the ultimate analysis, concluded Swinton, Pakistani policy
was 'almost certain to be Islamic rather than Commonwealth.'[38] This
consideration alone rendered the British indifferent to Pakistani supplications and grievances.

Nor would the British tidy up Pakistan's economic mess. In February
1953 they turned down a Pakistani request for credit on the grounds that
the British economy was being strained to the utmost, and the British faced
an uphill task in financing 'our own rearmament programme, without
having to pre-finance those of other countries as well: particularly
countries on whose active support in a war we cannot count.'[39] Patently
mistrustful of Pakistan's anti-Soviet professions, and critically surveying
her mounting political and economic disorder, British officials did not rate
her creditworthiness very highly. Pakistan's threats to go to the dollar
market could be taken with a pinch of salt because her sterling account had
been run down to a bare cover for existing commitments. The UK would
gain no advantage by extending her credit.[40] The sum of British arguments
was that they did not want to foot the bill for extricating Pakistan from her
financial straits. The general British attitude to Pakistan was one of indifference bordering on disdain, even contempt.

IV SNUBBING PAKISTAN WAS ONE THING, SNUBBING THE AMERICANS, ANOTHER ...

British policy towards Pakistan did not operate in a vacuum, and if
Pakistan could be rebuffed, the United States could not, if only because
the American interest in Pakistan portended American arms to Pakistan –
and a consequent loss of British influence on their traditional South Asian
turf. British lack of interest in Pakistan did not mean that they wished to be
elbowed out by the United States or other West European countries. The
point is of import partly because it fuelled British opposition to a Pakistani
role in Middle East defence and partly because the British inability or
refusal to give weapons to Pakistan was to lead to their dislodgement by
the US. Pakistan's pathological fear of India created her single-minded
determination to procure arms from anywhere – and this included the
United States. The British not only wished to fence out the US but also to
prevent Pakistan from drawing on the meagre dollar resources of the
sterling area. They were, therefore, perturbed at Pakistani attempts to
purchase American military hardware in the summer of 1952.[41] In June
1952 the cabinet agreed that India and Pakistan should be given enough
arms to prevent them from turning to the US. 'This has now become an
urgent issue.' If the British could not offer Pakistan aircraft immediately,
Swinton feared that the Pakistani air force would generally go over to
American equipment. But the Air Ministry claimed that Britain's own

needs and those of her allies in NATO deserved priority, and it was out of the question to meet Pakistan's exorbitant demands.[42]

Even as departmental differences stood in the way of Pakistan securing British aircraft, fortunately for the British, she fared no better with the Americans. Pakistan still ranked low on US strategic priorities. The State Department deprecated her excessive military spending and considered her defence demands irrational at a time when she was pleading financial near-bankruptcy.[43] Gratified at this 'helpful attitude' of the Americans, London took the unsurprising view that Pakistan should spend money in the sterling area rather than in the US or France. In the end the Pakistanis did not acquire what they coveted – a result of some adroit British stringpulling with the Americans, although the British themselves would not fulfil Pakistani demands. Naturally they did not want Karachi to know that they were trying to dissuade the Americans from selling arms to Pakistan.[44] Again, this British success in influencing the Americans would last as long as the Americans were amenable to that influence, and they were amenable as long as they did not themselves know what they wanted to do in Pakistan – and in the Middle East.

Indeed, it was vital that the Americans should wish to stand guard over Britain's niche in the Middle East, for the British could not do it single-handed. This meant, in turn, that American views on the Middle East had to be weighed carefully. On 18 June 1952, in a major review of Britain's overseas obligations, Eden informed the cabinet that the essence of a sound foreign policy was to ensure that a country's strength was equal to its obligations, and it was clear that the British government did not have the resources to meet theirs. Britain must determine how far her external obligations could be reduced, shared with or transferred to other countries, without impairing too seriously her world position and sacrificing the vital advantages flowing from it. For the Soviets would be 'only too ready' to step into any vacuum created by a British withdrawal. Britain's inter-national status would then be adversely affected, with a consequent shift-ing of the balance of power against the West. Any reduction in commitments would detract from Britain's claims to leadership of the Commonwealth, to a position of pre-eminence in Europe and to a special relationship with the US, and British prestige could fall into an abyss of decline. In the Middle East, the British should strive to make the Canal Zone an international responsibility. 'Hence every step should be taken to speed up the establishment of an Allied Middle East Defence Organisation.' The US was refusing to enter into commitments and 'it should be the constant object of Her Majesty's Government to persuade them to do so'. Britain should persuade the United States to assume the real burdens in such organisations, while retaining for herself as much political control as possible.[45] Eden's meaning was obvious: it reiterated the common British idea of American means to achieve British ends. Like many British officials, he overlooked, or was simply unaware of, the growing American dissatisfaction with British policy in the Middle East and South Asia, and he glossed over the British reluctance to go along with embryonic, though inchoate, American ideas of Middle East defence. Nasser's successful coup in July 1952, and the advent of Eisenhower's Republican administration to power in January 1953, were to push these contradictions to their logically inharmonious finale.

V AMERICA PARTS WAYS WITH BRITAIN IN THE MIDDLE EAST AND SOUTH ASIA

The advent of the Eisenhower administration to power in January 1953 altered neither American impatience with British policy in the Middle East, nor American interest in a Middle East defence grouping and Pakistan's participation in it. Anglo–Egyptian negotiations over Suez were deadlocked, and if MEDO could not take off, the US wanted another arrangement. The State Department's enthusiasm for defence parleys with Pakistan remained unbounded; 'the problem remains as to when and in what manner'.[46] In this, the Eisenhower administration followed the precedent, albeit nebulous, of the Truman government, and Eisenhower himself wanted an alternative to an Egypt-centred security arrangement. To make a personal assessment of regional problems and to appraise the viability of MEDO, Dulles (along with Harold Stassen, Director for Mutual Security) embarked on a three-week tour, the first made by an American Secretary of State, of the Middle East and South Asia in May 1953. Their prognosis of the future of MEDO was pessimistic, for British policy in the Middle East seemed sterile. As the US was Britain's ally, nationalist bitterness towards the British was rubbing off on the Americans. The diplomacy of most countries in the region also gave Dulles little cause for optimism; they seemed too preoccupied with their own internal affairs and too complacent about 'the Soviet threat'. It escaped Dulles that this might be because they did not perceive a Soviet danger to themselves, and Dulles himself did not offer any estimate of the nature of any Soviet threat to the Middle East or what would be necessary to confront it. He simply concluded that the old concept of MEDO, with Egypt as its corner-stone was certainly finished.[47] To the extent that the British were still commited to MEDO – if only because of their lack of an alternative – American enthusiam for British primacy in the Middle East was starting to wane, not necessarily with great forethought or purpose, but surely if somewhat fitfully.

How could Middle Eastern countries be saved from a Soviet menace they did not perceive? Dulles did not have to look far for the answer. Like McGhee, he thought Pakistan was a willing and staunch ally, who could soon enrol in a Northern Tier grouping, along with Turkey, Iraq, and Iran. The members of the Tier would form a regional alliance that would be far stronger than one based on Egyptian co-operation with the West. This idea, still in its infancy, marked sharply Dulles' differences with the British, even as it reflected the meagre American influence in the Middle East and their quest for regional surrogates. Playing the theme of the Northern Tier during his visit to Pakistan in May 1953, Dulles told Pakistani officials that any MEDO must have roots in the region itself, and that an alliance could not emerge out of a blueprint imposed by powers from outside.[48] Immensely impressed, on his own account, by the martial and religious characteristics of the Pakistanis, Dulles was convinced that Pakistan was 'one country that has moral courage to do its part in resisting communism'. Pakistan would be a stalwart of any Middle East defence scheme and 'we need not await formal defense arrangements as [a] condition to [sic] some military assistance to Pakistan'. He and Harold Stassen agreed that Pakistan was 'a potential strong point for us'. The general concept that Dulles brought home with him was that Pakistan could be made a strong defensive anchor; so, obviously, could Turkey.[49] Iran was the obvious weak spot in what could become a sturdy and stable Northern Tier alignment – and the CIA would soon put that right.[50] In spite of the general American anxiety about British policy in the Middle East, American (and British) attitudes were quite complex: they were at one on Iran but not on Pakistan.

The British were now notified about US misgivings over MEDO. On 17 June 1953, John Jernegan, Deputy Assistant Secretary of State, informed Harold Beeley, Counsellor at the British embassy in Washington, that MEDO was out of the question because of the political situation in the Arab states, so the best plan would be to work with Iraq, Syria and Pakistan, who were most disposed to co-operate with the West. Defence planning could be done by the nations concerned.[51] Beeley contented himself with reiterating the Foreign Office stance in favour of MEDO and did not solicit more information – an odd omission, one which was to have adverse consequences for the British. On 11 July Dulles expressed the same view to Salisbury in Washington. Salisbury's bland and unsuspecting response was that Indo–Pakistani friction would rule out Pakistan's participation in Middle East defence,[52] and he let the matter drop. Meanwhile, Stassen wanted survey teams to be sent to Syria, Iraq and Pakistan as early as possible to develop mutual security arrangements. But no commitment would be made at this stage, 'although of course the U.S. does become psychologically involved'.[53] Highly susceptible to Pakistani wooing, but uncertain how to respond to it, Dulles was 'nervous' about the possibility of being rushed on Pakistan. But he was not overly coy, and he asked the Department of Defence whether MEDO could be established even without Arab co-operation.[54]

By now the Americans were contemplating going ahead without the British. With Eisenhower's approval, the NSC, State and Defence Departments discussed the merits of the Northern Tier as an alternative to

MEDO, and they envisaged that a Turco–Pakistani pact would provide the initial impetus for a regional posse. NSC 155/1 of 14 July 1953 advised that the US should act with the UK but reserve the right to act with others or alone. It should '[t]ake leadership' in bringing the countries of the area into an organisation in which the Western powers would be participants or associates, while recognising that the political base for such an organisation did not exist and would have to be created. Evidently the Americans had decided that it was better to do something – anything – than nothing. Limited military assistance should be provided to pro-West governments, and special consideration should be given to Turkey, Iraq, Iran and Pakistan, in which the US would seek to obtain base rights.[55] NSC 155/1 was the formal expression of the American interest in Pakistani participation in a Middle East defence arrangement.

The conception of a Turco–Pakistani pact was muddled and hazy; it is evident from US records that American officials did not really know what they were about. But their determination to make a leap in the dark was underlined by their pre-emptive reaction to an anticipated Indian brouhaha over Pakistan's enlistment in Middle East defence. The Americans regarded nonaligned India as a nuisance, and, in the summer of 1953, they were trying to bar her from the Korean Political Conference.[56] But they could not ignore India, a democracy, and as such, the only substantial Asian counterpoise to communist China. According to Byroade, the US was 'buying democracy' with economic aid to India, and however annoying Nehru might be, he was the guarantor of Indian democracy.[57] Setting great store by Pakistan's help in manning US barricades in the Middle East, it is interesting that Washington braced itself for a row with New Delhi rather than London. American policy-makers did not anticipate a fracas with the British since the UK and US had agreed, in January 1953, on recruiting Pakistan in MEDO 'at the earliest politically feasible date'. But this citation of British views was selective, for, in conversation with Dulles on 6 March 1953 in Washington, Eden had opposed Pakistan's inclusion in MEDO because of Indo-Pakistani enmity.[58] And the Americans had not consulted the British on whether the present moment was 'politically feasible'; they chose the moment themselves and appear to have expected the British to fall in with them. By August 1953, two strands were discernible in American thinking towards the British: keeping them at arms length in the Middle East, while not excluding the possibility of co-operation with them; presenting the British with a *fait accompli* and expecting them to toe the American line. This was not for the first time: in November 1951 R.H. Scott had noted ruefully: 'We [British] do not always get a chance to influence American policy in the formative stages, and are apt to be confronted with a firm decision and a request for an immediate answer.'[59]

Pakistan's domestic maladies did not dishearten the Americans, rather they seem to have reinforced the US desire to shore up a very unstable government with economic and military largesse. In September 1953 the

Eisenhower administration granted Pakistan a generous wheat loan to stave off an impending famine. Clearly the State Department were determined to hold on to the Pakistani bird in the hand. Simultaneously, Pakistan was also moving away from the UK of her own volition. In September 1953, the government of Mohamad Ali complied with a decision by the constituent assembly that Pakistan would become an Islamic republic within the Commonwealth. Having done their unsuccessful best to forestall such an outcome, the British were dismayed that domestic pressures within Pakistan had dictated the issue. In contrast, American diplomats in Karachi hailed Pakistan's choice as a 'gradual shift away from dependence' on the UK and the Commonwealth and 'toward the United States'.[60]

Then, although the British did not know it, the trend towards a Pakistani role in the Northern Tier was slowly beginning to crystallise. Stopping in Ankara *en route* to Washington during the second half of September 1953, General Ayub Khan and Major General Iskander Mirza voiced their enthusiasm for military co-operation to the Turks. But neither side gave any inkling of the conversations to British diplomats. After his parleys with the Turks, Ayub matter-of-factly informed Avra Warren, now US ambassador in Ankara, that the Turks had shown no interest in substantive defence matters. He had not met the Turkish President, Prime Minister and Foreign Minister, only the Defence Minister who had not impressed him. The Turks notified Helm that Ayub had paid only a courtesy visit. Warren told Helm that he was sure that Ayub and Mirza had visited Turkey with some idea of ultimate defence collaboration. 'If they did, it was certain that they had received no encouragement', since the Turks were very suspicious of Pakistan's interest in "Islamic" associations.[61] In fact Turkey, Pakistan and the US all kept their counsel towards the British, for military co-operation between Turkey and Pakistan was discussed with the encouragement of the State Department, and Ayub's discretion probably resulted from a State Department warning to him against leaks to the press. But it was not only the British who knew nothing. Even Horace Hildreth, the US ambassador in Karachi was kept in the dark: he first came to know of the American stake in the Turco-Pakistan confabulations two months later, when he read the State Department's quarterly review of US-Pakistan relations which was dated 17 December 1953! The review hailed Ayub's visit to Turkey and his talks there on regional defence as the 'outstanding' event in Pakistan's relations with the Muslim world and as a 'positive step' by Pakistan to move closer to Turkey in a Northern Tier arrangement. This was 'an objective in which the U.S. has an affirmative interest'. All Hildreth could do was to protest at his being disregarded by the State Department,[62] while the British remained blissfully ignorant for the moment.

NSC 155/1 had envisaged but not detailed Pakistan's role in the Northern Tier, and Pakistan's interest in Middle East defence presented the Americans with an unprecedented opportunity to *do something*, even if they did not clearly know what. The Americans had not decided on military aid to Pakistan, but Ayub Khan's visit to Washington during the last week of September was having the effect of 'precipitating' a decision 'prematurely'. This was because the State Department did not want to rebuff Pakistan. The result was that 'we seem . . . to be on the point of deciding . . . [to] grant military assistance to Pakistan without at this moment knowing the full scope of our future plans for [a] grant [of] military assistance to Greece, Turkey and Iran as well as to other states in the lower tier.'[63] A memorandum by Byroade on 24 September confirmed that 'Pakistan's willingness to take the initiative in the promotion of Middle East defense arrangements may result in finally moving this project off dead center. We cannot risk the negative reaction which a rebuff at this juncture would involve.' Byroade was 'convinced' that the US should now offer some military assistance to Pakistan, in spite of the expected Indian outcry, which could be minimised by giving Pakistan equipment for an infantry division to serve in Korea.[64] Pakistan would not receive arms for home use immediately, so the military balance in South Asia would not be affected for the present.

The stage was now set for an affirmative American response to any Pakistani request for military funding. Meeting Dulles on 30 September 1953, General Ayub Khan made no bones about what he wanted – military assistance for the Pakistani army. Dulles responded encouragingly to Ayub. According to the State Department record, 'The Secretary observed, smilingly, that it was none of his business but he hoped General Ayub would get what he came for.' He was 'fully prepared' to help Pakistan, although he could not say whether or to what extent US would be able to supply the *matériel* needed. Ayub was assured that it would be possible to 'tell him something' when he returned to Washington on 15 October, after a tour of US military installations. Indian objections would be ignored; Dulles told Ayub that he did not consider India to be a 'controlling factor' in the situation.[65] The encouragment to Ayub was manifestly the brain child of the State Department; a note from Dulles to Bedell Smith on 1 October 1953 reveals that neither the American Chiefs of Staff nor the NSC knew what was happening.[66] Wanting a meeting between Ayub and Eisenhower when Ayub returned to Washington in mid-October, Dulles gratuitously "assured" Byroade: 'I will be glad to arrange such an appointment if you wish me to do so.'[67] Clearly Dulles intended to engineer a decision on US military aid to Pakistan.

But if any decision was to be made *de facto*, other departments had to be brought into the picture. On the same day – 1 October 1953 – Dulles advised Charles Wilson, Secretary of Defence, that the US position on the character and size of a possible Mutual Assistance Programme (MAP) to Pakistan and Egypt was 'urgently required for use in negotiations immediately pending'.[68] The basis for assistance to Pakistan also remained uncertain, as Ayub had not taken to the Korean idea. Ayub found much support among American officials, who thought the State Department should determine when it would be 'politically feasible' to widen the basis for military assistance to Pakistan. At a combined meeting on 6 October, the State and Defence Departments, FOA and Bureau of the Budget unanimously decided that Pakistan would get $15 million to 25 million in aid in the fiscal year 1954.[69] It was the first stumbling but definite American step towards gaining a military foothold in Pakistan.

VI THE BRITISH IN THE BACK-SEAT

It was only now that the British were briefed about American thinking. This was in accordance with the State Department's desire to keep the British posted about US intentions.[70] On 9 October 1953 Jernegan informed Beeley that the State Department had presented a strong case for US military assistance to Pakistan and that a decision had been taken to grant limited military aid amounting to $25 million. Indian objections had been fully considered, and to soften the blow to India the money would be used to equip a Pakistani brigade for service in Korea. Ayub had made a plea, and the State Department wished to give him an answer which, without going into detail, would be positive in principle.[71]

The British were stunned. Consultation was the essence of the Anglo–American relationship; the key to influencing their allies. And until now, the US had always consulted them on South Asia, which had been mutually regarded as a British domain. Quite apart from going against the spirit of the Anglo–American relationship, the Americans had now departed from their own precedent of consulting the British on South Asia.

Then there was the discomfiting truth that British diplomats in Washington, Ankara and Karachi had failed to get wind of what was going on. The first British reactions mirrored their anxiety about one of their best arms markets and their long-standing influence in Pakistan. From Karachi a bemused J.D. Murray, Acting High Commissioner, attempted to save face in a huff of moral righteousness: 'It would be most undesirable if the Pakistanis were bribed into a switch to United States equipment except possibly for some special items.'[72] The Foreign Office echoed unease whether a Pakistani brigade for Korea would be fitted out with British or US equipment. Should the British offer to supply arms, to be financed by the US, as an offshore purchase?[73] The Chiefs of Staff thought American munificence would be 'all to the good' if it took the form of offshore purchases of British weaponry. But the direct provision of American arms to a traditional British sphere of interest like Pakistan 'was bound to have serious effects on the economy of the United Kingdom'.[74]

Analysing American motives, the CRO noted that the State Department had for some time believed the British attitude to be too rigidly conditioned by Indian reactions and had been 'impatient' to encourage Pakistan's entry into Middle East defence. The Americans had discounted the possibility of Indian help; they were 'therefore unlikely to look very far ahead or to assess very carefully the benefits they can hope to obtain from the grant of military aid to Pakistan.'[75] But American assessments of the benefits of US assistance to Pakistan were myopic; military funding would spoil the chances of a settlement on Kashmir, which could provide 'the only real basis' for strengthening Pakistan and making her a valuable ally. At the same time, the West might lose all chances of contracting Indian help.[76] In Karachi, a more realistic Murray doubted that Mohammad Ali would be embarrassed by an offer of American aid. He would probably be eager to take it since the Pakistanis would assume 'this year's allocation to be the forerunner of regular and larger annual sums of military aid'.[77] Nevertheless the Foreign and Commonwealth Relations Offices drew false comfort from the illusion of Pakistani reluctance to accept American largesse and somewhat clumsily advised the State Department to await a specific Pakistani request rather than make an offer which Karachi 'might find . . . embarrassing to refuse'.[78] Although Washington had informed them that the initiative had come from Pakistan, the British sought to influence the Americans against military aid, for they knew that their position in Pakistan would only be impaired if the Americans gave in to Pakistan's clamouring for American weaponry. Strangely enough, they did not try to uncover why the Americans might wish to respond to Pakistan's importuning for arms.

The British sought Anglo–American consultations on what aid was to be given to Pakistan. The desire was not entirely futile, as the State Department felt it 'essential to be in step with the British if possible' because of their Commonwealth responsibilities and the more practical aspects of fitting American weaponry into an essentially British-equipped army. This could also serve as a pretext to 'delay our hand' in making a firm commitment to Ayub.[79] But the State Department made no promises to the British. Fearful of being left out in the cold, the British thought up several ideas to get round the Americans. Confidential exchanges between Nehru and Mohamad Ali were then under way, and British diplomats in New Delhi warned that military aid would block the prospects of a breakthrough on Kashmir.[80] Yet the British could not seriously have expected such an argument to gain a sympathetic American ear. Until now the British themselves had relegated the prospects of an Indo–Pakistani settlement to an unforeseeable future, and if military assistance were to await the coming of Indo–Pakistani fellowship it would never materialise! The essence of their predicament was that Pakistan's hankering for arms since her creation had stemmed from her animosity towards India, and it is surprising to find this fundamental ignored in British arguments against American military hand-outs to Pakistan. What the British did not seem to grasp was that the American response to Pakistan was rooted in American disapprobation of British policy in the Middle East. British blindness to reality led inexorably to self-delusion.

Another tactic was to tell the Americans what Britain could supply to Pakistan through offshore purchases. 'It would clearly be advantageous to get our thoughts across to the Americans before their own views have evolved too far',[81] advised the CRO. The Foreign Office instructed the embassy in Washington to inform the State Department of British reservations about US intentions, but if the Eisenhower administration still went ahead, the British 'would not wish to stand in the way'. According to the State Department record, Britain had conveyed certain anxieties, 'but it acquiesced to [sic] the US proposals'.[82] The *double entendre* of British statements made it possible for the Americans to put such a construction on British views. Moreover, the emphasis in British documents was now on offshore purchases of British weaponry by Pakistan, rather than on opposing US aid. The Foreign Office favoured an early indication of British willingness to meet Pakistani needs, and, at a joint meeting on 23 October 1953, representatives of the CRO, Foreign Office and Ministry of Defence agreed that Laithwaite should be instructed to find out what Pakistan wanted, and a list of offshore arms which Britain could provide drafted, to be sent to Makins in Washington.[83]

But the CRO dithered. On the absurd pretext that Pakistan was still undecided about accepting aid 'if offered', the CRO now wanted the British to refrain from forwarding their list of offshore items 'too precipitately' to the State Department. The list could be drawn up on a general basis and handed over to the Americans as part of a general exchange of information. The vacillation of the CRO stemmed from their fear of an Indian hue and cry, already discernible with unconfirmed rumours of military assistance, if British offshore equipment to Pakistan really materialised. As the CRO manoeuvred desperately to avert a row with India, the Commonwealth relationship seemed more of a mire in which the British had got stuck rather than a reflection of their grandeur. New Delhi's anger could not be assuaged by supplying similar amounts of equipment to India and Pakistan, for, as the Ministry of Defence pointed out, India could afford to buy what she wanted; Pakistan could only augment her military stockpile *with foreign funding*. And as the US was intent on bestowing largesse on Pakistan, the politic course for London would be to send a list of British items to Washington.[84]

Could the British draw up a list? Their newly born eagerness to supply offshore weapons was constrained by their ignorance of what Pakistan wanted and their inability to spell out delivery dates until this was known.[85] Even now, confronted with the prospect of losing their arms market – and their collateral military influence in Pakistan – the British would not take any initiative with the Pakistanis.

Meanwhile, the Americans made no formal commitment to Ayub Khan when he returned to Washington in mid-October, on the pretext that

American equipment would have to be discussed and co-ordinated with the British. Aware that the British also had a finger in the pie, the Pakistanis played on them to steer the US towards generosity to Pakistan, while the British played on Pakistan and the US against military assistance. It was a cat-and-mouse game and the Pakistanis revelled in it. On 4 November 1953, Iskander Mirza told Laithwaite, quite correctly, that he did not know the American position on arms for Pakistan. Laithwalte warned him that it would be 'very grave' from the Commonwealth point of view if US aid led to purchases of US equipment. Not wishing to drop Pakistan's British card while a formal American decision hung in the balance, the astute Mirza wondered aloud to an anxious Laithwaite 'what if any, strings were going to be attached to any such [American] gift'. Laithwaite averred that it would be better if the gift were food, unaccompanied for practical purposes by any conditions.[86] For, as a Cabinet Defence Committee paper of 9 November underlined, arms sales boosted British exports, they were an instrument of foreign policy and a means of keeping arms factories more fully employed.[87] India and Pakistan were lucrative markets, and the British wanted to retain their foothold on the subcontinent.

So, taking Mirza's preference for British equipment at face value the CRO and Foreign Office consoled themselves. But the British were hardly conversant with American thinking. The extent to which they were not *au fait* is revealed by a careful study of British and American reports of a series of developments from 8 to 13 November 1953, when Ghulam Muhammad, the Governor-General of Pakistan, visited Washington. During this period, the Americans themselves drew up new plans to recruit Pakistan and Turkey in Middle East defence. Early in November an American joint working group contemplated a four-power planning organisation along the lines of the moribund MEDO but without direct and overt Western participation. The ultimate objective would be a 'full defensive pact'; but for the moment, 'much could be accomplished toward the defense of the area without going that far'. Even if any two countries were willing to enter into such an arrangement – which might be confined to Turkey and Pakistan to begin with – military aid funds would be concentrated on them. This would give substance to Dulles's concept of the Northern Tier. The assent of the Defence Department to this strategic concept was vital, for Military Assistance Programmes (MAPs) had to be justified 'almost entirely on political grounds'. It would also be easier to persuade Congress if a political base could be laid on which to build a Middle East defence structure.[88]

If a four-power pact was feasible, what timing and procedures should be adopted? Should the US try to get Turkey or Pakistan to take the lead, 'while we lent discreet support in the background'? How should the British be brought into the picture? It would seem 'impossible' to leave them out where Pakistan was concerned.[89] Evidently, the State Department wanted the British to subscribe to an idea already in their mind and were not thinking of consulting them on the feasibility of the idea itself.

Perhaps this was because the State Department did not themselves know whether the provision of military assistance to Pakistan would 'assure' the development of a satisfactory Middle East defence arrangement, but without aid 'it is certain that no such arrangement will develop'. Still trying to invent an alliance, Dulles's personal championship of Pakistani participation in a Northern Tier grouping was obvious from his advice to Eisenhower on the eve of Ghulam Muhammad's lunch with the President. Dulles expected Ghulam Muhammad to raise the question of military assistance with Eisenhower. The US Joint Chiefs of Staff had not yet given their views, but Dulles's convoluted reasoning was that 'it would be a worthwhile move on our part . . . While we are not yet in a position to give the Governor General any firm assurances, I suggest that you express personal awareness that consideration is being given to providing military aid and that you will certainly give earnest thought to a proposal for such a program when you have been given a recommendation.' In Dulles's eyes, domestic instability in Pakistan amplified rather than diminished the importance of a sympathetic American response to the Pakistani quest for arms. 'The present government is pro-Western and against the adoption of a constitution which would be theocratic in nature', he counselled Eisenhower. The President could make known to Ghulam Muhammad his hope that Pakistan would continue to develop along modern and progressive lines.[90]

With the US Chiefs of Staff endorsing the Northern Tier concept on 14 November, the anticipated Indian uproar appeared to be the only spanner in the works. The subcontinent, commented Eisenhower plaintively if glibly, was 'one area of the world where, even more than most cases, emotion rather than reason seems to dictate policy.' Dulles was undeterred. The US, he counselled the President, might have to pay a price in a situation 'where it is difficult to help one without making an enemy of the other.'[91] With Dulles decided about whom the Americans would help, military aid to Pakistan was now on the anvil.

VII BRITISH INFLUENCE: SHADOW OR SUBSTANCE?

Meanwhile, the British displayed an unfortunate penchant for losing every iron in the fire. They *were* tipped off about American intentions by Arthur Ringwalt, First Secretary at the US embassy in London. On 9 November 1953, Ringwalt showed R.D. Fowler of the CRO a State Department telegram reporting a conversation between S.N. Haksar, the Indian Minister in Washington, and Byroade on 5 November. To Haksar, Byroade had denied reports in the *New York Times* on 1 November of a military alliance between Pakistan and the US, but he voiced American anxiety over Middle East defence and had indicated to Haksar that they were contemplating military aid to Pakistan within the framework of a regional pact. Uncertain what to make of the report, the CRO inquired whether the State Department 'have in fact' linked the question of military assistance with Middle East defence as the Washington telegram suggested.[92]

In Washington, the British embassy failed to unearth the real purpose of Ghulam Muhammad's visit. To their dismay, the State Department were 'not at all forthcoming' on what had transpired during the Governor-General's talks with US officials.[93] Left to their own devices, British diplomats satisfied themselves that Pakistani protestations that it was a private visit, 'incredible as they seem to be to the Press here, are true'. To underline this, the British embassy in Washington delayed their report to the Foreign Office 'until it was conclusive from both public statements, and from official sources in private', that the visit had 'not been decisive one way or the other' on military aid to Pakistan.[94] In this they were partly correct, since no *formal* decision, that is, by Eisenhower, had been taken. But they wrongly let the matter rest there, and did not follow up the important clue provided by Ringwalt.

The truth was that the British were still unaware of what was going on. During a visit to Turkey on 30 November, Ghulam Muhammad conferred with President Bayar, Prime Minister Menderes and Foreign Minister Koprulu, and he confided to Avra Warren that Bayar had confirmed Turkey's willingness to enter into a defence pact with Pakistan. However, Turkey would not countenance the inclusion of the Arab states. Turkish officials notified the British embassy in Ankara that the Governor-General had only paid 'a courtesy visit'. Helm suspected that there might be something in Turkish press excitement over the visit, for he had learned from Warren that Ghulam Muhammad had not been altogether discouraged by the Turkish reaction to his 'general feelers' about Iran's participation in a pact, though the Turks were 'distinctly icy' about including the Arab states in one. From Warren himself Helm heard that the Turks remained unsympathetic to any proposal for an Arab role in a regional coalition. On return to Karachi,[95] Ghulam Muhammed himself said nothing substantial about his visit when he met Laithwaite on 12 December 1953.[96] The British mistakenly assumed that no news was good news.

With the Americans, the Pakistanis pressed yet again for a military hand-out. Beating the anti-British drum, Prime Minister Mohamad Ali lamented to Ambassador Horace Hildreth on 2 December 1953 that the British could not be counted on; and, casting them as enemies of republicanism, he alleged that the British had subsidised trouble in East Pakistan to defeat the creation of a republic. This was an opening line to ingratiate himself with the Americans and to make known Karachi's disquiet at American procrastination on financing Pakistan's arsenal. Mohamad Ali voiced only one doubt about the US, and, according to Hildreth, it was 'with great feeling' that he made his only request during that conversation.

Take whatever time you need but for God's sake if you once make an affirmative decision, stick to it because we will have burned our bridges behind us and although we are not afraid and are determined in our policies it would be a tragic thing for us once the affirmative decision was made in cooperation with us if there were to be any reneging regardless of pressures.[97]

Pakistani officials pulled out all the stops when Nixon visited Karachi in the first week of December 1953. The talks were almost entirely devoted to military assistance and the Pakistanis did an 'intensive selling job' with Nixon.[98]

Far removed from American and Pakistani thinking, the British concentrated on how Eden should influence Dulles against military aid to Pakistan when they met at Bermuda in the first week of December.[99] In this the British acted partly of their own volition, partly at the request of the Indian government. Aware that the British were unhappy at the expansion of American influence in the Middle East,[100] the Indians may have hoped that the British would be able to dissuade the Americans from funding a Pakistani military build-up. On 30 November 1953, Raghavan Pillai showed Alexander Clutterbuck a telegram from G.L. Mehta, the Indian ambassador in Washington, reporting that, a fortnight earlier, Dulles had informed Mehta that the US wished to strengthen Pakistan with a view to associating her with Middle East defence. Pillai warned Clutterbuck that this would seriously impair Indo–US relations. Speaking on Nehru's behalf, Pillai entreated the British to influence the Americans against any such move.

He could only hope that we should be able to find [an] opportunity of holding the United States back from what would be both militarilly [sic] and politically a disastrous move and it was for this purpose [that] he was appealing to us in the Prime Minister's name and with the full force of his personal authority.[101]

Pillai wanted the appeal to reach Eden before he met Dulles at Bermuda.

Indian opposition was therefore a conspicuous theme in the British case against US military aid to Pakistan. 'We hold no particular brief for Nehru's views which are not entirely convincing', minuted Denis Allen on 3 December 1953. 'We do not wish to obstruct any U.S. effort to strengthen Pakistan.' But it was clear that the Indians felt strongly on the subject, and the risk of deteriorating Indo–Pakistani relations had also to be 'weighed in the other side of the balance'.[102] London's willingness to convey New Delhi's viewpoint to Dulles only revealed its unawareness of American intentions.

How ill-informed the British were about what had transpired in Washington and Ankara was reflected by Eden's anxiety to find out from Dulles at Bermuda what the Americans had in mind.[103] Meanwhile, the State Department gave no assurance on offshore purchases from Britain: they merely solicited British help in smoothing any ruffled Indian feathers.

All this only highlighted the gap between the US, Pakistan and Turkey on the one hand and Britain on the other. Time was not on the British side. A brief chronology of events may afford the best illustration of British ignorance of American designs and the process by which the Americans finally took a decision on military aid to Pakistan. On 7 December 1953 Dulles told Eden at Bermuda that the Eisenhower administration was still undecided on the form of such assistance and that Indian neutrality could not be allowed to veto the whole idea.[104] It was true that Eisenhower had yet to take a formal decision, but as we have seen, a series of departmental decisions had already prepared the way for military assistance to Pakistan within a Northern Tier alignment, although the Americans did not know exactly what they wanted or how they would achieve it. But they were not giving anything away to the British. The same day, Knox Helm wrote from Ankara that there had been 'more than a mere exchange of compliments' during Ghulam Muhammad's visit to Turkey. This was the first time that the British had got wind of it. Nuri Birgi, the Assistant Secretary-General in the Turkish Ministry for Foreign Affairs, told Scott Fox, Counsellor at the British embassy in Ankara, that the exchange had shown 'the most gratifying identity of views' on the Soviet threat to the non-communist world and the need for free world co-operation.[105] Even now the British did not grasp that the Turkish disclosure to Helm was only the tip of the iceberg.

Two days later, on 9 December, Vice-President Richard Nixon, wiring from Karachi, wanted the NSC to postpone taking a decision on aid until he had personally consulted Dulles and Charles Wilson on his return to Washington. If this was not possible, Nixon wanted to telegraph some of his impressions so that they could be recorded. Although this would delay a decision by the NSC, there was no reason to turn down his request.[106] Byroade expected Nixon to endorse military funding to Pakistan, for he recommended to Bedell Smith on 11 December that the Americans should move ahead as soon as Nixon returned to Washington and should seek 'an affirmative Presidential decision as soon as possible' after discussion with Nixon.[107]

Meanwhile the Foreign Office had realised, by 15 December, that there was no holding the Americans. Blaming the CRO for continuing 'to temporise, fending off' a definition of the British attitude by asking for more information about US intentions, the Foreign Office regretted that the British had not discouraged the United States at the outset, for it was now too late for them to intervene.[108] The question of nipping American plans in the bud did not even arise.

The truth had finally dawned on the British. Denis Allen surmised that the US must have discussed the scheme with Ghulam Muhammad in Washington in November; to Lord Reading, Minister of State for Foreign Affairs, it looked 'very much as if the plan had been put into Ghulam Mohammed's head during his visit to Washington'. On 17 December it struck the Foreign Office that this linked up with the US-Pakistani parleys on military aid and that the Americans visualised Pakistan and Turkey as forming two gateposts of a defensive system designed to counter a Soviet threat to the Middle East.[109]

It was a belated realisation, and the British still did not know how far their allies had gone. For Nixon, never an India-lover, had already turned the scales in favour of helping Pakistan; a day earlier, on 16 December he urged the NSC that he

was convinced that it would be a fatal mistake to back down on this program solely because of Nehru's objections. Such a retreat would cost us our hold on Pakistan and on many other areas in the Near East and Africa. We must always realize that Nehru was one sort of a character in his domestic position in India, and quite a different character in the realm of international relations.

Nehru was against military aid because a build-up of Pakistan would challenge his leadership in Asia and in parts of Africa. '[If] we at this point back down on our program of assistance to Pakistan, we can count on losing most of the Asian–Arab countries to the neutralist bloc.'[110] A week later, Nixon pursued his theme of winners and losers: 'I think Nehru likes nobody but Nehru . . . a policy of flattery is a great mistake . . . If we do not give aid to Pakistan, we've got to find a way to not give it without giving Nehru the victory.'[111] Nixon was simply reinforcing the American determination to ignore India which had been apparent even before the Americans decided in principle in September 1953 to subsidise and fortify Pakistan. As in the Asian cold war, Britain's "Indian pretext" had failed to impress or restrain the Americans in the Middle East, for in both cases basic principles of American strategy came into conflict with British interests. With Nixon coming down heavily on Pakistan's side, the case for alignment had carried the day in Washington.

VIII OPENING A NEW AMERICAN FRONTIER

The State Department now worked out the procedures to be followed if the Americans decided to move forward with military aid to Pakistan in the context of a Turco–Pakistani pact. On 23 December 1953 Dulles envisaged that local states might initiate some sort of regional defence co-operation. This would be important domestically and abroad to provide the rationale for aid and to uphold the US contention that assistance to Pakistan was directed towards defence against 'outside aggression' and not against India or Afghanistan. At the moment it would not be possible to progress beyond a Turco–Pakistani grouping, which would be looser than NATO, providing consultation and joint-defence planning. The US would not participate, only assist. The US would start by approaching the Turks and concert with them on tactics. To camouflage the American initiative, either Turkey or Pakistan could take the lead in proposing exploratory bilateral talks to the other. Such parleys might be secret at first but at some fairly early stage the two parties could publicly announce their intention to negotiate. Simultaneously or shortly afterwards Pakistan could formally request US military aid, and the Americans could justify their assent in public on the grounds that the proposed Turco–Pakistani pact would raise a security umbrella against communism.[112] Partly to assuage Indian feelings, partly to avoid being branded "imperialist" by nationalists in the Middle East, the Americans fastidiously veiled their own initiative in getting the Turco–Pakistani alignment off the ground. In doing so, they tacitly conceded their limited influence in the Middle East.

In keeping with their desire to brief (but not consult) the British, the State Department informed the British embassy in Washington on 29 December 1953 that there was now agreement in the US government to go ahead with military aid for Pakistan, if it could be set in an appropriate framework. The US government would therefore attempt to synchronise this with the initiation of some kind of collaboration between Pakistan and Turkey which would be a first step to setting up a collective defence system in the Middle East. The Americans would ask the Turks to make the first move by proposing discussions with Pakistan. They were not contemplating their own participation or that of any other Western power in the planning organisation. If the Turks agreed, and if their overture was favourably received in Karachi, the Pakistani and Turkish governments would declare their intention to start military talks. The US government could then refer to the Turco–Pakistani declaration when making public their own decision to respond to a Pakistani request for military aid. If the Turks refused, the matter would have to be reconsidered, but even in this event, it would be 'difficult' for the US government to withold aid.[113] Come what might, Pakistan would become an American ally.

Not for the first time, the British were taken by surprise. 'This is rather startling', minuted Eden on the telegram from Makins, 'and I have considerable doubts. Cabinet should discuss next week. Meanwhile what do we think?'[114] British officials were quite certain about what they thought. In their confidential exchanges, they unanimously condemned the American idea, 'on which they [Americans] have acted without prior consultation' with them, of linking aid to Pakistan with military collaboration between Turkey and Pakistan. In Karachi, an uninformed Laithwaite, who had been chagrined to learn about the proposed Turco–Pakistani compact from Knox Helm's letter of 7 December, now grumbled that the Pakistanis 'who are good, as you know, at keeping their own counsel when they want to, have let nothing leak that would be at all helpful to us'.[115] P.S. Falla berated 'this ill-defined framework of a regional defence system primarily as a means to justify their military aid to Pakistan.' Falla's minute formed the basis of a paper Eden presented to the cabinet on 5 January 1954. (It also inspired a draft telegram from Eden to Makins which was not sent.) The American idea was judged as 'positively harmful' primarily because it excluded Western participation. It would therefore lack the advantage of a British contribution to regional defence. It was 'surprising' that the US government should have launched this initiative without consulting the British. 'We were the originators of M.E.D.O., and are the only Western Power with forces in the area.' Emphasising British indispensability the Chiefs wanted to make clear to the Americans that 'we cannot accept exclusion from the organisation which might develop from their proposals.' Only planning without an alliance or commitments was envisaged. This would not by itself strengthen the anti-Communist front while being ostentatiously provocative to the Soviet Union.[116]

To the British the searing truth was that Dulles had not divulged anything to Eden 'more than very vaguely' about a pact when they had met at Bermuda.[117] But they had to make a show of strength, and from Eden downwards British officials thought they could still curb the Americans. Eden would take up the question with Dulles in Berlin. When asked by Jernegan whether this meant that Eden wished to be consulted before any further move was made, Beeley's pointed answer was that if the Turks replied favourably, the Americans 'could not retrace their steps', but if the Turks rejected the plan, Eden would like to be consulted before the Americans took any new initiatives. Neither Beeley nor Crawley raised any objection to American designs, though Jernegan sensed from the 'occasional implications' of their remarks, and from the nature of their questions to the State Department, that the British were 'not altogether happy'.[118]

Having failed to restrain the US from instigating the Turco–Pakistani arrangement, the Foreign Office now tried to manoeuvre the Americans on the manner and timing of its launching. The proposed alignment bore on Soviet interests at 'extremely sensitive points', and it was therefore 'surely not wise to advocate it publicly at this time just before the Berlin conference'. The conference seemed 'an added reason for not advocating, still less hurrying on with this plan at the present time.'[119]

Could the Turks be restrained? In Ankara, Knox Helm was offended that, '[t]hough not lacking opportunities' they had not broached the subject with the British.[120] Eden instructed Helm to seek 'a suitable opportunity' to probe Turkish thinking; to clarify that the British were not opposed to the US plan but that its implications, especially on timing, called for 'cautious examination'.[121] But the Turks were tight-lipped. On 9 January 1954, Koprulu told Helm that the American scheme was not 'practical politics' because Iraq would not have anything to do with it; he was scathing about Egypt and the Arabs, but gave no hint of US approaches to his government. Then, two days later, on 11 January, the Turkish Foreign Office informed Helm that they were agreeable to the American proposal since it would be a great step forward if the defence gap against the USSR could be closed. But prudence was called for because of Pakistan's enmity with India and Afghanistan and her own Islamic policy and identification with the Arab states. Iran did not count for much with Turkey, while an alignment between Iraq and the West was 'almost impossible'. The American proposal was premature and 'the Minister repeated . . . premature several times.' From this Helm deduced that nothing was happening for the moment.[122]

He was wrong. On the advice of the State Department[123] Eisénhower consented in principle to military assistance on 5 January 1954.[124] A final decision was pending but 'we are now in a position to act promptly on hearing from [the] Turks.' An affirmative reply from the Turks was not long in coming, and on 14 January 1954 Dulles notified Eisenhower that the Turks were ready to initiate talks on a coalition with Pakistan, and the US had reached the point where proceeding would be 'inadvisable' unless the US decision were definitely to go ahead.[125] For the Americans an opportune moment to swing into action had arrived. The next day, the State Department informed the British embassy in Washington that the Turks had accepted their scheme in principle. This did not square with what the Turks had told the British: they had obviously taken one line with the US and another with Helm – the difference was one of emphasis. Perhaps Helm had misunderstood something earlier – the Turks regarded the publicity given to the pact and not the pact itself as premature. But it would be futile for the British to take a 'purely negative attitude',[126] implying that the British must fall in with their allies.

Meanwhile the British continued to unravel the extent to which they had been ignored or misled by the US, Turkey or Pakistan. Jernegan's conversation with Joe Garner, Permanent Secretary at the CRO, on 16 January 1954 revealed to them for first time that a pact *had* been discussed with Ghulam Muhammad during his visit to Washington in November 1953: Jernegan confessed that the US had then been 'persuaded' to lend support to a Turco–Pakistani alignment. But both the State Department and Pakistan had previously assured the British 'most categorically' that American officials had not exchanged thoughts on any pact with Ghulam Muhammad. Unpleasantly surprised at Jernegan's revelation, the British found, to their discomfiture, that the Turks had been 'less lukewarm than we had supposed and the U.S. plan is now likely to make some headway'.[127] A reply to an anticipated question in the Commons showed how far the British would have to acquiesce, at least in public, in US proposals that were to their disadvantage. Any official reply would extol the granting of US aid to Pakistan as 'right and proper' and supportive of a fellow Commonwealth member. Indian objections would be brushed aside: India, it would be explained, was entitled to nonalignment. But British policy was 'different, and . . . we are convinced that the free world must be strong and united to defend itself'.[128] Having failed to rein the Americans in by using Indian arguments, the British now incorporated American answers to counteract any Indian hubbub over military subsidies to Pakistan. When it came to the crunch, the British had to walk in step with the US, even when they thought US policy was damaging to their interests.

It was not that the State Department were completely insensitive to British feelings. American officials were concerned that 'they [the British] feel they have been badly treated', and Raynor on the European desk observed that British politeness was a danger signal for Dulles–Eden relations. Raynor wanted the British to 'be with us on this matter 100% not only because it does neither of us any good to be pursuing different lines in the Near East', but because the British might create trouble in NATO.[129] But, having blazed a new Middle Eastern trail, the State Department would not stop in their tracks to offer the British any palliative; instead, they simply expected the British to jump on to the American bandwagon.

They were in fact racing ahead and wanted to make a public announcement of US support for the Turco–Pakistani arrangement. Eden intended to make an eleventh-hour attempt to dissuade the US from doing so when he met Dulles at the forthcoming Berlin conference, since the very survival of British influence in Pakistan and in the Middle East was at stake. Negative arguments would not impress Dulles, so Eden could stress the necessity of Anglo–American co-operation in Middle East defence and assert British primacy in the region. Eden could also remind Dulles that Britain would like Pakistan to use her American grant to buy British weaponry and that the British 'must' have advance warning of any final US decision on military funding to Pakistan.[130] It was a last, desperate British effort to save face. The attempt was also pointless, for the Americans wanted to inform NATO about their intentions. On 23 January Dulles told Eden at Berlin that the US was convinced that it should go ahead with military aid to Pakistan, although no formal decision had been taken. India would make a fuss, but the US could not surrender to neutralism, for all South and Southeast Asian nations would then take their cue from Nehru.[131] To set Indian fears at rest, Eisenhower would write a personal message to Nehru before any formal announcement was made in about three weeks' time. Having ridden roughshod over British interests in the Middle East and Pakistan, the State Department strove to avoid any British recriminations on relatively minor matters, such as the wording of Eisenhower's missive to Nehru. Eisenhower's draft letter to Nehru stated that the US 'admired the effective way' Nehru's government had ' "taken over from the British the direction of your military establishment." ' But the European section of the State Department had second thoughts. London, they cautioned, might interpret the remark 'as a pat on India's back for expelling the British Raj'.[132] So the sentence was omitted from the message Eisenhower finally sent Nehru on 25 February 1954. Such concern was a small detail in a policy that had undercut the British position in the Middle East and Pakistan. With Eisenhower taking the formal decision on 18 February 1954, military aid to Pakistan was soon to become a reality, and the stage was set for a new alignment of forces in South Asia and the Middle East.

The essential fact was that the British were floundering hopelessly. The Berlin brief, noted James Cable, no longer held good. The US had approved the Turkish proposals and would make a public announcement as soon as the Pakistani government agreed to start negotiations. The British wavered: their representatives in NATO and other capitals would want instructions, but at present, '*we do not know exactly what the views of H.M.G. are*'.[133] All that the British could do was to welcome the parleys and, having been left out for so long, reiterate the necessity for their participation.

While the sun had not yet risen on any American "imperium" in the Middle East, Britain's influence, even over her own allies, lay in the shadow. The Turks wanted the British to desist from pressing for a deferral of the American announcement until after the Berlin conference, especially in view of the leakages which had already occured. Also, the Pakistanis were calling for the earliest possible public statement. In the interests of forging an ever-elusive Commonwealth unity, the CRO backed the Turkish request for the waiving of British objections to the US announcement. Mohamad Ali, the CRO advised, was under considerable domestic pressure to wrap up an aid package, and would greatly resent any British action which would involve further delays. Under the circumstances, British insistence on postponing the statement would only embroil them with Turkey and Pakistan. The Foreign Office concurred and instructed the embassy in Ankara to thank the Turkish government for their draft anouncement and agreed, in view of 'what has already appeared in the Press', not to insist on its deferral. The Turkish announcement, affirmed the Foreign Office, was 'studiously mild'; it contained nothing the Soviets could take objection to, so there was no danger that the cold war would get hotter.[134]

With the British having been influenced rather than influencing, it was Makins who, surveying the situation from Washington, summed up their plight in a letter to Eden which was presented to the cabinet on 15 February 1954. On the British side, wrote Makins, there was 'a very understandable suspicion that the Americans are out to take our place in the Middle East.' Their influence had greatly expanded since 1945; they were now 'firmly established as the paramount foreign influence' in Turkey and Saudi Arabia; they were gaining 'a similar ascendancy in Persia, and it now seems that Pakistan may to some extent be drawn into their orbit'. Were the Americans consciously trying to don the mantle previously worn by the British in the Middle East? Makins thought not. The emergence of the Americans as the dominant power was not necessarily a foregone conclusion; much would depend on British efforts and 'in particular on the way in which we adjust ourselves to this new American factor in Middle East politics'. As the Americans extended their own military commitments, it would be inconsistent with their attitude towards Britain as their major ally deliberately to push her out of the Middle East. True, some Americans, spurred on by enthusiasm for their particular tasks, 'by a belief in the superiority of American methods or simply by vanity, are delighted to increase their own importance at our expense.' But these tendencies could be checked by 'a proper understanding' between London and Washington. The implication was that the British could only influence; and Makins – and the cabinet – at once recognised that their opinions would not necessarily carry weight with the Americans.[135]

How badly the British were hit by American sponsorship of the Turco–Pakistani alignment was revealed by their search for scapegoats for their ignorance and their failure to prevail upon the Americans. British officials blamed one other, their allies and the Indians for their débacle. From Karachi, Laithwaite sulked that a Commonwealth government had been so secretive and consoled himself that Pakistan's lack of frankness had not been in her own interests, while acknowledging that it had probably emanated from her fear that the British would 'crab [the] proposals' if they knew too much about them. In the Foreign Office, Tahourdin lamented that Pakistan's Commonwealth membership 'does not appear to count for very much when it is a question of telling us what she is up to with the Americans and the Turks.' W.J.M. Paterson also criticised Pakistan's behaviour as 'unbecoming' to a member of the Commonwealth.[136] All this conveniently glossed over the deaf ear the British had often turned to Pakistan's importuning for arms and to the tenuous Commonwealth link. It was not only the Pakistanis who were cagey. Because of the British penchant for secrecy, and their embarrassment at being outwitted and outpaced by their allies, the many telegrams exchanged between Washington, Ankara, Karachi and London were not distributed to old Commonwealth countries. Whatever the British rhetoric, equality and heart-to-heart confidences were not the bottom line of the Commonwealth relationship.

The soul-searching in London easily degenerated into fault-finding: the Foreign Office wondered how far the lack of information from Pakistan was the result of a deliberate policy pursued by Pakistan and how far due to insufficiently close ties between the UK High Commission and Pakistani officials. Questioning the competence of the CRO, Cable suggested that more Foreign Office members might be needed in the High Commission in Karachi, while Tahourdin agreed that 'matters appear to have been made worse by lack of zeal' in reporting on the part of the High Commission.[137] These views reflected Foreign Office contempt for the CRO, while turning a blind eye to the fact that the British embassies in Ankara and Washington had also been caught napping on more than one occasion.

The CRO, for their part, were merely concerned to keep up appearances. There had been no consultations with Pakistan, but they were 'anxious to conceal this lack of confidence on the part of the Government of Pakistan'. A reply to a question raised in the Commons on the pact was therefore relegated to a note for supplementaries, and on 22 February 1954 Eden merely welcomed 'this reinforcement' of the ties of friendship between Britain's ally, Turkey, and a fellow member of the Commonwealth.[138] It is a measure of their complete lack of realism, and consequently of their endless wait for the sun to rise on the Commonwealth, that senior CRO officials pouted that Mohamad Ali's speech on the Turco–Pakistani arrangements did not contain any reference to the Commonwealth![139] It was the unfortunate Laithwaite who summed up what the US had gained at Britain's expense. British policy, commented Laithwaite, had been rendered sterile because of Kashmir, and Pakistan had concluded that the US was the right horse to back. America had taken the initiative and was recognised as the power to be reckoned with. The British could do nothing but welcome US aid, even if its consequences were unpalatable to them. It would be the best way of 'strengthening the Commonwealth'. But – whatever the British might say in public – even this prospect was bereft of consolation. It was for Laithwaite 'a depressing and . . . rather humiliating analysis', but it was no use turning away from the facts.[140]

IX AMERICA IN BRITAIN'S PLACE

Overtaken by events, by mid-February 1954 the British had clearly acquiesced in US plans for military aid to Pakistan within the framework of a Turco–Pakistani alignment, while trying to salvage some of their influence by supplying offshore arms to Pakistan. Pakistani dissatisfaction with the amount of funding promised by the US raised British hopes of retaining some influence, so it is important to look at the differences between Pakistan and the US over military supplies.

Acting in accordance with American instructions Pakistan and Turkey signed a pact on 2 April 1954, but Pakistan found, to her dismayed surprise, that American assistance would fall far short of her expectations. Pakistani hopes had been high because no American official had taken issue with assertions by Ayub or Mirza that $50 million would be required annually from the US to build up the armed forces during the first phase of expansion. By April 1954, many Pakistani officials claimed that Pakistan's heavy defence burdens and the shortage of many essential goods had fomented political unrest. A surfeit of economic woes had made it impossible for Pakistan to carry out even the 1951 plan for strengthening her defences, and, because of the heavy slump in commodity prices, her annual foreign exchange earnings had fallen by $400 million. Pakistani officials wanted the US to equip Pakistan to meet the communist threat and not merely to make up the deficiency in her military capabilities.[141]

The Americans were not impressed. Brigadier-General William Meyers,

the head of the US military mission in Pakistan, said his charter was limited
to making existing Pakistani forces combat-worthy and did not take into
account the long-term programme. Pakistan's requirements and assets
would be considered and from this the deficiencies would be determined.
'These deficiencies must then be screened against lists of items considered
eligible for programming under *our* regulations.' It was clear that the
Americans would lay down the rules of the game; why did Pakistan accept
them? The answer was simple: some aid was better than none, and only the
Americans could dispense it. Meanwhile the Pakistanis continued to
badger the Americans. The US military attaché in Karachi noted 'complete
coordination' among Pakistani officials on a policy designed to bring about
an increase in American aid. In support of the policy past events were
distorted where necessary. For example, the Pakistanis were now alleging
that the US had taken the lead in setting up the aid programme, ignoring
the fact that 'Pakistan has been begging for military aid for the past two
years'. The Pakistanis also contended that military assistance had destroyed any chance of settling their disputes with India, 'a complete about-
face from earlier statements that a militarily strong Pakistan was the best
inducement to bring about successful negotiations with India'.[142] Hildreth
took up the Pakistani case, but the State Department, which had initiated
the whole idea of Pakistani participation in the Northern Tier, replied that
they would defer to the military. In part this reflected differences between
the State Department and the Pentagon over the aims of US policy with
reference to Pakistan's role in Middle East defence. The State Department
were convinced that aid to Pakistan had been 'compelled' by the 'logic of
events' and that 'this should be recognized as a basis of policy'. The
Pentagon, however, felt that US resources were inadequate to shoulder
new responsibilities and had 'consistently fought shy of this conclusion'.
These contradictions had not been reconciled.

Eisenhower, Dulles, Wilson and the US Chiefs of Staff all favoured
Pakistan's participation, but their views were probably unknown to what
Jernegan described as 'the operating level in the Pentagon', which was
intent on a policy of economy and caution. The result was that Brigadier-
General Meyers had taken the Pentagon line in Karachi – and there was
not much that the State Department could do about it.[143] On 15 April 1954
Bedell Smith advised Hildreth that long-term policies could best be considered against the background of the military mission report. Hildreth
should soothe the Pakistanis by recommending a one-year programme of
military assistance. Some delays in the initial period would be 'unavoid-
able' because of administrative delays in establishing a MAAG, placing
orders and effecting shipments. To begin with only the foundations would
be laid, and the achievement of long-term objectives would probably
require a programme of several years.[144] Pakistani officials were simultaneously humiliated and furious, but what could they do?

They could not reject American aid, but they could play their British card again. Less than three weeks after the formal decision by Eisenhower, Iskander Mirza told Lord Alexander that he was against mixing British and American weapons and that he would welcome offshore purchases.[145] On 3 April 1954, Ayub made it plain to the British military adviser in Karachi that Pakistan's first aim was to make herself self-sufficient for her own defence, (that is against India) and second, 'thereafter', to equip a force of sufficient size to participate in Middle East defence. Ayub remonstrated 'very sharply' that the US had encouraged expectations of generous assistance and exposed Pakistan to Soviet and Indian protests, but they were now giving only inconsiderable quantities. Ayub did not expect much from the British: they had never really been able to help Pakistan to build up her forces and they could have done 'much more' to back Pakistan over Kashmir.[146]

In the wake of his earlier discomfiture at the Pakistani silence, Laithwaite saw Ayub's disappointment with the US presenting the British with a fresh opportunity. Pakistan, he gloated, had 'only themselves to blame', since they had never been encouraged by the US to think that the aid would meet their grandiose expectations. Financially and in terms of supply Britain could not compete with the US, so he would not promise Pakistan very much. Whether the British could offer Pakistan any equipment 'over and above off-shore purchases from the American aid is not for me to say. But clearly we may expect a slight Pakistan [sic] reaction towards us which circumstances might enable us to take some advantage.'[147] Mutually – if differentially – resentful at the US, the British and Pakistanis tried to extract a favourable bargain from each other, hoping thereby to strike a successful deal with the Americans.

So when Zafrullah Khan told Laithwaite on 5 April 1954 that Pakistan wanted the British to lobby the Americans for more aid to her, Laithwaite was unctuous, nebulous and encouraging: the British government, he assured Zafrullah, favoured the strengthening of a Commonwealth country.[148] Meeting the British Chiefs of Staff in London on 7 April, Iskander Mirza said he favoured offshore purchases and sought their advice on a possible Pakistani contribution to Middle East defence in a war. In contrast to the previous British scepticism about such a contribution, General Sir John Harding envisaged Turkey and Pakistan as bastions of regional defence, co-operating with Britain and Iraq. Mirza cannily responded that this would depend on how much aid Pakistan received, and that the British Chiefs of Staff should nudge the US Chiefs towards generosity to Pakistan. He also expressed enthusiasm for liaison visits between British and Pakistani officers. The British Chiefs agreed to put in a good word for Pakistan, since a Pakistani expeditionary force capable of deployment at the head of the Persian Gulf on the outbreak of war would be of great strategic value. At the Cabinet Defence Committee meeting on 14 April, Swinton found it 'very encouraging' that Pakistan 'was beginning to show willingness to turn to us for advice' and to co-operate with the British in Middle East defence.[149] But the encouragement was short-lived, for Mirza threatened the British Chiefs that unless Pakistan could be assured of supplies she would reluctantly be forced to make purchases outside the Commonwealth.[150] Pakistan tried to play the British and Americans off against each other, threatening and pleading at the same time – apparently seeking advice from both and deriding one to the other. To Hildreth, Ayub alleged that the UK fancied isolating American influence in 'the whole area'; to the British he lambasted American procrastination and claimed that the Pakistanis were interested in early Anglo–American exchanges. The Foreign Office were taken in; the State Department, however, dragged their feet on the pretext that more thinking was needed on Middle East security,[151] and the Pakistanis bowed to the situation with bad grace.

What would Anglo–American exchanges yield?[152] Once again, the American ability to impose the rules, combined with the twists and turns of American policy-making portended unwelcome answers to both Pakistan and Britain. Neither the State Department nor the Mutual Security Administration were averse to offshore purchases from the British; such procurements would help to maintain a favourable British attitude towards defence arrangements 'in the area of Pakistan'.[153] The Pentagon, however, had other ideas. They decided that American equipment would replace serviceable British *matériel*, which would be 'retired' to the war reserve. Eventually, upon completion of the long-term programme the Pakistani army would be fitted out with American replacements, excluding those which could be procured through local manufacture or 'through known continuing British supply sources'. In the initial phase of training, American equipment would be introduced in existing units, and British weaponry known to be obsolete would be replaced.[154] There was no word of offshore arms.

News of Pentagon plans came as another blow to the British. The Chiefs worried that US equipment would be starting from scratch instead of supplementing what had already been provided. If this went on unchecked 'we should be ousted from our position of traditional suppliers.' The British should remind Washington of their position and of the items they could give Pakistan.[155] From Karachi, Laithwaite sent out the desperate signal that the American line of thinking was 'consistent with our gradually being elbowed out of our position in a Commonwealth country'. This had to be counteracted. Could British representatives sit in on talks between US and Pakistani officials? Laithwaite recognised the absurdity of his suggestion as soon as he made it: it would be awkward as the British would be objecting to American help because it cut across their supplying British equipment. Then there was uncomfortable knowledge that Mohamad Ali had an 'American slant', and rather than go without help, Ayub would grab whatever was offered.[156] The only option was to have a word with the Americans. At the CRO's bidding, Makins was instructed to warn the

Americans that the replacement of British by American equipment and organisation would not be good: 'this sort of revolutionary approach . . . must inevitably disrupt organisation, training and development of [the] Pakistan [sic] armed forces and set back considerably [the] date by which Pakistan might be capable of contribution [sic] to defence of [the] free world.' This would be 'inimical to our interests as well as to the best interests of Pakistan herself'. Makins should impress on the Americans the 'need to be frank with us'; he should 'in particular' seek an assurance that they would consult the British on supplies so that both could discuss how Britain's contribution could be fitted in.[157] Accordingly, Makins told Byroade that since the British and Americans had an 'identical' interest in the strengthening of Pakistan, 'I wondered whether we could not try to get this operation as far as possible on a tripartite basis.' Byroade made no promises, but he raised no objection, and the Foreign Office and CRO appear to have taken the absence of any objection at face value.[158]

The Pakistanis did not. While the British purported to be influencing the Americans in the interests of Pakistan, the Pakistanis fretted that British influence on the Americans might result in no arms for Pakistan. After all, the British had never given Pakistan what she wanted. To Ayub, the maintenance of traditional Anglo–Pakistani ties and the long-established organisation of the army were not ends in themselves, if only because the British were unreliable. Meeting Air Vice-Marshal Atcherley and General Price in Washington in October 1954, he bluntly told them that Pakistan would view any British attempt to stand between her and American aid as 'a very unfriendly act'. Atcherley assured him that was not the British intention: they wanted a tripartite review of Pakistan's needs and the best means of meeting them in the shortest possible time. In Atcherley's assurance Ayub saw a silver lining. The US, he whispered to Atcherley, was putting pressure on Pakistan to combine aid with the adoption of US military organisation, but Pakistan would not allow American funding to interfere with the existing British structure and hoped to restrict US influence to technical training. Then, offering an ace to the British, Ayub disingenuously declared that Pakistan really wanted offshore purchases as opposed to direct military aid, 'and he looked to us to help to persuade the Americans accordingly. He said firmly that he would prefer British equipment in the majority of cases.'[159] It was Pakistan's usual cat-and-mouse game.

The British did not see through it. Flattered and fortified by Ayub's interest in tripartite consultations and British equipment, Makins was prepared to broach both subjects with the State Department and to put forward specific proposals on the nature of the consultation, where they would take place and at what level. Pakistani opinion would be given weight. 'I assume that we would not make proposals of this kind to the Americans without first clearing them with the Pakistanis'[160] – a shift from the British habit of consulting the Americans first, since it was now the

Pakistanis who were telling the British what they wanted to hear.

Makins's suggestion was taken up by the Foreign Office, who initiated a meeting of the Defence, CRO, Foreign Office, Supply and Services on 28 October 1954. The Services favoured tripartite consultations in Washington. But what could consultations achieve? The British were uncomfortably aware that their shop was poorly stocked and badly run; in contrast, the Americans could offer Pakistan military equipment in the form of aid with immediate delivery. The Pakistanis would naturally jump at the American offer rather than 'our offer of delivery in a year's time'.[161] What the British feared to lose through their ragged competitive edge, they still hoped to salvage by making a show of importance. Quite absurdly, they expected the Americans to cater to *British* interests at the expense of their own. The Foreign Office instructed Makins to tell the Americans that it would be 'helpful' if American service people in Karachi could be 'restrained in their attempts at high-pressure salesmanship' of US equipment which was 'merely embarrassing to everyone', if the new Pakistani Minister of Defence was, 'as he says, firmly wedded to British equipment'.[162] Evidently the British failed to make, even to themselves, a convincing case for offshore purchases by Pakistan, and expected the Americans to refrain from pushing for *their* equipment. There could not have been a more fatuous self-delusion, and it is hardly surprising that Makins failed to elicit any assurance from Stassen when he discussed offshore purchases with him in Washington.

For the Americans clearly held the whip-hand over both the British and Pakistanis. Ayub's request for funding to recruit up to 40,000 men to fill the gaps in the proposed new Pakistani army was brushed aside by the Americans with the terse order that US economic aid would provide the wherewithal in increased Pakistani exports and profits to produce this. Furious, Ayub thundered: ' "it was like telling a Commander to sell onions in order to pay his troops".'[163] Pakistan could only sulk at American niggardliness and endure her discontentment with the US because the meagre dispensations of American aid would amount to much more than she would ever get from the British.

Therein lay the irony of the situation. While Pakistan was manifestly unhappy about the $40 million aid announced by the Americans in October 1954, she had, nevertheless, entered America's sphere of influence. The British offered too little, too late to make a winning bid, and the knowledge hurt them. Commenting on the enthusiastic reception accorded to Mohamad Ali during his visit to Washington in October 1954, Makins grudgingly acknowledged the new closeness between the US and Pakistan which had been achieved at the British expense:

Pakistan is the kind of ally particularly dear to the American heart. The American/ Pakistan relationship at the moment has the nice, simple, honest, uncomplicated character which the United States would be only too relieved to find in their more complex relationships with some of their more important allies. Pakistan, like Turkey, has stood up and been counted, and is not afraid to say so.[164]

Yet Pakistan's move into the American orbit was not inevitable. Until 1950, the Americans not only imbibed British ideas of South Asia but saw British influence over the region as a political and strategic asset. The idea of Pakistani participation in the Middle East was first mooted by the Pakistanis and was taken quite seriously by the British to begin with. Eventually, however, the British and Americans both turned a deaf ear to Pakistan's professions of her desire to join forces with the West – the British because they were not willing to pay the price of a guarantee against India and to finance a perenially unstable and bankrupt state, the Americans out of sheer lack of interest in Pakistan.

The Americans responded to Pakistan after the outbreak of the Korean war, during the course of which they started to question whether their customary reliance on the British was really serving their interests in the Middle East and Asia. By 1951, the American move away from traditional British conceptions of South Asia and the Middle East and the response to Pakistan were intertwined. Military ties were forged between the US and Pakistan only when the American interest in defending the Middle East converged with the Pakistani craving for arms against India and recast the American image of Pakistan from a strategic non-starter to a loyal military asset.

The question of timing is also important. Since the Americans had started to doubt the value of the British role in South Asia by 1950–1, why did they wait until 1953–4 to decide on military aid to Pakistan? This question can be answered at several levels. From 1951–2, the British were able to head off the Americans essentially because the Americans themselves had no idea of how to replace what they saw as a barren British strategy in the Middle East. The Americans could not conjure up a regional coalition by the mere desire or thought of Pakistani participation. Apart from Pakistan, what other countries were ready to police America's barricades in the Middle East? Turkey had already lined up but wanted to avoid entanglement in any schemes for "Islamic" defence, so beloved of an insecure Pakistan seeking to strengthen and reinforce her identity against India. Other countries, as the Americans themselves noted, were either unable or unwilling to participate. This in itself reflected the lack of American influence in the Middle East, even as the dearth of other partners rendered Pakistan an attractive prize.

As long as nationalists in the Middle East associated the US with British imperialism, the Americans would remain distrusted. Anxious to win allies, the Americans reckoned that standing back from the British would refurbish America's image, clear the decks to political and military compacts with Middle East nationalisms and stabilise the region to the benefit of the West. The idea stemmed from their flawed self-image as supporters of "freedom" in general, and they conveniently forgot that, until very recently, they had shored up British power in the Middle East against regional nationalisms. It is not clear that they actually intended or wished to displace the British; they simply thought they had better ideas to safeguard Western interests in the area. And since something could be done with Turkey and Pakistan, the Americans were determined to do it – although they were unable to detail that "something", which was as unimaginative as it was myopic, for it ignored the possibility that Middle East nationalisms might wish to be as independent of the Americans as of the British.

In the event, American plans for giving military subsidies to Pakistan within a Turco–Pakistani Northern Tier arrangement were half-baked. They never fortified the Pakistani army for a confrontation with the Soviets, and the Pakistanis never knew what was expected of them. But it is significant that these ill-conceived American ideas and parsimonious military hand-outs were enough to dislodge the British from Pakistan in 1954. With all their experience of Pakistan, the British failed to keep their ear to the ground on more than one occasion between October 1953 and February 1954. Even when provided with valuable clues, they showed surpisingly little initiative in uncovering what the Americans and Pakistanis were up to. It is difficult to account for this, especially as the British had jealously guarded their position in South Asia and the Middle East against the Americans since 1945. The most plausible explanation appears to be that American ideas of the Turco-Pakistani arrangement defied their wildest imagination,[165] so they were unable to formulate a response when, little by little, the truth dawned on them. There were at least four reasons why the British discovered too little, too late. First, there was the question of what the US, Pakistan and Turkey thought they were doing; second, what they told the British they were doing; third, what the British thought their allies were up to; and fourth, what the Americans, Pakistanis, Turks – and British – actually did.

Had the British been better attuned to what was going on, would they have been able to manipulate the Americans or Pakistanis? Even that was uncertain. The Americans turned to Pakistan because they were uneasy at Britain's inability to secure a vantage point for the West in the Middle East; to that extent the American swing towards Pakistan was a move away from the British. They did want to carry the British with them but this did not involve hammering out new policies in concert with the British, only informing them of plans that were already under way. In any case, the vagaries of American decision-making often resulted in the NSC or Defence Departments not being conversant with what the State Department were up to – let alone the British – and the mutual non-admiration between the Turks and Pakistanis hardly facilitated regular consultations.

The British could not drive a good bargain with Pakistan because even the niggardly American aid was more than the British could ever have offered. American tightfistedness made Pakistan turn to the British again, since arms in hand were of greater consequence to Pakistan than their source. But the British could not turn Pakistan's dissatisfaction with the Americans to their advantage because British indecision and inability to deliver blunted their competitive edge. The American penetration of Pakistan first reflected the distance between the US and Britain over Pakistan and the Middle East, then widened the gap and finally confirmed America's success in supplanting Britain as the primary foreign influence in Pakistan.

Neither American military assistance nor the displacement of the British gave Pakistan security against India. Pakistani participation in American-sponsored defence pacts did not safeguard the Middle East, if only because the Americans were never really clear about what they were trying to safeguard and against whom. Undercutting the British in the Middle East did not win over regional nationalisms or stabilise the area in favour of the West – indeed, Soviet penetration of the Middle East began soon after the Americans had erected the Turkish and Pakistani gateposts of the Northern Tier. The whole American exercise can be likened to a pilot whose aeroplane is supposed to soar high into the sky, but since no one knows where the aeroplane should land, it never takes off. In 1954, the main American achievement was to dislodge the British from Pakistan and simultaneously to quicken the ebbing of British influence in the Middle East. It was an ironic and unintended outcome of a British policy which had hoped to transfer real burdens on to American shoulders while retaining the primary influence for Britain.

5. India, the cold war in Indochina, and the Anglo–American relationship, 1954–6

The American attitude towards China is the product of emotional, political and military pressures. These make many Americans disinclined to accept the fact that Communism in China has come to stay . . . the United States Administration find it difficult to pursue a realistic policy towards China . . . In some American quarters impatience is expressed with the 'neutralism' of India, Burma and Indonesia and it is sometimes claimed that the only friends who matter are those with large armies and strong anti-Communist convictions. [C (53)330, 24 November 1953, CAB129/64]

We discussed . . . the conditions on which the United States might intervene in Indo-china . . . in terms of the implication that we might conceivably go ahead without the active participation of the United Kingdom . . . while this had its grave disadvantages in indicating a certain breach, there were perhaps greater disadvantages in a situation where we were obviously subject to [the] UK veto, which in turn was in Asian matters largely subject to [the] Indian veto, which in turn was largely subject to [the] Chinese Communist veto. Thereby a chain was forged which tended to make us impotent, and to encourage Chinese Communist aggression to a point where the whole position in the Pacific would be endangered and the risk of general war increased. [Memo by Dulles of conversation with Eisenhower, 11 May 1954]

I INTRODUCTION

The American irritation at Britain's "Indian pretext" did not alter the British image of India's importance in diplomatic containment in Asia. As in Korea, the British made use of Indian ideas to bring peace to Indochina in 1954 and to allay China's fears of Western threats to her territory. However, Indo-British relations were not a one-way street; they were criss-crossed by differences on other issues such as SEATO and the Bandung conference. On those two matters, the British found a greater coincidence of outlook with the US than with India. As this chapter will show, whether working with or against India, the British sought to achieve their paramount aim of preserving Western influence and containing communism, without increasing their own military involvements in Asia. It will also highlight India's place in British strategy and the extent to which it helped or hindered their attempts to influence the US.

Korea was only one aspect of the Asian cold war. The case of Indochina was more complex. Unlike Korea, it did not involve a clear-cut issue like resisting communist aggression but the possible replacement of the French empire by nationalists with communist leanings. Like Korea, Indochina was not traditional British turf, but cold war contingencies meant that they could not be indifferent to what happened there. By 1949 communist successes were most widespread in Vietnam, where, under the leadership of Ho Chi Minh, the Vietminh had extended their control over the northern half of the country. Aware that the war against the communists could only be won with popular support, the French government invited the ex-Emperor Bao Dai, who had abdicated in 1945, to return to Vietnam early in 1949 as head of a national government. Under the agreement of 8 March 1949 he was recognised as emperor. The French Council ratified the settlement on 5 June, and Vietnam became an Associated State within the French Union. Similar agreements were also signed with Laos and Cambodia.

But this piecemeal political advance was of little consequence, for the French retained authority for defence, foreign affairs and currency. It was also too late and hardly endeared itself even to the moderate nationalists in Laos and Cambodia who were not as strong as Vietnamese nationalists. There was hardly any enthusiasm for the agreement in Vietnam, where the French confronted the greatest challenge to their empire. The French ruled over less than half of a truculent population, while the Vietminh had established an effective administration in areas under their sway. Militarily, the 100,000 Vietminh were more than a match for the troops under French command – an uncomfortable mix of Foreign Legionnaires, soldiers from various parts of the French union and badly trained Vietnamese. To the ebbing fortunes of the French empire was added a Chinese advance to the Tongkin frontier in December 1949. The British and Americans were thoroughly alarmed. The British remembered how the Japanese had used Indochina as a base for the invasion of Malaya in 1942. Acheson declared that Chinese activities constituted a threat to international peace and security; an American military team was sent to Saigon for talks in January 1950, and Congress appropriated $75 million in military aid to France. Indochina had become another battlefield in the global cold war.

The reality of Vietminh successes was crowned by the recognition, in January–February 1950, of the "Democratic Republic of Vietnam" by communist powers. The recognition of Ho by the communists made him, in Acheson's words, 'the mortal enemy of native independence in Indochina', and a significant and ominous portent of Stalin's intention to 'accelerate the revolutionary process' in Southeast Asia.[1] It will long be debated whether Western recognition of Ho Chi Minh might not have steered him away from the Soviets and Chinese. Ho was a communist, but he initially asked for independence within the French union, and it was only after the transfer of power to Bao Dai that he turned to the Chinese and Soviets for help. The nationalist in him harboured a traditional Vietnamese loathing of the Chinese, and he received from them only a fraction of the aid that the US was disbursing to put more backbone into the French. But his was the winning star, and by the beginning of 1950 both the Americans and British realised that a French defeat was on the cards.

Reality could be acknowledged, but not surrendered to, so it must be changed and a new reality created. In May 1949 Malcolm Macdonald had propounded his "domino theory", warning that the fall of Indochina to the communists would be followed by Thailand, Malaya and India. The cold war meant that the British and Americans could not recognise Ho. To offset the communist recognition of Ho's government, they recognised, in February 1950, the State of Vietnam, comprising areas not under communist control, and urged the French to grant a more substantial independence to Indochina. But the relinquishment of imperium did not come easily to the French, and a painful combination of military reverses and Anglo–American pressure could only squeeze minor concessions out of them. Indeed, the subservient status of Bao Dai was one of the few points of accord among the British, Indians and Americans; the Indians reviled him as a French stooge, while Acheson fretted that the US 'might lose out' if it identified with 'old-fashioned colonial attitudes'. But Bao Dai was the only alternative to the communists; backing him would avoid the appearance of propping up French imperialism; so the US might gently nudge France into making symbolic concessions to the Vietnamese army. The Americans upgraded their consulate in Saigon to a legation; the initial British recognition did not go so far and was limited to conferring the rank of Minister on the Consul-General because, as Bevin explained to the Commons on 24 May 1950, 'we were anxious that rather more independence should have been given to the Bao Dai government than has, in fact, been given.' Nationalism, Bevin noted in August 1950, was the best answer to communist subversion. The French should follow the same enlightened policies that the British had in India in 1947 to transform nationalist opponents of French imperialism into friends of France.[2] In Indochina, the "anti-colonialism" of the British stemmed to some extent from the knowledge that they did not have the wherewithal to bail out the French, but most of all from their wish to concentrate on defending their imperial stake in Malaya and Hong Kong.

It was in relation to the growing fortunes of the Vietminh that the British wanted India to recognise Bao Dai's government. At one level, British officials thought that India had considerable influence in Asia and that Indian recognition of the royalist–nationalist governments could give a fillip to non-communist nationalists in Indochina. The theme of Indian influence is strong in many official memos, but the validity of this assumption is questionable. An Indian – or rather, Hindu–Buddhist – political and cultural influence in Southeast Asia dated from the second century AD, especially in the area around modern Laos, Cambodia, Thailand and Indonesia.[3] But how did this translate into political reality in the early fifties? There were Indian communities in Indochina, but they were not necessarily influential. Nor did New Delhi seem particularly interested in a larger Indian role in the region; communist involvement had rendered Nehru's government wary of espousing nationalism in Indochina. For example, in 1947 they turned down a Vietminh request to raise the question of Vietnamese independence in the UN.[4] With a French defeat in the offing after 1949, the British held that the political expediency lay in assisting the development of Vietnam, Laos and Cambodia as stable, independent states. India did not have diplomatic ties with any nationalist government in Indochina, and this is precisely what the British sought to encourage after 1949. But they came up against Indian reluctance to recognise either nationalists with communist links or nationalist leaders who appeared to be colonial lackeys. The problem was illustrated in Vietnam, where the Indians refused to recognise a French puppet – 'none of us Asians would be seen dead with these French colonials' – and they thought Ho Chi Minh would eventually emerge the winner. Since the situation was uncertain, they would not recognise either side. As Subimal Dutt, the Indian Foreign Secretary, told Frank Roberts, in New Delhi in January 1950, India's dilemma was that while she had no wish to see communism expand in Indochina, she could not recognise Bao Dai, as this would be contrary to the instincts of Indian public opinion. The anti-communist inclinations of the Indians were reflected in their acceptance of a South Vietnamese representative in New Delhi at the end of 1949, while they had no intention of welcoming a Vietminh envoy, and Nehru resisted parliamentary pressure to come out more forcefully against the French and in favour of the Vietminh.[5] Anti-communism and anti-colonialism were both prominent strains in Indian policy in Indochina.

The Indian refusal to recognise Bao Dai annoyed some British officials, who attributed it to Nehru's 'sentimental regard' for communism.[6] There was a tendency to dub Nehru as soft on communism when his ideas on dealing with communists were at variance with those of the British. Such strictures probably reflected the momentary irritation of British policy-makers at Nehru's refusal to subscribe to their views and should be seen in this context. Had the British seriously considered Nehru or India to be sympathetic to communism, it is unlikely that their interest in Indian influence in Asia would have cropped up, time and again, in official memos. Criticism of the Indians often ran parallel to receptivity to some Indian ideas, and the occasional exasperation with Indian policy did not lessen official keenness to acquire Indian support for a British stance. At the same time, it is unlikely that the British were susceptible to Indian ideas for their own sake or as a matter of principle.

The Indians were aware of but unmoved by the Western proclivity to label them soft on communism, for they felt that the Western countries themselves had combined with or opposed communism out of political expediency and not moral principle. As Raghavan Pillai observed in January 1954, the Indians could not forget that it was the British and Americans who had befriended and allied with the Soviet Union during the Second World War. The USSR was not very different then: there 'is nothing known today about Communist policies or Communist ambitions that was not known in 1942!' More than that, in India the British Raj had joined up with the communists against the Indian National Congress in 1942 and had helped them to gain control of labour unions. Or, as Nehru reportedly reminded the American Ambassador, George Allen, in New Delhi in April 1954, '"you were hand in glove with [the] Commies when I despised them as traitors."' As for Indochina, the Vietminh struggle against France started during the period when the Soviets were still aligned with the West; the Vietminh had consolidated their position before the communists gained power in China, and the forces presently battling against the Vietminh were predominantly French. And Western backing for the French took on the character of support for colonialism. The Indians found it difficult to swallow the claim that the West was defending "freedom", if this "freedom" involved the preservation of Western empires.

It is often asked [wrote Pillai] why India and other Asian countries are so loud in their protests against European colonialism, while they are silent about the colonialism of the Soviets. The answer is clear. The Soviets have never claimed that they represent the free world and have never asked India or any other country to join forces with them. Their ideology is different, and so long as they do not force their views on us, we do not force our views on them. But the case of the free world is different. It is claimed that by refusing to line up with the free world we are doing something morally reprehensible and politically bad. It therefore becomes important for us to know what the free world represents. Such a question does not arise with regard to the Soviet Union, as we know what Communism means and have been fighting it even while others were fraternizing with Moscow.[7]

Differing political interests, moral values and perceptions were inextricably interwoven into the fabric of relations between India and the West, and they were to impinge upon Britain's aim of influencing the US in favour of her Asian cold war strategy.

II THE ROAD TO GENEVA

Armistice lulled the fighting in Korea in July 1953. But in November of that year Eden held that communism had made its 'greatest gains' in East

Asia and was still making 'strenuous efforts there'. The fall of the French empire was a matter of time, but it should not be replaced by communism. To check communism, Eden envisaged the alignment of the policies of the UK, Commonwealth and Europe on the one hand and the US on the other. Anglo–American differences were not of aim but of method and over the choice of friends to be used to contain communism. Sceptical that Western military intervention would frighten the Chinese into disengagement from Indochina, Eden was both apprehensive and irritated at talk by some American officials of military action to the extent of helping the Chinese people to liberate themselves from communism. Communist China was there to stay, and Eden was firm that she should not be provoked into war, while any Sino–Soviet divergences should be exploited by the West.[8] Here his thinking followed that of Bevin.

If diplomacy was to be the primary means of containing China, it is not surprising that Eden, like Bevin, doubted that reliance on countries with 'large armies and strong anti-Communist convictions' would accomplish the purpose. A recurrent theme in official papers is the role envisaged for India in Indochina because of her 'influence' in Asia. It is not always clear how widespread officials considered Indian influence to be or exactly what they expected of India. But Eden seems to have gone further than Bevin in his hope of Indian participation in a collective defence organisation, although this might be slow to evolve. As he informed the cabinet in November 1953, 'important Asian countries such as India and Indonesia are not yet ready to participate in an anti-Communist defence organisation'.[9]

The Korean truce intensified domestic pressures on the French government for a negotiated settlement of the war in Indochina. By the autumn of 1953 the French controlled the Red River delta and a few towns including Hanoi, Haiphong, Hué, Tourane and Saigon. The rural areas outside the cities were in the grip of the Vietminh, who now wielded authority over more than half of Vietnam – most of north and northwest Tonkin, Central Annam and many sectors in the Mekong delta and Cochin China. And in December 1953 a Vietminh thrust into Laos threatened the French position there.

As the French faced defeat by the beginning of 1954, the British favoured a diplomatic solution, and at the Foreign Ministers' Conference which opened in Berlin on 25 January 1954 they managed to persuade the superpowers to put Indochina on the agenda. The way was now open to a negotiated settlement in Indochina.

The next question was what could be negotiated. The British toyed with the idea of partition as a practicable way of ending hostilities in Vietnam. But it was not to give succour to the French. 'My chief concern was for Malaya', recollected Eden in 1960. Eden wanted an effective barrier as far north of Malaya as possible.[10]

The rationale behind British interest in a possible partition of Indochina was summed up in a Foreign Office memorandum by B.R. Pearn on 26 February 1954. The British assumption was that the key to the problem in Indochina was to be found in the Chinese attitude. The Vietminh depended on them, and a cessation of the war in Indochina could only be achieved with the concurrence of the Chinese government.

Historically, the Chinese had perceived Korea and Indochina as 'satellites' in their sphere of influence. The collapse of the Vietminh would involve the establishment, indirectly, of American power on the very frontiers of China, and the Chinese would not accept such a situation in Vietnam any more than they had in Korea. The urge to maintain a Vietminh zone was therefore an essential part of Chinese policy and strategy. Partition appeared the only solution which would reconcile Chinese aims and simultaneously save 'something . . . from the wreck of the Associated State [sic] system.' Partition was far from being the ideal solution, but the alternative would be the take-over by the communists of all of Indochina instead of only a part.[11] For the moment, the communists had the military vantage in Indochina, so the British were against an immediate cease-fire. They were therefore unresponsive to Nehru's call for one on 27 February 1954. To get round this, Eden held that a political settlement should precede a cease-fire.[12] In other words, the British were searching for a way which would enable the French to retreat without dishonour, while extracting from the Vietminh a negotiated compromise which would play down the extent of their military successes. This would entail some accommodation with the communists, but it was the only way to prevent the whole of Indochina from falling into their hands.

The question of a compromise with communists marked the single most important difference between British and American tactics in Indochina. To the Americans, global communism had to be resisted, but how? On 12 January 1954 Dulles had enunciated his principle of massive retaliation – of depending primarily upon 'a great capacity to retaliate, instantly, by means and at places of our choosing'. In the age of the bomb, this raised the frightful spectre of an atomic war, which was not diminished by Dulles's assertion that local defences alone could not contain communism; local defences must be backed up by a "community security system". Dulles's meaning was nebulous and did not really reflect the difficult options confronting US policy-makers. In discussion with the NSC on 8 January 1954, Eisenhower was 'bitterly opposed' to any unilateral American military action in Indochina. The Americans would earn a colonial stigma, and the Vietnamese 'could be expected to transfer their hatred of the French to us . . . this war in Indochina would absorb our troops by divisions!' America was fighting for a losing cause, if only because of the strength of communist morale and the Western inability to win local friends. Eisenhower wondered why 'one of the outstanding failures of the Western world in Asia was its inability to produce good fighting material in the Asian countries for which Western powers were responsible. The

Communists were more effective. They got hold of the most unlikely people and turned them into great fighters.'[13]

This theme was echoed on 24 February 1954 by Edmund Guillon of the PPS. Even with American aid, he wrote in a memorandum for the Geneva negotiations,[14] Bao Dai was not likely to win. The Vietminh had fought the war very effectively without Chinese assistance for three to four years, using 'mere pickup stocks.' After 1950, American aid to the Associated States 'was scores of times greater in tonnage than Chinese aid to the Viet Minh; we had more men under arms, better communications, and a great food supply base in our territory. Yet all this superiority has not been translated into offensive gains by our side.'

Of the possible solutions to the conflict, Guillon saw a cessation of arms aid by both belligerents as the only proposal on which the Chinese, Vietminh and French might agree. Partition would offer 'the vague hope' of later improvements, but it would be construed as 'the ultimate sell-out' by most Vietnamese; the US would be held responsible for a multilateral partition of Indochina and would lose all standing in Asia. The US Chiefs concurred. Any coalition or partition would represent 'at least a partial victory for the Viet Minh and would constitute recognition of a Communist territorial expansion'; it would also cast doubts on the ability of anti-communist forces to stop the advance of communism in the Far East.

A neutralised zone was the least dangerous alternative but one the communists were unlikely to accept. An outright victory was impossible, but any compromise solution smacked of defeat to the Americans; it would therefore be better for the Geneva conference to end inconclusively than for the US to countenance a sell-out. The French should be told of American opposition to any such settlement; the war should continue, but if the French decided to quit then the war should be internationalised under the UN, knowing that if US forces took part, China might retaliate massively. What Guillon envisaged was a continuation of the war and the hope of allied support for and even participation in it. Would the allies join forces with them? Eden's behaviour at the Berlin conference in February 1954 had not been promising: he did not want the language of any resolution to impugn the good faith of the Chinese, and the British wanted the Western position at Geneva to be defensible in the eyes of as many nations as possible.

The Vietminh siege of Dienbienphu on 27 March 1954 raised the question of military intervention by a Western-led coalition. On 29 March Dulles called for "united action" to combat the prospect of communist control. Dulles's meaning was hazy: one of his advisers later dismissed his sabre-rattling as a calculated bluff to frighten the Chinese. The Americans were not spoiling for a fight: the Eisenhower administration had turned down three French requests for US military intervention between March 1953 and April 1954. Congressional and public opinion were also slanted against US military intervention. On 4 April Eisenhower's blunt response to the French plea was that in the absence of Congressional approval, such action would be 'unconstitutional & indefensible', and the US could not risk its prestige in a defeat. Dulles emphasised that there must be a 'full political understanding' with other countries; Congressional authorisation for intervention would be necessary, and such action could only be contemplated on a 'coalition basis' which would include the active participation of the Commonwealth countries, in view of their great stake in Malaya, Australia and New Zealand. On 6 April in the NSC, Eisenhower ruled out unilateral intervention by the US, but he authorised military planning for a possible intervention later if the required political conditions were met.[15] In effect, intervention was not ruled out if the US could rally its allies. And Eisenhower clearly wanted their support. He pleaded with Churchill for British adherence to a coalition that would be 'willing to fight' communism in Indochina. In his public enunciation of the "domino theory" on 7 April, he admonished that the fall of Indochina to the communists would result in the rest of Southeast Asia 'go[ing] over very quickly', so the possible consequences of the loss were 'just incalculable to the free world.'[16] But *joint* allied intervention would be necessary. The American reluctance to intervene single-handed, coupled with their desire for intervention by an allied coalition explains why Dulles spurned French entreaties and made overtures for British participation in "united action" in the same breath.

The British were filled with consternation. Dulles seemed to want their support for a military intervention in principle, while the British emphasised the uses of diplomacy. They sought international backing for the Western negotiating stance, as yet undefined, at Geneva. Dulles's summons to a 'united will to resist aggression', combined with Nixon's talk of sending 'our boys' to Indochina, raised their fear that the US might drive the Western alliance into a war. Three concerns now dominated official British thinking. First, they wished to avert any involvement in Indochina. The Chiefs of Staff counselled that Britain did not possess the resources to undertake any military commitment in Indochina. Second, increased commitments would be 'inevitable' in the event of joint allied action in Indochina, while the British defence programme was governed by financial shortages and entailed a reduction of commitments of the armed forces. Finally, Eden himself was against being 'hustled' into 'hasty decisions' or a military commitment and wanted to give the Geneva conference a chance of success. Knowing that the odds were stacked against the French, Eden, the Foreign Office and the Chiefs seriously contemplated the idea of a partition to forestall a communist takeover of the whole of Indochina.[17]

In fact a wide schism defined British and American ideas about the nature and timing of collective defence. The British were not minded to rescue the French from an Asian Waterloo and Churchill was quite clear why: 'I do not see why we should fight for France in Indo–China when we have given away India.'[18] The British, reckoned Eden, should give the French all diplomatic support, and if a settlement was reached, the UK would join the US and Southeast Asian countries in guaranteeing that settlement. Eden's aim was to fashion an agreement at Geneva and then to secure Asian support for it. The fall of the French empire would not lead to communist mastery of Southeast Asia: the British, Eden pointedly and condescendingly reminded Dulles, had twenty-two battalions in Malaya. At the same time communism had to be contained. In 1952 Eden had in mind the formation of a Far Eastern regional association on the lines of NATO. Some sort of collective defence was desirable, but Eden was undecided about its form. Dulles was dismayed and not a little annoyed at the British attitude. To him, and to many US officials, the stark choice was between an all-out allied effort to preserve the French position and a communist walk-over in Indochina, and it seemed that the unhelpful British attitude would propel the French into capitulation. Dienbienphu could not be saved, but the French must have some hope of *future* support.[19] American officials wanted to forge some kind of coalition with Thailand, the Philippines and Western countries as soon as possible. The British stalled. Collective defence, argued Eden, would provoke China and would spoil the chances of the success of the Geneva conference. Eden's tactic was to suggest Five-Power talks to keep the American idea of collective defence at bay,[20] for the Five Powers would exclude America's Asian allies. Whether the Americans divined the intention behind the "Five-Power tactic" is unclear, but they were certainly indignant, for a Five-Power pact would savour of Western imperialism rather than team-work by Asian and Western countries to roll back communism. Eden also wanted wide Asian participation in collective defence but disagreed with the Americans about who counted in Asia. The British were convinced that it was India, though whether India would enter a coalition was another matter. In a Foreign Office paper on the Commonwealth and Southeast Asia in March 1954, John Tahourdin predicted that educating India would require great patience on the part of the British. 'To achieve this we should be prepared to devote in New Delhi something of the effort we have expended in the last 15 years in Washington over the Americans. Results would no doubt take time and we might be unsuccessful.' Eden, however, was personally keen to have India in a joint defence scheme. To Denis Allen's advice on 8 April that India and Pakistan were unlikely to respond to any call to enrol in collective defence, Eden insisted, 'But we ought to try to get them.' Consultations with India were urgent: 'something must be arranged either through Delhi or here before I leave for country' [sic]. The Americans also wanted Asian participation, but their hopes did not centre round India, and Eden was clearly sour at Dulles's 'ignoring my insistence' that India be included in a coalition.[21]

Indian officials were dismayed at the allied statement of 13 April 1954 which called for an examination of the possibility of collective defence. Nehru was incensed at Dulles's blustering about massive retaliation and united action, and he brooded that it would require an incurable optimist to suppose that any good could come out of the Geneva conference with the US threatening military action. Pillai warned that China might call the bluff of any US threat. The Indian view was 'not very far' from the British one.[22] Eden sought to persuade Nehru of the need for collective defence and to maintain a dialogue with him on it. Nehru's strictures of collective defence appear to have annoyed him greatly, sparking off an outburst that, 'Within your lifetime, India will have . . . gone Communist while he [Nehru] fiddles around, complaining about the Americans.' Nehru had to be kept 'on the rails' about collective defence,[23] so on 15 April, Eden made known to Nehru his concern at the 'mounting violence' of the Vietminh, supported by 'massive aid' from China. Britain wanted a settlement at Geneva, but if it failed to materialise, non-communist states should show 'a united determination' to thwart communist aggrandizement in Southeast Asia. He assured Nehru that the British wanted 'genuine national independence' for Indochina and that they were impressing this on the French.[24]

How realistic was Eden's hope of Indian participation in collective defence? Indian officials were put off by the loud American talk of war and perceived the Americans to be 'ignorant . . . drunk, and hopelessly unreliable'. Pillai made clear to Alexander Clutterbuck, then High Commissioner in New Delhi, India's firm opposition to any concept of collective defence in Southeast Asia under Western leadership. Collective defence was aimed at buttressing French imperialism. Nehru held that collective defence would mean the encirclement of India by the US and its associates, while the Chinese would not cave in to threats involving loss of face.[25] The depth of Indo–US antipathy also rendered Eden's hopes of Indian participation a pipe-dream. Indo–US acrimony was at a high point in April 1954. Ostensibly to defend freedom the US was bolstering a colonial puppet in Vietnam. The conflicting and multifarious connotations of "freedom" were symbolised by the Indian government's refusal, in April 1954, to allow US aircraft carrying French reinforcements to cross India. This had been their policy over the last three years, and Indian officials were aware that it would be misunderstood by the Americans. On 5 April Pillai expressed his 'deepest regret' to the US Ambassador, George Allen, in New Delhi that this matter had arisen since 'it could not fail to worsen Indian–American relations'. Then there was an exchange between Nehru and Allen on 6 April. Informed by Nehru that his government could not renege on promises made to Parliament for three years, Allen's sententious response was that India would not wish to leave her neighbours open to communist aggression. The sensitive Nehru smarted and asked Allen 'if I [Allen] was trying to get him to change his policy'. Allen was. 'I said I was trying to consider what was in India's over-all national interests, as well as that of the free world.'[26] Such an attitude could not reduce the verbal sniping between India and the US. Congressional hostility to India, manifested in demands for cuts in economic aid to India, added fuel to the fire and infuriated Nehru into declaring that India would not barter away her freedom or independence of action 'under any pressure or threats'. To Nehru, it seemed as if the US was trying to act as a world leader and telling everybody what to do. The US hoped to bring China to an all-out surrender by threatening an all-out war; the US expected the communists to capitulate although they held the military advantage in Indochina. American sabre-rattling was increasing tension and the prospect of war.[27]

The British were disturbed by the increasing bitterness between India and the US. In Washington, Makins was 'much concerned with this extraordinary hostility to India and the Indians in the United States.' From the point of view of Commonwealth solidarity it could have 'by indirection, an increasingly deleterious effect on our position in the United States as well'. He was uncertain what the British could do. But British diplomats in Washington would keep trying: 'when I or members of my staff are asked questions about India, we begin by saying that we cannot speak for India and then do our best indirectly to give the Indians a boost.'[28] At the Foreign Office, James Cable doubted that the British could do much. The problem was the 'fundamental divergence' in the policies of India and the US which, 'given the ineradicable addiction in both to lecturing the rest of the world, no amount of diplomacy will ever smooth over.' India was 'the only important country' (with the possible exception of Argentina) that had not acquiesced in the view of the superpowers of the division of the world into two camps led by those two powers. As long as India maintained her independent attitude, there would be more irritation and friction in her relations with the US. The only remedy was for the British to forge closer ties with India and so to narrow the gap between India and the US. Their chances of success were slender, but 'they are nevertheless far greater than those offered by any direct attempt to improve Indo/American relations'. Tahourdin concurred: a British mediatory role would become all the more important in the context of US proposals for collective defence.[29]

How would the British repair the breach between India and the US on collective defence given their own differences with the US on its nature and timing? Dulles wanted arrangements to be made before the Geneva conference to make it clear to the communists that they would not succeed 'in their presumed grandiose plans in Southeast Asia.'[30] This reflected his belief, expressed later to Ambassador G.L. Mehta in Washington, that 'the only thing that moderates the Communists is a strong position on the other side.'[31] This attitude was apparently similar to that of Eden; the crux of the difference lay in what was meant by strength. Like Nehru, Eden did not think the Chinese would be intimidated by the spectre of collective defence, and there was no point in threatening China if the West was not prepared to use the threat.[32] This the British certainly did not want.

But the British were not against the idea of collective defence in itself – the question was its form and timing – and they found themselves at one with the Americans in wanting to foil any Indian endeavours to censure it openly. Concerned about a possible Indian attack on collective defence at the Colombo conference of Asian prime ministers from 27 April to 2 May 1954, Dulles initiated diplomatic moves to resist it. On 9 April he told Amjad Ali, the Pakistani ambassador in Washington, of his hope that the Colombo conference 'would not take a course counter to our objectives at Geneva'.[33] Amjad Ali expressed satisfaction at being so informed. Dulles followed up with instructions to the US ambassador in Karachi to express his hope to Mohamad Ali, the Pakistani Prime Minister, that the Colombo conference would not undercut Western efforts at Geneva. An obliging Mohamad Ali assured the Americans of his government's 'full cooperation'.[34] Indo-Pakistani antagonism provided his rationale for doing so. Engaged in forming an alliance with the US, Pakistan was eager to stop Nehru from beating 'the neutralist drum' at Colombo. On the British side, Gilbert Laithwaite picked up the thread in Karachi. On his advice that Pakistan be supplied with British views before the conference, Eden sent a personal message to Mohamad Ali, expressing his hope that Pakistan would alert her colleagues at Colombo to the communist menace to Southeast Asia and that the Colombo powers would not reject collective security. Sir John Kotelwala, the Ceylonese Prime Minister, was expected to oppose any concluding statement hostile to a military grouping.[35] With their differences over collective defence, the coincidence of the Indian and British preference for diplomatic containment was not taken for granted by Eden, as he joined Dulles in blunting the edge of any possible Indian offensive against an allied coalition.

Despite their differences on collective defence, Nehru's speech in the Indian parliament on 24 April was intended to be conciliatory to the British. Against collective defence and massive retaliation, Nehru welcomed the Geneva conference which would start on 26 April. He called for a cease-fire by the French, Associated States and the Vietminh; a non-intervention agreement stopping aid to both sides to be signed by the US, UK, USSR and China; and for any settlement to be enforced by the UN. The British were relieved: Lord Reading, Minister of State at the Foreign Office, held Nehru's statement to be 'better than we had expected'. Eden knew that the statement would nettle the French and Americans, but at the same time he hoped to bring them round to the advantages of a solution similar to that suggested by Nehru – a negotiated settlement backed by 'some subsequent guarantee'.[36] The differences and concurrences of outlook between Eden and Nehru ran parallel to one other; evidently Eden was quick to take up those of Nehru's ideas that he deemed advantageous to diplomatic containment in Indochina.

Eden was not about to edge closer to American views on collective security. On 25 April 1954 he showed Dulles a British plan for the partition of Indochina and reiterated that the British were not prepared to countenance any collective defence which might commit them to fight in Indochina.[37] Finding it hard to swallow British objections, American officials were determined not to be reined in by them. To Eisenhower the

British stance was only explicable on the grounds that the British feared that 'if the fighting continues we – and possibly other countries – might become involved and so tend to increase the danger, in the British opinion, of starting World War III'. But a coalition could exclude the British, for Eisenhower believed that 'the British government is showing a woeful unawareness of the risks we run in that region'.[38] On 29 April Nixon told the NSC that the British should not be allowed to veto the Americans, and held that America's relationship with the British in the Far East was a 'real liability'. American officials contemplated parting company with the British. Dulles asserted that the US should be ready 'to take the leadership in what we think is the right course. This did not imply a bold or war-like course.' But what would leadership entail? To Eisenhower, the concept of leadership implied associates. 'Without allies and associates the leader is just an adventurer like Genghis Khan.'[39] And for the moment America's allies were not minded to play follow-my-leader. Caught between two stools, the Americans could neither reconcile themselves to negotiating with the communists nor to a French defeat; they knew a French victory was unattainable, but a compromise with the communists would be unacceptable.

III THE GENEVA CONFERENCE: THE BRITISH CONCEIVE DIPLOMATIC CONTAINMENT ON THE BRITAIN–INDIA–CHINA CIRCUIT

Thus at the start of the Geneva conference on 27 April 1954, the Anglo–American rift over the nature and timing of collective defence could not have been deeper. The Americans were reluctant participants at Geneva. Parleys with communists were unsavoury; negotiations with communist China were anathema to them. The American attitude was symbolised by Dulles, who would not shake hands with Chou En-lai, and whose general behaviour was redolent of 'a Puritan in a house of ill repute'.[40] The British on the other hand were committed to a settlement. The personal animosity between Eden and Dulles was intense, not merely because of the contrast between Eden's sartorial elegance and Dulles' rumpled look, or because Eden irritated Dulles by addressing him as 'my dear' while Dulles, slurring in speech, could only invoke 'Ant-ny', but because Dulles felt let down by the British. They seemed to be fairweather friends. At the end of the first week of the conference, Dulles was enraged that the British delegation had sat back quietly when the communists had accused the Americans of imperialism; then Eden 'had the gall to come to the airport to bid Dulles farewell, and be photographed with him, although he never said a word in defense of the US at the Conference'.[41]

Indeed, Anglo–American bipartisanship in blocking Indian criticism of collective defence could not disguise their differences over Indochina, and the Colombo conference seemed destined to push the British and Americans further apart. Indochina held the minds of the Colombo powers (India, Pakistan, Indonesia, Burma and Ceylon) from 27 April to 2 May. At the Colombo conference Nehru sought support for his six points of 24 April. He won over Prime Minister U Nu of Burma by agreeing that the Colombo powers would request China to give satisfactory assurances to Burma that she would not aid communist rebels in Burma. To assuage Pakistan, the final resolution of the conference was worded so as not to imply criticism of Pakistan's new association with the US. British and American officials interpreted the absence of any criticism of collective security in the Colombo proposals as a defeat for Nehru. But they under-rated his determination to secure a unanimous resolution on Indochina which would be considered representative of an *Asian* viewpoint. Nehru secured unanimous backing for a resolution urging that Indochina be allowed to settle its own future without interference by the great powers.[42] Nehru himself believed that peace with China was possible. The Sino–Indian agreement of 29 April 1954, based on the Five Principles, had created an environment in which China would find it difficult to break her word, and China had demonstrated that she was prepared to meet India half-way.

The Indian government, Nehru wrote Eden on 5 May, considered that a 'major responsibility' now rested on them in contributing to a solution in Indochina.[43] Indian officials remained concerned about any extension of the conflict and were applying their minds to containing it. On 8 May Krishna Menon hinted to Escott Reid, the Canadian High Commissioner in New Delhi, how far the Colombo proposals might go. His suggestion of a cease-fire echoed that of Nehru: a cease-fire should be accompanied by a non-intervention agreement between the USSR, UK, US and China, who would pledge not to provide troops or *matériel* to any of the belligerents. The Geneva conference should set up a Neutral Nations Commission (NNC) to patrol the cease-fire line and to verify the observance of the non-intervention agreement. This commission might include Mexico, Sweden, Argentina and India. Each member of the commission would be invited to send troops to Indochina to enable it to discharge its responsibilities. With the cease-fire, non-intervention agreement and NNC serving as the starting point for discussions, the Geneva negotiations could be held in a peaceful atmosphere and the chances of agreement enhanced. When approached by Clutterbuck, Pillai replied that Menon's ideas probably reflected those of Nehru. Pillai added, significantly, that Indochina being nearer to India than Korea, public opinion would support a despatch of troops to see fair play and to prevent a recurrence of hostilities.[44]

The Colombo proposals and Indian ideas were in line with Eden's own inclinations. They presented him with diplomatic alternatives to end the conflict in Indochina, and he quickly took them up. On 10 May he wrote to Nehru that he found 'encouraging' the Indian government's sense of

responsibility for a settlement in Indochina. In the Indian suggestion Eden
saw an arrangement similar to the Locarno treaty whereby the guaranteeing powers would undertake to oppose any violation of the agreement by
any party. 'If this is so, and if India would be prepared to join in such a
multilateral guarantee, I should certainly like to give it serious study, for I
have always felt this to be the best solution available.' From the Commonwealth Relations Office, Lord Swinton concurred. The Indians would not
support Western-led collective defence, but they might play 'a helpful part'
in a cease-fire or an armistice, and it would be 'especially useful' if India
provided forces to supervise the carrying out of a cease-fire or an
armistice.[45]

Eden found the Colombo communiqué 'of real value', and it inspired his
'practical questions' to the Geneva conference on 12 May. The first task
was to stop the fighting 'in an orderly way', and then to associate the UN
with the implementation of any agreement reached at Geneva. To end the
hostilities, Eden asked the conference whether all agreed that all troops on
both sides should be concentrated in determined areas and the irregulars
withdrawn. Did the conference accept that Laos and Cambodia were in 'a
special category' and that the Vietminh would pull out from them? What
form should any international supervision take? Eden noted that the
Colombo powers had favoured the use of UN machinery to carry out
decisions on Indochina. 'When we say United Nations we do not mean the
combatants or necessarily any of us round this table. There could be an
agreed panel of countries from whom these United Nations countries could
be drawn.'[46] Apparently the Indian idea of a Neutral Nations Commission
had struck a chord with Eden.

The closeness of the Indian and British outlooks was illustrated yet again
with Pillai's query on 17 May to Clutterbuck whether the British would like
New Delhi to approach Peking with a view to the Chinese intervening with
the Vietminh against new military operations. New Delhi feared that the
Vietminh might be out to 'seize all the ground they can' before a cease-fire,
and it 'entirely' shared the British view that this would be both wrong-
headed and dangerous. In their original proposals on 24 April, the Indians
had entreated both sides to refrain from stepping up the tempo of the war
and they were ready to speak to the Chinese ambassador in New Delhi.
Eden affirmed that such an approach to China would be 'very helpful at
this stage'. In particular, it would be useful if the Indians emphasised that
Laos and Cambodia should be left alone. By now, the Indian view about
the timing of a French withdrawal seems to have shifted closer to that of
the British. On 17 May Pillai also told Clutterbuck that continued stationing of French troops would not be inconsistent with the full political
independence of the Associated States if it was limited in time and on a
diminishing scale. Clutterbuck pointed out that this represented 'a considerable change' from the previous Indian demand that all vestiges of
colonialism should be removed as soon as possible.[47]

Colombo in fact revealed more clearly than ever the gap between British and American thinking. The Americans saw the Colombo proposals as giving way to the communists, and their failure to draw the British nearer to their viewpoint left them angry and frustrated and, not for the first time, drove them to question the worth of their British partner. Dulles fulminated about '[the] UK veto, which in turn was in Asian matters largely subject to [the] Indian veto, which in turn was largely subject to [the] Chinese Communist veto. Thereby a chain was forged which tended to make us impotent, and to encourage Chinese Communist aggression.'[48] This was a simplistic account of the very real Anglo–American differences on Western strategy in Indochina. The British were not about to save the French empire: Churchill bluntly told the Americans that since the British had let India go, 'they would not be interested in holding Indochina for France.'[49] The British were concerned to hold on to Malaya – a narrow aim, according to Dulles, which did not show adequate regard for other areas of the Far East including Japan. To London, the French empire was a burnt-out case, and wisdom dictated that the French should quit Indochina.

However, India and Britain were not about to make common cause. They did agree on a "Locarno" pact – but that was as far as they were in tune with each other. To Eden the desirablity of a "Locarno" arrangement did not obviate the need for a "NATO-type pact" in Asia. One reason was that the British would be included in it, so that any Asian pact would be an improvement on ANZUS which excluded them and the 'free and friendly countries of South Asia'. Here Eden clearly had Ceylon, Pakistan and, above all, India in mind. But reference to a 'Far Eastern NATO' would be avoided as it would only frighten off Asians. And Asians would construe any Western-sponsored organisation as a means to expand Western military influence in Asia. So the issue would be postponed, even side-stepped for the moment. Instead, emphasis should be placed on the purpose of the Geneva conference: to bring the conflict to an end. Once this had been accomplished, measures could be taken to build up a political and military deterrent to the communists.[50] This did not imply a British preference for military containment in Indochina. Eden thought that war would only be a stopgap deterrent to Chinese expansion and would have to be replaced by an alliance of South and Southeast Asian countries strong enough to make aggression unprofitable. His hopes about India remained. 'Only India and Pakistan . . . have the resources and the martial tradition to make such an alliance militarily viable, but it will take time and patience to bring them along.'[51] As he told Dulles on 26 June, he was searching for some arrangement in which Asians would join the West in telling the communists, ' "Thus far and no farther".'[52] Eden knew that there was no meeting ground with the Americans on this point. The American idea of including Thailand and the Philippines was myopic: it would provoke China without making any significant addition to Western military strength. He feared

that this 'token Asian support' would enable the Eisenhower administration to justify military intervention in Indochina, 'but this is just what I
want to avoid.' The Americans appeared to contemplate an organisation
that would enable them to reconquer Indochina; the British 'would not be
prepared to participate in such a venture.'[53]

By now – 22 May – Eden was certain that some concessions would have
to be made to the communists. This might entail creating a buffer zone on
China's southern border. 'This would be excluded from the South East
Asia defence organisation I envisage.'[54] The Americans were on a different plane; for they were now ruminating over the establishment of military
aid missions to the Indochina states. The arrival of Krishna Menon in
Geneva in an unofficial capacity did not gladden their hearts; Dulles
thought he was a ' "pretty bad fellow" '; Eisenhower prophesied that
whatever Menon did was 'not likely to be acceptable' to the US. This was
in stark contrast to Eden's opinion of Menon's activities. As Menon
sounded out the chances of Chinese agreement, Eden appreciated 'how
helpful' and discreet in his contacts Menon was.[55] Talking to Eden on 3
June, Menon was optimistic that China would use her influence with the
Vietminh to agree to an armistice in Vietnam. Two days later, Eden was
impressed that Chou En-lai was a man of wide outlook and receptive to
ideas different from his own. Chou did not contest the fact that the
Vietminh had invaded Cambodia and Laos and that their withdrawal was
an essential condition for peace. Provided that no military bases were
established in Laos and Cambodia, China would be prepared to recognise
their independence and unity. This recognition by China, noted Eden,
would enable the French to quit honourably.[56]

Such terms for peace were on a collision course with American thinking,
although the US had no alternative to offer. The British were exasperated;
Dulles, commented Makins tartly, seemed to be 'thrashing around for
policy like a whale in a pont [sic].'[57] Eden informed Dulles on 17 June that
the Chinese were willing to recognise the "Kingdoms" of Laos and
Cambodia as independent states ' "in the same manner as India and
Burma" '; they would consent to Laos and Cambodia maintaining their
relationships with France, but their major worry was the American intention of establishing bases in those countries for an assault on China. Dulles
would not make any commitment: he was against giving China any impression that an agreement would exclude the possibility of enrolling Laos
and Cambodia in some collective security association or making 'military
arrangements' implicit in such an association. A "Locarno" treaty, he
contended, would imply a moral approval of Communist successes. 'This
was unacceptable.' Dulles wanted consideration to be given to the possibility of the Indochina states developing non-communist governments if
they received no substantial help from outside. Therefore, 'the degree of
neutralization or demilitarization, affecting military training missions,
equipment and advisors, was very important.'[58] It was an attitude that did

not augur well for the success of diplomatic containment in Indochina.

By 21 June Eden was aware that American intransigence might obstruct a settlement. He was persuaded that the Soviet Union and China wanted an agreement but might have difficulty in restraining the Vietminh who were in a position to demand a high price. This would not be the only obstacle: 'It may prove even more difficult to persuade the Americans to accept whatever settlement can eventually be reached.'[59] But he went ahead, and it is in relation to Chou's conciliatory attitude and the commonality of the official Indian and British outlooks on containing communism through diplomacy that Eden's appeal to Nehru of 23 June should be seen. On the eve of Chou's visit to New Delhi – for which the initiative had come from Chou himself – Eden hoped that Nehru would take the opportunity to obtain 'these same assurances' from Chou, 'since I am convinced that you will attach the same importance to this issue as I do.' China's role would be 'crucial'. The French wanted a settlement, but they could not capitulate. 'The chances of success depend as much on China as on France.' If China used her influence on the side of moderation, Eden was hopeful of an accord.[60]

In New Delhi, Nehru warned Chou of the dangers to the Geneva negotiations if Vietminh operations increased. To Pillai, Chou gave the impression that China could order the Vietminh out of Laos and Cambodia. Chou agreed with Nehru that large states like India and China had to allay the fears of their smaller neighbours, and he was ready to give assurances based on the Five Principles to Burma and to China's other neighbours. China desperately needed peace on her borders so that she could get on with the task of internal reconstruction. China would be content with an independent and sovereign Cambodia and Laos, provided they were not used as bases for military operations against China, and she would give them assurances on this point. Chou's conciliatory attitude was evident again when he told Eden on 13 July of China's willingness to recognise the independence of Laos and Cambodia. Eden agreed with him that they should not be used as military bases against China and that their arms imports should be restricted to what their governments deemed necessary for self-defence. The chances of a settlement now seemed near at hand. Eden told Chou that the Colombo powers would support a settlement on the lines of the Locarno system 'though that name should be avoided'. The states of Indochina 'might be a protective pad having advantages to both sides'. Chou averred that Southeast Asia presented special opportunities for peace on a collective basis, and he agreed that Indochina could become 'a protective pad'.[61]

The question remained, who would monitor the peace? Eden wanted the Colombo powers to play a supervisory role, and he found 'comforting' the opposition of the Vietminh on the ground that three of them – India, Pakistan and Ceylon – were members of the Commonwealth. The idea appealed to Pillai, who thought it would strike a chord with Asian opinion.

It would also offer a viable alternative to the Soviet demand that Poland and Czechoslovakia be included on a Neutral Nations Commission. Krishna Menon, however, was dead set against the inclusion of Pakistan, through whom the US could meddle in the commission's work. Nehru himself thought the communists would take exception to Pakistan, since she was receiving US military aid, and he also felt that it might be generally difficult for India and Pakistan to co-operate. Eventually, a consensus was reached on an international commission comprising Canada, Poland and India, who would also chair the commission.[62]

Yet the possibility of failure loomed large almost until the last minute. The main stumbling block was the Vietminh insistence on drawing the cease-fire line in Vietnam at the 16th parallel, whereas the French wanted it at the 18th. The Vietminh also looked askance at French intentions on elections. Menon advised Eden that if the Vietminh could be given an assurance on elections, they might be shifted from their insistence on drawing a cease-fire line at the 16th parallel.[63] Menon's confabulations with both sides helped to bring about a settlement, and the Geneva accords, signed on 21 July 1954, ended the fighting in Indochina.[64] The parties to the conflict – France, Cambodia, South Vietnam and the Vietminh – agreed on a cease-fire and on the recognition of the independence and territorial integrity of Vietnam, Cambodia and Laos. Vietnam was partitioned along the 17th parallel. Although the Vietminh's military vantage point gave them a strong claim for influence throughout the whole of Vietnam, they succumbed to heavy pressure for a compromise from the Soviets and Chinese, neither of whom wanted a long-drawn-out war in Indochina. The division of Vietnam was intended to be temporary; it was to be reunified by elections in 1956 which would be supervised by an international commission composed of India, Poland and Canada. The final declaration of the Geneva conference, which was also issued on 21 July but not signed by any of the delegations, endorsed the Geneva agreement.

What really concerned China was the elimination of an American military presence from Indochina, since she believed that American activities would be directed against her and not in defence of the territories the US purported to be helping. Thus, Vietnam, Laos and Cambodia would become independent, but they could not enter into military alliances or permit foreign bases on their soil except in cases where their security was threatened. As we shall see, this provision was to stir up differences between India, the US and Britain about what military assistance could be given to the newly independent states, especially Cambodia.

IV INDIA, THE WEST AND SEATO

Geneva marked the first occasion on which China participated in a major international conference since the triumph of the communists in 1949. It was a diplomatic succcess for Britain in that she extracted an agreement from the communists, who did not take full advantage of a military situation that was favourable to them. But it was only a partial success – in fact the country from which Britain won the highest praise was India, which had not been officially represented at the conference, although the efforts of Krishna Menon, behind the scenes, did contribute to the agreement. Problems could be anticipated with other countries. South Vietnam never accepted the accord because it made possible the partition of Vietnam. That ultimate bulwark of Western security in Asia – the United States – disassociated itself from the agreement on the pretext that it was a compromise with communism, but it promised not to try to change anything through force. The American attitude stemmed from their reluctance to guarantee communist conquests, as they had done at Yalta, but their open rejection of any accord would have left them exposed as the power responsible for blocking a settlement. In Dulles's words, 'There would have been more talk of too many stiff-necked Presbyterians, of sanctimoniousness, and of invoking lofty moral principles.'[65] The Americans disliked the provisions relating to the status of bases in Indochina since they wished to establish their own. The provision for elections in Vietnam left them cold, since they expected the Vietminh to win a majority. Some form of American military intervention – as yet unknown – seemed to many US officials to be the only way to save Vietnam from communism. How could the US, not militarily omnipotent, create a deterrent to Chinese expansion in Asia? That dilemma in US foreign policy could not be resolved. Its existence did not, however, lessen American dissatisfaction with the Geneva accord or with the British policy of diplomatic containment which had contributed to the agreement. In the American disapprobation of Geneva lay the seeds of their subsequent unilateral involvement in Vietnam.

The Americans were determined to go ahead with SEATO, but they were not contemplating military and economic aid to potential Asian allies on a scale analogous to NATO or the Marshall Plan in Europe. Having averted Western military action during the Geneva negotiations, the British were now ready to cast in their lot with SEATO. The Americans would press on, come what may, and, politically, the British could not afford to stay out. As Anthony Nutting had affirmed in May 1954, unless the British were to abdicate their position in Southeast Asia, SEATO 'will have to happen'. SEATO in fact offered the only opening through which the British could remain visible in the region; and Churchill looked on it as a way of overcoming their exclusion from ANZUS.[66]

Once the British decided to join SEATO, it is interesting how Anglo-

American wrangling over India evaporates from official memos. Since the British had entered SEATO in the face of Indian opposition to it, American officials did not now complain of an Indian influence over Britain's Asia policy. Perhaps it is because they, like the British, hoped for at least a favourable Indian attitude to SEATO. For their part, the Indians had hoped that in the wake of the Geneva accord, the British would give up the idea of SEATO or at least ensure that the Americans did not act precipitately.[67] Despite Indian antipathy to SEATO, the British told US officials that 'the most important problem was to get India with its 330,000,000 uncommitted people into a pact.'[68] If Japan and Korea enrolled in an Asian alliance, then it would be necessary to bring in Formosa, and this would preclude Indian participation. Was this a ruse to keep Japan and Korea out of SEATO, as their inclusion would have been a red rag to China? Some American officials did ponder over the British idea of giving time to the Colombo powers to join SEATO or at least to be well disposed towards it. Charles Wilson, Secretary of Defence, thought that without the Colombo powers, 'we wouldn't have much in Southeast Asia.' Robert Cutler of the NSC inquired whether the US could begin with an economic treaty, thereby attracting those Asian nations who would not sign a military agreement and giving the whole project 'an Asian flavor' from the start. Charles Ogburn, Regional Planning Adviser in the Bureau of Far Eastern Affairs, felt that if an arrangement could be devised that would increase the solidarity of Asian countries, including the neutrals, 'we should have accomplished something of outstanding value and significance and have imposed a formidable obstacle to further Communist expansion.'[69] But these views did not carry much weight. The US Chiefs of Staff did not want the Colombo powers in SEATO, and Radford entertained some notion that the US 'would wish to strike at China'. Less pugnacious, Dulles and Eisenhower were convinced of the necessity of *some* deterrent; Dulles thought 'it would be an unmitigated disaster' to abandon a Southeast Asian pact.[70] By the end of July 1954, Eden knew that the Indian response to collective defence would be negative, but it was 'most important . . . that Nehru's reaction should be as favourable as possible'.[71] This was not to be. Nehru thought it could only promote suspicion; China could not swallow up her neighbours without risking a major war. The majority of Asian countries would not combine with the West, so SEATO would look like 'an attempt of the powerful nations of the West to protect territories outside their own.' It was not similar to ANZUS, which 'comprised of [sic] countries which can claim to be themselves concerned.'[72] Oddly enough, Dulles concurred, albeit unwittingly. He thought that 'the Western coloration of the proposed pact was unfortunate . . . the principal members would be the United States, the United Kingdom, France, Australia, and New Zealand – all Western powers. It was true that Thailand and the Philippines presumably would adhere but their influence was limited and the adherence of additional Asian countries would be desirable.'[73]

If the British interest dictated that they eventually come round to a SEATO without India, they shared with the Americans a lack of enthusiasm for having only Pakistan in the organisation, and were embarrassed by Pakistan's eagerness to join, for the West would scarcely benefit from her membership. But if Pakistan wished to enrol she could hardly be stopped from doing so. Dulles anticipated a stiffening of Indian opposition if Pakistan alone entered SEATO. If Pakistan did not come in as an initial participant, she might even exercise a 'constructive influence' on the other Colombo powers and marshal their support for SEATO. In any event, the Americans did not expect much of Pakistan; the State Department visualised 'no special role' for her in SEATO 'other than attendance [at the conference] and eventual signing – a step we believe in [the] interest [of] Pakistan's national security'. This last phrase presaged that Pakistan would not gain what she coveted most: British and American guarantees against an Indian attack. Arguing against specifying that communist aggression would be the only type of armed attack which SEATO would resist, Eden contended that a more appropriate alternative would limit obligations undertaken by any one of the parties to the treaty to ' "taking such action as it deems necessary" '. This limitation would enable the US or Britain or any other party 'to take only diplomatic action in the event of the dispute being of a purely local character (e.g. Kashmir)'.[74]

As it turned out, both India and Pakistan had their own reasons to be dissatisfied with SEATO. Pakistan neither got the assurance of security against India that she desired nor the arms she craved. And contrary to British hopes, SEATO only drove India and the US further apart. To Nehru it represented the expansion of Western military influence in Asia and a corresponding diminution of the freedom of Asian countries. By provoking China, it could ignite a new conflagration; it would enhance insecurity rather than security in Asia. India saw the organisation as being inspired by the Americans, so it was they, rather than the British, who were the target of Indian criticism. Nevertheless, British participation in SEATO symbolised their long-term differences with India over a Western military presence in Asia. It also implied that their association with the American-sponsored SEATO, whatever its limitations, was necessary if they were to maintain their credentials as an Asian power. For there was no doubt, after the Korean war, that it was the US which was the dominant, though not omnipotent, Asian military power. Therefore the American dislike of the Geneva accord, which was masterminded by the British, was an ominous portent for the working of that accord and for Britain's Asian cold war strategy.

V WHO GAINED AT THE BANDUNG CONFERENCE – BRITAIN, THE US, INDIA . . . OR CHINA?

The perception of India as the key to containment in Asia could not obscure the fundamentally divergent aims between a Britain which saw her participation in SEATO as essential to sustain her Asian and global influence and an India whose opposition to colonialism and to military intervention by the great powers in Asia was grounded in her own struggle for independence. The Afro–Asian conference at Bandung from 25 to 29 April 1955 showed how easily this contradiction could come to the fore and how an anticipated Indian challenge to British imperialism could transform, and run parallel to, the British image of India from a much needed pro-West influence in Asia to an *enfant terrible* to be quietened. Bandung was one of the few issues in the Asian cold war on which there was a congruence of American and British interests in checking Indian nonalignment and anti-colonialism. The question is, why?

The Bandung conference was the brainchild of the Indonesian Prime Minister, Ali Sastromojo. Indian officials were lukewarm about what they expected to be a nebulous, unwieldy gathering of some twenty Afro–Asian nations, but they did not wish to offend the Indonesians and lent their support to the conference. They then sought to avoid fruitless bickering over contentious issues such as Israel and Palestine. Instead, with the Geneva conference and SEATO in the background as manifestations of decision-making by the great powers on Asian affairs, India hoped that Bandung might afford an opportunity for Asians and Africans to make their own voice heard on matters affecting their interests, and she wished to foster a consensus on such matters.[75]

The Bandung conference is sometimes described as the birthplace of Third World neutralism, but this description is both misleading and inaccurate. Thirteen of the twenty-eight countries which attended the conference were allied with the West; the neutralism of two of the most prominent participants, India and Egypt, predated the conference. Bandung was one of the few Asian issues on which the British and Americans concurred in devising stratagems to counter any criticism of their policies by India, whose nonalignment represented in the first instance a move away from Britain, and, by implication, from the West. Many countries, including the Colombo powers, were newly emerged from colonial status; others, including Iraq, Lebanon, Thailand, Turkey, Japan and Iran had not recently been colonies. The imperial power of Turkey was defeated only during the First World War, while the humbling of Japanese imperialism had hoisted the US to military primacy in the Far East after 1945.

With the participants having such varied backgrounds and foreign policies, it is interesting that both the British and Americans assumed that the conference would be "anti-West". Perhaps it was because India and China, the two Asian countries most likely to speak out against the West, had, in Nehru and Chou En-lai respectively, leaders of outstanding intellectual and political calibre, and Western officials worried that their own allies would not be able to stand up to them. Dulles conjured up visions of 'Asian elements [especially India] . . . pushing for a pan-Asian movement which would be by its very nature and concept anti-Western',[76] and he wanted British co-operation in checking such elements. Race, racism and political interest were interwoven in the British concern that the participants would 'have little in common except colour'[77] – an odd observation, for participants ranging from China and Japan to Turkey could hardly have shared a common colour – the only thing common to them was that they were not white. Perhaps this rendered British officials, consciously or unconsciously, apprehensive that the one subject which the countries were likely to agree upon was anti-colonialism, which was bound to become the theme of the conference. They did not welcome this prospect. On 24 November 1954, Ivone Kirkpatrick commented:

The world may be in some danger of moving into "Alice through the Looking Glass". The aspirations and the national feelings of the colonial territories are very well understood here and we have sympathy for them. But the march of events is causing many of the oldest, the most civilised and the wisest nations to abandon elements of their sovereignty and to move towards greater international co-operation. It would be an anomaly if, at the same time, exaggerated nationalism took hold of the less developed territories . . . The *reductio ad absurdum* would be no sovereignty and no nationalism for the old, cultivated and civilised states; complete sovereignty and exaggerated nationalism for barbarians.[78]

Kirkpatrick's anachronistic and imperialist attitude appears strange in the context of the many official memos in which the British had congratulated themselves on the 'achievement' of decolonisation in South Asia and had advocated that the French follow the same enlightened course in Indochina. But such memos may have been inspired more by a refusal to squander resources on a disintegrating French empire than by anti-colonial fervour. Or, the contrapuntal themes of enlightened or progressive decolonisation (when perceived as a necessity) and preservation of imperium were both woven into official thinking, and the contradiction between them was not recognised. Thus the same Churchill who was determined not to liquidate the British empire in 1941 could observe admiringly in June 1954 that the US, 'even at the height of its present power, has not attempted to acquire territory and that made him very proud of his blood connections'. Yet, his last wish when he laid down office in April 1955 was that his colleagues would weave 'still more closely the threads which bound together the countries of the Commonwealth or, as he still preferred to call it, the Empire'.[79]

The news of Bandung raised the imperialist hackles of the British. What especially disturbed them were the invitations to the Gold Coast and the

Central African Federation, still parts of the British empire, and their annoyance was directed at Nehru who had been the prime mover in getting these colonies invited.[80] But Nehru's logic was that the Gold Coast and the CAF were on the verge of independence, and the invitation to the CAF was partly inspired by a desire to avoid the appearance of a conference based on colour.[81] A suggestion by G.H. Middleton in New Delhi that their presence at the conference might add a credit to Britain's liberal record did not find favour with the Foreign Office. The regressive attitude of the Foreign Office stemmed from 'our reluctance to permit any avoidable strengthening of the existing links between Asian and African nations'.[82] However, the British could not openly inveigh against the conference, as this would play into the hands of the USSR which had welcomed it and which would adroitly espouse the anti-colonial cause. But they should not leave the field clear to those powers who would attack colonialism. Instead, the British should discourage friends who consulted them from attending the conference and encourage them to resist assaults on colonialism; and Swinton advised Godfrey Huggins of the Central African Federation not to participate. But the British were mindful of the the benefits of good relations with India, and Swinton counselled Huggins not to tell Nehru that he had consulted them.[83] Summing up the official British view at a cabinet meeting on 13 January 1955, Eden deprecated the invitations to the Gold Coast and the Central African Federation (CAF) as 'an unfortunate initiative' which seemed likely to result in resolutions condemning colonialism. There was general agreement in the cabinet that, 'this Asian intervention in African affairs [a reference to Britain as an African power] was not to be welcomed.' It would be 'preferable' that governments of British territories in Africa should not be represented at the conference, and 'discreet steps' should be taken to discourage them from attending the conference. And 'guidance' could be given 'to those of the Governments invited to it who were likely to accept advice from us'.[84] The CAF did not participate; much to British dismay, the Gold Coast did.

The Indian initiative in inviting China to the conference also ruffled the West. Engaged in tortuous negotiations over the detention of US prisoners in China, the Americans were apprehensive that China would use the conference as an anti-American platform. Nehru urged the Chinese to show greater flexibility on the issue, even as he provided China with an opportunity to persuade the participants at Bandung that she was not a threat to international peace. A hint by Eden that the presence of China would create a bad impression on the US was dismissed by an indignant Nehru. The world was larger than Britain and the US, and account had to be taken of views and reactions in the rest of the world. 'For us to be told, therefore, that the United States and the United Kingdom will not like the inclusion of China in the Afro–Asian conference is not very helpful. In fact, it is somewhat irritating. There are many things that the United States and the United Kingdom have done which we do not like at all.'[85]

British and American energies were now directed at prodding their friends to counter any Indian or Chinese offensives against colonialism or collective security. Their feud with India made the Pakistanis eager to oblige the West and even turned them into ardent well-wishers of Dutch imperialism in New Guinea. Preparing for a diplomatic war with India, Pakistani officials wanted as much 'ammunition' as possible on the Sino–Soviet treaty, alleged violations of the Geneva settlement and SEATO. Appreciative of Pakistani partisanship, the Foreign Office noted that the British 'can rely on Pakistan to take a sensible attitude at Bandung'. Other friends, including Iraq and Turkey, could also be expected to resist any attacks on collective security, while Kotelwala's anger at the Soviet veto on Ceylonese membership of the UN would render him sympathetic to any Western causes.[86]

The British and Americans also attempted to deflect Indian strictures of Western imperialism by instigating their associates to flay Soviet colonialism. How successful was this strategy? Iran first alluded to Soviet colonialism and received strong support from Iraq, Turkey and Pakistan. Nehru was aware that countries allied with SEATO or NATO had been briefed in detail for the occasion and represented fully 'the pure American doctrine'.[87] The NSC happily confirmed that the Prime Ministers of Pakistan and Ceylon were 'inspired' by a US decision 'to influence the Bandung Conference by encouraging friendly countries to participate and supplying guidance as appropriate to those representatives'. The Prime Ministers of Pakistan and Ceylon 'played particularly helpful roles in supporting free world positions'.[88] But Nehru's report on the Bandung conference does not reflect any knowledge that the British had also primed their friends. For example, John Kotelwala's onslaught on Soviet colonialism in East Europe and the Baltic states was fed with information from the Foreign Office. But British officials considered him somewhat unreliable since he tended to choose his words to please his audiences. So Malcolm Macdonald exhorted him 'to be sure to deliver' his attack on the Soviets and urged Turkish and Pakistani officials 'to put courage into men like Kotelwala'. The prodding worked; the Foreign Office was satisfied with his performance, and a smug James Cable gloated that 'Sir John Kotelwala made good use of his brief'.[89]

Nehru reacted rather sharply to the contention about Soviet colonialism on the grounds that the countries of the Soviet bloc were recognised as independent by the UN and could not be labelled colonies. Whatever the strength or weakness of his argument, his stand against colonialism was not based on the mere wish to embarrass the West. When, for example, Pakistan's desire to strengthen her credentials with "Muslim" countries inspired her to launch a stinging attack on French colonialism in North Africa, Nehru exercised a restraining influence on the wording of the resolution against France. British and American records are silent on this point. Perhaps because British and American officials had wrongly and

unimaginatively typecast Nehru as "anti-West", they could not accommodate themselves to different facets of his policies. Nehru's keenness to
secure the largest possible measure of agreement inspired his formula of
opposition to 'colonialism in all its manifestations' which was accepted by
the conference.[90] Even the Americans could not object to this: 'its references to colonialism were in accord with what we feel in our hearts (though
we are unable to say them publicly)', observed Dulles to the cabinet on 29
April 1955.[91]

Even as the British consoled themselves that they had not been singled
out for condemnation on colonialism, the Foreign Office held the resolution on colonialism to be the 'least satisfactory element' of the communiqué and regretted the singling out of West New Guinea, Aden and French
North Africa – all Western colonies – for special mention. They also knew
that few Western allies would stand up to attacks on colonialism: even
Turkey supported anti-colonial resolutions to avoid isolation. The Colonial
Office deplored the bracketing together of colonialism and communism as
evils of the same order: this would make it more difficult to justify colonial
responsibility and also to prove that anti-colonialism played the communist
game by promoting instability and disorder. Future conferences with an
anti-colonial theme would be embarrassing to the British.[92] Even if Nehru
had reacted a shade too sharply to the equation of Western and Soviet
colonialism and failed to persuade others that the two should not be
confused, there was no doubt that the cause he championed was the one on
which both allies of the West and neutral countries could unite.

If muffling Nehru was in the British and American interest, it must be
doubted whether the emergence of Chou as the star of Bandung was really
to their liking. Indeed, with Nehru's help, and occasionally at Nehru's
expense,[93] Chou achieved exactly what the Americans had feared: he
disarmed even their own allies and persuaded them that China was eager
for peace, and most of them made a distinction between the Soviet Union
as representing an expansionist brand of communism and China as a peace-
loving nation. Instead of seeking support for Chinese stances on many
issues, Chou proffered China's sympathy for the grievances of America's
friends and dispelled their fears of China's policies. The Lebanese concluded that he was 'très fin'; Turkey saw India with her upbraiding of
alliances and colonialism as the main troublemaker; the Pakistanis were
ecstatic that Chou had given them 'virtually everything we asked for. We
found nothing to fight'; 'a new political ABC.' had to be learned. Bandung
marked the emergence of a new rapport between Pakistan and China, and
Moscow's approval of it was probably reflected in the omission from the
Soviet press of Pakistan's anti-Soviet tirade at the conference. The Foreign
Office surmised that China's influence in Asia was much augmented and
that anti-communism as distinct from non-communism was proportion-
ately diminished. Consequently there was little chance that more states
would be attracted to SEATO, and a growing tendency towards Indian

neutralism could be expected.[94] This was at variance with Dulles's cock-sure and not very accurate assertion that the conference was dominated 'by a group of friendly Asian nations who believed in association with the West'. It was Chou En-lai who stole the show; he persuaded most Western allies, as he had already impressed on Nehru, that coexistence with China was possible. Even Dulles confessed that he had to "salute" Chou's performance at Bandung a (although he doubted his sincerity).[95]

Interestingly, both the British and Americans noted that the conference had produced an Afro–Asian consensus on many issues without being anti-West. Their pre-emptive fears of the conference mirrored their knee-jerk suspicion that anything in which the West was not included was automatically anti-West. They also reflected a certain inability to adjust to the foreign policies of newly independent states and to the ongoing diffusion of power in an international system still dominated by the West. Anglo–American fears of the the conference revealed the *mentalité* of cold warriors and their moral defensiveness about Western imperialism, even as they sought to preserve their influence through local partners. The conference underlined the American dislike of nonalignment and British annoyance at Indian anti-colonialism. Yet the British were not about to discard India, though whether they would work with or against India would depend on whether she would advance or thwart their ambitions. On the whole, their interest in India as an instrument of their diplomacy in Asia endured.

VI ALIGNMENT OR NONALIGNMENT? INDIA, CAMBODIA AND THE ANGLO–AMERICAN RELATIONSHIP

Despite India's unconcealed dislike of SEATO and her performance at the Bandung conference, British interest in India as a counterpoise to Chinese influence in Asia prevailed. Churchill summed up the British line in glowing terms to Nehru in February 1955, even as the British worked against the anticipated Indian stance at Bandung.

I hope you will think of the phrase 'The Light of Asia'. It seems to me that you might be able to do what no other human being could in giving India the lead, at least in the realm of thought, throughout Asia, with the freedom and dignity of the individual as the ideal rather than the Communist Party drill book.[96]

The British also valued India as an intermediary with China. During the winter of 1954–5, the CRO and Foreign Office noted that India and Britain shared a belief in democracy and a desire for international peace. As with the United States, India's differences with Britain related to means rather than to ends: Britain believed that strength was the way to deal with communism, while India held that military alliances only increased tension and wanted to build up a psychological pressure on communist countries which she hoped 'may force them to honour an agreement into which they have entered'. Whatever the merits of such a policy, 'one thing is clear: India has succeeded in getting herself recognised as a genuine neutral and is therefore accepted as impartial by the Communist world.' This had enabled India 'to intervene effectively' with China and to assist in bringing about settlements in Korea and Indochina. As such the 'close and intimate relations between the United Kingdom and India serve a valuable purpose in interpreting East and West to one another.' They were a unique force in international diplomacy. 'Acting in concert the United Kingdom and India could do more than any other power or agency to bridge the gulf between China and the United States.' This would not be easy: India's emotional antipathy towards the US was 'unfortunate', and the British should not allow it to spoil their relations with either India or the US. But the Americans themselves were often to blame through 'the heavyhandedness of their approach to many Asian problems'.[97]

So, in the summer of 1954, Clutterbuck advised Donald Kennedy, then American Chargé d'Affaires in New Delhi, that the Indians did not like being told what to do; it would be best to consult Nehru and to try and influence him indirectly. Other Western ambassadors in New Delhi suggested to Kennedy that the US might occasionally applaud India's peacemaking efforts. Kennedy's reply was revealing. It would be difficult, he explained, for the Americans to follow this advice, since the Indians 'always seemed to scrutinize US statements to see what they could find to criticize, while examining Chinese statements for things to praise'.[98] American sensitivity to Indian strictures, and their seeing in this criticism a tendency to give communists, whether of the Soviet or Chinese variety, the benefit of every doubt, was to plague Indo–US relations for more than thirty years. It remains to be seen whether the end of the cold war will end the intermittent sparring between an America which has perceived her military strength as underwriting "freedom" and an India which has discerned American alliances as a threat to *her* independence.

The theme of an Indian role in Indochina recurred in British memos after the Manila treaty. British policy-makers were keenly interested in Nehru's visits to China and Indochina in November 1954 and were impressed by his warnings to Chou and Ho Chi Minh not to upset the Geneva accord.[99] In response to a question from Chou, Nehru had averred that India was dealing with Cambodia and Laos 'for all practical purposes' as independent states. Meeting Prince Norodom Sihanouk in Pnom Penh, Nehru was convinced of his patriotism and intelligence and recognised that Cambodian independence was a reality. On his return to New Delhi Nehru decided that India should have full diplomatic representation in Pnom Penh.[100] British officials were pleased, since they had encouraged Indian recognition of non-communist governments in Indochina since 1949.

The establishment of diplomatic relations between New Delhi and Pnom

Penh amplified British interest in Indian influence in East Asia. Following a visit to Indochina in November–December 1954, Malcolm Macdonald advised London that India could play a significant part in deterring the Vietminh from interfering in Cambodia. If, following Nehru's warnings to Chou and Ho, India could perform this role, that warning would be 'greatly reinforced'. The British should do 'all in our power' to persuade New Delhi to appoint as soon as possible an ambassador in Pnom Penh. A simultaneous Indian recognition of the Royal Government of Laos would have the 'maximum effect'.[101]

The Americans also favoured Indian diplomatic influence to counter the Chinese in Indochina. On 20 June 1954 news that New Delhi was about to recognise the Royal Government of Cambodia was welcomed by Bedell Smith, who surmised that China would play her cards carefully with Laos and Cambodia because of the 'sympathy' they entertained in India and Burma. The communists were not disposed to irritate India; although militarily weak, India enjoyed great moral stature and influence in Asia.'[102] Sihanouk himself saw advantages in Indian recognition of his government and was encouraged by Robert McClintock, the US Chargé d'Affaires in Pnom Penh. Racking his brains for ideas as to how Sihanouk could impress Nehru, McClintock advised the king to speak to Nehru in Cambodian, not French, so that Nehru would not conclude that he was under French influence. The advice displayed a dubious talent for fine detail, which was uninformed about the complexities of nationalism in colonial settings: Nehru's own mastery of English prose may have reflected a British cultural influence, but it had never made him a British stooge. As it turned out, Sihanouk asked the French embassy to translate his speech from French into English, so that he could practice his English pronunciation before trying it out on Nehru. But time ran short, no translation was made; the speech was ultimately delivered in French – and Sihanouk nevertheless hit it off with Nehru. McClintock was pleased with Nehru's warnings to Ho and Chou, for he thought that they evinced India's interest in her own sphere of influence which would act as a counterbalance to a Chinese one. It might also exacerabate Sino–Indian rivalry – a prospect McClintock entertained with much relish.[103]

It is, however, unlikely that the British and Americans had the same idea about the extent to which they desired Indian influence in Indochina and the purposes each expected it to serve. To the British, Indian influence was a means of containing China through diplomacy. Indian influence would not compete with theirs, since Cambodia was not a British domain. But could Indian influence have the same meaning for American officials who were ruminating on the desirability of extending US influence to "save" Indochina from communism? For the Americans, the diplomatic option did not foreclose a military engagement in Cambodia – the question was what form this should take. The general idea of becoming militarily involved had been bruited by Nixon at the NSC meeting of 8 January

1954[104] and had been given fresh impetus by a Cambodian overture to the US on 20 May and a Vietnamese approach on 18 June.[105] Since the Americans had ruled out any kind of unilateral military intervention, and would only give aid if asked by the Associated States, the Cambodian and Vietnamese requests opened the way to augmenting America's military clout in Indochina.

This might have seemed exactly what the US had been waiting for, but there were obstacles in the way of American military missions in Indochina. The French were not the least of these. Talking to the NSC on 22 July 1954, Dulles saw them as the real obstacle to an American military mission; 'he would almost rather see the French get completely out' of Indochina and thus permit the United States to work directly with local leaders. The desire was echoed by the Joint Chiefs of Staff who thought a MAAG should be set up if the Associated States requested the US to assume responsibility for training their forces. In that event, the Chiefs wanted all French advisers to be withdrawn. But Dulles and other State Department officials knew that it would be difficult to translate such wishes into reality; the Chiefs were being 'too legalistic and unrealistic', and a policy aimed at ousting the French would 'most certainly cause violent French reactions involving European matters as well as Indochina'.[106]

However the Americans would go ahead, and they would inform the British about their intention to set up a MAAG in Cambodia. American policy-makers were suspicious of the nature of the assurances Eden had given Chou En-lai in Geneva. At a meeting with Eden and Harold Caccia in Washington on 27 September 1954, State Department officials pressed Caccia as to why there should be any objections to a US military mission in Cambodia in the context of the Geneva accord. According to the State Department record: 'Mr Caccia's somewhat evasive answers tended to confirm the suspicions that the British had given side assurances to the Chinese Communists regarding the U.S. training missions in Laos and Cambodia.' On 9 October, Dulles was unsure whether the British had promised Chou that they would oppose a MAAG as a violation of the Geneva accord, and a few weeks later, on 22 November, McClintock was advised by British officials that it would be preferable for the US to refrain from establishing a military mission in Cambodia.[107]

The British preference was for an Indian military mission. The Americans recognised the benefits of India regarding Laos and Cambodia as belonging to the sphere of Indian culture, especially if it prompted Nehru's government to support the independence of these two countries. However, it is most unlikely that the Americans and the British shared the same expectations of the Indians. A comparison of British and American records of a meeting between Eden and Dulles in Paris on 16 December 1954 reveals some differences of interpretation. According to the Foreign Office record, Eden found Dulles receptive to the idea of an increased Indian influence in Indochina. The United States 'had no desire to play a role there and would be well content if India could step in her place.' Eden agreed with Dulles, whose views he would pass on to Nehru. The nuances of the State Department record are not quite the same. It cites Dulles as saying that, 'if India would be willing to effectively guarantee Laos and Cambodia against Communist domination, the U.S. would be glad to bow out of the picture.' Eden said it would be 'very helpful if he could pass on to Nehru the Secretary's thoughts about the importance of the role which India could play . . . and the Secretary agreed that he could do so'. The British, said Eden, would see what they could do to persuade India to interest herself in Laos and Cambodia in order to remove Chinese suspicions of American intentions in Indochina. With Dulles's agreement, Eden would write to Nehru.[108]

British attempts to coax Nehru's government to enhance India's profile in Cambodia continued. A brief prepared by J.C. Cloake, and taken by Denis Allen for Eden at the Mallaig conference on Southeast Asian security in February 1955, argued that historical and cultural links between India and Indochina would facilitate Indian influence in those countries. This in turn would discourage communist adventurism in Laos and Cambodia, which would form with Burma a *cordon sanitaire* between China and the Vietminh on the one side and Thailand and Malaya on the other. Moreover, any communist attempt to gain control over them might nudge India to take more seriously the communist menace to Southeast Asia and consequently to look more favourably on SEATO. Indian 'protection' could of course do nothing to save these countries in the event of aggression but, except for the threat of action under the Manila Treaty, there was little direct help that US military aid could give. 'Neither country is properly defensible from a military standpoint.'[109]

This last point was reaffirmed in a Foreign Office memorandum on the Manila Treaty which stated that with fifteen Vietminh divisions backed by two million men of the Chinese army in Vietnam, neither China nor the Vietminh had cause for alarm at the Manila treaty or at measures taken by the US government to train and reorganise the South Vietnamese army. The inference was that the independence of Laos and Cambodia would hinge on the Chinese abiding by the Geneva agreement. This accorded with the Indian view. The British did not really want SEATO to be used – an attitude which caused considerable heartburning on the American side.[110] Meanwhile the Mallaig conference favoured the extension of an Indian role in Indochina, and Cloake's brief was also used by Denis Allen and Harold Caccia during Eden's visit to New Delhi in February 1955.

For their part the Indians were willing to give technical and financial aid to Cambodia. More significantly their interest in a military mission arose from their interest in safeguarding Cambodian independence and encouraging Cambodian neutrality. But they were reluctant to do anything unless approached by Cambodia herself and their mission supported by the great powers.[111] This reflected Indian acknowledgement of their insignificant influence in Cambodia, for, without the concurrence of the great powers and Cambodia, an Indian military mission could achieve precious little.

China's reaction to the idea of an Indian military mission was of great import to the British. Presented with the idea by U Nu, Chou agreed that an Indian presence 'in practice removed apprehensions on both sides'.[112] So on 13 May 1955, Eden urged Nehru that the ideal solution would be an Indian military mission backed by US financial and military assistance and that India might assume greater responsibility in Laos and Cambodia.[113] In other words, the allaying of China's insecurity about her own sphere of influence offered the best chances of her curbing the Vietminh, and it would be the most efficacious long-term check on communist expansion in Indochina.

But Indo-US friction – this time, about the implementation of the Geneva accord – threatened to upset the applecart. This was partly because the Indians suspected that the US was working against the accord. By early 1955, the Indians were concerned that US arms to Vietnam, and the inclusion of Vietnam in the area to be defended by SEATO, violated the Geneva agreement. In their self-appointed role as the bridge between India and the US, the British assured the Indians that this aid did not contravene the Geneva accord, for the Manila powers had unilaterally decided to include Vietnam in their area of defence; Vietnam, therefore, had not violated the agreement.[114] At another level, American officials alleged that G. Parthasarthy, the Indian chairman of the International Supervisory Commission was soft on communist violations of the Geneva agreement, while suspicious of any move by Cambodia and Laos to strengthen military ties with the West, even when these were fully in accordance with the agreement.[115] There seemed no sign that India and the US would bury the hatchet.

It is hardly surprising, then, that India frowned upon the US–Cambodian military treaty of 16 May 1955. The US stipulated that direct military aid should be conditional on assignment to the US of responsibility for training the Cambodian army.[116] The Indians alleged that the American demand was contrary to the Geneva accord. Eden remained anxious to get the Indians into Cambodia by reconciling Indian assistance with what the Americans were doing. Meanwhile the problem was complicated by Sihanouk's preference for French military training which could be traced partly to his dislike of American pressure on him to abandon Cambodian neutrality, partly to French influence over him and to the French determination not to be pushed out by the Americans or Indians. Eden assured Nehru that the supply of US *matériel* to Cambodia was not inconsistent with the Geneva agreement. The problem for the British was to lessen Indian mistrust of the US and simultaneously to overcome American 'distaste for Indian intervention'.[117] In his talks with Nehru on 8 and 9 July 1955, Eden impressed on Nehru 'the great importance' he attached to Indian training of the Cambodian army. An Indian presence in

Laos and Cambodia would dissuade the communists from making trouble there. 'This was perhaps the only way in the long run to maintain the independence of Cambodia and Laos.'[118]

Given the tendency of American officials to believe that American MAAGs offered the best chances of strengthening Cambodia against communism, and their desire to eliminate the military influence of even their French ally, it is unlikely that the American interest in an Indian role implied an Indian lead in Cambodia. McClintock warned that Indian influence would nurture Cambodian neutrality which was not to the American liking. The Americans 'must not forget the fixed and inverterate [sic] hatred of Nehru, Krishna Menon and company for [the] SEATO pact'. Situated between Thailand and Vietnam, Cambodia would become, under Indian tutelage, a military factor firmly opposed to SEATO. For this reason alone 'I would oppose an Indian military mission'. It would also be difficult to imagine the US Congress voting funds for a Cambodian army trained by India.[119]

Talk of Indian training for the Cambodian army eventually fizzled out because of Sihanouk's preference for the French, Indo–US antagonism and Sihanouk's indignation at the Indian démarche, and on 8 December, the Indian Minister in Pnom Penh informed McClintock that an Indian military mission was ' "a dead duck" '. In a rare condemnation of Indian attitudes to Indochina, Littlejohn Cook, who had been an enthusiastic advocate of an Indian mission in Cambodia, blamed the Indians for upsetting the Cambodians. Earlier, on 1 August, Anthony Rumbold at the Foreign Office criticised the Indians for annoying the Americans, who would supply the money and equipment, the French, who at present provided training, and the Cambodians, who would use them all. By the end of 1955, Denis Allen saw little point in British efforts at bringing about an Indo–US rapprochement.[120]

These British opinions missed the point that India was not at the helm of affairs in Indochina. Even before the end of 1955, the successful working of the Geneva accord was also in doubt. South Vietnam had never accepted the agreement, and its attitude was summed up by the slogans which greeted Nehru on his visit to Saigon in November 1954: ' "Welcome to the Prime Minister of India and tell him no co-existence." '[121] It was persistently hostile to the International Supervisory Commission in Vietnam, and the government of Ngo Dinh Diem connived in demonstrations against the Commission in June and September 1955. Facing great personal risks, and resentful of the Diem government's animus against the Commission, the Indian commissioner – and the Indian government – contemplated India's withdrawal from the Commission. As S. Dutt, the Indian Foreign Secretary, pointed out, the Commission was being used to maintain a stalemate when one party to the cease-fire had no intention of carrying out the Geneva agreement. Privately Eden agreed.[122] In June 1956, Eden informed Commonwealth Prime Ministers in London that a stalemate persisted in Indochina but that it would be best if the settlement were given a chance.[123]

To the British idea of containing communism through diplomacy in Indochina was linked their hope that SEATO would never engage in a war. This was the background to their talk of "Indian influence" in Indochina. The Indians were neither influential nor popular with the French, the US or South Vietnamese. Sihanouk was ambivalent towards them – although he believed that neutrality afforded the only course to avoid provoking China and to safeguard Cambodia's independence. ' "I am using Nehru's penicillin because it seems to be good for what ails us" ' – was his pithy summing up of the rationale behind Cambodian neutrality.[124] At the same time he resented what he sometimes saw as Indian arrogance. The British concept of Indian influence to check China, then, was open to question. It is curious that so many British officials wrote of 'Indian influence' as if it already existed, when in fact they desired an increase in Indian influence in order to contain China. Curiously they said little about what the Cambodians or Vietnamese themselves might want.

Then there were problems with Britain's own allies in Indochina. The French did not want to be elbowed out of Indochina by the Americans or anyone else; India and the US remained mutually antagonistic; the US was lukewarm if not hostile to the Geneva agreement. By 1956, some American officials perceived Britain and France as having abdicated their positions in the Far East; they saw the US bearing the major burden of defence against communism in the region and being 'the only Western power prepared to fight'. Consequently the views of the United States and its allies in the Far East should prevail.[125] Convinced of the indispensability of a military intervention by the US to save Indochina from communism, the Americans were on the verge of a long-drawn-out involvement in Vietnam. British officials conceived a tentative diplomatic solution to the conflict in Indochina on the Britain–India–China circuit, but the complexities of the Asian cold war extended far beyond that.

6 The limits of influence

. . . much will depend on the extent to which we in the United Kingdom save and invest our savings in Commonwealth countries. The initial urge to do this, and to develop commercial relations with the Commonwealth, has to be present in United Kingdom industry as a result of our general financial policies. If it is there, we can help it along . . . If it is not, we shall inevitably see others penetrating commercially into our terrain. [S. Garner to J.D. Murray, 28 September 1954]

We must not . . . overlook the danger of finding ourselves trying to outbid every uneconomic offer the Russians like to make; nor indeed the risk that Pakistan and perhaps other allies may draw unfavourable comparisons between the advantages offered by such agreements as the Bagdad [sic] Pact and the bargaining position apparently afforded to India by her neutralism. Nevertheless it is clear that the recent visit to India of Krushchev and Bulganin has not been without some success, and this is therefore not the moment to remain inactive. [Home to Eden, 14 December 1955]

I BRITAIN'S WESTERN COMPETITORS IN SOUTH ASIA

If by 1956, the Americans saw themselves as guardians of Western interests in Asia, what did they think of the British role on the subcontinent? In contrast to the years 1947–50, when they had seen South Asia as essentially a British concern, by 1956 there is hardly any sign that they still took that view. It is not that South Asia rose on their list of priorities; nor does there seem to be any conscious or well-thought-out American debate about why or how their perception of the British position in South Asia should change or had changed. Britain remained the most important ally of the US, but the Americans now regarded themselves as the anchor of Western security in Asia, and there is scant evidence that they still perceived the British as the corner-stone of the Western position. One can deduce a variety of reasons why this was so. One was the divergence between British and American perceptions of India's role in the Asian cold war and the American feeling that British susceptibility to Indian influence ran contrary to American interests. Second, British advice on the need to mend fences with India wore thin on American officials in the face of an Indo–US friction which reflected the contradiction between Indian nonalignment and the American demand for alignment. Third, the US had supplanted Britain as the primary influence in Pakistan in 1953–4. Although the US had not consciously aimed at displacing Britain, it acquired political and military clout in Pakistan at Britain's expense as it emerged as the primary military and economic aid donor to Pakistan. Pakistan's entry into the British-sponsored Baghdad Pact in September 1955 did not augment British leverage with her, if only because the British had no intention of increasing military or economic assistance to her which might have improved the UK's position in relation to the US.

On the British side, there had always been the knowledge that American help to the UK and good Indo-US relations were vital to the success of British strategy in the Asian cold war, but this had never implied a wish to see the US enhance its standing on the subcontinent. There is a limited sense in which the disharmony between nonalignment and the American emphasis on alliances was beneficial to the British: Indian nonalignment had been a move away from Britain, but it also ruled out the likelihood of India joining the American camp. And despite India's poor relations with both superpowers, the dialogue with Britain remained constructive. It was a position that the British were keen to maintain, not least because they saw their rapport with India as a key to preserving Britain's credentials as an Asian power.

The Commonwealth also came into the picture. With decolonisation in Malaya and Ghana on the anvil by early 1955, the question was what form the Commonwealth should take. The Commonwealth was still seen as an instrument of British influence and claims to world-wide status, even if, as officials admitted, it had few financial or military teeth. Debating the future of the Commonwealth in October 1954, there was no coyness about why the British wished to keep it as a going concern: 'If we are to maintain our influence as a world power we must increasingly rely on our position as *primus inter pares* in a group of independent Commonwealth countries.' The inference was that Britain's leadership of a loosely-knit organisation, rather than economic or military strength, would bolster her claim to global influence. The British did not pretend that the Commonwealth really implied a relationship among equals. Following decolonisation in South Asia, a two-tier Commonwealth had come into existence. Much information was not passed on to the new dominions – some was even withheld from the old dominions – but the experience with India and Pakistan had shown that such a Commonwealth could be managed without adverse effects. However, the formalisation of a two-tier membership would create resentment among those relegated to second-class status in the Commonwealth, while a denial of membership to newly independent African states might disrupt the Commonwealth and provoke a walk-out by Asian members, leaving them free to make claims to leadership of 'aspiring African colonies'. Therefore, secession from the Commonwealth was not to be encouraged; it would be tantamount to 'deliberately weakening our own strength and authority in world councils by a series of self-inflicted wounds'.[1] The presence of a republican India in the Commonwealth had actually enhanced Britain's prestige as a bridge between East and West.

British attitudes to the US remained ambivalent. Culturally, they assumed that the US was a non-starter in South Asia. Early in 1954, James Cable discounted the value of anything the US might have to offer in the cultural field. Referring to the desire of Senator Charles Howell from Connecticut to make Indians aware of the cultural aspects of American life, and his suggestion 'as an experiment, to send Bing Crosby on a tour among India's youth', Cable wrote smugly: 'I was initially puzzled by the reference to cultural missions, wondering what the United States had to show India in that field, but the penultimate paragraph makes all clear: the reference is to Bing Crosby!'[2]

On another plane, American anti-colonialism aroused British indignation. There was considerable annoyance at a speech made by Ambassador Chester Bowles in New Delhi in December 1953: his condemnation of colonialism and reference to the exploitation of colonies were 'objectionable' to the Foreign Office. In India, Vice-President Nixon's emphasis on the common achievement of independence by India and the US also irritated the British. Cable alleged that the Americans were 'trying to curry favour with Indians by describing both peoples as having escaped from the British colonial yoke'.[3] Fortunately for the British, the Indians were not taken in by such rhetoric. At another level, Indian disapproval of US military alliances was not taken amiss if an Indian official implied that Britain could play a constructive role in Asia. For instance, in November 1953, the words of a senior Indian diplomat in London – that Britain should enhance her profile in Asia – were what British officials wanted to hear, and they indulged in a round of self-congratulation. John Tahourdin subjectively thought the remarks reflected 'a somewhat more realistic and less detached attitude on the part of India towards our general policy in South East Asia'. Denis Allen saw the Indians becoming increasingly aware of the need to build defences against communism, 'but they cannot yet take the lead themselves and would prefer our leadership to that of the Americans.' Perhaps this was why some officials viewed the growth of India's influence as being to Britain's advantage, especially as the Anglo–Indian conflict over colonial problems diminished. Indian influence could be simultaneously anti-American and pro-British, and British and American interests were not necessarily identical.[4] At the same time the British saw themselves bridging the gap between India and the US to the extent that, when Nixon toured Asia in November 1953, Makins and Strang urged British envoys in Tokyo and Seoul to 'do what they can' to make Nixon appreciate the importance of keeping India on the Western side. British diplomats on the spot were to counteract the anti-Indian sentiments Nixon would 'doubtless' hear from US military commanders and Syngman Rhee.[5] According to Makins, the US expected Britain to promote and improve the American understanding of India. British officials placed the onus for Indo-US altercations on the Americans: Makins wrote that, 'The antipathy with which most leading Americans regard most leading Indians often seems abnormal.' Home lamented that 'America, with all her money and strength, makes no headway in winning their [Indian] confidence.' This rendered the British indispensable: 'In so far as any country from the West can exercise influence the task of holding them [India] lies upon us.' The British linked American irritation with India to the American dislike of the Commonwealth as an independent entity or as a possible Third Force and to the American fear that the new Commonwealth could pull Britain away from the US.[6] The inference was that American anti-Indian sentiment indirectly reflected American annoyance at British independence in diplomacy. From these different strands of thought, London happily concluded that Britain's continued influence in South Asia was essential to bridge the Indo–US chasm in the long-term interests of containing communism.

Economically, too, South Asia's membership of the Commonwealth remained important to Britain. In September 1953, South Asia contributed over half the total UK export trade and nearly half the import trade with the Far East region; and the Commonwealth accounted for some 82 per cent of her exports and 79.7 per cent of her imports from the Far East. The Far East itself accounted for 14.2 per cent of British world exports and 10 per cent of imports. The only region to exceed this position was Europe in the case of exports. India, Pakistan, Ceylon, Malaya and Burma together contributed 44.5 per cent of the dollar earnings of the whole sterling area and 17 per cent of other non-sterling earnings. As late as 1958, India was Britain's fourth-largest market in the world.[7]

Britain was India's largest trading partner,[8] and British investments in India rose during the early fifties. Yet the British feared for their economic stake in India, partly because the Indian government imposed restrictions on foreign investment, partly because independence offered more economic choices to India. Consequently Britain faced more competition from other countries on the Indian market. The Commonwealth–Empire did not recover its pre-war importance in South Asia in spite of the emergence of Pakistan as a new trading unit within the Commonwealth. The share of the Commonwealth in India's total imports from the UK declined from 47 per cent in 1950–1 to 41 per cent in 1952–3.

Despite Indo–US discord, the most significant increase of any single country in India's trade was the United States. In 1937–8 the American share of India's imports had been 7 per cent; in 1949–50 it was 15.7 per cent. Indian exports showed a similar pattern: in 1938–9 the sterling area had absorbed 53 per cent of Indian exports and 42 per cent in 1948–9; the figures for the dollar area were 12 per cent in 1938–9 and 25 per cent in 1948–9. In addition, there was a relative decline in India's trade with

Britain and a relative rise in her trade with Australia, Canada, West Germany and Japan.

Economic competition, even from Western allies, therefore alarmed the British. For example, in 1953, they faced a challenge from West Germany in India, where Mercedes Benz were trying to manufacture tanks. To some British policy-makers, it was not merely a question of straightforward competition: 'It is only one more instance in an alarming, long-standing and general tendency for the U.K. to lose her markets in India to foreigners.' Pressure needed to be applied on departments in Whitehall if they wanted to maintain Britain's traditional position as India's main supplier of capital goods and war munitions.[9] The Defence Ministry, FO and CRO reckoned that the best way to tackle the problem was to sharpen the competitiveness of British exports. Meanwhile the Defence Ministry urged 'doing all we can' to encourage Leyland to frustrate the efforts of Mercedes Benz to establish themselves in India, and 'no doubt we shall again have occasion to encourage enterprise and energy on the part of our manufacturers if they are to retain or exploit the Indian market.' Could anything be done to forestall a Mercedes bid to make tanks in India? The Board of Trade answered that they had done 'a little canvassing in Whitehall, which has certainly revealed uneasiness, but equally, has not disclosed anything which could be done'. The Foreign Office were dismayed, and not without a tendency to fault Britain's foreign competitors for unscrupulousness, perhaps as a small consolation in the face of the relatively poor competitiveness of British industry or slow decision-making. 'Is there really nothing that can be done?', lamented R.A. Burrows on 23 December 1953. 'We seem to be competing in kid gloves against rivals who will use all devices to secure their own advantage.' Noting New Delhi's complaints about red tape in Whitehall, the Foreign Office recognised that, in the circumstances, the Indians 'will naturally prefer our foreign competitors' – but then there was a self-righteous dig at the supposed lack of discrimination of foreign competitors 'who are eager to sell anything to anybody'.

II KEEPING THE SOVIETS AT BAY: THE BRITISH NEED AMERICAN HELP

Losing out to Britain's friends was bad enough; losing out to the Soviets was worse, yet it appeared possible after 1953. Until India demonstrated, during the Korean war, that she was not a protégé of the West, the Soviets had vilified her and Pakistan as camp-followers of Western imperialism. The implacable hostility and ignorance of the Soviets only served to block the chances of any improvement in their relations with India and Pakistan, and consequently of any enhancement of Soviet influence in South Asia. But it is worth remembering that a chilly Indo–Soviet connection ran parallel to sour Indo–US relations, that the irreconcilable contradictions between alignment and nonalignment had made American officials perceive India as pandering to communism. British officials took the same line when India did not go along with them, but perhaps the Commonwealth connection made them realise that nonalignment had a pro-Western edge. It could hardly have been otherwise. During the fifties, India took almost all her military imports from the West, and Britain was her largest trading partner. As for the Asian cold war, there seemed to be a disjunction between Indian rhetoric about the need to bring China into the international fold and the limited economic contact between India and China. In fact it was "aligned" Pakistan whose volume of trade with China was more than four times that of India in 1954–5; Turkey, Ceylon and Britain herself had larger volumes of trade with China.[10] However, it was India's political stance which solidified the Western image of India, and as the Colombo and Bandung conferences showed, any anticipated opposition to the West was easily construed as pro-communist. Probably this was because the Western hold over India was not secure. Independence, after all, implied political and economic options. How receptive the Indians would be to Soviet courtship would depend on what the Soviets had to offer in comparison with the West.

Soviet overtures to the Third World, and a mellowing of their animosity towards India, started in earnest only after Stalin's death in March 1953. Two years later, in February 1955, the Soviets offered India a steel plant on credit at the very favourable rate of interest of 2.5 per cent, which was better than anything the British could offer. To offset this, all that the CRO could suggest was a steel mission to investigate the chances of a British steel plant under the Colombo Plan.[11] Coming soon after the announcement of the Bandung conference, which the British and Americans expected to be anti-West, the news of the Indo–Soviet steel plant agreement added to Western apprehension about India. The agreement marked the first large-scale development programme in India to be financed by a communist government and the beginning of Soviet penetration of the Indian economy. It also signalled the first major Soviet economic challenge to the West in South Asia.

The British and Americans were both filled with consternation. The State Department regarded the Soviet offer as 'an unfavourable political development, though it could contribute to our over-all economic objective of strengthening India's basic economy.' The State Department gloomily prophesied that American aid would compare favourably with Soviet, but the concentration of 'so much Soviet assistance in one large tangible structure will no doubt lend itself to Communist publicity about Soviet as compared to American economic aid'.[12] From New Delhi, Malcolm Macdonald warned that India would judge the friendliness of countries by their economic generosity to her. Britain's own abilities were constrained, and containing the Soviets called for early discussions with the Americans.[13] If competition from allies gave the British a start, competition from the Soviets introduced a tangible cold-war dimension into British attempts to safeguard their political and economic interests in India. The British and Americans now came together to counter the Soviets, especially on sales of military equipment to India.

The British and Americans watched, with bated breath, the tenor of Nehru's visit to the USSR in June 1955. From Moscow, William Hayter reported a Soviet reception unparalleled in anyone's experience of the USSR. Never before had any foreign visitor been driven through the streets of Moscow in an open car with a Soviet leader and greeted by 'obviously enthusiastic' crowds, who frightened Bulganin by throwing bunches of flowers into the official car. Nehru was accorded unprecedented honours; he was accompanied by the entire Soviet presidium publicly on no less than twelve occasions, and he addressed an audience of 80,000 at the Dynamo stadium. Hayter thought his speech innocuous, but one which would please the Soviets, for there was 'nothing in it that could not equally well be subscribed to by a satellite Prime Minister'. But he took the view that Nehru's private talks with Soviet leaders had been salutary. In London, the CRO were pleased at Nehru's reception in the Soviet Union. He had built up a wealth of experience and contacts which enhanced his ability to act as a bridge between East and West and as an interpreter of one to the other.[14] Perhaps the CRO thought Nehru's enhanced prestige reflected well on the Commonwealth, implying that they saw a parallel between Nehru's diplomatic accomplishments and the Commonwealth's purpose as an instrument of British influence.

Khrushchev and Bulganin returned the visit with a tour of India in November–December 1955, and it was clear that they would concentrate on loosening India from the West. The Indians were well prepared for a Soviet diplomatic offensive. Pillai told Malcolm Macdonald in the strictest confidence that the Indian government intended to have the minimum of serious discussions with the Soviets during the visit; the programme had been filled with 'an almost continuous succession' of social, ceremonial and similiar functions so as to reduce the time for more substantial conversations. The Indians would be cautious, though they could not take an 'entirely negative' attitude. Pillai anticipated one or two economic agreements between India and the USSR, but 'in most cases' the Indians intended to make non-committal replies to Soviet offers of aid. Any Soviet proposals about financing the gaps in India's second Five-Year Plan would be examined in relation to offers from other countries.[15]

It followed that the Indian government would not welcome Khrushchev and Bulganin with entirely open arms and that the ability of the Soviets to make a dent in India's relations with the West would hinge on what they could offer her and also on the extent of Indian pleasure or displeasure with Western policies. Politically the West could not have been on more slippery ground. The visit coincided with the first meeting of the Baghdad Pact council on 21 and 22 November 1955. As Pakistan was a member of the Pact, the Indians felt affronted at the council's denunciation of neutralism as dangerous to the 'homogeneity' of West Asia. In Nehru's words, this was 'in direct opposition' to nonalignment. As if this were not enough to annoy India, Britain had formally aligned herself to the Pact and to Pakistan; she had come 'perilously near to . . . taking an unfriendly step towards India', since she was associated with a country hostile to India.[16] Eden assured Nehru that the pact was defensive[17] and that Pakistani aggression against India would not be supported. But Nehru was not mollified, and the meeting of the Pact council contributed to the backdrop against which Khrushchev and Bulganin visited India in November–December 1955.

Avowing the independence of his government, Nehru made clear to them that India's interests did not dovetail with those of the Soviet Union simply because of their mutual dislike of the Baghdad Pact, but he did not get much help from the West. Nehru spurned a Soviet offer to nominate India as a permanent member of the Security Council. Faced with a heavy Soviet barrage against the US, Nehru's response was double-edged: 'I don't see why a strong man should always go about showing his muscles.'[18] Oblivious of the hint, the Soviet leaders discomfited their Indian hosts with anti-West diatribes, including a stunning accusation by Khrushchev that the West, especially Britain, had sent Hitler's divisions to invade Russia.[19] Even as Indian officials recovered from their embarrassed astonishment, Dulles gave the Soviets a boost by declaring US support for the 'Portguese provinces' in Asia. Indian annoyance at Soviet behaviour was replaced by anger at Dulles's insensitivity. The timing and content of his statement played straight into Soviet hands. Seizing their opportunity Khrushchev and Bulganin publicly asserted Soviet backing for India's stand on Kashmir and Goa. The Indians were taken by surprise, but they could hardly give the Soviets the cold shoulder. Waking up to the offence he had caused the Indian government, Dulles tried to conciliate them by clarifying his statement – only to blunder on 6 December that, 'as far as I know all the world regards it [Goa] as a Portuguese province.' It was the turn of British officials to be astounded at Dulles's clumsiness. Nothing could have been more calculated to alienate Indian opinion than this 'amazing statement' by Dulles. From Moscow, Hayter commented that, 'American timing certainly does seem to have been extraordinarily bad throughout the visit.'[20] Once again the British blamed the Americans for an Indo–US fracas.

Actually, Nehru was chagrined at this time by both the British alignment with Pakistan in the Baghdad Pact and with Dulles's endorsement of the Portugese empire. 'People in England and America are very courteous to us and friendly but, in the final analysis, they treat India as a country to be humoured but not as an equal.'[21] Generally he thought that the UK and US had both created adverse impressions by their policy of military alliances which were encircling India; neither was able to adapt to changed circumstances in Asia. America's financial and military might had made them look down on almost everybody, 'friend or foe, and they have developed a habit of irritating others by their overbearing attitudes'. Nehru perceived Britain as being trapped in an imperial time-warp so that the Soviet Union had the great advantage of not coming into conflict over any issue of 'the old colonial type' and could denounce colonialism without any injury to itself.[22]

Even with the West seemingly doing their best to alienate India, Nehru's government were determined to stand their ground with the Soviets. The final communiqué covering the Soviet visit was drafted by the Indians and committed the Soviets to the Five Principles.[23] By acquiescing in the Indian provision for non-interference in internal affairs, the Soviets were, in effect, renouncing Cominform. Nehru turned down a Soviet suggestion that both sides reject the policy of military blocs and stay out of coalitions directed against each other. This would be a negative alliance and, as such, it would not be acceptable to India. From New Delhi, G.H. Middleton was of the opinion that the British could not object to the communiqué, except on opposition to military blocs and Indochina, but on these points India was only reaffirming her existing policy.[24] On Nehru's advice, the Soviets withdrew their veto on the admission of new members to the UN, and on 14 December, sixteen countries were admitted to the UN on their initiative.

To the British, the economic communiqué of the visit revealed its 'only concrete result' – the intended purchase by India of one million tons of steel from the USSR between 1956–8. This was not to the liking of the British, who could not offer India economic aid on such favourable terms. Macdonald reported that the Indians were alive to the dangers of Soviet courtship, but they were so keen to push ahead with economic development that they looked to every quarter for assistance. The British, he warned, could no longer assume a preferential Indian friendship; they would meet with competition from elsewhere and must have a planned policy to counter it. British investments in India totalled £260 million, but the Soviets and West Germans were likely competitors. 'Prestige and political considerations aside, neither the Russians nor anyone else should be permitted to oust us in this steel manufacturing department, which lies at the core of the next Five Year Plan.'[25] The motives underlying the aid would count with India; Denis Allen thought British assistance to India should be represented as help to India herself 'and not simply as part of our Western struggle against Soviet imperialism'. This was 'fundamental', and Dulles's talk of aid to counter the Soviets was 'an object lesson in the way not to handle this whole problem'.[26] Again the British censured the Americans for messing things up.

News of a Soviet military offer to India had surfaced shortly before the Khrushchev–Bulganin visit. In the wake of India's resentment and indignation at the West, the news startled the British, who were India's main arms supplier and remained so until 1962. India was reportedly considering a Soviet offer of IL-28 aircraft, rather than the Canberra which was on offer from Britain. Indian interest in the IL-28 had been aroused during Nehru's visit to the USSR in June 1955, when Indian Air Force officers had been impressed with its performance. The big attraction of the IL-28 was the price – £135,000 as compared to £210,000 for the Canberra. The Soviets were also promising delivery within three months, whereas it would take ten months for the Canberra to be delivered. Speaking on Nehru's authority, Pillai told Macdonald on 16 November 1955 that the Indian government wanted the Canberra offer to be brought closer to the Soviet one, otherwise the substantial advantages of the Soviet machine might make it impossible to persuade the cabinet not to sanction its purchase.[27]

Coming on the heels of a Czech arms sale to Egypt two months earlier, which had broken the Western monopoly on arms supplies to the Middle East, the news of the Soviet aircraft offer to India galvanised the British to action. Eden regarded the matter 'as of the greatest importance'.[28] On his instructions, Macdonald assured Nehru that the British would be able to make their offer more attractive. He expressed British concern about India buying the IL-28. Nehru observed that India should be free to buy machines from wherever she thought best. Macdonald explained that the security of British military information was involved: Soviet technicians would come to India to ferret out the secrets of British aircraft supplied to India and there would be 'political objections' to India becoming dependent on the USSR for military supplies.[29]

The British government now despatched D.W. Haviland, Under Secretary in the Ministry of Supply, to New Delhi. Haviland reported that the Indians wanted a navigational device called "Green Satin", which incorporated technical details of US origin and would require clearance from the US. Eden's reaction mirrored his sense of urgency: 'Is that so difficult?' 'Then agree subject to this.' On Haviland's advice that the important thing was to find out the basis on which to make a deal, Eden pressed: the 'important thing is to make an offer'.[30]

The British chafed at the need for American permission to offer "Green Satin" to India; Home lamented that it could make all negotiations – and good relations – with India ' "subject to American clearance".' So the British must plan 'two bites at this cherry' – the first exploratory to counter Soviet claims and clarify India's requirements and the second, 'I would hope, definite and conclusive.'[31] The success of the British in getting the better of the Soviets would make it easier for them to combat Soviet offers in other fields.[32] Eden now approached Eisenhower for the release of material to India. The Russian intervention made it essential to clinch business with India as soon as possible and to forestall further Soviet inroads into India.[33]

Then there was the problem of delivery dates. The early supply of Canberras to India would delay deliveries to the Royal Air Force by nine months. This delay could be permitted only if it were 'absolutely essential' to make an offer to India and provided that the US accepted the reasons for it before an offer was made to India. The need for discussions with the Americans arose because £75 million in aid to the RAF was linked with the completion, by a fixed date, of a plan which included two Canberra squadrons. Details of the plan had been given in writing to the Americans. The RAF were willing to let the Indians have "Green Satin", but on condition that this would involve a delay of eighteen months, so as not to prejudice the secrecy of the device.[34] In that event, the British might not be able to satisfy the Indians on timing.

The British broached the subject with the Americans during the NATO meeting in Paris on 20 December 1955. Charles Wilson recognised the importance of preventing the sale of Soviet aircraft to India, and he agreed to delay the build-up of Canberra in the RAF, but he wished to consult Washington before releasing "Green Satin".[35] On 28 December the Defence Department consulted the Office of Munitions Control, who advised them that the information was classified. The matter would have to be taken up by the State-Defence-Military Information Committee, who would consider whether an exception could be made to the 'national disclosure policy' in order to permit the UK to sell "Green Satin".[36] The British continued to press the Americans – this time in New Delhi, where Ambassador John Sherman Cooper was sympathetic to the British view and urged the State Department to make an immediate study of the problem.[37] The State Department wanted to know how firm the Soviet offer was and whether the British could steal a march on the Soviets by selling the Canberra to India.[38] Cooper assured Washington that the Soviet offer was definite and the Indian consideration serious. A mild element of Anglo-American competition was also involved. To prove the optimal worth of their offer, the British High Commission had, 'ironically', told the Indian government that the Canberra would be quite effective against the F-86 – which the Americans were rumoured to be supplying to Pakistan – but the IL-28 would not stand a chance.[39] To news from Macdonald of Pillai's warning that unsatisfactory answers would impel the Indians to buy the IL-28, Eden pressed: 'Please let me know urgently what can be done about this.'[40] On his part, Cooper confirmed that a long delay in taking a decision would strengthen the hands of those Indian officials in favour of the IL-28. His advice had some effect in Washington. At a State-Defence-Military Information Control Committee meeting on 23 January 1956 the State Department put their weight behind the release of "Green Satin", arguing that the purchase of the IL-28 would signify a severe setback to the Western position in Asia and encourage other neutralist countries to follow India's example. The US Joint Chiefs of Staff thought security objections should be waived to keep Soviet aircraft out of India. But the US Air Force contended that the release of "Green Satin" would sacrifice its confidentiality and lead to similar requests in the future.[41] The British were on tenterhooks as the American decision hung in the balance.

The British cabinet were now brought into the picture, and they decided that the British government would waive part of the research and development levy on the Canberra which the English Electric Company (EEC) was planning to sell to India. From the economic viewpoint the sale of Canberras represented a significant deal in an important market and it would be better to forego the development levy, if by doing so the British could secure an export order worth more than £12 million, rather than lose the business altogether – 'in which case we should not get any levy either'. Four days later, Home informed the cabinet that the EEC had agreed to bring down by £10,000 their original price of each aircraft and they would reduce it by a further £20,000 if the Ministry of Supply were ready to meet this by a corresponding abatement for the levy payable on export sales on account of research and development costs. The cabinet agreed that the political considerations in favour of completing the contract outweighed the financial objections mentioned in the memoranda.[42]

By the end of January 1956 there was still no answer from the Americans, and it was now proposed to deal with them at the highest level.[43] On 1 February 1956 Eden wrote Eisenhower that the British had had 'a real struggle' to get the Indians to buy the Canberra. To win the order the British had 'cut our prices mercilessly' and switched Canberra bombers due for delivery to the RAF, and they would lose half a million pounds to get the order. Eden was clear about his priorities. 'There is no question of money in this, but only of security.'[44]

On 2 February Eisenhower and Dulles discussed the British plea on the telephone. Dulles's response was negative, but Eisenhower did not want to make an outright rejection; 'he would like to say that we had the matter under study'. A few minutes later, Dulles spoke to Radford on the telephone. The next day Radford informed him that the Air Force 'had O.K.d the British request'. Eisenhower was satisfied: 'fine, go ahead and tell Eden,' he instructed Dulles; and Dulles delivered the letter containing the news to Eden at the airport just before the latter's departure from Washington.[45]

However, Anglo–American agreement on the need to release "Green Satin" in order to prevent India from buying Soviet aircraft did not mean that the British had won out. They still had to contend with the Indian suspicion that the UK was an unreliable supplier of arms and might stop supplies in the event of war. Macdonald wanted authority to confirm that export licences for Hunters, which the British were also trying to sell India, would not be withheld in any circumstances and that spare parts for Canberras, Hunters and Gnats would not be held back because it was clear from his talks with Indian officials that 'this request was a breaking point in the negotiations'.[46] Then there was the possibility that the Indians might buy both the Canberra and the IL-28. Eden was firm that the supply of "Green Satin" to India would have to be reconsidered in that case.[47] But Home was worried about the implications of such a decision. The British might risk asking the Indians to make 'a direct choice in this field of modern military aircraft between East and West'. Also, the British must take a decision on supplies during a war. 'The issues are primarily political.'[48] Eden reiterated that concessions could not be made to the Indians if they acquired Soviet aircraft as well, and it would be impossible to give them any guarantee on continued supplies. But Macdonald should be discreet; he should not raise the matter with the Indians. If, however, he was pressed, he could say that 'all contracts would, of course, be honoured unless entirely new circumstances arose'.[49]

Dulles now lent the British a helping hand. On an official visit to New Delhi, he told Nehru on 10 March 1956 that whatever the technical justification might be for buying the IL-28, it would have a 'very bad effect' on Indo–US relations.[50] British officials were happy that Dulles 'had helped our cause'.[51] Selwyn Lloyd and Mountbatten impressed the British view on Nehru in New Delhi a few days later, and, as a friendly gesture, Nehru said his government would not buy the IL-28. However, the Indian government refused to make any long-term commitment that they would not purchase Soviet aircraft in the future.[52] With American help, the British had foiled the Soviets on this occasion, but they could take nothing for granted.

Soviet offers of economic and above all military assistance brought the whole question of India's ties with the West to the fore. India was the one Asian nation that could be built up as a counterpoise to China, and Home considered it 'vital' that India's links with the West be maintained and strengthened. It was encouraging to the British that Nehru had proclaimed India's attachment to the Commonwealth in the midst of the Russian visit, but the Soviets were out to gain a foothold in India, and, 'if we are to resist them, special efforts on our part will be required.'[53] Home outlined his plans which included more consultations, liaisons between the British and Indian armed forces, and visits by British statesmen to India. He proposed that the Freedom of the City be conferred on Nehru and that the British try to contribute to a settlement on Goa. But he turned down a suggestion by Macdonald for some statement of support for the Five Principles, in view of the propaganda uses to which they had been put by communist countries. Instead, it could be stressed that Commonwealth co-operation went further than the Five Principles in its mutual trust and joint consultation. The UK must participate in India's economic development to counter the Soviet economic offensive in Asia.[54]

Soviet economic penetration of developing countries troubled the Americans as well. It was an issue that occupied Eisenhower's attention 'for part of every waking hour I have'.[55] To Dulles, the problem assumed the magnitude of a crusade. In February 1956 he urged Eden in Washington that the West 'must be more vigorous than we have been in combatting the idea of neutralism', and he predicted that it would be difficult to prevent a communist take-over of neutral governments if they continued to adhere to their view that 'the world problem is merely a power struggle between two blocs which does not affect their countries. This kind of thinking fits right into the whole Communist conspiracy to take them over . . . he was afraid that they would eventually succumb unless they could develop a crusading spirit against the evil forces of Communism.' The US did favour countries 'that are lining up with us' and 'we should not treat neutrals better than these. But that is quite a different thing from doing nothing at all. India is a case in point.'[56] Giving aid to India was never without complications: Congressional irritation with India was only one of these. Moreover, the West might face an uphill task: in New Delhi, Cooper was struck by the skill with which Khrushchev and Bulganin had touched every sore spot with the purpose of creating ill feeling against the West. He thought the Indians were uneasy and did not want to be driven to the Soviets for assistance, and they were watching very eagerly to see what measure of help they would get in the immediate future from the West. But he feared that Indians felt 'a more natural affinity' with Russia and China than with Europe and would 'turn East naturally' for economic aid. Here Cooper was wrongly confusing ideology, political choices and race. While hoping that more American largesse would be forthcoming for India's second Five-Year Plan, he forecast that the West would not be able to match every Russian enterprise.[57] Nine years after Indian independence, Britain and the US remained India's main aid donors, yet it was impossible to predict whether their munificence would really bring her closer to the West.

III COULD THE BRITISH FIND THEIR WAY THROUGH THE INDO–US–PAKISTANI TANGLE?

Economic assistance was not the only unknown in relations between India and the West. The recurrent juxtaposition of disparate Indian and Western diplomatic interests created many a stumbling block. The Pakistan factor also remained as an obstacle to better Indo–US relations and therefore to the containment of Soviet influence in South Asia. Pakistan's alliance with the US did not render her altogether immune to neutralism, if only because of her dissatisfaction with the meagre hand-outs she received from the West. The British were embarrassed by Pakistani carping that neutralism was enabling India to obtain material from both blocs, while Pakistan was not getting what she wanted from her Western allies. The British knew it would be awkward if they paid more attention to nonaligned India than to their ally Pakistan. In spite of Pakistani membership of SEATO and the Baghdad Pact, neutralist tendencies were strong in Pakistan in the winter of 1955–6, partly because of a feeling that nonaligned countries like India and Egypt were adept at extracting the best from both worlds, while Pakistan was treated shabbily by Britain and the US. Annoyed that the British were taking her for granted and paying 'so much attention to those not so friendly',[58] Pakistan became, in March 1956, an Islamic republic within the Commonwealth, clearly dashing British hopes of forestalling this very eventuality.

It was left to the Americans to stem the unwelcome neutralist tendencies surfacing in Pakistan in 1955–6. US diplomats in Karachi noted that it was 'fashionable to be outspokenly critical of the United States'. The Pakistani people, reported the American embassy, were swayed by the same basic 'anti-Western, anti-white prejudices as are the Indians and the Near Eastern peoples who have been under colonial rule'[59] – again, political affinities of non-Western countries were simplistically identified with race. On 15 February 1956 Hildreth bluntly told Iskander Mirza that neutralism would put Pakistan at a disadvantage in relation to India. Pakistan could hardly expect preferential treatment if she followed India's example; 'if it [Pakistan] resorted to the same game then it would seem to us who were friends of Pakistan that inevitably the result must be that interest in Pakistan would diminish and the interest in India increase, due to the size and resources of India.'[60] Pakistani complaints about economic generosity to India were shrugged off by the Americans, and Dulles impressed on Mirza on 6 March 1956 that US aid to neutrals was intended to keep them from falling wholesale into the Soviet orbit. At the same time the US would not enter into a contest trying to outmatch the Soviets. 'This would be foolhardy because all the Soviets would have to expend was a little paper and ink, making an offer which they did not intend to keep and then the United States by accepting the challenge would have to spend real money or real assets.' He also made it plain that Pakistan should not be ungrateful to the US for whatever she was getting. The US was spending 'a good many billions of dollars' each year to maintain a strong, mobile striking force, which was the greatest deterrent to Soviet aggression. All the nations allied with the United States were recipients of 'this great benefit and protection to them, but too often the peoples, at least of other nations, did not realise this benefit because it did not show up as tangible evidence in their particular countries'.[61] This confirmed the Pakistani suspicion that neutrals were treated better than partners: Mirza complained that Dulles had spent six hours in conversation with Nehru and only one hour with Mohamad Ali.[62] Pakistan's dissatisfaction with the West was mirrored in her efforts to improve relations with China, and Ali advised Dulles that recognition of China by the Americans would fracture the communist bloc. Dulles remained unyielding: a Sino–Soviet quarrel would have come, 'just as ultimately there would have been a breach as [sic] between the Axis Powers, but we did not want to give the Axis Powers victory merely on the theory that later they would quarrel about the spoils.'[63] One point does emerge: the possiblity of India moving closer to the Soviets did result in the West thinking long and hard about how best to check it. The same careful consideration was not accorded to Pakistan. Perhaps because Pakistan was already in the Western camp – a disgruntled member but not likely to walk out, especially as she was quite isolated in the Middle East after she joined the Baghdad Pact – the West could ignore her complaints. This seems to have been the Anglo–American attitude to Pakistan in practice, even if it was never clearly spelt out as such. And it was evident that it would be the US which would call the tune with Pakistan.

But the American propensity to antagonise India, and so to increase Indian susceptibilities to Soviet advances, continued to worry the British. On his visit to New Delhi in March 1956, Dulles informed Nehru that the US would help Pakistan to build up five and half divisions. The programme was in arrears, and the Americans intended to speed up delivery. The Indians were uneasy, probably because they were not aware that the American commitment was to equip five and half *existing* divisions. But Indian fears were not entirely unfounded. According to the State Department, Pakistan would obtain 'more modern military equipment under the United States military aid program, which might give it a partial advantage until India obtains comparable equipment'.[64]

Having averted a purchase of Soviet aircraft by the Indians, the British were, nevertheless, keeping a watchful eye on India, as her annoyance with the West on Goa, Kashmir and alliances could make her more responsive to Soviet overtures. Home urged consultations with the US about current issues in Indo–Pakistani relations and especially on US arms supplies to Pakistan. He wanted to find out what the US was providing. Makins was 'very ready' to take up the subject with Dulles and would propose an exchange between London and Washington on their respective arms supplies to India and Pakistan. On 1 May Makins explained Indian fears to Dulles.[65] The Secretary of State was sure he had done no more than mention to Nehru the general plan and its dimensions and the fact that the US aid programme to Pakistan was well in arrears. On Eden's instructions, Makins asserted that the British needed to know how much the Americans were giving Pakistan so that they could deflate Indian anxieties and also meet Indian demands for more arms to match alleged deliveries to Pakistan. The US and UK, urged Makins, must take 'a common line' with India on this matter. The Americans should exchange information with the British on a 'very confidential basis', and the British would reciprocate about what they were giving India. They would not disclose to New Delhi what the US was supplying to Pakistan – they merely needed the information to calm Indian fears.[66]

Dulles was not very enthusiastic: side-stepping the issue, he told Makins that the Americans 'might feel a little shy' at having to disclose how far they were behind in their commitments to Pakistan. In any case they had contemplated giving India information about their arms shipments to Pakistan but had dropped the idea on the advice of Ambassador Hildreth in Karachi. For the moment they had sent only a quarter of what they had promised.[67] Nevertheless the Americans would ask the Pakistani government for permission.[68] In Karachi, Hildreth feared "heavy going" from Pakistan on the matter. The Commander-in-Chief of the Air Force was British, and the Pakistanis assumed that the British knew all that was happening 'on the air side'. But they did 'cherish the illusion' that they were safe regarding some elements of the army. Hildreth's attitude was criticised by Symon as 'thoroughly defeatist',[69] but it proved correct. On 5 June William Rountree, Deputy Assistant Secretary of State, notified the British embassy that the Pakistani government had 'categorically rejected' the proposal that Washington give London details of US military aid to Pakistan because they feared that the information might be passed on to New Delhi. The State Department did not see fit to press the matter further.[70]

Pakistani mistrust of British intentions had been clear in 1953; what was significant in 1956 was that the Americans spurned British advice that they jointly assuage Indian fears. This was in sharp contrast to American suggestions to the British during the Korean war, and on the issue of Pakistan's participation in Middle East defence in 1951, for joint Anglo–American approaches to India and Pakistan respectively. As they had wished to preserve what they saw as their special position in South Asia, it had been the *British* who earlier had held out against joint overtures.

By the summer of 1956, the tide seemed to have turned; it was the Americans who were now upholding their independent connections with India and Pakistan, in a manner that did not always please the British. In the event, British influence over the US in South Asia was simultaneously constrained by Indo–Pakistani animosity at one level and at another by the American judgement of their own interests. This worked in favour of the British on foiling Indian purchases of Soviet aircraft and against the British on information about military supplies to Pakistan. The Suez crisis was to expose further the limits of British influence in South Asia and over the United States.

IV SOUTH ASIA, THE ANGLO–AMERICAN RELATIONSHIP AND THE SUEZ CRISIS

How could we possibly support Britain and France if in doing so we lose the whole Arab world? [302nd NSC meeting, 1 November 1956]
This is a declaration of independence for the first time that they [British and French] cannot count upon us to engage in policies of this sort. [Dulles to Nixon on telephone, 31 October 1956]

If keeping Soviet bombers out of India brought home to the British that the attractiveness of their offers would be crucial to preserving their influence in India, and that American co-operation would be essential to head off the Soviets, the Suez crisis showed how easily the influence of the British could wane in the absence of a shared outlook with not only nonaligned India but also Pakistan, their ally in the Baghdad Pact, and the United States – the mainstay of their post-war foreign policy. It confirmed the trend, discernible in Korea and Indochina, that friends were more amenable to influence if they had common goals *and* similar ideas about the means to achieve them; if the interests of Britain were seen by her friends as too disparate from theirs, the odds were against British views carrying much weight.

Eden and Home were bitter at India and the US for their lack of support during the Suez operation, while, much later, Macmillan claimed that India and Pakistan had shown 'remarkable sympathy [towards Britain] in spite of their natural doubts'.[71] A study of the diplomatic interaction between London, Washington and New Delhi after Nasser's nationalisation of the Canal on 26 July 1956 will demonstrate whether the Eden–Home plaint or the Macmillan gloss was justified, what attention the British paid to the opinions expressed by American and Indian officials between July and October 1956 and whether they deluded themselves into thinking that the US and India were on their side. This account will also focus some attention on Pakistani reactions to the Suez crisis because British records reveal that the fissures between Pakistan and Britain went deeper than those between the UK and India, to the extent that the government of H.S. Suhrawardy was on the verge of succumbing to public pressure to quit the Commonwealth in November 1956. Much has been made of a crisis in the Commonwealth resulting from an Indo–British rift, while differences with Pakistan have barely received a passing mention, although the CRO admitted in December 1956 that in Pakistan the public reaction 'was if anything more hostile than that of India'. In this section, the main focus is on what the Suez crisis revealed about the extent of British influence in South Asia and over the United States.

Nasser announced the nationalisation of the Suez Canal on 26 July 1956, just after returning to Cairo from Brioni, where he had conferred with Tito and Nehru. The immediate cause of the nationalisation was the withdrawal of American aid for the Aswan dam, and Nasser had shown Nehru on their flight from Brioni to Cairo the text of Dulles's speech announcing the suspension of American assistance for the dam. Nehru was struck by Dulles's arrogant tone. But Nasser had said nothing about nationalisation to either Tito or Nehru at Brioni, and Nehru was certain that he took the decision to nationalise the Canal only after returning to Cairo. The chronology of events bears this out: the American statement was made on 19 July; Nasser had been out of Egypt for ten days before that, Nehru had left Cairo on 21 July – five days before the nationalisation was announced. Nehru was unpleasantly surprised when he read the news on his return to New Delhi. His first thought was that the Egyptian government was 'undertaking more than it can manage and is being pushed by some extremist elements and by angry reaction to American and British refusal to help the Aswan dam project'. Under the Convention of 1886, Egypt had a right to nationalise the Canal, but the manner in which it was done and the offensive tone of the Egyptian government's declaration made it difficult to reach any agreement acceptable to both sides under which the Canal would remain an open waterway. It was important not to inflame international tensions. India could not champion Nasser out of a blind anti-imperialism, for she was a member of the Commonwealth and had close ties with Britain. For the moment, India would simply avoid taking sides.[72]

In Britain, it is clear that, on 27 July 1956, the cabinet had decided to reverse the nationalisation by force of arms if necessary. On the same day the Egypt Committee of the cabinet decided that 'while our ultimate purpose was to place the canal under international control, our immediate objective was to bring about the downfall of the present Egyptian government'.[73] These decisions should be seen in the context of the British desire to retain primacy in the Middle East, which they equated politically and emotionally with the very survival of Britain herself. Although the cabinet acknowledged that Nasser had done nothing illegal – he was only buying out the shareholders – to admit this publicly would not accord with Britain's interests. The cabinet saw Britain waging a life and death struggle with Nasser, an apocalyptic vision fed by British intelligence reports since the signing of an arms deal between Egypt and the USSR in October 1955. Nasser was a cat's-paw of the Soviets.[74] For that reason alone, every effort to depose him would be justified.

The British then sought American support for their designs. Writing to Eisenhower on 27 July 1956, Eden urged that 'we must be ready, in the last resort, to use force to bring Nasser to his senses.'[75] This statement of intent worried the Americans. Although Eisenhower voiced his grave concern at Nasser's invectives against the US,[76] the Americans deemed the nationalisation to be within Egypt's rights, and until her operation of the Canal proved incompetent, 'there was nothing to do.' In conversation with Nixon on 30 July, Dulles feared that the British and French were 'really anxious to start a war and get us into it'. He was doing his best to make them realise they might have to do it alone.[77]

The next day came the news that the British had taken a firm decision to take military action in six weeks' time. Eisenhower deprecated this as unwise and 'out of date', since the situation could easily take on the colours of a conflict between nationalism and colonialism. The tension should be defused; Nasser should not be given 'undue stress', since he embodied the demands of the people of the area for independence and for ' "slapping the white Man down" '. Military action might 'array the world from Dakar to the Philippine Islands against us'. In any case, military intervention was probably unnecessary: in Dulles' memorably inelegant phrase, Nasser could be made to 'disgorge what he has seized, and agree to internationalize the Canal'. Dulles recognised that such a policy 'would not serve the French and British interests in the Middle East and Africa so dramatically . . . they felt a bolder action was necessary. Such [action] did not necessarily represent our interest, however.'[78] The consensus among American officials was that internationalisation could be achieved without force, and Eisenhower communicated this view to Eden on 31 July 1956.[79] Any measures to internationalise the Canal should be taken on the broadest possible basis, involving all the maritime powers and the Americans should steer clear of precipitate action with the British and French. The British should try to carry world opinion with them.[80] On Suez the Americans were just as determined to avoid military action as the British had been in Indochina two years earlier. The American desire to secure the widest possible support for international control of the Canal was reminiscent of the British wish for broad support for a negotiated settlement at Geneva in 1954. In both cases, British and American attitudes were shaped by their perceptions of their respective interests. The American concern for keeping the Canal functioning as an international waterway was not identified with *Britain's* survival – whether as a great or little power. Nor were the Americans persuaded that Nasser was the handmaid of the Soviets; Eisenhower, in fact, thought nothing should be done to push Nasser into a Soviet embrace. There was every possibility of negotiating with him, and force was ruled out. Both in aim and in method the Americans distanced themselves from the British within less than a week of the nationalisation.

So did other British allies including Canada and Australia. Some ambivalent backing for the British position came, interestingly enough, from Pakistan, whose government was the most unstable in the Commonwealth. Domestic instability partly accounted for the Pakistani stand. The government of H.S. Suhrawardy was torn between its desire for military links with the West and its political need to identify with the 'Muslim' world, especially against the background of India's friendliness with Egypt. But Pakistan's accession to the Baghdad Pact in 1955 had aroused the hostility of Egypt, and top Pakistani officials had no qualms about running Nasser down. The animosity between Pakistan and Egypt precluded Pakistani mediation between the UK and Egypt, whereas good Indo–British and Indo–Egyptian relations cast India in a mediatory role between her two friends. That role put India in the limelight and could explain Home and Eden's bitter resentment of India, given that their expectations – however illusory – of her were greater than of Pakistan. Picking up the British picture of Nasser as a Soviet agent, Pakistani officials craftily contrasted public Soviet support of ' "so-called neutrals" (e.g. India, Saudi Arabia and Egypt)' with the hesitation and even refusal of Western countries to side with their friends. The Pakistanis confided that they supported the British but they could not show a lack of sympathy with ' "another Muslim people" '. At the same time they affirmed that the nationalisation of the Canal was legal and that Britain would be isolated if she resorted to force against Nasser.[81]

But the advice of many friendly countries against military action fell on deaf British (and French) ears. (This account will concentrate on the

British.) Having met Eden, Salisbury, Macmillan and Pineau in London on 2 August, Dulles was worried that Britain and France were bent upon military intervention unless Nasser accepted international control of the Canal. Dulles thought that he had, for the moment, persuaded Britain and France to make a 'genuine effort' to mobilise world opinion in favour of an international solution, but when it came to applying the principles, 'they are inclined to procedures which I fear will in fact alienate world opinion.'[82]

This was borne out by the British posture in their talks with Indian officials in New Delhi and London. For his part, Nehru was anxious to calm the situation, and he implored Nasser to take some diplomatic initiative. The British had agreed to Dulles's suggestion to convene a Conference of Maritime Nations (London Conference) to discuss international control of the Canal, and they had hopes of getting round India. On 2 August Macdonald reported that Indian views were still in a formative stage, and there was 'a chance of our influencing them in our favour'.[83] But Macdonald's own reports from New Delhi reveal that an Indo–British rift was in the making. On 4 August Menon and Pillai told Macdonald that the crucial question was whether Egypt would accept the invitation to the London Conference. This should not include any prior conditions. In a letter to Eden on 5 August, Nehru emphasised the futility of laying down any prior conditions about the acceptance of an international authority by Egypt.[84] Eden assured Nehru that attendance at the conference did not imply prior acceptance of internationalisation; 'though of course we shall seek agreement on that principle at the Conference.'[85]

Although Indian officials were critical of the manner in which Nasser had nationalised the Canal, they thought he should not be provoked but given the opportunity to rethink his policy. In any case, Indian and Asian public opinion would make it impossible for India to side with Britain against Egypt, and opposition to Nasser could prejudice the chances of India persuading him to modify his policy. For the moment, the Indian government were uncertain as to what could be done. They were, however, concerned at the talk of military measures in Britain. To the Indians, Nasser himself appeared inflexible at times; and he wanted India to team up with Egypt in boycotting the London Conference. After some hesitation about attending a conference at which Egypt would not be represented, Nehru turned down this suggestion on the plea that India would work for conciliation. This was the need of the hour, and there was a dose of rebuke in Nehru's advice to Nasser that any unilateral action by one country or group of countries would spoil the chances of conciliation and compromise.[86] For their part, the Egyptians were simultaneously worried and piqued at what they saw as Nehru's intellectualising, his desire to weigh all sides of the question and to be all things to all men.[87]

Playing the role of the honest broker, India seemed fated to annoy both Egypt and Britain. The outlook for conciliation seemed gloomy, as Eden and his colleagues had conjured up the horrifying vision that Nasser could 'strangle us at will'.[88] Nehru's attitude angered the British: his parliamentary speech on 8 August was considered one-sided by Malcolm Macdonald, evidence of the Indian tendency to express public sympathy with anti-colonialists quarrelling with the West, 'without being as fair in public as in private to the West'.[89] But Macdonald consoled himself – and possibly his audience in London – that Nehru could not publicly reveal his 'sympathy' for the British. Yet the gap between New Delhi and London was becoming more evident, as Pillai and Menon urged recognition of Egypt's right to nationalise the Canal if there was to be a peaceful and amicable settlement.[90] But to Eden, who was determined to bring down Nasser, it appeared that India was striking a balance between the West and Egypt, in spite of Nasser's "Hitlerian" methods, and he departed from the circumspect tone normally used by British officials in their diplomatic memos: 'It would seem hardly surprising that we should be concerned at a man with this record having his thumb on our windpipe.'[91] Blinkered by their memories of the thirties, Eden, Lloyd, Home and Macmillan among others saw Britain locked in a life-or-death struggle against an Egyptian Hitler or Mussolini. The Indians did not go along with this opinion of Nasser. Nehru's 'tentative estimate' was that Nasser was inexperienced and narrow-minded as was to be expected of an army officer who had not been outside his country until eighteen months ago – nothing worse, while Menon did not consider him a paranoiac. Both tended to believe that he had moderated his cabinet's attitude to Israel and that he was not basically hostile to the West.[92]

But with talk of war in the air, the Indians were becoming suspicious of British motives. On 14 August 1956 Pillai asked Norman Brook, secretary to the cabinet, whether the British wanted international control of the Canal or whether their 'real objective' was to overthrow Nasser. Brook's not very subtle answer was that Britain's 'primary objective' was to establish a satisfactory international control of the Canal, but they would not be sorry if such an arrangment 'destroyed' Nasser's position in Egypt and the Middle East. It would be dangerous 'for us all that Nasser should become a successful leader of the Arab world'.[93] Eden had notified Eisenhower on 27 July and 5 August about the British desire to topple Nasser, but Brook's conversation with Pillai was probably the first inkling given to the Indians of this intention.

In fact, the British and French had started military talks in early August, and on 10 August the Chiefs of Staff presented the Egypt Committee with a plan named "Musketeer", which envisaged a straightforward assault on Alexandria on 15 September and the overthrow of Nasser.[94] Knowing that Britain would mobilise little support – either from the Commonwealth or from the US – for such a venture, the Suez Committee deliberately sought to avoid any discussion at the forthcoming London Conference on the Indian point about Egypt's right to nationalise the Canal.[95]

A rare meeting of minds had emerged between India and the US in attempting to restrain Britain. In Washington American officials welcomed Nehru's parliamentary statement of 8 August. It was one of those exceptional occasions when Nehru even earned applause from Dulles, that hater of "immoral" nonalignment, and Nehru was pleased to receive from him 'a very friendly personal message'.[96] Nehru's political calibre had also impressed Eisenhower, who hoped that he and the Indian Prime Minister would be able to ease some of the tension.[97]

Involved in 'the most difficult and dangerous situation in international affairs [that] we have faced since independence', Nehru's government concentrated their energies on breaking the deadlock. It proved a thankless task. Nasser, for one, was a difficult customer. Miffed at Nehru's tepid support for Egypt, Nasser feared that he might influence other nonaligned countries. En route to the London Conference, Menon stopped at Cairo. To Menon, Nasser acknowledged that he had been precipitate, but he was unyielding on international control of the Canal.[98] All did not seem lost to Menon, and he still hoped to secure a compromise. In London, Menon sought to persuade the West to negotiate with Egypt on the basis of her sovereignty – only to be embarrassed by the unexpected Soviet endorsement of India's stand. The reasons were not far to seek. The Indian recommendations were at variance with an American proposal, which called upon Egypt to accept operation of the Canal by an international board on which she would be represented but would not control. In effect, the management of the Canal would be taken out of Egyptian hands. This reflected Dulles's conviction that the international board 'should not be wholly under Egypt's political control', for he held that 'there could be no universal confidence in Egypt's ability alone' to administer the Canal. At the same time, the British and French should not be led to believe that the Americans would support 'any kind of precipitous [sic] action they may take.'[99] Dulles regarded the Indian position as untenable, and his cold warrior mind visualised, not very accurately, that 'the ultimate line-up will be almost entirely the West on one side and Asia on the other side with the Soviet Union on the Asian side.'[100]

On 20 August 1956 Menon formally presented the Indian proposals to the London Conference. They suggested minority representation of international user interests on an Egyptian corporation running the Canal, a consultative body of user interests, and submission by Egypt of annual reports to the UN. Dulles thought the proposals were 'all right as generalities' which could be accepted by Nasser without any assurance whatsoever that the Canal would not merely cater to Egypt's political interests. He dismissed Menon's references to international bodies as 'pure scenery'.[101] The British were furious because they thought the Indian proposals indulged and extenuated Nasser and hardly went beyond reaffirming Egypt's sovereignty over the Canal and the need to rely on her word.[102] If the international boards only had an advisory function, Nasser could discriminate against individual nations or act arbitrarily in raising dues.[103] Nehru understood British misgivings but stressed that no solution could be imposed on Egypt. The real dilemma, as he saw it, was not the Suez Canal but all the fears and apprehensions, the vested interests and the new urges that lay behind the conflict between a rising Arab nationalism and such Western control as existed in the Middle East. For Indian officials, the problem was how to coax Egypt into negotiations and then to accept a reasonable settlement in the course of the negotiations. Designed to achieve the first of these purposes, the proposals presented by Menon in London were 'necessarily couched in general terms and did not contain the last thoughts of India on the details of a settlement'. The Indians hoped that once diplomatic parleys began, it might be possible to talk Nasser into making further concessions. But it would be politically impossible to get Nasser into negotiations which postulated that he would have to undo the nationalisation.[104]

Nasser's dislike of the Indian proposals went undetected by both Britain and the US. Nasser was unhappy with the suggestions that one-third of the directors of the international boards should be from user countries and that if Egypt's decision to bar Israeli ships from the Canal as an act of war provoked a dispute, she should abide by the verdict of the International Court of Justice. His objections went so far that Menon had to tell him to counter the impression that India had no influence in Cairo. But it was in vain, and Nehru sadly recognised the limits of Indian influence on Nasser.[105]

The US, meanwhile, had its own axe to grind. Dulles wanted the US proposal to be accepted by the London Conference, but without the agreement of India and Egypt, it could easily acquire shades of "colonialism". To avoid charges that the US was bolstering imperial allies, Dulles persuaded Pakistan, Turkey and Iran to introduce the American proposal as their own with some nominal amendments. Thus obliged, he was satisfied that these countries were 'now definitely committed to our program', making it 'not just a Western program but one with Asian and African support'.[106] Appearances obviously counted, and the Americans were satisfied when eighteen out of the twenty-two countries attending the conference voted for their proposal.

But Anglo–American agreement on international control of the Canal never meant US endorsement of military action, as many British officials, including Eden, Lloyd and Home seem to have inferred. How they assumed this is mystifying, given that Dulles told them more than once that the US would not countenance 'a military venture'.[107] Also, in his missives to Eden, Eisenhower was continually unimpressed by British allegations that Nasser was acting at Russia's behest; he repeatedly tried to dissuade Eden from using force, and on 8 September he warned Eden that force against Nasser 'might have consequences even more serious than causing the Arabs to support Nasser. It might cause a serious misunderstanding between our two countries.'[108]

A group from the London conference, led by Sir Robert Menzies, the Australian Prime Minister, now went to Cairo to persuade Nasser to accept the Eighteen-Power Proposals. The Egyptians would not budge. Dulles was sympathetic to Britain and France on international control of the Canal, and he thought the British and French would argue that they had gone as far as they could but had been rebuffed by Nasser. To avoid a stalemate, he suggested the formation of a Suez Canal Users' Association (SCUA), which would attempt to keep up the momentum of the London Conference. The SCUA would hire pilots, collect fees and manage the Canal. Neither he nor Eisenhower were sure that it would work, but Dulles thought 'we had to keep the initiative and to keep probing along various lines, particularly since there was no chance of getting the British and the French not to use force', unless viable alternatives were presented to them.[109]

What could be done now? Nasser himself seemed interested in breaking the deadlock, and he approached Nehru to get negotiations started on the basis of the legitimate concerns of user interests but without international control. On 10 September Nehru welcomed the Egyptian proposals and urged Eden and Eisenhower to press for a negotiated settlement. But he did not get anywhere even with the Americans, who were still far removed from the Egyptian position. Anxious to stave off a diplomatic breakdown, Nehru and Menon tried to persuade Nasser to accept the SCUA,[110] but they encountered no success. As Nehru had foreseen, both sides were displeased with India.

The British now saw themselves parting company with India, who in their view favoured Egypt: Home grumbled that India's role had been helpful to Egypt and the consequences could be serious. This reveals Home's bias better than anything else, for one has only to read Heikal's account to recognise Egypt's annoyance at what she saw as Indian vacillation. From the hindsight of more than thirty years, it seems strange to read that Indo–British differences had made Home 'anxious that we should not break with India'.[111] But if he saw a break coming, it was probably because the extreme ideas of overturning the nationalisation by force and the destruction of Nasser were in his mind. For Home, making his first foray into international relations following his appointment as Secretary of State for Commonwealth Relations in April 1955 and fed with advice from Laithwaite, now Permanent Under Secretary at the CRO, was – along with Eden and Macmillan – among the most hawkish of British officials. Satisfied that British sabre-rattling was upsetting India, Home conjured up the possibility that the more the Indians feared war, 'the more inclined they will be to turn their pressure on to Nasser'.[112] In other words, the British were threatening war to bring Nasser to heel. Nehru was dismayed at Eden's belligerent speech in the Commons on 13 September and urged him not to put the clock back in respect of the national status of newly independent nations.[113] Perhaps the British were hoping that India could bring Nasser over to their viewpoint under threat of war. This explains Home's counsel to Eden that India could be the instrument of their policy – which does sound rather odd given his concomitant thought that India was pandering to Nasser. Home prepared for Eden a draft letter to Nehru, urging him to see the merits of British policy and to impress them upon Nasser. Eden himself added in the draft words to the effect that Nehru had 'great' influence with Nasser and suggested that Menon visit Cairo and endeavour to persuade him that 'our proposals are consistent with Egyptian sovereignty. I am sure he could make an immense contribution'.[114] In fact, this really implied that the British had no intention of accepting any compromise, and authorities as varied as the Pakistani government and Dag Hammarskjöld, the UN Secretary-General, feared that they had abandoned negotiations.[115]

While Eden and Home sulked over the limited Indian support for their plans, trouble was brewing with Pakistan. Domestic support for Nasser had made it impossible for Suhrawardy's government to back Britain openly – which they claimed they wanted to do – and Pakistan disapproved of the attempt to impose the SCUA on Egypt. The functions of the Association had been announced without consulting other countries, and it looked like 'a preliminary to shooting it out with Egypt'. Pakistan might not even attend the Users' conference in London. Firoz Khan Noon, now Pakistani Foreign Minister, clarified that his government sympathised with the British, but they could not give 'open help as the people of Pakistan were ignorantly and violently pro-Nasser'.[116] Caught between his government's professed desire to side with the British and a rabidly anti-British public opinion, Noon was the only representative at the London conference to inveigh against the Users' Association. An actual vote by Pakistan against the SCUA would have been most embarrassing to the British, and it is a measure of their lack of influence in Pakistan that they now approached the Americans to head off a Pakistani attack on the Association.

On 20 September 1956 the CRO instructed Morrice James, the Acting High Commissioner in Karachi, to make the 'most urgent representations' to Suhrawardy and President Iskander Mirza to authorise Noon to say that a Pakistani decision on the SCUA would be taken when Noon returned to Karachi. Dulles concurred with this approach, and the next day he and Lloyd jointly drafted a telegram to Hildreth and James, instructing them on 'an urgent basis' to point out to the President and Prime Minister of Pakistan 'the catastrophic effects' of any change in Pakistani foreign policy.[117] James spoke to Hildreth, both met Suhrawardy, and Hildreth practically ordered Suhrawardy: ' "I take it that [the] Pakistan Cabinet will give a final decision on [the] S.C.U.A. after Noon comes back and reports." ' Suhrawardy would then direct Noon to use the following formula at the conference: ' "The revised proposals will be referred to my

Government." ' Both Hildreth and James were satisfied that this was the maximum that could have been achieved. To Eden, it meant little: 'Not much gain, I fear'.[118] Suhrawardy obeyed Hildreth's instructions grudgingly, and James suggested that a personal message from Eden might flatter his streak of 'inordinate vanity'.[119] Suhrawardy resented being treated as a pawn in the game and might respond well if he thought he had a personal role to play. A missive from Eden could be flourished in the National Assembly as a personal success and might help him to keep his extremist supporters at bay. Acting on James's advice, Eden duly wrote Suhrawardy a suitably honeyed note on 23 September. Dulles also sent Suhrawardy a message, exhorting him that the solidarity of the Baghdad Pact was of vital importance for its future.[120]

Leaving nothing to chance, Hildreth and James then met President Iskander Mirza. According to Hildreth's account, Mirza had stressed that Suhrawardy must support the West and that he would back Suhrawardy 'so long as Suhrawardy did not cross him on foreign policy'. The substance of James's message to the CRO was quite similar. James recounted that Mirza had echoed the Pakistani military's dislike of Suhrawardy and asserted that he should not be deterred from supporting 'Pakistan's true friends'. He repeated with great firmness 'his determination to keep Suhrawardy on the rails and to take strong action if necessary'. He would even dismiss Suhrawardy – his 'keen hope [was] that if he had to take over the country people in Britain and America would not say he had done so for personal ends'.[121] It was all too clear that the limited British influence in Pakistan meant that American help was necessary to prevent Pakistan's domestic imbroligios from unleashing a diplomatic storm. The Americans used their clout over the Pakistani elites to stop them from succumbing to Pakistani public opinion. As the Americans had initiated the plan for a SCUA, their own interests were also at stake, and it was one of the few occasions on which they and the British acted in concert during the Suez crisis.

For the rest, the Americans found the British intransigent, and they doubted whether the British really wanted a peaceful solution. Something might be afoot against Nasser, and Eisenhower was firm that the Americans would not join any covert operations against him.[122] Thinking that Nehru might be able to help, Eisenhower wondered if the Americans should be 'more specific in our communications with Nehru in the hope that he could influence Nasser into negotiations'.[123] No firm decision was taken, but the Americans assumed that India would continue her efforts to talk Nasser into modifying his stand.[124]

The Indians, however, did not get very far with either the Egyptians or the British. Menon made it clear to Humphrey Trevelyan, British Ambassador in Cairo, that the establishment of an international operating board would amount to the creation of a new Canal company which would be inconsistent with nationalisation, which India recognised as being within

Egypt's sovereignty. Finally, he added that if the real issue was 'the dangers of Nasser to Western interests', India would not be able to help.[125] The Indians and British were talking at cross purposes. Eden and Home were obsessed by the vision of Nasser accepting one agreement but repeating the whole performance at some later date.[126] Eden was adamant that Nasser should not be judged by the world to have got away with it. This was a constant refrain in Eden's missives to Nehru and Eisenhower. On 2 October Menon made another suggestion, which would enable Egypt to enter into co-operation with a SCUA. Such co-operation would include advice, consultation and liaison.[127] Britain found the proposals 'nebulous and incomplete' and stood firm on the Eighteen-Power proposals.[128] Having at first called for Menon to mediate with Egypt, Eden, Lloyd and Home now questioned his role. The only 'useful function' he might have would be in trying to discover Nasser's views and to impress upon him the need to accept the Eighteen-Power proposals.[129]

A ding-dong exchange ensued between Indian and British officials, with Nehru and Menon stressing that no settlement would be possible on the basis of the Eighteen-Power proposals; and the British sticking to their view that Egypt should not be left in unfettered control of the Canal and that it should be impossible for a future Egyptian government to repeat the 'act of brigandage' of which Nasser had been guilty.[130]

In Washington the mood was pessimistic, and American officials did not want the British and French to expect too much of the US. Dulles felt the British and French were irritated because they had realised that they could not count on the US outside NATO 'automatically', but the US should not try to buy pro-American sentiment by leading them to feel that 'we will blindly support them in any course which they may wish to pursue'.[131] London emphasised the need for military measures on the grounds that the Middle East was menaced by Egyptian and Soviet-instigated subversion, but Eisenhower was determined that the Americans would not join them, and he contemplated issuing a statement containing 'a frank warning that the United States will not support a war or warlike moves in the Suez area. It would insist that negotiations must be continued until a peaceful but just solution is reached – regardless of how long is [sic] takes.'[132]

By mid-October there were unconfirmed reports that Nasser had accepted the Indian proposals.[133] But these rumours were unduly optimistic. For the British and French had started talks with Israel on staging a military operation to occupy the Canal. On 29 October Israel attacked Egypt, and Britain and France intervened on the pretext of keeping the Canal open to international traffic. Under the terms of the Tripartite Agreement of 1950, the US, Britain and France were to defend Egypt, but the British and French were now evasive about invoking their commitments, and on 30 October they vetoed a US-sponsored resolution condemning Israel in the UN.

The Americans were outraged: 'nothing justifies double-crossing us',[134] thundered Eisenhower. The general feeling in Washington was that Britain had tried to force the Americans into a position in which they would have to choose between their European allies and the Arabs; she had assumed that the US would not let its partners 'go under economically' and would take extraordinary measures to help them. Extremely angry, Eisenhower 'did not see much value in an unworthy and unreliable ally . . . the necessity to support them might not be as great as they believed'.[135] The British and French 'should be left to work out their own oil problems – to boil in their own oil, so to speak'.[136] The President reportedly vowed that he would never forgive Eden for what he had done.[137] Britain and France had acted 'deliberately contrary to the clearest advice we could possibly give them'.[138] The US had everything to lose by siding with them and everything to gain by opposing them. The Americans had found more international support for their position 'than we have secured at any time in our history'. Until now the Americans had walked the tightrope between their colonial allies and independent states. They could not walk the tightrope any longer. If they did, Afro–Asian countries would turn to the USSR. It was really a question of preventing the Soviets from seizing the mantle of world leadership, since most Afro–Asian nations hated at least one of the three – Britain, France or Israel. The global primacy of the US was at stake; 'the United States would survive or go down on the basis of the fate of colonialism'.[139] Suez came to be seen as a colonial issue by the Americans – 'this action is in the mid-Victorian style' – and not a cold-war contest, as the British presented it. The British had taken military action to survive as a great power; the Americans saw the Anglo–French intervention as impairing *their* global hegemony in the cold war. The two allies were clearly acting at cross-purposes: Britain invoked the cold war to draw in the US; the US invoked the cold war to take a stand against Britain in 1956.

The situation had to be defused, if only because the Soviet invasion of Hungary on 29 October 1956 had threatened to make the "real" cold war hot. At this juncture, the Americans did not want Britain and France to bear the brunt of condemnation for imperialist aggression,[140] and they discussed the possibility of a joint appeal for peace by Nehru and Eisenhower. Suez momentarily appeared to have buried old Indo–US antipathies. Before the Suez crisis, it had usually been the British who wanted Indian representation in diplomatic parleys and the Americans who had objected to it. The Americans had similar hopes of Nehru during the Suez crisis as the British had had in the Asian cold war – to restrain their ally. The difference was that earlier it had been the British who had tried to rein in the Americans; now it was the Americans who were trying to moderate the British. Nonalignment appeared to have demonstrated its uses as an instrument of diplomatic prudence and sanity. Eisenhower's respect for Nehru was evident from his willingness to meet Nehru '[i]f the UN would want him to' because he thought that he and Nehru 'came closer to commanding the respect of the world and it would make it difficult for the world to turn down our proposal'.[141] On 6 November 1956, Eisenhower sent a message to Nehru imploring him to use his 'great influence with the British government' to urge them to accept the American cease-fire plan. India should also serve on a UN peacekeeping force – 'your action would have a most calming and beneficial effect upon the entire situation.'[142]

The stakes in winning over India extended beyond Suez. In the wake of the Soviet assault on Hungary, American policy-makers saw a fresh opportunity to sharpen the anti-communist edge of nonalignment. Having found a rare coincidence of outlook on the Suez crisis, American officials were somewhat disappointed at Nehru's slow and muted reaction to the Soviet aggression in Hungary. To Eisenhower the explanation was that 'Nehru thinks of only one thing, which is colonialism, by which he means the white over colored people.' He would nevertheless write to Nehru to say they were witnessing 'colonialism by the bayonet' in Hungary. Even Nixon, who had earlier warned against hailing Nehru as the voice of Asia, saw in the Soviet invasion an unprecedented opportunity to win Nehru over to the West. If Nehru could line up with the West over Hungary, 'Russia would be ruined in Asia', and he wondered if Nehru's visit to the US could be expedited.[143]

For the moment, the Indians were preoccupied with the Suez crisis. Nehru was shocked that Britain and France had associated themselves with aggression and intervention – he did not know that they had actually colluded with Israel – and, in the circumstances, there was no question about Indian support for Egypt.

It was Pakistan, Britain's ally in SEATO and the Baghdad Pact, who turned sharply against the British and stirred up the greatest turmoil in the Commonwealth. Suhrawardy warned that the Anglo–French intervention would have 'calamitous consequences'. Britain and France had thrown down the gauntlet before all Arab countries, who would unite against the West, and the Pakistani government might find it difficult to remain in the Baghdad Pact. The Pakistani government would endorse the summoning of the UN General Assembly and the official US stand. Privately, Pakistani officials had backed the British: on 31 October, Noon had said that without the use of force Nasser would not come to the negotiating table. But the Pakistanis were critical of Britain's choice of allies: the French who were 'burning to revenge themselves on Nasser' because he supported nationalists in their North African colonies; and the Israelis who would completely compromise Britain's position in the eyes of the Muslim world. Pakistan was also stunned by the British veto of the American resolution condemning Israel. With an eye on Kashmir, Pakistani officials pointed out that if the founding members of the UN defied it, it would hardly be possible for small states to survive.[144]

Suhrawardy's own party put pressure on his government to take Pakistan out of the Commonwealth. A soothing message from Eden had little effect on him, and on 2 November Suhrawardy told Morrice James that he might have to make an announcement very soon. Playing for time, James asked Suhrawardy to give him a chance to notify Eden to consider the position before making a public statement. Suhrawardy was unwilling to make such a promise. Meanwhile, a sharp outburst of anti-British feeling in Pakistan compelled the Pakistani authorities to advise the cancellation of Attlee's forthcoming visits to Lahore and Peshawar.[145]

It was now the Americans and Australians who came to Britain's rescue. Apprehensive that Pakistan's departure from the Commonwealth would harm the West, the State Department did not want the Soviets to acquire diplomatic benefits from the Suez crisis.[146] The Commonwealth loyalist, Sir Robert Menzies, dissuaded Pakistan from quitting and from making an anti-Commonwealth statement. On 9 November Suhrawardy agreed to Menzies' request to refrain from making any statement until the Baghdad Pact meeting, but he pointed out that the Anglo–French intervention had endangered the safety of all small nations. There could be no question of a Baghdad Pact when one of the parties to it had committed aggression. It would be difficult to remain in the Commonwealth 'when its very head is regarded throughout the Muslim world from which Pakistan cannot divorce itself as an aggressor'.[147] It was obvious that *British* influence had not been sufficient to hold Pakistan in the Commonwealth.

A.C.B. Symon, the High Commissioner in Karachi, was not slow to learn this painful lesson. Suez had impressed upon the Pakistanis that the UK 'is no longer able singlehanded, to maintain its position and succour its allies in the Middle East. It is felt that we tried "to go it alone" and failed and that henceforward we shall never be in a position to try . . . again.' Pakistan would emphasise co-operation with the US, and look to the US 'for many of the things (including physical protection and even moral leadership) that she formerly expected to obtain from the United Kingdom'. This, in turn, would have an effect 'on the relative standing of the United Kingdom and the United States in Pakistan'.[148]

Meanwhile, the Australian and New Zealand governments supported Britain, but there was no public rallying to Britain in any Commonwealth country. From the CRO Gilbert Laithwaite observed, with some understatement, that 'the effect of our actions had been greater than had been expected'. But a CRO note admitted that the British 'took the decision to go into Egypt with full awareness how strong Indian and Pakistani reactions would be'.[149] In India there was a wave of hostility to Britain and the Commonwealth, and even conservative politicians demanded that India withdraw her membership. Nehru quickly scotched rumours that India would leave the Commonwealth and added for good measure that such a serious step would not be taken on the spur of the moment. Defending his government's stand, Nehru argued that the operation reflected the aberration of Eden's government and did not necessarily mirror the wishes of the British people as a whole.[150]

The Commonwealth remained intact, but the CRO blamed India and Pakistan for their tendency to assume that, 'any action taken in the name of nationalism is justified and that any attempt to prevent the damage which comes from the abuses of nationalism is to be resisted.' Relations with them should be re-established 'on a basis of frankness and realism'.[151]

What would the new frankness imply? From London, Vijayalakshmi Pandit, now High Commissioner and a confirmed Anglophile, was saddened that it would take the British a long time to recover their prestige in India, but they were 'still more popular and more trusted than the Americans'. But from New Delhi, Malcolm Macdonald reported on the vehemence of Indian feeling, the sense of shock at the British action. Indian officials from the Army, Navy and old Indian Civil Service had been appalled at the intervention. The 'tragic truth' was that Britain's moral authority in Asia had plummeted, and Macdonald thought the US and Canada had taken the UK's place as the countries 'most trusted by India in international affairs'.[152] St. Laurent of Canada also noticed room for a much better understanding between India and the US.[153] The Americans themselves noted that Suez marked the first occasion when they and the Indians had been on the same side against their Western allies and thought that the moment was propitious for India and the US to sink their differences and come closer to each other.[154]

The irony was that their common opposition to Britain had given Indo–US relations a fresh lease of life. British officials no longer wrote of acting as a bridge between India and the US – in fact they had failed to narrow the gap when India and the US had divergent interests and outlooks. It was the Americans who were now taking the initiative to exploit the opportunity provided by the Suez crisis and the Soviet invasion of Hungary to woo India more definitively to the Western bloc.

As for the Anglo–American relationship itself, British officials saw themselves renegotiating it. The British case would be strengthened if the Suez crisis were portrayed as a part of the cold war. The Americans, minuted Paul Gore-Booth, should not give 'aid and comfort to a combination of Russia and Colonel Nasser at the expense of the United States' Western allies'. But there was little regret or recognition that Britain might have followed the wrong course, rather a lament from Hankey that without US opposition the operation might have been more successful than it was and, 'Nasser might well by now have been out of power and the whole Middle East situation transformed.'[155]

Suez became an emotive and rancorous issue in Anglo–American relations. Harold Caccia, who had replaced Makins as ambassador in November 1956, was glad that the post-war period of ' "old boyism" ' was at an end. 'We have now passed the point where we are talking to friends. We are negotiating a business deal . . . we are dealing with an Administration of business executives who rightly or wrongly consider that they are animated by the highest principles.' The alliance should be renegotiated, issue by issue, on China, NATO, sterling, 'but without mincing matters at any point'. Caccia displayed the emotional dramaticism which had characterised so much official language during the Suez crisis: 'I do pray in the bowels of mercy that we shall say what we cannot do, as well as what we can . . . They have always pleaded Congress. Now perhaps we can plead Parliament?'[156] From the UN, Pierson Dixon also advocated a new relationship based on hard bargaining. The past weeks had shown that the American government was 'impervious to arguments and appeals to sentimental ties'. There was also the tendency, common when nations have not secured much support in the UN, to conclude that the UN had served little purpose. The crisis had shown 'how fatal it would be to leave the General Assembly as the arbiter of our world wide interests'. The Security Council was 'useless', except for carefully prepared exercises on the Palestine question.[157] Mindful, perhaps, of the American perception of Suez as a colonial misadventure, Caccia thought the British should make it plain to the US that they would not tolerate more lectures on their international morals and that American attacks on colonialism only helped communists and split the alliance.[158]

After 1945, the British knew that they were not the equal of the superpowers; but they were still a great power, and they considered the US as the bastion of their security. With this security assured, they would remain the dominant global influence. India had been seen as the key to containing communism in Asia through a programme of regional economic collaboration under the invisible but indispensable aegis of the British. But in November 1956 Malcolm Macdonald, one of the originators of Britain's Asian cold-war policy, calmly noted that India's acceptance of a long-term Soviet credit was motivated by economic considerations and did not indicate any political move towards the USSR. Suez had done 'irreparable damage' to Indo–British relations, but Australia, the US and Canada could steer her away from the Soviet Union, and of course, the Indians themselves would be cautious in their dealings with the Soviets.[159] Between 1947 and 1956, the wheel had turned full circle; the British themselves realised that their influence was not a fundamental to keeping India and the Soviet Union apart. Influence, in any case, could not easily work its way through the maze of disparate interests among Britain and her friends. Neither the Anglo–American nor the Anglo–South Asian–Commonwealth relationships could sustain Britain as a great power; in 1956 Britain dispensed with the illusion that these relationships would enable her to remain the principal international influence.

Conclusions

Writing in the aftermath of the Suez débâcle, Geoffrey Crowther observed that the illusion that Britain was a great power was entertained only by Britons in their clubs or foreigners who passed through these clubs on their way to their tailors in Savile Row.[1] What was true of Britons and foreigners in clubs was not necessarily true of British officials. Labour and Conservative ministers between 1947 and 1956, officials from the Foreign and Commonwealth Relations Offices, Ministry of Defence and the Treasury all knew that Britain was not the equal of the superpowers and that she lacked the capacity to retain all her imperial possessions. But they were determined nevertheless that Britain should keep what she could. To them, the Empire–Commonwealth was inextricably interwoven with Britain's survival – indeed with her very identity – as a great power. Knowing that that power was limited, British policy-makers conceived a 'special relationship' with the United States after 1945 and tried to harness the relationship to Britain's interests. Influence would cover the gap between Britain's goal of remaining a front-rank power and the diminished means she possessed to achieve it. There were at least two connotations of influence in the Anglo–American relationship. At one level, it meant the superiority of British experience, character and brains over American money. It also implied the intention that Britain should be the peer of the superpowers or, at the very least, appear as their equal. Britain would claim the top international rank through association and membership of a very exclusive club of which the United States, the world's most powerful country, was the only other member.

The club instinct was important to the British in upholding their global status and in exercising influence; in actual fact they knew that the Commonwealth was merely The Other Club, which would display their international credentials but would not impart much substance to their power, so it took second place to their relationship with the United States. But its very existence was evidence of their global stature, and the point was continually underlined, not least to the Americans. The effort was not in vain. The Americans welcomed the help given by the Commonwealth in steering newly independent countries away from the Soviet Union; they welcomed it as a surrogate, a collaborator in South Asia, and they valued it, conjointly with the preservation of Britain's world status, as an indispensable partner in the crusade against communism. The shrill Soviet denunciations of India and Pakistan as henchmen of Western imperialism suggest that the façade had impressed Britain's arch-enemy as well. That Britain should be the primary Western influence on the subcontinent after 1947 was the common desire of both the British and Americans.

However, the Anglo–American relationship was not destined for smooth sailing, despite the shared outlook on Britain's world role in general and on South Asia in particular. Britain and the United States were two independent global powers with their own resources, historical traditions, memories, visions and perceptions of the world, and they would devise individual policies towards South Asia. British diplomacy had to work through several currents and cross currents: Anglo–American, Anglo–Indian, Anglo–Pakistani, Indo–US, Indo–Pakistani, and more broadly, Asian and Middle Eastern. Anglo–American agreement on an extended British role in South Asia for some time after decolonisation could not in itself assure British predominance in the subcontinent; that was also contingent on India and Pakistan, newly independent in August 1947 and having diplomatic options.

Between 1945 and 1947, the political and military imperatives of the cold war dictated the retention of an undivided India within Britain's global defence network, but the political aspirations of Indian and Pakistani nationalisms blocked the fulfilment of that aim. Independence and partition sounded the Last Call of the imperial security system; Britain's domestic preference for butter rather than guns ended it *sotto voce*. In the long run, India and Pakistan did not endorse Britain's international primacy or share Britain's vision of the Commonwealth as a mirror of her grandeur. Both stayed in it for their own reasons. Before the partition of the subcontinent, Muslim League leaders had declared that Pakistan would remain in the Commonwealth, but this was largely to steal a march on the Congress which was then advocating the severance of all Indian ties with the Empire–Commonwealth. Pakistan hoped that dominion status would secure her international support against India. After independence, the determination of the Congress to break with the Commonwealth was tempered by the realities of a bipolar world and by India's wish to avoid both the power blocs as well as diplomatic isolation. At that time, the Commonwealth offered India the only escape from both a stifling American economic embrace and a communist bear hug. Confident that the Commonwealth would not restrict her freedom of action, India became its first republican member in April 1949.

This was made possible by the British cabinet's unprecedented decision, a few weeks earlier, to allow an Indian republic in the Commonwealth. They knew that India's membership was unlikely to result in any military tie. Indian nonalignment ruled out any chance of Britain recovering the vital link of her pre-1947 power through the New Commonwealth. The

Empire–Commonwealth could not establish Britain as the equal of the superpowers or as leader of an independent Third Force. By 1949 a series of domestic and international crises, including the Berlin blockade, the communist takeover of Czechoslovakia and communist insurrections in Southeast Asia had convinced the British that their dependence on the US in Europe and Asia would endure. But the New Commonwealth Club was kept going by an increasingly impoverished Lady Britannia because it upheld her global status and made her feel at home in a fast-changing world. Members owed the club no fees or obligations, but they still expected services from the insolvent club owner and grumbled at her inability to provide them. But Britannia preferred to have some international friends to show off, even if they were a bit quarrelsome. How such a club would function was anybody's guess; Britain's uncertain hopes were summed up in the words of Noel-Baker in March 1949, when he defended the presence of a republican India in the Commonwealth – 'we shall be making an act of faith'.[2]

The New Commonwealth, then, was less the result of British influence than of a coincidence of rather disparate interests in its existence among the UK, India and Pakistan. It was not long before the British came face to face with the discrepancy between the appearance of unflappability and their inability to reconcile differences between the US, India and Pakistan. Two points are worth making. By May 1950 the British realised that the Commonwealth would have limited influence over India and Pakistan. India went her own way, while Pakistan, frustrated at her failure to rally the Commonwealth against India, did her best to ingratiate herself with the US. Juxtaposed with this was the American grievance, especially after the communist triumph in China in October 1949, that Britain's susceptibility to India's baneful influence in Asia was a complication in the Anglo–American relationship. India came to symbolise Anglo–American differences over the means of containing communism in Asia, to the extent that she led the Americans to question their traditional reliance on Britain and the Commonwealth in Asia *and* the Middle East. How would the British exert their influence over such politically diverse friends? The answer lay in their priorities and the means they conceived to achieve them; past inheritance, present position and visions of the future together made up a kaleidoscopic prism through which their images of the US, India and Pakistan were refracted.

The one perception that the British and Americans shared was that there was no Soviet military threat to South Asia. On the British side, this was in marked contrast to their oft-professed "responsibility", before decolonisation, for the subcontinent against the Russians. The end of the Raj in August 1947 and the onset of the European cold war did away with the notion that the subcontinent could easily fall a prey to the Soviets. It was a revealing example of how the perception of a threat could be discarded mentally by changed political circumstances.

The British derided what they saw as India's narrow outlook because she did not identify her strategic interests with theirs, but it was no great misfortune. The subcontinent was not a major theatre of the cold war; the British saw no Soviet military threat to South or Southeast Asia, which ranked third on their strategic priorities, after Europe and the Middle East. Britain could not provide large-scale military aid to India and Pakistan – but these countries did not need it since they were not menaced by the Soviets. Elsewhere in Asia the situation was different: in Malaya the British waged war against communist guerrillas to defend their stake there, while in Burma, the Philippines and Indochina communism reared its head in the form of internal subversion, and this danger lent importance to India's presence in the Commonwealth.

Britain's vision of India's cardinal role in the Asian cold war took shape before the communist victory in China. The part assigned to India was an extrapolation of the traditional role India had played as the strategic base of the empire. India did not align militarily with Britain after independence, but she was situated at the centre of a line of communications controlled largely by Britain from the Middle to the Far East, so any British policy in Asia had of necessity to take account of India.

Unlike the Americans, the British were convinced of India's anti-communist and pro-Western credentials. In January 1949, just before Strang spelled out his Asian cold war strategy, he appreciatively took note of Nehru's condemnation of communist methods as evil. Their success at forging a coalition with the Malay elites against communist guerrillas made the British receptive to Indian advice that nationalism would not only be a counterbalance to communism but might even turn the scales against it. An independent India in the Commonwealth would not only serve as an anti-communist example to other Asians; it would also persuade them of Britain's progressive intentions.

The Indian character reference, along with the effort made by Britain to resist the challenge to her position in Malaya, would also serve as an expedient excuse to avoid rescuing some of her European allies in Asia from their quagmires: Britain would let the French empire in Indochina die some as yet undefined natural death at the hands of communist-nationalists. The French should take their cue from Britain's sagacious act of decolonisation in India. The British, however, would hold their ground in Malaya, Hong Kong, their bases in the Middle East and their African empire. The British considered their own imperialism – which they called influence – essential to save Asia from communism. This did not render them willing to rebuild tottering European empires in Asia. The British emphasis on recognising Asian nationalisms mirrored their reluctance and inability to pay the price of extended military involvement and also their hopes of wooing those nationalisms to the Western side. 'Nationalism', affirmed a Foreign Office brief in 1955, 'remains the most potent single force throughout Asia. If we can convince the peoples of Asia that nationalism and Sino–Soviet communism are fundamentally incompatible we shall have done much to frustrate the Communist threat to Asia.'[3] Whatever the rhetoric, British colonialism and anti-colonialism emanated from circumstances rather than from mere principles. Political exigency determined the transfer of power in India and the British refusal to shore up the crumbling French empire, while the will to remain a great power inspired their imperialistic posture over Suez in 1956. At another level, having assisted the French to a safe exit from Indochina in 1954, the British, together with the Americans, worked covertly against anticipated Indian denunciations of Western colonialism at the Bandung conference in April 1955. For the British, as for the Americans, colonialism and anti-colonialism were mere instruments of containment, the goal of which was simultaneously to forestall communist advances and to extend their own influence. The thrust of Britain's Asian containment policy was to guide Asian countries into an anti-communist front, based on regional economic collaboration and financed by American cash. In this way, Britain could remain a great Asian power without undertaking expensive military engagements. The British cut their coat according to the cloth they possessed, even as they hoped their friends would provide them with a cloak of imperial grandeur.

How did this go down with their rich American friends and their considerably poorer Indian ones? On the face of it, there should have been few problems. For the Americans regarded the British as their surrogate and collaborator in Asia. Also, there seemed a reasonable chance of empathy between India and the United States. Both had won independence from the British, both prided themselves as idealistic champions of anti-colonial movements, and India acknowledged her economic dependence on the US. After October 1949, the Americans perceived India as the only viable counterpoise to communist China, and, on another plane, some American officials were also well-disposed towards India. For example, Eisenhower's interest in India dated from his boyhood days; his awareness of the limits of American power prompted his thought that neutrality was not such a bad thing and that the Americans would not have the resources to ally with India, and it induced him to advise an American journalist in 1955 not to be too harsh on India.[4] But these reflections were minor details which could neither sweeten a perenially sour, even acrimonious Indo–US relationship nor translate into a well-considered policy. India's need for economic largesse from the US proved a hurdle to a pleasant relationship, if only because she never got as much as she wanted. In American eyes, Nehru himself posed part of the problem. Identifying Indian foreign policy with Nehru, American officials were, at best, baffled by him. 'Prime Minister Nehru is far from being a typical Indian.' the State Department advised Eisenhower on the eve of Nehru's visit to the US in December 1956. 'He thinks and reportedly even dreams in English.' Nehru's *amour-propre* and sensitivity made him a tricky customer. 'It was indicative of Nehru's pride of position,' commented the State Department, 'that President Eisenhower's invitation for the visit had to be specifically renewed at least two times before it could be fulfilled.'[5] At worst, many American policy-makers simply misunderstood, ignored or even disliked Nehru and the foreign policy he was devising for India. To give a few illustrations, it was the Eisenhower administration which decided on military assistance to Pakistan in 1954 which India considered, not unreasonably, as directly harmful to her interests, since it was Eisenhower's Vice-President, Richard Nixon, who justified the aid as necessary to counter Indian neutralism. The same administration pressed its allies to exclude India from the Korean Political conference in 1953. It also stood aloof from the Geneva accord, towards the achievement of which India made an offstage contribution. In addition, legislators on Capitol Hill were frequently more hostile to India than officials in the Truman and Eisenhower administrations. The sum of all this was an indefinite, continual downturn in Indo–US relations which could never be halted, and it did not augur well for British hopes to promote their influence in Asia.

Indo–US acrimony was noticeable even before the communist triumph in China; while the Soviet Union was still hostile to India and before the US started giving military aid to Pakistan in 1954. The conflicting interests of India and the United States during the cold war had a greater impact on their relationship than their common historical experiences as rebels against colonial rule, and their self-images as supporters of freedom movements. Paradoxically, India and Britain enjoyed a very cordial rapport until 1956, in spite of Britain's recent overlordship of India and the continued possession of the rest of her formal and informal empire. Nonalignment shattered British hopes of retaining the substance of Pax Britannica, but the unexpected, unprecedented amicability between India and Britain signalled that birds of different feathers could flock together. In contrast, Indo–US relations seemed fated to perennial discord: nonalignment was fundamentally at odds with American bipolarism. Since their world view was bipolar, the Americans underestimated the extent to which newly independent India was determined to preserve her independence of the Soviet Union *as well as* the US. In other words, India believed that lining up with the Americans would actually curtail her independence. The Americans anointed themselves as defenders of "freedom" – only to find themselves assailed, every now and then, by the Indians, to whom American support for European empires did not savour of freedom and to whom freedom implied the right to disagree with the Americans and to choose and define India's place in the world. The Indians prided themselves on judging issues on their merits, which, in their eyes, included criticising American policies when they so pleased. Such criticism did not denote any softness towards communism. The Americans realised that India was not in the Soviet camp, but their perception of their 'defence of the free world', and their articulation of it through a series of alliances, put them on a collision course with a nonaligned India who did not think that military compacts with the US were necessary to preserve *her* freedom. To India, which wanted an end to great power decisions on the fate of Asia, post-war US military expansion in Asia was unwelcome and sparked off many bad-tempered exchanges between the two countries. Cheering their own crusade against communism, the Americans seethed at what they saw as the Indian tendency to equate them with the Soviets by pronouncing a "plague-on-both-your-houses", and they branded nonalignment as immoral. The propensity of both the Indians and Americans to inject a strong dose of morality into their respective justifications for their political interests created a dissonance that jarred on the ears of both rather than harmony between the world's two largest democracies.

The recognition of communist China was the first major bone of contention in both the Anglo–American and Indo–US relationships and the biggest single point of agreement in the Anglo–Indian relationship. What, for the US, marked the start of the Asian cold war was, for India, simply a question of doing business with her powerful Asian neighbour. Like the Indians, some officials in the Truman administration thought that recognition of communist China offered an opportunity to influence her and to engineer a split in the communist camp. The debates for and against recognition did take place in Washington; it was the argument against accommodation which ultimately carried the day. By December 1949 the Americans saw India as the best Asian counterpoise to communist China, but they simultaneously ruled her out as the bulwark of their strategy in Asia. In other words, the possibility could not be translated into reality, American style. Nonaligned India could not be the linchpin of a policy which emphasised military containment, defining the Ryukyus, Japan and the Philippines as America's frontline by December 1949, and identifying Formosa as crucial to its defensive perimeter strategy in June 1950.

Military containment also portended little or no American enthusiasm for Britain's strategy of diplomatic containment centring round India and led the US to spurn requests by both India and Britain for more aid to India. Washington bluntly told New Delhi and London that the American distrust of nonalignment ruled out munificence to India. Indo–US animosity presaged that Britain's strategy of containment through American-backed regional economic collaboration rather than greater military involvements was in for a rough ride.

The Korean war sharpened further the Anglo–American differences symbolised by India. Neither India nor Britain had any qualms about condemning North Korean aggresssion, but both were uneasy about endorsing Truman's declaration of 26 June 1950 which not only threatened to embroil the UN in an unwarranted and unwinnable conflict against China but also to trigger off a world war. British and Indian efforts were directed at limiting hostilities in Korea. This infuriated the Americans, not because they were reckless warmongers – indeed they debated at length the pros and cons of limiting and expanding the conflict – but because limiting the conflict was never an end in itself for them as it was for the British and Indians. Because of that common Indo–British interest, the Americans alleged that the British were susceptible to Indian influence. The American charge was probably fuelled by the frequent British references to the need to have Asian, meaning Indian, support whenever they disagreed with the Americans, and the British used their "Indian pretext" whenever they wished to restrain the Americans. On the whole, though, the American allegation was simplistic and unfair. During the first phase of the Korean war, until January 1951, even a cursory look at the Nehru–Attlee exchanges reveals New Delhi's disappointment at its inability to influence London, especially on admitting China into the UN and on that most important Indian plea – that UN troops should not cross the 38th parallel. This did not win London any thanks from Washington; instead, the Americans were frequently piqued that, under Indian influence, the British were deviating from the trail blazed by the United States. Pique turned into anger during the negotiations over the POWs' resolution in November 1952, when Acheson furiously rounded on the British for supporting an Indian resolution in preference to an American one.

American anger at Britain's "Indian pretext" stemmed in part from their view of Indian diplomacy as distinctly harmful to the US and as a bad influence on the British. There was a touch of paranoia in this outburst, for it credited India with a leverage she did not possess. It is difficult to see how officials of the calibre of Attlee, Bevin, Dening and Strang could have been swept away by "Indian influence". The British stood fast on their priorities: India may have been a member of the Commonwealth and the key to British strategy in Asia, but the US, not India or the Commonwealth, was the undisputed corner-stone of British security.

It is arguable that the use of the "Indian pretext" by Britain was self-defeating. It never swung the Americans to the Indian or British point of view, and, as the controversy over POWs in Korea showed, it probably intensified American dislike of Indian diplomacy and prejudiced them against any idea that emanated from the Indians. The British brushed aside American objections to the Indian resolution on the POWs partly because they were convinced that it offered the only chance to resolve a seemingly endless conflict in Korea, partly because they were able to win the support of other allies and partly because the Indian government were able to word the resolution to accommodate the American stance against forced repatriation of prisoners of war while allowing the communists to save face. The ill-judged Soviet attack on the Indian formula finally ensured American support for the Indian resolution, but it enhanced neither their liking of nonalignment, nor their responsiveness to British advice to pay heed to Indian opinion. In the summer of 1953 the success of the Americans at excluding India from the Korean Political Conference demonstrated that British endeavours to bridge the Indo–US gap were in for a long haul.

It was not that the British were torn between India and the US; the point is that India and the US mirrored British interests at somewhat different levels. The Indian emphasis on limiting the conflict struck a chord with a Britain who could not defend any of her major interests singlehanded or squander her meagre finances on problematical military engagements in Asia as a *quid pro quo* for the Americans to stand guard over Europe. The British interest in an American role in Europe and in limiting the conflict in Asia were separate but integral parts of a single policy. The problem for the British was that the Americans and Indians fulfilled different needs of that policy.

Indochina and SEATO again illustrated that. Much to India's disappointment, Britain entered SEATO in 1954. But seeing that Indian diplomacy could promote their interests in Asia, the British wanted an enlargement of Indian influence in Indochina, first to bolster noncommunist nationalists, and then, after the signing of the Geneva accord, to reassure China that there was no Western threat to her territory. At Geneva the British seized the initiative in negotiations not because of their influence over the French, the Indochina states or the US, but because in the confused situation after Dienbienphu they wished to steer clear of an American-instigated military intervention. This made them determined to find a tenable if tentative substitute for it. The Americans smarted in dismay at the British refusal to participate in any coalition, and the grapes tasted sourer as the Americans realised that they could not make a convincing case for unilateral intervention in Indochina.

Unlike the United States, Britain thought that the fighting in Indochina could be contained through negotiation, and the Geneva agreement was a triumph for independent British diplomacy, acting in secret concert with India. British diplomacy, drawing upon Indian ideas and trying to achieve peace with China, paved the way for an honourable French retreat from Indochina. To that extent, British influence was a force to be reckoned with in Asia. But it did not go far enough. British officials – and the Geneva accord – said very little about the wishes of the Indochina states. One upshot was the adamant opposition of South Vietnam to the agreement because of the partition of Vietnam. The accord was also disliked by the Americans because it did not "free" North Vietnam. So they disassociated themselves from it, and, in contravention of the spirit of the accord, made plans to increase their military involvement in Indochina. The subsequent American engagement in Vietnam was to epitomise their predilection for military solutions.

The case of Cambodia illustrated their emphasis on military means at another level. Established as an independent neutral state by the Geneva agreement, the question was how Cambodia could arrange for her defence without antagonising China. The British thought the answer might lie in an Indian military mission in Cambodia, but their own allies were loath to endorse this formula. It was disliked by the French, who already trained the Cambodian army, and the Americans, who saw the advantages of an Indian training mission to assuage Chinese fears but fundamentally distrusted the Indians and were disturbed at the likelihood of a "neutral" Indian influence on Cambodia. The issue was finally resolved by Cambodia's decision to stick to the French. All this laid bare the complexities involved in ending the Indochina war on a Britain–India–China circuit if that circuit was not favoured by Britain's own allies, who wished to preserve and widen their own influence in Indochina and had their own ideas of how to do it. The limits of British influence stood revealed.

Nevertheless, some caution is necessary before one chastises the British for illusions about their influence. Although they operated under manifold constraints, they accomplished a veritable *tour de force* at Geneva in 1954. The establishment of independent neutral states on China's borders "removed" threats to her territory and dissuaded her from expansion. Neutral and nonaligned states had their uses. Nonalignment, reflecting India's determination to practice and to safeguard her independent foreign policy, did not make her the primary Asian power economically or militarily, but it impelled her to resist communism and to remain a political democracy. The problem was that while neutral states were acceptable, even desirable, to the British as a means of containment, they won little applause from the Americans; the "will to fight" seemed all-important to the United States in 1954–6. The historical record suggests that American support for the Geneva agreement might have stabilised Indochina and saved the US from a costly, unproductive and painful intervention in Vietnam. Alliances and American military engagement could not deliver Indochina from communism – but the Americans were not inclined to believe this between 1954–6. The American readiness to fight was not a guarantee of a successful strategy; the British inability to enforce the Geneva accord and to influence the US in its favour did not necessarily imply a wrong policy.

Differences over India showed the Americans at variance with the British insistence on limiting Western military interventions in Asia. In the Middle East and Pakistan, too, American dissatisfaction with British policy led the US to embark on a course which not only exposed the limits of British influence on the US but also cut the ground from under the British position. For Britain, the Middle East was second in importance only to the UK and Europe; it was an area which symbolised her power all the more after the loss of India but which she could not defend without US support. The problem here was that the threat to British interests came not from communism but, as on the Indian subcontinent, from regional nationalisms. Demanding a British pull-out from the Suez base, Egyptian nationalism posed the greatest challenge to British imperialism: the two were at daggers drawn, for Egypt was the nucleus of Britain's "post-India" Middle East defence system. The British attitude to the US was ambivalent, seeking to arouse and engage American backing for their interests in the region, while being wary of US attempts to undermine Britain's status. The US and Britain initially had the same goal – to safeguard Western access to Middle East oil, and the US endorsed Britain's claim to station troops in Egypt. Contrary to their self-image, the Americans were hardly unswerving opponents of colonialism: in the Middle East as in Asia, American anti-colonialism took on the forms prescribed by American strategic interests and on the ways in which the US sought to fulfil those interests.

The idea of a Pakistani contribution to Middle East defence had tempted the British since Pakistan's overtures to them in 1948, but Anglo–Pakistani parleys had always broken down because of the Pakistani insistence on guarantees against India. Pakistan also turned to the Americans, but it was without avail, for they were not very interested in either Pakistan or the Middle East.

Events in Korea and Iran in 1950–1 altered US policy in Pakistan's favour. Mired in Korea and observing the surge of nationalism in many Middle East countries, the US started to question seriously Britain's capacity to man the barricades for the West in the Middle East and Asia. The conclusion, crudely drawn, was that British policy lacked the cutting edge. Old-fashioned imperialism was *passé*, for it was "winning" enemies rather than friends in the Middle East. In the circumstances, it was imperative that the Americans extend their influence, but how could they do it? The realisation that most Middle East countries did not share their perceptions of a Soviet threat – the extent and nature of which the Americans did not define – made the Americans painfully aware of *their* limited influence in the Middle East. The only alternative, *faute de mieux*, was to make do with whatever was available. The Americans now set about finding allies in the Middle East. Turkey was an obvious choice; Pakistan, the rejected but ever patient suitor now appeared a worthy partner, and, in 1951, the Americans interceded with the British in favour of Pakistan's recruitment in a Middle East alignment.

The idea had its attractions for the British, especially in the wake of the Iranian oil crisis and Egypt's refusal to join a Middle East command in 1951, but they could neither picture a Pakistani lead in it nor contemplate basing their Middle East strategy on an unstable Pakistan which had very little influence in the area. In a nutshell, Pakistan could not satisfy British needs in the Middle East. The British therefore refused to give Pakistan guarantees against India, for this would have meant upgrading Pakistan's place in their priorities and spoiling their relations with India without ascertaining the preservation of their now fragile ascendancy in the Middle East.

The Americans, however, did not have a position to defend but influence to acquire. How best could they achieve it? All they were certain of was the necessity of distancing themselves from the British and assuming leadership in the Middle East. They had little idea of what they would lead, how and what should be done. NSC 155/1 of July 1953 envisaged a role for Pakistan in Middle East defence, but it left unspecified what that role would be. The basic desire to enlist Pakistan rendered the Americans receptive to Ayub's overtures for military aid in September 1953, although they did not know what they expected in return. The India factor was weighed, all the more carefully since the Americans were pushing for India's exclusion from the Korean Political Conference at this time, but it was discarded, with some thought of softening the blow for India by vague talk of a Pakistani contribution to the UN effort in Korea. But the Pakistanis would have none of it, and the Americans did not press the point, since their real objective was to engage Pakistan in the Middle East.

Having decided to act independently of the British, the Americans did not consider themselves hostile to them – or at any rate did not wish to appear at loggerheads with them. Justifying their decision to enrol Pakistan in Middle East defence they claimed that they were acting in accordance with an Anglo–American decision of January 1953 that Pakistan should be recruited when the time was ripe. Without consulting the British, the Americans decided that the time was ripe. They wished nevertheless to make a show of concern for British sensitivities and to keep the British posted as Pakistan was a member of the Commonwealth. In practice they merely conveyed to the British a decision that had already been taken in principle. Throughout the period from 30 September 1953, when the State Department took the informal decision, to 25 February 1954, when Eisenhower set the seal on it – there is evidence that the Americans wanted to tell the British what they were doing. Instead, they sprang one surprise after another on London, partly because they informed the British of decisions that had already been made, partly because they – and Turkey and Pakistan – were tightlipped about what was happening among all three. Additionally, British diplomats in Washington, Karachi, Ankara and London failed to detect what was going on. This brought out the differing British and American ideas about what was meant by consultation. Apparently the Americans wished to keep the British informed, but only after certain decisions had been taken. To the British, consultation meant being associated as much as possible with the formulation of decisions and policy.

Part of the problem was knowing what actually constituted American policy. The State Department had no blueprint for Middle East defence: it took the decision to give military assistance to Pakistan without really knowing in what framework the aid would be used, and even the NSC and US Chiefs were not always conversant with the State Department's thinking. Moreover, uncertainty whether Turkey's lack of enthusiasm for "Islamic" Pakistan would enable *anything* to get off the ground accentuated the need to maintain strict secrecy; the Americans were stumbling in the dark and did not want to fall with a crash. In any case, when the British were tipped off they tried to rein in the Americans; not consulting the British saved time and simplified what were already tortuous procedures in the initiation of a scheme in which the Americans did not want to reveal their hand. Day-to-day improvisations constituted American policy.

The British were stunned at the news of US military assistance to Pakistan in October 1953, and their attempts to stop the Americans demonstrated their misgivings about the very goals of America's new and inchoate Middle East strategy. The British did not consider its timing right, if only because they did not know what would become of their military influence in Pakistan and because it would antagonise India. They tried to find out whether they could salvage their position by supplying offshore equipment to Pakistan, but they never received an answer from the Americans.

Even as the British tried to recover some ground and restrain the Americans between October and December 1953, the Americans were forcing the pace with schemes to link Pakistan and Turkey in an alternative to MEDO; the British came to know of American designs only at the end of December 1953. Why did this happen? Hints that the Americans were trying to cobble together an alliance which would include Pakistan were dropped by American officials off and on, but they were mysteriously not followed up by the British. Part of the reason is that the British found the idea so far-fetched, so inconceivable, that they simply shrugged it off. Nor do they seem to have got wind of the basic American impatience with a barren British policy in the Middle East. This may not have seriously occurred to them since the Americans had connived with them in over-throwing Mossadegh in Iran in August 1953, and the British may not have sensed American disagreement on other issues in the Middle East. One result of their failure to divine American intentions was that the British expended considerable effort on criticising the Americans and discouraging them from giving military aid to Pakistan – while assuring them that the British were not really opposed to the aid! This *double entendre* was futile; it only facilitated an early American claim that the British had acquiesced in their plans to subsidise Pakistan's armed forces. The British acted on the assumption that by appearing to walk in step with the Americans they could keep them on British rails; instead the Americans happily concluded that the British were in line with them. The British failed to find out what their allies were really up to because they missed the wood for the trees. Thinking that the Americans were merely impatient with them on Pakistan, they were slow to sense that the root cause of American interest in Pakistan was American disapprobation of British policy in the *Middle East*.

The question arises how the Americans managed to enlist Pakistan without giving her a guarantee against India. This is important, since British negotiations with Pakistan had always foundered on the rock of support against India. Pakistan's own diplomatic style provides a partial explanation. Infructuous negotiations with Britain had driven home to

Pakistan the futility of importuning for guarantees against India. Made wiser by the experience, Pakistan did not broach the subject with the US but concentrated on making the right anti-communist noises and persuaded the Americans, who wished to be persuaded against much British advice, of her anti-communist fervour. Once the Americans were lured by Pakistani overtures, the ball was in the US court. On knowing of American interest, Pakistani hopes of military largesse soared even though the Americans had not made any promises. American procrastination in formalising the decision kept Pakistan on tenterhooks; the Americans secured Pakistan's agreement to military assistance within the framework of a Turco–Pakistan pact without making any commitment about the exact amount. By the end of November 1953, concern over whether they would get *any* aid overshadowed Pakistani considerations of how much they would receive. In any case, since the Americans had never discouraged their expectations, they assumed they would obtain as much as they wanted. Once the formal decision was taken, Pakistan secured no guarantees against India and far less aid than she had expected. But having gone thus far, Pakistan could not withdraw because a niggardly sum of money was better than none. Moreover, the Americans alone could dole out military subsidies, and they held the purse-strings.

The Pakistani choice for alignment, however unsatisfactory that alignment, was evident from their efforts to flatter the British that they really preferred offshore British equipment to American weaponry. On this point there was a coincidence of interest between Britain and Pakistan: the British because they wished to retain their arms market and collateral military influence in Pakistan; the Pakistanis because they were desperate for military hardware from *any* quarter. But the British made no headway, partly because the Pentagon laid down the terms on which American *matériel* would be supplied to the Pakistani army. Additionally, the little the British could offer Pakistan could only be offered too late; the paltry aid that trickled in from the US was still more than she would have ever received from Britain. Fearful of losing one of their best customers, the British then tried to talk the Americans into toning down Washington's forceful salesmanship! Once again, the British hoped to achieve by influence what they could not achieve through a ragged competitive edge.

American military largesse to Pakistan reflected the British failure to satisfy the Pakistani need for security as well as American dissatisfaction with British policy in the Middle East. Those were the crucial points in the American dislodgement of the British from Pakistan. The colossal American ignorance of Pakistan did not prevent the US from gaining a military foothold there. The extent to which Pakistan was unknown territory to Dulles, even after becoming 'America's most allied ally in Asia',[6] is revealed in his defence of Pakistan's inclusion in SEATO to Walter Lippmann, soon after the signing of the Manila Treaty on 9 September 1954:

'Look Walter,' Dulles said, blinking hard behind his thick glasses, 'I've got to get some real fighting men into the south of Asia. The only Asians who can really fight are the Pakistanis. That's why we need them in the alliance. We could never get along without the Gurkas.'

'But Foster,' Lippmann reminded him, 'the Gurkas aren't Pakistanis, they're Indians.'

'Well', responded Dulles, unperturbed by such nit-picking and irritated at the Indians for refusing to join his alliance, 'they may not be Pakistanis, but they're Moslems.'

'No, I'm afraid they're not Moslems, either, they're Hindus.'

'No matter,' Dulles replied, and proceeded to lecture Lippmann for half an hour on how SEATO would plug the dike against communism in Asia.[7]

British experience, know-how and traditional influence in Pakistan and the Middle East did not matter a fig if they could not fulfil American and Pakistani demands. This was the logic behind the US derailing the British from Pakistan within seven years of decolonisation in South Asia, an area which the British had ruled for some 200 years, and which they and the Americans had traditionally regarded as a British sphere of influence.

This brings us to the question of whether the Americans were responsible for the decline of British infuence in South Asia. If one looks at the period 1947–51, before the Americans got interested in Pakistan and the Middle East, British influence had already taken a few knocks. Unconditional independence and partition, nonalignment and Kashmir themselves mirrored an ebbing British influence and power. At another level, British fears that they might lose their economic and military markets to the US and other allies reflected their apprehension that they did not always have the best to offer. They were therefore aware of their weakness in competition and also of the reality that British influence was circumscribed by the very fact of India and Pakistan having choices.

The alternatives did not always injure the British. India's choice of nonalignment may have unhinged Britain's imperial designs, but it also ruled out the chances of India running into the American embrace. Nor was American wire-pulling always detrimental to the British. On at least two occasions the Americans used their good offices to Britain's advantage. Britain's winning of the aircraft offer against the Soviets in 1955–6 revealed both her resentful dependence on the US to make the offer more attractive to India and also American decision-making in the British interest. Then, during the Suez crisis, the greater American hold over Pakistan forestalled a Pakistani attack on the SCUA and Pakistan's withdrawal from the Commonwealth, thus preserving the unity of the Commonwealth.

Where the Americans considered it to their advantage to support the British, they did so; where their interests ran counter to those of Britain, they worked against her. South Asia illustrated the importance of a congruence of interests *and* agreement on means in the Anglo–American relationship. In 1954, the British resisted American pressure to collaborate in an undefined military intervention in Indochina; during the Suez crisis the Americans were just as determined not to embark on any military adventure. In both instances, the decisive factor was the perception of its interests by each side. Sometimes Britain's viewpoint coincided with India's, sometimes with that of the US – and India and the US were often at cross-purposes. Thus the long-term Indo–British interest in diplomatic containment led the US to believe that British and American interests in Asia were at variance. American interest in Pakistan after 1951 showed that the upholding of British ascendancy in the Middle East was no longer vital to the US; it was a hindrance rather than a help to them. It took the Suez crisis to bring home the point to the British and to destroy their illusion of influence. The hyperbolic American 'declaration of independence' in October–November 1956 was the definitive symbol of the divergence of British and American goals in the Middle East. By then it was too late for the British to prevent the Americans from undercutting them as the United States forged their own way ahead. America's "independence" of Britain would not assure the success of US strategies in the Middle East or Asia – but that story lay in the future.

Notes to Preface

1. The historiography of the Anglo–American relationship is reviewed by D. Reynolds, 'A "Special Relationship"? America, Britain and the International Order since the Second World War', and 'Rethinking Anglo–American Relations', *International Affairs*, vol. 62, 1986, and vol. 65, 1988/9, pp. 89–111 respectively. Reynolds lists the most important works on the subject.

   Critiques of American historiography of the cold war include: D. Reynolds, 'The Origins of the Cold War: the European Dimension', *Historical Journal*, vol. 28, 1985, pp. 497–515; R. J. McMahon, 'Eisenhower and Third World Nationalism: a Critique of the Revisionists', *Political Science Quarterly*, vol. 101, 1986, pp. 453–73, and 'The Cold War in Asia: Toward a New Synthesis?', *Diplomatic History*, vol. 12, 1988, pp. 307–28; D. Cameron Watt, 'Britain and the Historiography of the Yalta Conference and the Cold War', ibid., vol. 13, 1989, pp. 67–98; G. Lundestad, 'Empire by Invitation? The United States and Western Europe 1945–1952', *Journal of Peace Research*, vol. 23, 1986, pp. 263–77, and 'Moralism, Presentism, Exceptionalism, Provincialism and Other Extravagances in American Writings on the Early Cold War Years', *Diplomatic History*, vol. 13, 1989, pp. 527–46, and in his *The American "Empire"*, (Oslo and Oxford 1990), pp. 11–29; J.L. Gaddis, 'New Conceptual Approaches to the Study of American Foreign Relations', *Diplomatic History*, vol. 14, 1990, pp. 425–32.

   However, there are a number of American 'depolarisers'. To name only four: R.M. Hathaway, *Ambiguous Partnership: Britain and America, 1944–1947*, (New York 1981); T.H. Anderson, *The United States, Britain and the Cold War, 1944–1947*, (Columbia 1981); F.J. Harbutt, *The Iron Curtain: Churchill, America, and the Origins of the Cold War*, (New York 1986); and R.J. Best Jr. *'Co-operation with Like-Minded Peoples': British Influences on American Security Policy, 1945–1949*, (New York 1986).

2. American interest in the settlement on Korea in 1945 and the sending of the Wedemeyer mission to China in 1946 did reveal concern over communism in Asia, but an active US involvement in containment in Asia really dates from October 1949. On the Wedemeyer mission see W.W. Stueck, 'The Marshall and Wedemeyer Missions: A Quadrilateral Perspective', in H. Harding and Yuan Ming (eds), *Sino-American Relations 1945–1955: A Joint Reassessment of a Critical Decade*, (Wilmington 1989), pp. 96–118.

3. For a short introduction to the debate on Britain's 'decline', see A. Sked, *Britain's Decline: Problems and Perspectives*, (Oxford 1987).

Notes to Introduction

1. This story was told by Sir Oliver Franks at the National Press Club, Washington, 8 June 1948, FO371/68045G.
2. Among the works that I have found useful are: H.C. Allen, *Great Britain and the United States 1783–1952* (London 1954), M. Beloff, 'The Special Relationship: An Anglo–American Myth', in M. Gilbert (ed.), *A Century of Conflict: 1850–1950: Essays for A.J.P. Taylor* (London 1966), pp. 151–71; C. Thorne, *Allies of a Kind* (London 1978); D. Cameron Watt, *Succeeding John Bull: America in Britain's Place 1900–1975* (Cambridge 1984); W.R. Louis and H. Bull (eds), *The Special Relationship: Anglo–American Relations since 1945* (Oxford 1986).
3. Cited in M.J. Hogan, *The Marshall Plan: America, Britain and the Reconstruction of Europe, 1947–1952*, (Cambridge 1987), p. 213.
4. COS(48)26(0), 'The Problem of a Future War and The Strategy of War with Russia', memo by Montgomery, 30 January 1948, FO800/452.
5. JCS 1641/3, 13 March 1946, cited in D. Dimbleby and D. Reynolds, *An Ocean Apart*, (London 1988), p. 171.
6. Memo from Deputy Under Secretary to SS on questions to be discussed with Lord Franks, 7 March 1950, DS file 611.41/3–750, and DS policy statement on UK, 7 June 1950, DS file 611. 41/6–750.
7. J. Colville, *Fringes of Power: Downing Street Diaries, 1939–1955*, (London 1985), p. 564.
8. J. Kent, 'Bevin's Imperialism and the Idea of Euro-Africa, 1945–49', in M. Dockrill and J. Young, *British Foreign Policy, 1945–56*, (London 1989), pp. 47–76.
9. CP(48) 'The First Aim of British Foreign Policy', memo by Bevin, 4 January 1948, CAB129/23.
10. Cited by A. Adamthwaite, 'Britain and the World, 1945–9: the View from the Foreign Office', *International Affairs*, vol. 61, 1985, pp. 228–9, 232.
11. Cited by V. Rothwell, 'Britain and the First Cold War', in R. Crockatt and S. Smith (eds), *The Cold War Past and Present* (London 1987), p. 67.
12. For example, the quip during the loan negotiations of 1945 was: 'It's true *they* have the money bags, But *we* have all the brains.' Cited by Reynolds, 'Rethinking Anglo–American Relations', p. 96. Writing to Harold Macmillan on 9 July 1955, Roger Makins observed that the American fear of being outwitted by 'the subtle and unscrupulous foreigner' was 'heightened by the thought that their side is captained by an amateur, while ours is led by a professional' (FO371/114364).

13. C(52)202, 'British Overseas Obligations', 18 June 1952, CAB129/53.
14. C.W. Kegley Jr and E.R. Wittkopf, *American Foreign Policy: Pattern and Process* (Macmillan paperback, 1987), p. 40; P. Darby, *Three Faces of Imperialism* (New Haven and London 1987); M.H. Hunt, *Ideology and US Foreign Policy* (New Haven and London 1987); M. Leffler, 'The American Conception of National Security and the Beginnings of the Cold War, 1945–1948', and the comments on it by J.L. Gaddis and B.R. Kuniholm, and Leffler's reply to them, *American Historical Review*, vol. 89, 1984, pp. 346–400; J.L. Gaddis, *Strategies of Containment*, (New York 1982); S. Ambrose, *Rise to Globalism*, (Penguin Books, 1983); D.W. White, 'History and American Internationalism: the Formulation from the Past After World War II', *Pacific Historical Review*, vol. 48, 1989, pp. 145–72.
15. See chapter 2 of this book.
16. For some reflections on the American tendency to use military means in Asia, see C. Thorne, *American Political Culture and the Asian Frontier, 1943–1973*, (London 1988), pp. 373 ff.
17. See chapter 5 of this book.
18. Ibid. In 1954, British opposition to military intervention obliged the Americans to shelve 'united action', but it also led them to consider the idea of going ahead without the British at some future date.
19. To give just three instances of the debate over Suez, David Reynolds cautions against making too much of the Anglo–American rift in 1956 in his 'Eden the Diplomatist, 1931–1956: Suezide of a Statesman?' *History*, vol. 74, 1989, pp. 76 ff. Roger Louis, on the other hand, highlights the differences between Dulles and Eden over the use of force in his 'Dulles, Suez and the British', in R.H. Immerman (ed.), *John Foster Dulles and the Diplomacy of the Cold War*, (Princeton 1990), pp. 133–58. See also W. Scott Lucas, *Divided We Stand: Britain, the US and the Suez Crisis*, (London 1991).

Notes to Chapter 1

1. CCAC, memo by Lord Privy Seal, 3 November 1947, CAB134/54.
2. See chapter 2 of this book.
3. Cited in C. Thorne, *Allies of a Kind*, p. 649 and A. Bullock, *Bevin*, p. 65.
4. Quoted in *Notes for Speakers and Workers 1945: General Election 1945* (London 1945), p. 108; *General Election 1950: the Campaign Guide* (Conservative Party), (London 1949), p. 16; See also F.W.S. Craig, *British General Election Manifestos 1918–1966*, (Chichester 1970), pp. 88, 105, 113. For the similarity of Labour and Conservative views on the Middle East during the election campaign of 1951, see W.R. Louis, *The British Empire in the Middle East 1945–1951*, (Oxford 1984), pp. 739–40.
5. V. Rothwell, *Britain and the Cold War, 1941–1947*, (London 1982), p. 409. See also John Kent, 'Bevin's Imperialism and the Idea of Euro-Africa, 1945–49', in M Dockrill and J. Young (eds), *British Foreign Policy, 1945–56*, pp. 47–56, and 'The British Empire and the Origins of the Cold War, 1944–49', in A. Deighton (ed), *Britain and the First Cold War* (London 1990), pp. 165–83.
6. K. Morgan, *Labour in Power* (Oxford 1984), p. 228 and K. Harris, *Attlee* (London 1982), p. 362.
7. How she hoped to achieve this is the subject of Louis, *Middle East.*
8. For two recent studies of the subject, see R.J. Moore, *Escape from Empire* (Oxford 1983) and my *Origins of the Partition of India 1936–1947*, (Oxford University South Asian Studies series, New Delhi, 1987, 1989, paperback 1990, 1992).
9. This is discussed more fully in my 'Decolonisation in India: The Statement of 20 February 1947', *International History Review*, vol. 6, 1984, pp. 191–209. For recent general studies of decolonisation, see J. Darwin, *Britain and Decolonisation*, (Macmillan 1988), R.F. Holland, *European Decolonization*, (Macmillan, 1985). Both contain useful bibliographies.
10. For interwar politics in British India, see R.J. Moore, *The Crisis of Indian Unity 1917–1940*, (Oxford 1974), and D. Page, *Prelude to Partition*, (New Delhi 1982).
11. Louis, *Middle East*, on an analogous British strategy in the Middle East.
12. Interview between cabinet delegation and Jinnah, 16 April 1946, N. Mansergh and P. Moon (eds), *The Transfer of Power* (referred to hereafter as *TOP*), vol. 7, pp. 284–5.
13. *Hansard*, col. 581, 1946, vol. 430 and Bullock, *Bevin*, p. 66.
14. As in note 4 above.

15. S. Sarkar, *Modern India 1885–1947*, (New Delhi 1983), p. 414, and B. Chandra *et al.* (ed.) *India's Struggle for Independence*, (New Delhi 1987), pp. 473 ff.

16. See for example, K. Morgan, *Labour in Power*, and A. Sked and C. Cook, *Post-War Britain: A Political History*, (Penguin 1979), pp. 24 ff.

17. D. Potter, 'Manpower Shortage and the End of Colonialism', *Modern Asian Studies*, vol. 7, 1973, pp. 47–53.

18. Home Establishments File no. 30/11/46, and some reflections on official propaganda by H.V. Hodson, Reforms Commissioner, 26 August 1942, Reforms Office file 143/42-R, National Archives of India, New Delhi. See also note by Conran Smith, 19 October 1942 and Maxwell to Laithwaite, 24 October 1942, *TOP*, vol. 3, pp. 160–1, 156–8.

19. Linlithgow to Amery, tel. 104-S, 21 January 1942, *TOP*, vol. 1, p. 49.

20. John Connell, *Auchinleck* (London 1959), pp. 949, 945.

21. Auchinleck to COS, 22 December 1945 and 18 January 1946; CDC meeting, 11 January 1946, *TOP*, vol. 6, pp. 675–6, 813–14, 763–4 respectively.

22. Alanbrooke to Auchinleck, 4 February 1946, L/WS/1/1008 and CCOSC meeting, 22 February 1946, CAB79/45.

23. Cabinet delegation to cabinet office, 25 March 1946, *TOP*, vol. 7, p. 6 and note of meeting between cabinet delegation and Viceroy's executive council on 26 March 1946, ibid., p. 7.

24. The following account is based largely on my 'Imperial Defence and the Transfer of Power in India 1946–1947', *International History Review*, vol. 4, 1982, pp. 568–68.

25. See chapter 2.

26. R.J. Moore, *Churchill, Cripps and India 1939–1945*, (Oxford 1979).

27. *TOP*, vol. 1, pp. 314–15.

28. B. Bond, *British Military Policy Between the Two World Wars* (Oxford 1980), p. 126.

29. Moore, *Churchill, Cripps and India*, pp. 114–16; S. Gopal, *Jawaharlal Nehru: A Biography, vol. 1, 1889–1947*, (London 1975), pp. 279 ff.

30. Linlithgow to Amery, 26 January 1943, *TOP*, vol. 3, p. 543.

31. Amery to Churchill, 16 April 1943, ibid., p. 895; Amery to Wavell, 26 March 1944, *TOP*, vol. 4, p. 838.

32. First draft of paper for cabinet by Bevin, 21 June 1943, Bevin papers, cited in P.S. Gupta, 'Imperial Strategy and the Transfer of Power, 1939–51', in A.K. Gupta (ed.), *Myth and Reality: The Struggle for Freedom in India, 1945–47*, (New Delhi 1987), p. 5.

33. War Cabinet India Committee papers, I(44)10, 28 December 1944, and 1(45)5, 9 January 1945, *TOP*, vol. 5, pp. 381, 339–40.

34. P. Darby, *British Defence Policy East of Suez, 1947–68*, (London 1973), pp. 11 ff; R.J. Moore, *Making the New Commonwealth* (Oxford 1987), pp. 12–13. See also Washington (Halifax) to FO, tel. 7516, 10 November 1945, FO800/470, and chapter 2.

35. Quoted in Connell, *Auchinleck*, pp. 830–1, emphasis mine; CP(46)96, 7 March 1946, ibid., pp. 1125–6; meeting between cabinet delegation and Wavell, 15 April 1946, *TOP*, vol. 7, p. 267; for example *New Statesman and Nation*, 22 March 1946, p. 149.

36. Enclosures 1 and 2 in Wavell to Pethick-Lawrence, 13 July 1946, *TOP*, vol. 8,

49–57; M.M. Gowing, 'Britain, America and the Bomb', in D.Dilks (ed.), *Retreat from Power* (London 1981), vol. 2, p. 126; CCOS(46)133rd meeting, 30 August 1946, *TOP*, vol. 8, p. 348; annex to CDC paper DO(46)104, 4 September 1946, ibid., pp. 415–16; Pethick-Lawrence to Attlee, 20 September 1946, ibid., p. 551. See also Gowing, *Independence and Deterrence: Britain and Atomic Energy, 1945–1952*, vol. 1, (London 1974), pp. 331–2; and J. Lewis, *Changing Direction: British Military Planning for Post-war Strategic Defence, 1942–47)*, (London 1988), pp. 159–60, 264–6, 315–17, 329.

37. Among the many statements by Nehru on this, see *National Herald*, 5 March 1946; confidential note for AICC by Nehru, 15 March 1946, S. Gopal (ed.), *Selected Works of Jawaharlal Nehru*, vol. 15, (New Delhi 1982), p. 106; *Hindustan Times*, 6 April 1946.

38. Monteath to Machtig, 8 November 1946, *TOP*, vol. 9, p. 31.

39. See chapter 4 of this book.

40. Note by Pethick-Lawrence and enclosure, 13 February 1946, *TOP*, vol. 6, pp. 951–63; note by Lt-Gen. Sir Arthur Smith on interview with Jinnah, 28 March 1946, *TOP*, vol. 7, p. 21; enclosure to Wavell to Pethick-Lawrence, 6 February 1946; *TOP*, vol. 6, pp. 892–8; note by Croft and Turnbull, 9 April 1946, *TOP*, vol. 7, pp. 196–8; memorandum by Cripps, undated but around 9 April 1946, ibid., pp. 174–80 and meeting between cabinet delegation and Wavell, 10 April 1946, ibid., pp. 209–12.

41. Enclosure to Wavell to Amery, 20 September 1944 and war cabinet India committee meeting, 26 March 1945, *TOP*, vol. 5, pp. 38–9, 735–6.

42. Note by Wavell, 7 September 1946, enclosed in Wavell to Pethick-Lawrence, 8 September 1946, Wavell to Pethick-Lawrence, 23 October 1946, and Wavell to Attlee, 30 October 1946, *TOP*, vol. 8, pp. 455–9, 794–9, 839–40 respectively.

43. Pethick-Lawrence to Wavell, 28 September 1946, *TOP*, vol. 8, pp. 620–2; Pethick-Lawrence to Wavell, 25 November 1946, *TOP*, vol. 9, p. 173.

44. Cabinet meeting, 5 June 1946, *TOP*, vol. 7, pp. 818–19; Downing Street meeting, 23 September 1946, *TOP*, vol. 8, pp. 570–1; undated notes by Attlee, *TOP*, vol. 9, pp. 68–9. Cf. Louis, *Middle East* on cabinet opposition to phased withdrawal from Iran, pp. 670ff.

45. IBCM, 11 and 17 December 1946, *TOP*, vol. 9, pp. 332–7 and 358 respectively.

46. IBCM, 11 December 1946, ibid., p. 335.

47. Confidential annex to CM(46) 108th conclusions, 31 December 1946, ibid., p. 428. Emphasis mine.

48. Annex to IBCM, 24 February 1947, ibid., p. 799, and note by Mountbatten, 11 February 1947, ibid., p. 674. Emphasis mine.

49. *Hansard*, vol. 434, 1947, cols. 507, 541.

50. Wavell to King George VI, 24 February 1947, *TOP*, vol. 9, p. 809.

51. Governor of Punjab to Viceroy, tel. 28-G, 5 March 1947, R/3/1/176, and Jenkins to Mountbatten, 4 August 1947, R/3/1/89. A fuller discussion can be found in my *Origins of Partition*, pp. 217ff.

52. Viceroy's personal report no. 11, 11 July 1947, L/P&J/10/81, and Mountbatten's *Secret Report of the Last Viceroyalty, 22 March–15 August 1947*, (London 1948), pp. 90, 172.

53. Harris, *Attlee*, p. 384; emphasis in original.
54. Viceroy's staff meeting, 28 March 1947, *TOP*, vol. 10, p. 35; Liaqat Ali Khan to Mountbatten, 7 April 1947, Mountbatten to Liaqat Ali Khan, 9 April 1947, interview between Liaqat Ali Khan and Mountbatten, 11 April 1947, Liaqat Ali Khan to Mountbatten, 13 April 1947, ibid., pp. 151–2, 165, 200–1, 220–1 respectively. See also interview between Mountbatten and Jinnah, 9 April 1947, ibid., p. 163, Defence Committee of India meeting, 25 April 1947, ibid., pp. 434–5.
55. SS to Viceroy, 3 July 1947, L/P&J/10/21; Stapleton to Monteath, 13 June 1947, ibid, COCCR, 8 August 1947, CAB134/117. See also Auchinleck to Mayne, tel, 14 September 1946, L/WS/1/1060, Pethick-Lawrence to Wavell, 26 September 1946, *TOP*, vol. 8, pp. 597–604; COSC report by Joint Planning Staff, 'Withdrawal of Indian troops', 27 May 1947, DEFE4/4; COCCR meeting, 8 August 1947, CAB134/117; Strategic Summary, 16 October 1947, DEFE4/8; CDC meeting, 4 August 1947, CAB131/5; note on defence arrangements in India by Minister of Defence, 3 July 1947, CAB134/34.
56. Enclosure, 'Chiefs of Staff Requirements of India and Pakistan', in H.C. Cowe (War Office) to D.F.C. Blunt (Treasury), 18 September 1947; H. Wilson-Smith (Treasury) to E. Speed (War Office), 4 October 1947, T225/23.
57. IB(47)135, 'Defence Arrangements in India', by Minister of Defence, 3 July 1947, CAB134/346; JP(47)47 (Final), 27 May 1947, DEFE4/4 and JP(47)93 16 October 1947, DEFE4/8.
58. Bevin to CIGS, 18 October 1947 (based on a minute by Orme Sargent), and Bevin to CIGS, 25 October 1947, FO800/451. During the Anglo–Iranian oil crisis in 1951, the Chiefs lamented the unavailability of the Indian army. See Louis, *Middle East*, p. 666.
59. Bevin to CIGS, 18 and 25 October 1947, FO800/451; CDC paper DO(49)66, memorandum by the Minister of Defence on 'The Requirements of National Defence: Size and Shape of the Armed Forces 1950–1953', 18 October 1949, CAB131/7.
60. CCAC meeting, 14 October 1947, Ismay's report on situation in India and Pakistan, CAB134/54; note by A. Carter of conversation with Jinnah on 1–3 October 1947, dated 8 October 1947, ibid; memorandum by SSCR, 'Indian–Pakistan Dispute', 26 October 1947, CCAC, ibid; Moore, *New Commonwealth*, pp. 21ff., p. Ziegler, *Mountbatten*, (Fontana paperback, 1986), pp. 443 ff. Gopal, *Nehru*, pp. 26 ff.
61. UK-Karachi to CRO, tel. 126, 13 October 1947, and Grafftey-Smith to A. Carter, 5 December 1947, Grafftey-Smith papers, Middle East Centre, St Antony's College, Oxford.
62. For better or worse(!), a thorough discussion of the Kashmir conflict is beyond the scope of this book, and I will simply list some references that I have found useful. General Scoones (CRO) was 'convinced' that Britain 'ought to back Pakistan in the interests of imperial defence', while Mountbatten and Cripps thought the opposite. Note by Gordon-Walker on Kashmir, 29 December 1947. On 4 April 1948, Gordon-Walker wrote that the CRO 'tends to be pro-Pakistan and originally produced a policy of bringing Pak troops into K[ashmir]. N[oel]-B[aker] has in fact become anti-Indian on this issue because if fighting is to be stopped & Pakistan is to be got to get the tribesmen out of K. this can only be acheived if India makes great concessions

and abandons in effect the rights deriving from K.'s accession to India.' File 1/6, Gordon Walker papers, Churchill College, Cambridge.

63. Grafftey-Smith to Addison, 3 September 1949, Grafftey-Smith papers.

64. Attlee was annoyed that Noel-Baker had got Britain into a position where they would have to take a very anti-India stand. Note by Gordon-Walker, 4 April 1948, Gordon-Walker's note of 21 April 1948, file 1/6, Gordon-Walker papers, and the exchange of telegrams between Attlee and Noel-Baker between 12 March to 7 April 1948 in FO800/470. See also Krishna Menon to Attlee, 17 February and 1 September 1948, boxes 67 and 73 respectively, Attlee papers, Bodleian Library, Oxford; Rajagopalachari to Cripps, 18 October 1948, CAB 127/146; US–New Delhi to SS, tel. 848, 17 September 1948, DS file 845. 00/9–1748.

65. Mountbatten to Gordon Walker, 27 February 1948, file 1/7, Gordon Walker papers; Secretary, COSC to CRO, 7 January 1948; COS(48) 4th meeting, 9 January 1948, DEFE4/10.

66. Orme Sargent to PM, 6 January 1948, and Ivone Kirkpatrick to PM, 13 January 1948, FO800/470.

67. Memorandum by SSCR, 'Indian–Pakistan [sic] dispute', 26 October 1947, CCAC, CAB 134/54.

68. CCCR, note by SSCR, 'The Commonwealth Relationship', 9 March 1948, CAB134/118; Attlee to Nehru, 11 March 1948, PREM8/820; CDC meeting, 16 September 1948, CAB131/5; Pethick-Lawrence to Mountbatten, 4 April 1947, TOP, vol. 10, pp. 6–7; CDC meeting, 19 December 1947, CAB131/5; CCAC meetings, 31 October and 14 November 1947, CAB134/54.

69. Secretary, COSC to CRO, 9 January 1948, annex 1, COS(48) 4th meeting and minute 2 of same meeting DEFE4/10; CCAC CA(47) 3rd and 4th meetings, 31 October and 14 November 1947 respectively, CAB134/54.

70. IBCM, 3 July 1947, CAB134/136 and COSC meeting, 12 November 1947, DEFE4/8; JP(48) 1 (S) (Final), enclosure to COS(48) 44th meeting, 3 March 1948, DEFE4/11.

71. Record of conversation between SSCR and Cawthorn, 18 September 1948; and extract, COS(48) 136th meeting, 24 September 1948, PREM8/997.

72. See chapter 2.

73. COS(49)39th meeting, 9 March 1949, DEFE4/20; Noel-Baker to Attlee, 13 April 1949, ibid.

74. COS(49)65th meeting, 4 May 1949 PREM8/997 and COS(49)76th meeting, 23 May 1949, DEFE4/22; H.L. Godfrey to J.L. Pumphrey, 2 June 1949, PREM8/930. On the other hand, Strang, Dening, and Macdonald did not expect any military links with India.

75. COS(49)96th meeting, 4 July 1949, DEFE4/22. Emphasis in original.

76. Grafftey-Smith to Noel-Baker, 24 June 1949, PREM8/1219.

77. Ibid., and Addison to Grafftey-Smith, 23 August 1949; CRO note, 'Proposed military guarantees to India and Pakistan', PREM8/1219; CDC paper, DO(50)27, 'Implications of War between India and Pakistan', 6 April 1950, CAB131/9; COS(50)208th meeting, 15 December 1950, DEFE4/38; C. Costley-White to S.J.L. Olver, 29 January 1951, FO371/92872.

78. Memorandum by SSCR, 'Defence burdens and the Commonwealth', 20 December 1949, DO35/2577.

79. Shone to Noel-Baker, 30 July 1948, FO371/69734.

80. COSC JPS JP(48)71, 3 July 1948, discussed at ministers' meeting, 28 July

1948, and annex 1 to the same meeting, FO800/444.

81. Extract from COS(48)160th meeting, 10 November 1948, FO800/454; W.S. Anderson (London) to SS, 28 December 1948, DS file 841.00/12–2848.

82. Cited in N. Mansergh, *The Commonwealth Experience* (London 1969), pp. 19–22; W.D. McIntyre, *Colonies into Commonwealth*, (London 1966), pp. 143–4; P. Gordon-Walker, *The Commonwealth* (London 1962), p. 15.

83. JP(47)93, 16 October 1947, DEFE4/8; CDC paper DO(48)12, 'Statement Relating to Defence', 23 January 1948, CAB 131/16, and note by Gordon Walker, 6 October 1947, file 1/6, Gordon-Walker papers.

84. JP(47)93, 16 October 1947, DEFE4/8, and CDC paper DO(48)12, 23 January 1948, CAB131/6, and CCCR meeting, 15 September 1947, annex D, note by Norman Brook, 'Defence and Commonwealth relations', CAB 134/117.

85. Annex to COSC meeting, 10 September 1947, DEFE4/47; Rothwell, op cit., p. 409; Thorne, op. cit., p. 342; CIBC meeting, 28 May 1947, *TOP*, vol. 10, p. 1019; memo of conversation between J.S. Sparks (SOA) and US ambassador to Pakistan, 26 December 1947, *FR, 1947*, vol. 3, pp. 177–78.

86. CP(49)67, 17 March 1949, CAB129/33, part 2. See also Grady to SS, tel. A-106, 22 March 1948, DS file no. 845.00/3–2248. Also see K.P.S. Menon, *The Flying Troika*, (London 1963); T.N. Kaul, *Diplomacy in Peace and War*, (New Delhi 1979), and V. Pandit, *The Scope of Happiness: A Personal Memoir*, (London 1979); Nehru's report on Commonwealth conference, 7 May 1949, cited in Gopal *Nehru*, vol. 2, p. 46.

87. Entry for 15 October 1948, B. Pimlott (ed), *The Political Diary of Hugh Dalton 1918–40, 1945–60* (London 1986), p. 443.

88. See my 'Economic Consequences of India's Position in the Commonwealth: the Official British Thinking in 1949', *Indo-British Review*, vol. 11, 1984, pp. 106–11; and C.G. Ramasubbu, 'India and the Sterling Area', *India Quarterly*, vol. 5, 1949, pp. 244–53, B.R. Tomlinson, 'Indo-British Relations in the Post-Colonial Era: The Sterling Balances Negotiations, 1947–49', *Journal of Imperial and Commonwealth History*, vol. 13, 1985, pp. 142–62, and chapter 6 of this book.

89. The following account is based on COCCR papers GEN 276/1 to 276/4. Most of the material from these papers was incorporated into GEN 275/6, 22 February 1949, CAB130/45. See also M. Kidron, *Private Investment in India* (London 1968), pp. 97 ff.

90. *SW*, vol. 7, p. 625; emphasis mine.

91. As in fn. 89 above.

92. FO memo, COCCR, GEN276/2, 16 February 1949, CAB130/45.

93. Guidelines for coming UN General Assembly session, 12 September 1948, *SW*, vol. 7, pp. 611; SW, vol. 8, pp. 288–9, 329–30; See also FMM(50)3rd meeting, 10 Jan. 1950, CAB133/78. Indian reservations about an Asian union were summed up by H. Venketasubbiah, 'Prospects for an Asian Union', *India Quarterly* vol. 5, 1949, pp. 212–28.

94. GEN 276/6, 22 February 1949, CAB130/45.

95. COCCR, memo by Colonial Office, 17 February 1949, GEN 276/4, CAB130/45.

96. Enclosure, Laithwaite to N. Brook, 5 August 1948, CAB21/1818.

97. GEN 276/6, 22 February 1949, CAB130/45.

98. COS(49)25th meeting, 14 February 1949, DEFE4/19; COS(49)31st meeting,

21 February 1949, DEFE4/20; COS(49)53rd meeting, 8 April 1949, DEFE4/21.

99. CP(49)53, 14 March 1949, CAB129/33, pt. 1; Noel-Baker to Attlee, 20 April 1949 and annexes A and B to same, CAB21/1824. For discussion on changes in nomenclature, see PREM8/802, DO35/2187 and DO35/2250. For some Indian views of the New Commonwealth, see, *SW*, vol. 8, pp. 245 ff, and V.K.R.V. Rao, 'The New Commonwealth – Will It Endure?', *India Quarterly*, vol. 6, 1950, pp. 3–17.

100. Statement in the Commons on 6 March 1947, cited in M. Gilbert, *Winston S. Churchill, 1945–1965*, vol. 8, p. 299; memo of conversation between Eden and Acting SS Grew, 16 May 1945, DS file 711. 41/5–1645.

101. Shone to Noel-Baker, 30 July 1948, FO371/69734.

102. ibid.

103. Annex to minsters meeting, 28 July 1948, and JP(48)71, 3 July 1948, FO800/444.

Notes to Chapter 2

1. Annex to JP(48) 56 (Final), 9 June 1948, DEFE4/13.
2. Nye to Cripps, 20 December 1948, CAB127/43; Bevin to F. Roberts, 27 February 1951, FO800/470.
3. This was despite the fact that Pakistan remained a dominion until 1956, while India became a republic in 1950.
4. Strang, Macdonald and Dening did not think that India would enter into any alignment, while Attlee, A.V. Alexander, and the Chiefs continued to entertain such hopes for some time after India decided to remain in the Commonwealth as a republic.
5. This section is based on CP(49)67, 17 March 1949, CAB129/33, part 2; Dening's brief on Southeast Asia and the Far East, enclosed in Dening to C. Syers, 18 March 1949, FO371/76023; Macdonald to Bevin, 23 March 1949, FO371/76033; record of FO meeting on 24 May 1949, FO371/76034; PUSC reports, 28 July and 20 August 1949, FO371/76030. See also the essays by D.C. Watt, 'Britain and the Cold War in the Far East, 1945–58', T. Yoshihiko, 'The Cominform and South-east Asia', in Y. Nagai and A. Iriye (eds), *The Origins of the Cold War in Asia*, (Tokyo 1977), pp. 89–122 and 362–77 respectively. On Malaya, see A.J. Stockwell, 'Insurgency and Decolonization during the Malayan Emergency', *Journal of Commonwealth and Comparative Politics*, vol. 25, 1987, pp. 71–81. The Malayan communists formally ended their struggle in November 1989.
6. CP(49)67, 17 March 1949, CAB129/33; PUSC reports, 28 July and 20 August 1949, FO371/76030. See also N. Tarling, 'The United Kingdom and the Origins of the Colombo Plan', *Journal of Commonwealth and Comparative Politics*, vol. 24, 1986, pp. 3–34; and R. Ovendale, 'Britain and the Cold War in Asia', in his *Foreign Policy of British Labour Governments, 1945–51*, (Leicester 1984), pp. 121–47 and his *The English-Speaking Alliance*, (London 1985), pp. 145 ff.
7. Maclennan to Dening, 21 March 1949, FO371/76023.
8. Dening to C. Syers, 4 April 1949, FO371/76031.
9. PUSC(53) Final Approved, 20 August 1949, FO371/76030.
10. Macdonald to Bevin, 23 March 1949, FO371/76033; minute from Bevin to Attlee, 21 April 1949, FO800/462, and enclosure on South Asia by Bevin, 14 April 1949, FO800/445. See also Singapore to FO, tel. 928, 6 November 1949 and minute by Strang, 30 November 1949, FO371/76010.
11. Draft by Reading on economic development in South and Southeast Asia, 2 November 1954, FO371/111915.

12. CP(50)200, 30 August 1950, CAB129/41.
13. Minute by R.H. Scott on British Policy in the Far East, 30 October 1951, FO371/92065.
14. H. Isaacs, *Scratches on the Mind*, (New York 1958), pp. 38, 67, 89, 239–41, 302–13. When Dean Rusk took up his post in the intelligence section of the War Department in 1941, the principal file – marked confidential – on 'British Asia' was a tourist handbook on India and Ceylon. T.J. Schoenbaum, *Waging Peace and War: Dean Rusk in the Truman, Kennedy and Johnson Years*, (New York 1988), p. 75.
15. See R.G. Good, 'The United States and the Colonial Debate', in A.C. Wolfers (ed.), *Alliance Policy in the Cold War*, (Baltimore 1959), especially pp. 224–69; G. McT. Kahin, 'The United States and the Anticolonial Revolutions in Southeast Asia, 1945–50', in Nagai and Iriye (eds), op. cit., pp. 338–61; R. McMahon, *Colonialism and the Cold War*, (Ithaca 1981); J. Sbrega, 'The Anticolonial Policies of Franklin D. Roosevelt: A Reappraisal', *Political Science Quarterly*, vol. 101, 1986, pp. 65–84; K.J. Clymer, 'Franklin D. Roosevelt, Louis Johnson, India and Anticolonialism: Another Look', *Pacific Historical Review*, vol. 57, 1988, pp. 261–84; M. Kahler, 'The United States and the Third World: Decolonization and After', in L. Carl Brown, (ed.), *Centerstage*, (New York 1990), pp. 104–20.
16. M.S. Venkataramani and B.K. Shrivastava, *Roosevelt–Gandhi–Churchill: America and the Last Phase of India's Freedom Struggle*, (New Delhi 1983), pp. 314–52.
17. Chargé d'Affaires, US–New Delhi to SS, tel. 1039, 7 December 1945, DS file 711.45/12–745, and Donovan (Bombay) to SS, tel. 755, 8 December 1945, DS file 711.45/12–845.
18. CIA report SR-21, 16 September 1948, 'India-Pakistan', and CIA report ORE 25–48, 3 September 1948, 'The Break up of the Colonial Empires and its Implications for US Security', TL.
19. Grady to Truman, 19 July 1947, PSF Subject file, Truman papers and Truman to Grady, 8 August 1947, ibid., TL. See also D. Merrill, 'Indo–American Relations, 1947–50: A Missed Opportunity in Asia', *Diplomatic History*, vol. 11, 1987, pp. 203–26.
20. Grady to SS, despatch no. 237, 16 March 1948, DS file 745.00/3–1648.
21. DS Policy Statement on India, 20 May 1948, DS file 711.45/4–248.
22. CIA report SR-21, 16 September 1948; Oral History Interview with J. Wesley Adams, 18 December 1972, pp. 90–2, TL.
23. Washington to FO, tels. 1904 and 1905, 24 March 1946, and minute from Attlee to Bevin, 25 March 1946, FO800/470.
24. CIA reports ORE 25–48, 3 September 1948, 'The Break-Up of the Colonial Empires and Its Implications for US Security', p. 6; SR-25, 7 December 1949, 'United Kingdom'; ORE 93–49, 23 December 1949, 'The Possibility of Britain's Abandonment of Overseas Military Commitments', all TL; NEA Department to MEA Department, 31 January 1946, DS file 711.45/-3146.
25. NEA to Middle East department, 31 January 1946, DS file 711.45/1–3146; report of SANACC Subcommittee for Near and Middle East, Appendix B, *FR, 1949*, vol. 6, p. 13. See also Washington to FO, tel. 7516, 10 November 1945, FO800/470; *Documents on British Policy Overseas*, series I, vol. 3, pp. 138–40; and American JCS reports on US requirements for bases and military

rights, dated 27 September 1945, 30 June 1946, JPS report, 8 January 1946, RG 218, series CCS 360 (12–9–42), JCS 570/34, 570/52, and JPS 781 respectively, cited in Leffler, op. cit., p. 353.

26. Enclosure 1 to secret despatch no. 8, from Henderson to DS, 3 January 1949, DS file 845.00/1–349.

27. CIA report, SR-25, 7 December 1949, TL.

28. *FR, 1949*, vol. 6, p. 16. While I do not share some of the views of H.W. Brands, 'India and Pakistan in American Strategic Planning 1947–54: the Commonwealth as Collaborator', *Journal of Imperial and Commonwealth History*, vol. 25, 1986, pp. 41–55, I have found the article stimulating.

29. Appendix B to SANACC subcommittee report, 19 April 1949, *FR, 1949*, vol. 6, pp. 16–17, and memo from JCS, 24 March 1949, ibid., p. 30.

30. Cited in Venkataramani, *American Role in Pakistan*, p. 21; JCS memo, 24 March 1949, *FR, 1949*, vol. 6, pp. 30–1; report of SANACC subcommittee for rearmament, 18 August 1949, *FR, 1949*, vol. 1, pp. 262–3; Policy Paper approved by Foreign Assitance Correlation Committee, 7 February 1949, *FR, 1949*, vol. 1, pp. 253–4; SANACC report, 19 April 1949, *FR, 1949*, vol. 6, pp. 21–2.

31. *FR, 1949*, vol. 6, pp. 25–6.

32. Ibid.

33. PPS report, 24 February 1948, *FR, 1948*, vol. 1, part 2, pp. 523–6, and *FR, 1949*, vol. 6, p. 30.

34. SS to Acting SS, 29 October 1948, *FR*, 1948, vol. 5, part 1, pp. 435–6 and *FR, 1949*, vol. 6. pp. 17, 41.

35. Grady to SS, 9 July 1947, *FR, 1947*, vol. 3, pp. 160–1. On 12 May 1947, Baldev Singh, Minister of Defence in the interim government, told Merrell that India would prefer closer economic relations with the US than with the UK. US–New Delhi (Merrell) to SS, tel. 324, 12 May 1947, DS file 845. 00/5–1247.

36. Memo of conversation, 26 December 1947, DS file 845.00/12–2647.

37. Nehru to Krishna Menon, 26 June 1948, cited in S. Gopal, *Jawaharlal Nehru: A Biography, vol. 2, 1947–56*, (London 1979), p. 45.

38. US–New Delhi to SS, tel. 184, 3 March 1948, DS file 745.45F/3–348, and memo of conversation between Bajpai and Henderson, 2 April 1948, DS file 711.45/4–248; memo of conversation between Bajpai and Lovett, 2 April 1948, ibid.; memo of conversation by Mathews, 28 April 1948, *FR, 1948* vol. 5, part 1, pp. 501–6. See also memo of conversation between B.R. Sen, (Indian Chargé d'Affaires Washington), and J.S. Sparks, 29 April 1949, DS file 845.00/4–2949.

39. *FR, 1948*, vol. 5 part 1, p. 504, and DS Policy Statement on India, 20 May 1948, DS file 711.45/4–248.

40. S. Gopal (ed.), *SW*, vol. 1, pp. 572–3.

41. SS to Acting SS, 16 October 1948, *FR, 1948*, vol.5, part 1, pp. 516–17.

42. Henderson to SS, 3 January 1949, file 890.00/1–349, and Kennan to Henderson, enclosed in Lovett to Henderson, 5 January 1949, DS file 890.00/1–549.

43. See Nehru's memos and letters on Indonesia in *SW*, vol. 8, pp. 373ff; Gopal, *Nehru*, pp. 59; and DS (Acheson) to US–Bangkok, 26 January 1949, DS file 890.00/1–2649.

44. DS memo of conversation between Bajpai and Henderson, 2 April 1948, DS 711.45/4–248. See also H. Venkatasubbiah, 'Prospects for an Asian Union',

part 2, *India Quarterly*, vol. 5, 1949, pp. 212–28.

45. Gopal, *Nehru*, vol. 2, p. 59; emphasis in original.

46. T.G. Paterson, 'Foreign Aid Under Wraps: the Point Four Program', *Wisconsin Magazine of History*, vol. 56, (Winter 1972–3), pp. 119–26, quoted in Dennis Merrill, *Bread and the Ballott: The United States and India's Economic Development, 1947–1963*, (Chapel Hill and London 1990), p. 34. See also A. Rotter, *The Path to Vietnam*, (Ithaca 1987), pp. 18–20.

47. Memo by Acheson of conversation with Bevin, 4 April 1949, *FR, 1949*, vol. 6, p. 53.

48. Franks to FO, 10 May 1949, FO371/75566; Nye to Franks and Dening, 20 July 1949, FO371/76100: Garner to Roberts, 27 July 1949, DO35/2579; Douglas to SS, 29 July 1949, DS file 898.00/7–2949; record of conversation, 12 September 1949, in Dening to Scarlett, 17 September 1949, FO371/76032. The DS version of this conversation is in *FR, 1949*, vol.7, part 2, pp. 1197–203. See also Dening to Strang, 15 September 1949, FO371/76024, and minute, 16 September 1949, FO371/76037.

49. US–New Delhi despatch no. 272 (from Donovan) to SS, 28 March 1949, DS file 845.00/3–2849. See also *FR, 1950*, vol. 6, pp. 2, 27–8, 35–6, 122.

50. Dening to Strang, 15 September 1949, FO371/76024 and FO minute, 16 September 1949, FO371/76037.

51. Oral History interview with John F. Cady, Chief of the South Asian section of NEA affairs 1945–7, p. 31, TL. British diplomats in New Delhi considered Mrs Henderson a liability to her husband. Nye thought Henderson was 'much handicapped by his wife . . . who sees the nefarious hand of the Kremlin everywhere and who is, in addition, extremely indiscreet and tiresome'. Frank Roberts thought that she 'is of course a public menace'. Nye to Syers, 15 March 1950 and Roberts to Gore-Booth (Washington), 13 November 1950, DO35/2932. Henry Deimel, Special Assistant to the Director of the NEA, 1945–9, thought that Henderson was 'very much disturbed by the fact that India recognized Red China while he was there [in India].' Oral History interview, 5 June 1975, p. 99, TL.

52. Henderson to SS, 22 December 1948, file 845.00/12–2248 and Henderson to SS, 3 January 1949, DS file 890.00/1–349.

53. Memo of conversation between Jessup and Mrs Pandit, 17 August 1950, DS file 611.91/8–1750. Nye and Roberts were aware of the poor relations between Henderson and Nehru; as in note 48 above. See also Nehru to Henderson, enclosure 2 to confidential despatch no. 40 from Donovan to SS, 10 January 1949, DS file 845.00/1–1049.

54. This paragraph is based on US–New Delhi to SS, tel. 26, 8 January 1949, DS file 711.45/1–849 and Henderson to SS, secret despatch no. 361, 30 April 1949, DS file 845.00/4–3049; Henderson Oral History interview, pp. 64, 171–2, TL. See also Grady to SS, secret despatch no. 237, 16 March 1948, DS file 745.00/3–1648. At least one British diplomat confirmed that there was *some* justification for the American allegation that the British were behind Indian opposition to the US. 'There is . . . no denying the fact that there may be some truth in this.' D.L. Cole (New Delhi) to D.J.C. Crawley (Washington), 21 December 1953, FO371/112212.

55. Henderson Oral History interview, pp. 169–70.

56. Grady to SS, despatch no. 237, 16 March 1948, DS file 745.00/3–1648;

CP(49)67, 17 March 1949, CAB129/33; part 2, Nye to Syers, 15 March 1950, DO35/2932.

57. Memo of conversation between Bajpai and Henderson, 2 April 1948, DS file 711.45/4–248.

58. Memo of Acheson's conversation with Mrs Pandit, 30 August 1949, Acheson papers, box 64, file: memos of conversations Aug–Sept 1949; Dean Acheson, *Present at the Creation*, (New York 1969), p. 334, and memorandum by Jessup, Fosdick and Case to SS, 2 September 1949, DS file 711.90/9–249; Johnson to Acheson, 9 September 1949, DS file 845.002/9-949.; Webb to Johnson, 8 October 1949, DS file 845.002/9–949; Mathews to McGhee, 6 September 1949, DS file 845.002/9–649.

59. Memo of conversation between Nehru, Mrs Pandit, Bajpai, Kennan, Jessup, McGhee and others, 13 October 1949, Acheson papers, box 64, TL; and memo to certain American diplomatic and consular officers, 20 January 1950, DS file 691.00/1–2050.

60. Memo of conversation by Acheson, 13 October 1949, PSF subject file, Truman papers, TL.

61. Gopal, *Nehru*, vol. 2, pp. 60–1; Oral History interview with Fraser Wilkins on 20 June 1975, p. 75, TL; Acheson to Henderson, 21 November 1949, DS file 845.61311/10–2749; CIA memo by R. Hillenkoetter, 'Observations of Pandit Nehru on international affairs with particular reference to India's relations with the United States, Great Britain and the Soviet Union', 20 December 1949, PSF Subject file, CIA intelligence, Truman papers, TL. The US embassy in New Delhi commented acerbically that the Indian press had exaggerated the importance of India and Nehru in American eyes. US–New Delhi to SS, tel. 1241, 14 October 1949, DS file 845.00(W)/10–1449.

62. For recent debates on the US recognition of China, see Warren Cohen 'Acheson, His Advisers and China, 1949–50', in D. Borg and W. Henrichs (eds), *Uncertain Years: Chinese American Relations 1947–1950*, (New York 1980), pp. 15–52; N. Tucker, *Patterns in the Dust: Chinese–American Relations and the Recognition Controversy, 1949–1950*, (New York 1983), R. Blum, *Drawing the Line: The Origin of the American Containment Policy in East Asia*, (New York 1982); D. McLean, 'American Nationalism, the China Myth and the Truman Doctrine: The Question of Accommodation with Peking', *Diplomatic History*, vol. 10, 1986, pp. 25–42; E.M. Martin, *Divided Counsel: The Anglo–American Response to Communist Victory in China*, (Lexington 1986); Yuan Ming, 'The Failure of Perception: America's China Policy, 1949–50', in H. Harding and Y. Ming (eds), *Sino-American Relations, 1945–1955: A Joint Reassessment of a Critical Decade*, (Wilmington 1989). pp. 143–56, and G. Chang, *Friends and Enemies*, (Cornell University Press Ithaca 1986).

63. *Hansard*, vol. 469, 1949, cols. 2225–6, D.C. Wolf, 'To Secure a Convenience', *Journal of Contemporary History*, vol. 18, 1983, pp. 299–326.

64. *Survey of International Affairs 1949* (London, 1953), p. 336; Robin Edmonds, *Setting the Mould* (Oxford, 1986), p. 147; and P. Lowe, *The Origins of Korean War*, p. 109.

65. See the many letters written by Nehru between December 1948 and September 1949 in his *Letters to Chief Ministers*, vol. 1, especially on pp. 231–2, 260–2, 308–9, 323–4, 354–5, 369–70, 374–5, 467.

66. For a fuller discussion of this point see John Gaddis, *The Long Peace*, pp. 165 ff.
67. CM(18)49, 8 March 1949, CAB 128/15.
68. The nuances of the debate are illuminating, but they should not be confused with the real thing – the decision itself – and its effects on international relations. For example, John Gaddis's identification of Dulles as a prime mover behind the strategy of increasing pressure on China in order to exacerbate Sino–Soviet tensions leads him to come close to crediting Dulles with forging the Sino–American *rapprochement* in 1972. See Gaddis, *The Long Peace*, p. 174, and the comments by Richard Immerman, 'In Search of History and Relevancy: Breaking Through the "Encrustations of Interpretation" '; *Diplomatic History*, vol. 12, 1988, p. 353. See also NSC 48/1, 25 October 1949, PSF, file NSC meeting no. 50, 29 December 1949, and DS background memoranda on Nehru's visit, PSF Subject file: India – Pandit Nehru, Truman papers, TL.
69. Report by Frank Roberts on conversation with Bajpai, 21 November 1949, F0371/76097.
70. The following account is based on CM(49)62nd conclusions, 27 October 1949, CAB 128/16; note by Bevin on conversation with Nehru, 12 November 1949, FO371/75822; Noel-Baker's record of his conversation with Nehru, 13 November 1949, FO371/75823; minute by Scarlett, 14 November 1949, FO371/75822; CRO brief for Noel-Baker, 14 November 1949, FO371/75824; Indian government memo on recognition of the new regime in China, enclosed in Krishna Menon to Bevin, 21 November 1949, FO371/75823; UK–New Delhi to CRO, 16 November 1949, priority tels. 1947 and 1948; FO to Washington, tel. 10979, 23 November 1949, FO 371/75822 and minutes from Strang to Bevin, 24 and 25 November 1949, F0371/75824; CP(49)244 and CP(49)248, 26 November and 12 December 1949 respectively, CAB129/37 part. 3.
71. Ibid.
72. Ibid., and minute by Bevin of conversation with Nehru, 12 November 1949 FO 371/75822.
73. UK–New Delhi to CRO, 1 December 1949, tel. immediate X2031, FO371/75825.
74. UK–New Delhi to CRO, tel. X2049, 3 December 1949; ibid; Nehru to Attlee, 19 December 1949, text of message from Attlee to Nehru, 19 December 1949; statements by Bevin and Nehru at Colombo conference, FMM(50)3rd meeting, 10 January 1950, CAB 133/78; and minute by P. Scarlett, 22 December 1949, FO371/75829.
75. Ovendale, *The English-Speaking Alliance* p. 200.
76. NSC 48/1, 23 December 1949, PSF, Subject file, box 207, file NSC meeting no. 50, 29 December 1949, Truman papers, TL.
77. Policy Statement on UK, 7 June 1950, DS file 611.41/6–750.
78. See chapters 3 and 5 below.
79. As in note 76 above.
80. Oral History interview with Joseph C. Satterthwaite, then US ambassador to Ceylon, 13 November 1972, p. 36, TL.
81. Ibid., pp. 39–40. Bevin, however, thought that 'adequate steps' were taken to ensure that the US government were kept informed of the proceedings of the Colombo conference. Bevin's draft note, enclosed in Dening to Garner, 17 February 1950, DO35/2773.

Notes to Chapter 3

1. US officials recognised early that Commonwealth consultations were not always in the American interest. 'The greater the degree of United Kingdom resistance or dislike to a given request, the more certain complete consultation with the Commonwealth will be.' Satterthwaite to Perkins, Labouisse and Thompson, 3 November 1949, DS file 711.411/11–349. See also Henderson's memo of his conversation with Sir Rama Rau, 6 February 1950, DS file 611.91/2–650. Interestingly British officials also doubted that the Commonwealth would influence India to come on the side of the West in a war. From New Delhi, Roberts commented, 'It would be over-optimistic to suppose that India would intervene on our side from considerations other than her own security interpreted in a narrow sense, and the fact of the Commonwealth connection would not be likely to influence her in deciding her policy.' Roberts to Liesching, 27 May 1950, and confidential annex to COS(50)103rd meeting, 6 July 1950, D035/2580.
2. Memo by Henderson of conversation with Nehru, enclosure 3 to despatch no. 332, 9 February 1950, DS file 691.00/2–950.
3. Cited by B. Shiva Rao and C. Kondapi, 'India and the Korean Crisis', *India Quarterly*, vol. 7, 1951, p. 301.
4. The sheer length of the historiography of the Korean war is formidable; to list only a handful of the works that I have found most useful: B.J. Bernstein, 'New Light on the Korean War', *International History Review*, vol. 3, 1981, pp. 256–77; A. Bullock, *Ernest Bevin: Foreign Secretary*, pp. 790 ff., M. Dockrill, 'The Foreign Office, Anglo-American relations and the Korean war, June 1950–June 1951', *International Affairs*, vol. 62, 1986, pp. 459–76; R. Foot, 'Anglo-American Relations in the Korean Crisis', *Diplomatic History*, vol. 10, 1986, pp. 43–57: J.L. Gaddis, *Strategies of Containment*, pp. 89 ff; B.I. Kaufman, *The Korean War*, (New York 1986); E.C. Keefer, 'President Dwight D. Eisenhower and the End of the Korean War', *Diplomatic History*, vol. 10, 1986, pp. 267–89; C. Macdonald, *Korea: the War Before Vietnam*, (New York 1986); R. Ovendale, *The English-Speaking Alliance*, pp. 211 ff; W.W. Stueck Jr, *The Road to Confrontation*, (Chapel Hill 1981); and 'The Korean War as International History', *Diplomatic History*, vol. 10, 1986, pp. 291–309. See also Rosemary Foot's review of the historiography of the Korean war, 'Making Known the Unknown War: Policy Analysis of the Korean Conflict in the Last Decade', *Diplomatic History*, vol. 15, pp. 411–31. Some other works consulted are listed in the notes below.

5. For the official British account, see A. Farrar-Hockley, *The British Part in the Korean War*, vol. 1, (London 1990).

6. SS to US-New Delhi, 27 June 1950, *FR, 1950*, vol. 7, p. 210; Henderson to SS, 28 and 29 June 1950, ibid., pp. 218–19, 230–1 and 234–6 respectively; Henderson to SS, 7 July 1950; ibid., p. 244; Nehru, *Letters to Chief Ministers*, 2 July 1950, vol. 2, pp. 118 ff.

7. CP(50)159, 5 July 1950 CAB129/41; minute by Dening, 7 July 1950, and minute by Pierson Dixon, 6 July 1950, FO371/84085.

8. Nehru to Attlee, 8 July 1950, FO371/84090; Acting UK–New Delhi to CRO, tels. 1836, 1837, 1838, 8 July 1950 and Acting UK–New Delhi to CRO, tel. 1866, 11 July 1950, FO371/84089; Nehru to Attlee, 10 July 1950, FO371/84088. See also *FR, 1950* vol. 7, pp. 235–6, 284.

9. R. Foot, *The Wrong War* (Ithaca 1985), pp. 64 ff, P. Lowe, *The Origins of the Korean War* (London 1986), pp. 163 ff.

10. Douglas to SS, 8 July 1950, *FR, 1950*, vol. 7, p. 331.

11. Ibid., pp. 329–31, 284, 340–1.

12. Ibid., 342–3, 359–60; memo of conversation with President on 10 July 1950, file: Memo of conversations, July 1950, box 65, Acheson papers, TL; SS to London, 10 July 1950, *FR, 1950*, vol. 7, pp. 347–51.

13. Douglas to SS, 11 July 1950, ibid., pp. 361–2; Douglas to SS, 14 July 1950, ibid., pp. 380–4; minute by Strang, 15 July 1950, FO371/84091.

14. Nehru to Attlee, 10 July 1950, FO371/84088; Acting UK–New Delhi to CRO, tel. 1880, 13 July 1950, FO371/84090; Moscow to FO, tel. 611, 14 July 1950, FO371/84087; *FR, 1950*, vol. 7, pp. 401, 408.

15. Nehru to Attlee, 14 July 1950, FO371/84049.

16. Minute by Bevin, sent as FO to Washington, tel. 3243, 18 July 1950, FO371/84088. Minute by R.E. Barclay, 12 July 1950, FO371/84086, see also minute by Younger, 11 July 1950, FO371/84091; Attlee to Nehru, 14 July 1950, in FO to Washington, tel. 3193, FO371/84088; Washington to FO, tel. 2003, 19 July 1950, FO371/84089; FO to Moscow, tel. 667, 24 July 1950, FO371/84091.

17. *FR, 1950*, vol. 7, p. 408; R.E. Barclay to D.H.F. Rickett, 18 July 1950, FO371/84089; Attlee to Nehru, 18 July 1950, in FO to Washington, tel. 3246, FO371/84088.

18. Acting UK–New Delhi to CRO, tel. 1917, 18 July 1950, FO371/84089; Kirk to SS, 1 August 1950, *FR, 1950*, vol. 7, pp. 512–13.

19. Nehru to Attlee, 21 July 1950, CAB127/143; Burrows (Karachi) to Maclennan (CRO), 21 July 1950, FO371/84093; note by Lord Ogmore, 1 August 1950, FO371/84096; Strasbourg (Bevin) to FO, tel. 5, 3 August 1950, conveyed by Strang to Chancery, Washington, 5 August 1950, ibid.

20. Nehru to Attlee, 21 July 1950, CAB127/143. See also his *Letters to Chief Ministers*, 15 July 1950, vol. 2, pp. 138–47; Roberts to Liesching, 5 August 1950, FO371/84091.

21. Minute by Strang, 10 August 1950, FO371/84095; minute by P.C. Homer, 12 August 1950, FO371/84094.

22. CP(50)200, 30 August 1950, CAB 129/41.

23. Henderson to SS, tel. 393, 14 August 1950, *FR, 1950*, vol. 7, p. 580.

24. M. Trachtenberg, 'A "Wasting Asset": American Strategy and the Shifting Nuclear Balance 1949–1954', *International Security*, vol. 13, 1988/89 pp. 18, 28. and Foot, op. cit, p. 37.

25. *FR, 1950*, vol. 5, pp. 202–3, and J.J.S. Garner to Roberts, 26 September 1950, FO371/84094.
26. Nehru, *Letters to Chief Ministers*, 14 Sept. 1950, p. 196.
27. *FR, 1950*, vol. 7, pp. 742–3; Henderson to SS, 23 September and 27 September 1950, ibid., pp. 763 and 790–2 respectively; Nehru to Bevin and Bevin to Nehru, 29 September 1950, FO371/84109; Attlee to Bevin, 28 September 1950, in tel. 1488, FO to New York; and Attlee to Nehru, 29 September 1950, FO371/84097, Nehru to Bevin, sent in UK–New Delhi to CRO, tel. 2765, 28 September 1950, FO371/84098.
28. Oliver Franks Oral History interview, TL, pp. 24–5; Bevin to Nehru, in New York to FO, tel. 1232, 27 September 1950, FO371/84097; Attlee to Bevin in FO to New York, tel. 1488, 28 September 1950, ibid; Nehru to Bevin, in UK–New Delhi to New York, tel. 2765, 28 September 1950 and Bevin to Nehru, in New York to FO, tel. 1258, 29 September 1950, FO371/84098.
29. *FR, 1950*, vol. 7, pp. 793–4, 810; Acheson to Bevin, 28 September 1950, ibid., pp. 811–12. See also Ronald Steel, *Walter Lippmann and the American Century*, (London 1981), p. 472.
30. Henderson to SS, tel. 812, 30 September 1950, *FR, 1950*, vol. 7, pp. 831–2, 7 October 1950, ibid., pp. 902–3.
31. Memo of conversation between Younger, Jebb and Allison, 4 October 1950, ibid., pp. 868–9.
32. UK–New Delhi to CRO, tels 2804 and 2805, 3 Oct. 1950, FO371/84109; and tel. 2807, 4 October 1950, FO371/84110.
33. MacArthur to Joint Chiefs of Staff, 28 November 1950, *FR, 1950*, vol. 7, p. 1237. On China's decision to intervene, see J.D. Pollack, 'The Korean War and Sino–American Relations', in H. Harding and Y. Ming (eds), *Sino–American Relations, 1945–1955: A Joint Reassessment of a Critical Decade*, (Wilmington 1989), pp. 213–37.
34. Mrs Pandit to Nehru, 18 December 1950, cited in Gopal, *Nehru*, vol. 2, p. 109.
35. The text of Pearson's message to Nehru is in FO371/84106. See also Nehru to Attlee, in FO to Peking, 5 December 1950, tel. 2071, FO371/84134. On Bevin's interest in Indian mediation, see his minute of 6 December 1950, FO371/84105.
36. UK-New Delhi to CRO, tel. 3401, 5 December 1950, FO371/84106; Nehru, *Letters to Chief Ministers*, 1 February 1951, vol. 2, pp. 315–16. Nehru's opinion is corroborated by evidence from Chinese sources. Chou En-lai wrote:

    'By using the bases in Japan, the United States inherited the adventurism of the Japanese militarists, following the history since the war of 1895 and took the track of conquering China, namely, to occupy North-east China before annexing China and to occupy Korea before grabbing North-east China . . . . For us, the Korean question is not simply a question concerning Korea, it is related to the Taiwan issue . . . after occupying North Korea, they [the US] will come to attack China.' *Selected Works of Zhou Enlai*, vol. 2, p. 52, quoted by Hao Yufan and Zhai Zhihai, 'China's Decision to Enter the Korean War: History Revisited', *China Quarterly*, no. 121, 1990, p. 103.

37. New York to FO, tel. 1932, 4 December 1950, FO371/841120; tel. 1933, 4 December 1950, FO371/84105; UK-New Delhi to CRO, tel. 3401, 5

December 1950, FO371/84106. See also FO minute, 'Far Eastern Section of Washington Brief, Section V: Korea', 4 December 1950, FO371/84122.

38. UK-New Delhi to CRO, tel. 3401, 5 December 1950, and Peking to FO, tel. 1975, 7 December 1950, FO371/84106.

39. Nehru to Attlee, 3 December 1950, FO371/84123. Attlee was 'very anxious to keep in the closest possible touch' with Nehru. Draft letter from Attlee to Nehru is in Emery (CRO) to Hunt, around 14 December 1950, FO371/84108. See also minute by Bevin, 6 December 1950, FO371/84105.

40. *FR, 1950*, vol. 7, pp. 1374, 1383, 1385.

41. *FR, 1950*, vol. 7, pp. 1398, 1384; Washington to FO, tel. 3281, 4 December 1950 and Attlee to Nehru, in Washington to FO, tel. 3294, 5 December 1950, FO371/84105.

42. FO to PM (Ottawa), tel. 1334, 9 December 1950, FO371/84105.

43. Minute by J.S.H. Shattock, 10 December 1950, FO371/84123. New York to FO, tels. 1999 and 2000, 9 December 1950, FO371/84122.

44. Minute by Bevin, incorporated in FO to New York, tel. 2295, 10 December; tel. 2012, 11 December; tel. 2303, 12 December 1950, FO371/84122.

45. New York to FO, tel. 2012, 11 December 1950, ibid., and New York to FO, tel. 2016, 12 December 1950, FO371/84123.

46. Peking to FO, tel. 2023, 13 December 1950, ibid., and PMM(51)3rd meeting, 5 January 1951; PMM(51)7th meeting, 9 January 1951, CAB133/90.

47. Minute from Gordon Walker to Attlee, 7 October 1950, and draft telegram to UK-New Delhi, undated but probably early October 1950, PREM8/1352. Washington to FO, tel. 2, 1 January 1951, and PM's personal minute to Bevin, 4 January 1951, PREM8/1350 and FO800/445; PMM(51)2nd meeting, 4 January 1951, and 3rd meeting, 5 January 1951, CAB133/90; minute by Strang, 3 January 1951, FO371/92067.

48. Minute by Strang of Bevin–Nehru conversation, 5 January 1951, FO800/462.

49. PMM meetings on 4, 8 and 9 January 1951, CAB133/90; Gopal, *Nehru*, vol. 2, pp. 134–6.

50. P. Lowe, 'Great Britain, the United Nations and the Korean War 1950–3', *International Studies*, 1987/1, pp. 8–11.

51. Minute by Dixon, 29 January 1951, FO371/92067.

52. Nehru, *Letters to Chief Ministers*, 1 February 1951, vol. 2, pp. 318, 320.

53. Minute by Strang of Bevin–Nehru conversation on 5 January 1951, FO800/462.

54. Gifford (London) to SS, 20 January 1951, thought that in the interests of Commonwealth solidarity, the British would avoid any action 'which might alienate India as potential leader [of] non-Communist Asia', *FR, 1951*, vol. 4, p. 896. See also Henderson's statement at conference of US ambassadors in South Asia in Nuwara Eliya, 26 February to 3 March 1951, McGhee Papers, TL, (referred to hereafter as Nuwara Eliya). See also Nye to SSCR, 15 December 1950, DO35/2838; D.W. Kermode (Jakarta) to Younger, 20 July 1950 and Macdonald to Bevin, 2 August 1950, DO35/2976.

55. Cited in Nehru, *Letters to Chief Ministers*, vol. 2, n. 13, p. 239.

56. The next three paragraph are based on McGhee to Acheson, 3 November 1950, DS file 611.91/11–350.

57. As early as 29 June 1950 Nehru had informed Henderson of this problem. *FR, 1950*, vol. 7, p. 236.

58. This paragraph is based on *FR, 1950*, vol. 5, pp. 196–200; and final draft, NSC 98/1, 25 January 1951, PSF, Subject file, Truman papers, TL.
59. Memo from Acheson and Harriman to Truman, 5 June 1952, *FR, 1952–1954*, vol. 11, part 2, pp. 1646–7. For a fuller discussion of US policy, see Dennis Merrill, *Bread and the Ballott: the United States and India's Economic Development, 1947–1963*, (Chapel Hill and London, 1990). The importance to the British of the Colombo Plan was reiterated in a paper presented to the cabinet by Eden, Butler and Ismay on 20 December 1951. They underlined the importance

in the struggle of ideas in Asia to persuade the people of the region that their true interests are best served by continued association with the free world. To this end it is necessary . . . to convince them that the Western Powers are sincerely and actively interested in helping them to improve their living standards, and the Colombo Plan has been our main effort in this direction. . . . The importance of the Plan as a means of fostering the Commonwealth connection . . . is a strong argument for the United Kingdom to continue to play, and to be seen to play, a major rôle in working for its success . . . its centre of gravity is, and will obviously remain, in the Indian subcontinent. Any patent weakening of United Kingdom initiative or support would reduce United Kingdom influence in the Commonwealth countries in particular, and in the area of South and South-East Asia in general. [C(51)51, and annex to, CAB129/48]

60. Summary of meeting of State, Agriculture and Budget departments and ECA, 15 January 1951; summary of SS' daily meeting, 16 January 1951, DS file 891.03/1–1751.
61. Memo of conversation between Acheson, McGhee, and Mrs Pandit, 29 December 1950, box 65, Acheson papers, and memo of conversation with Mrs Pandit by McGhee, 29 December 1950, DS file 611.91/12–2950. See also DS memo of conversation between Mrs Pandit and McGhee on 6 September 1950, DS file 611.91/9–650.
62. *Jawaharlal Nehru's Speeches* (New Delhi, 1957), p. 138. See also McGhee to SS, 25 January 1951, DS file 611.91/1–2551, and DS memo of conversation between Acheson, McGhee, Mathews and Mrs Pandit, 27 January 1951, box 66, Acheson papers, TL.
63. See *Executive Sessions of the Senate Foreign Relations Committee, 1951*, vol. 3, part 1, pp. 25–45; State Department report on 'India's Request for Foodgrains: Political Considerations', in McGhee to Acheson, 24 January 1951, *FR, 1951*, vol. 6, part 2, pp. 2085–6, and R. McMahon, 'Food as a Diplomatic Weapon: the India Wheat Loan of 1951', *Pacific Historical Review*, vol. 56, 1987, pp. 361–2, 372–3, and Merrill, *Bread and the Ballott*, pp. 46 ff. For Nehru's views, see his statements in the *National Herald*, 7 April and 13 June 1951, and *Letters to Chief Ministers*, 2 May 1951, vol. 2, p. 384.
64. Nuwara Eliya meeting, McGhee papers, TL.
65. Ibid.
66. Memo of conversation between C.M. Walker (British embassy, Washington) and E.G. Mathews (Director, SOA), 2 September 1950, DS file 611.91/9–250; Roberts to Garner, 7 November 1950; see also H.A. Graves (CRO) to R.H.

Scott, 8 September 1950, DO35/2838, and Roberts to Liesching, 5 August 1950, ibid.

67. *FR, 1950,* vol. 7, pp. 882–3; DS file 891.00/1–851; and *FR, 1951,* vol. 6, part 2, p. 2115.

68. Nuwara Eliya, McGhee papers, TL.

69. Ibid., and *FR, 1951,* vol. 6, p. 1668

70. J.J.S. Garner to Lt Gen. Sir Neville Brownjohn, 2 March 1951; FO minute by J.S.H. Shattock, 1 March 1951, FO371/92831; CDC DO(51)7th meeting, 2 April 1951, CAB131/10; UK–New Delhi to CRO, tel. 540, 7 April 1951, FO371/92834.

71. CRO to UK–Karachi, tel. 484, 5 April 1951 and UK–Karachi to CRO, tel. 393, 7 April 1951, FO371/92834.

72. Note by H.H. Phillips, 4 September 1951, FO371/92884.

73. Ibid.

74. Draft letter by Frank Roberts to F. Tomlinson, 7 September 1951. Emphasis in original.

75. See chapter 4.

76. P. Lowe, 'The Settlement of the Korean War' in J. Young (ed.), op. cit, pp. 207–31, and R. Foot, *A Substitute for Victory: The Politics of Peacemaking at the Korean Armistice Talks,* (Ithaca 1990).

77. Summary of telegrams, 19 and 21 May 1952, Daily Briefs, Truman Naval Aide files, Truman papers, TL.

78. Summary of telegrams, 19 May 1952, ibid., and *FR, 1952–1954,* vol. 15, part 1, pp. 206–7.

79. Lowe, 'The Settlement of the Korean War', p. 216, and record of conversation between Eden and Menon, 21 May 1952, FO800/781; *FR, 1952–54,* vol. 15, part 1, pp. 227, 247–51

80. Summary of telegrams, 19 and 23 June 1954, Daily Briefs May–June 1952, Truman Naval Aide files, Truman papers, TL, and *FR, 1952–1954,* vol. 15, part 1, pp. 340–1 and 344–8.

81. Ibid., pp. 344–8.

82. *Korea: A Summary of Further Developments in the Military Situation, Armistice Negotiations and Prisoner of War Camps up to January 1953,* Cmd. 8793, p. 4.

83. H. Isaacs, *Scratches on the Mind,* pp. 314–15; opinions more favourable to Menon are in personal and confidential minute from Lloyd to Milner, 20 August 1956, FO371/123590, and Escott Reid, *Envoy to Nehru,* (New Delhi 1981), pp. 43–4. Loy Henderson's Oral History interview, p. 173, TL. See also Gopal, *Nehru,* p. 144 and M. Brecher, *India and World Politics,* (London 1968), for Menon's view of the world.

84. Acheson's memo of his conversation with Lloyd on 28 October 1952, file memo of conversations, October 1952, box 67a, Acheson papers, TL.

85. New York to FO, tel. 808, 15 November 1952, FO371/99589, and Lester Pearson, *Memoirs: 1948–1957, vol. 2,* (London 1974), p. 316.

86. C(52)441, 15 December 1952, PREM11/406.

87. SS to DS, *FR, 1952–1954,* vol. 15, part 1, pp. 586–7.

88. C(52)441, 15 December 1952, PREM11/406.

89. Memo of conversation, 13 November 1952, file: memos of conversations November 1952, Box 67a, Acheson papers, TL.

90. Memo of conversation with Lovett, 15 November 1952, ibid.
91. Summary of telegrams, 10 November 1952, Daily Briefs, Truman Naval Aide files, Truman papers, TL; *FR, 1952–1954*, vol. 15, part 1, pp. 590–1.
92. Ibid., pp. 616–25, 629–32, 654–9, 662–3; and *Korea: The Indian Proposal*, Cmd. 8716, 1952, p. 13.
93. Memo of conversation between Truman and Eisenhower, 18 November 1952, file: memo of conversations, box 67a, Acheson papers, TL.
94. Summary of telegrams, 19 November 1952, Naval Aide files, Truman papers, and SS to President, 20 November 1952, *FR, 1952–1954*, vol. 15, part 1, pp. 662–3, 666; E. Shuckburgh, *Descent to Suez*, pp. 54, 56–7.
95. *FR, 1952–1954*, vol. 15, part 1, p. 668.
96. Meeting between Acheson and Canadian PM, 22 November 1952, file: memo of conversations, box 67a, Acheson papers.
97. Gopal, *Nehru*, p. 145.
98. *FR, 1952–1954*, vol. 15, part 1, p. 703.
99. C(52)441, 15 December 1952, PREM 11/406.
100. London to DS, tel. 3465, 21 February 1952 and memo of conversations by Henkin, 22 February 1952, DS files 795.00/2–2152 and 795.00/2–2252 respectively. *FR, 1952–1954*, vol. 15, part 1, p. 132; Dulles–Lodge telephone conversation, 20 June 1953, Dulles papers, Telephone calls series, box 1, file: Tel. memos May–June 1953 (1), EL. See also CC(53)46, 28 July 1953, CAB128/26 and New York to FO, tel. 553, 28 July 1953, PREM11/405.
101. Conversation between Dulles and Rhee on 5 August 1953, *FR, 1952–1954* vol. 15, part 2, pp. 1470–1.
102. SS to Lodge, 13 August 1953, ibid., 1492–3.
103. Salisbury to Jebb, 14 August 1953, FO800/798; Dulles–Lodge telephone conversation, 12 August 1953, Dulles papers, Telephone calls series, box 1, file: Phone memos July–October 1953 (4), EL.
104. Dulles telephone conversations, 24 August 1953, Dulles papers, Telephone calls series, box 1, file: phone memos, July–October 1953 (4), EL. See also minutes of cabinet meeting, 27 August 1953, AWF/Cabinet series, box 2, file: cabinet meeting of 27 August 1953, DDE papers, EL.
105. Ibid.
106. Conversation between Lodge and Menon, 14 August 1953, ibid., p. 1494, Ambassador in India to DS, 26 August 1953, *FR, 1952–1954*, vol. 15, part 2, pp. 1500–1.
107. Dulles telephone conversations, 28 August 1953, Dulles papers, Telephone calls series, box 1, file: phone memos, July–October 1953 (3), EL.
108. State Department Quarterly Review of US–Indian relations CA-2156, 19 October 1953, DS file 611.91/10–1953.
109. Nehru to Mehta, 28 August 1953, cited in Gopal, p. 172.
110. Churchill to Nehru, 29 August 1953, PREM11/457.
111. Dening shared the common official British view that in Asia the British had 'influence without power'. See his report to Secretary of State for Foreign Affairs, 1 May 1951, DO133/140; minute by R.H. Scott on British policy in the Far East, 30 October 1951; FO minute, 1 November 1951, and minute by Scott on Anglo–American co-operation in the Middle and Far East, 2 November 1951, FO371/92065
112. *FR, 1951*, vol. 4, part 1, p. 940.

Notes to Chapter 4

1. The idea of a strong "British" influence originated in Selig Harrison, 'India, Pakistan and the U.S.-I', *New Republic*, 10 August 1959, pp. 10–17. It was refuted by M.S. Venkataramani and H.C. Arya, 'America's Military Alliance with Pakistan: the Evolution and Course of an Uneasy Partnership', *International Studies*, vol. 8, 1966, pp. 84–5.
2. Nehru, *Letters to Chief Ministers*, vol. 3, pp. 457–8.
3. For example R. Ovendale, *The English-Speaking Alliance*; B.H. Reid, 'The Northern Tier and the Baghdad Pact', in J.W. Young (ed.), *The Foreign Policy of Churchill's Peacetime Administration 1951–1955*, pp. 159–80; D. Devereux, 'Britain, the Commonwealth and the Defence of the Middle East 1948–1956', *Journal of Contemporary History*, vol. 24, 1989, pp. 327–45. G. Aronson, *Britain's Moment in the Middle East*, (Boulder 1986), has stray references to Pakistan in the Northern Tier, but he focuses on Egypt and does not make use of much unpublished archival material on the subject.
4. R. McMahon, 'US Cold War Strategy in South Asia: Making a Military Commitment to Pakistan 1947–54', *Journal of American History*, vol. 75, 1988, pp. 812–40 and M.S. Venkarataramani, *The American Role in Pakistan*, (New Delhi 1984). For a discussion of recent literature on the subject, see Gary Hess, 'Global Expansion and Regional Balances: the Emerging Scholarship on United States Relations with India and Pakistan', *Pacific Historical Review*, vol. 56, 1987, pp. 259–95.
5. A. Jalal, 'Towards the Baghdad Pact: South Asia and Middle East Defence in the Cold War 1947–55, *International History Review*, vol. 11, 1989, pp. 409–33; A. Eden, *Full Circle* (London 1960), p. 64; H. Macmillan, *Tides of Fortune 1945–1955*, (London 1969), pp. 630–1; B.H. Reid, 'The Northern Tier and the Baghdad Pact', in J.W. Young, *The Foreign Policy of Churchill's Peacetime Administration 1951–1955*', pp. 159–80.
6. The following account is based on E. Ingram, *The Great Game in Asia* (Oxford 1984); W.R. Louis, *The British Empire in the Middle East 1945–1951*; P.L. Hahn, 'Containment and Egyptian Nationalism: the Unsuccessful Effort to Establish the Middle East Command 1950–53', *Diplomatic History*, vol. 11, 1987, pp. 23–40; A. Nachmani, 'It is a Matter of Getting the Mixture Right: Britain's Post-War Relations with America in the Middle East, *Journal of Contemporary History*, vol. 18, 1983, pp. 117–40
7. *FR, 1951*, vol. 5, p. 2.
8. Background Memoranda on visit to the US of Liaqat Ali Khan in May 1950,

prepared by DS, 14 April 1950, Truman PSF, Subject File: Pakistan, Truman papers, TL.

9. *FR, 1950*, vol. 5, pp. 1498–9; *FR, 1949*, vol. 6, pp. 30–1.

10. *FR, 1950*, vol. 5, p. 204.

11. *FR, 1951*, vol. 5, pp. 4–6, pp. 6–14, 24.

12. Ibid., pp. 4, 24–7.

13. Ibid., pp. 94–5, 109–110, and CC(51)1st meeting, 23 January 1951, DO35/ 2452; Lt–Gen. Sir Neville Brownjohn to Gen. Sir Brian Robertson, 5 February 1951, WO216/724.

14. *FR, 1951*, vol. 6, part 2, p. 1667.

15. *FR, 1951*, vol. 5, p. 120; record of conversation between McGhee and Foreign Office, 3 April 1951, FO371/92875. The American record of the conversation is in *FR, 1951*, vol. 6, part 2, pp. 1689 ff.

16. Minutes by S.J.L. Olver, L.A.C. Fry, R.J. Bowker and R.H. Scott, 6, 10, 14, 18 and 24 April 1951, FO371/92875; note from Garner to Gen. Scoones, 24 Oct. 1950, DO35/3006; JP(50)147, 15 December 1950, CRO final draft, incorporating FO views, 'India and Pakistan in relation to Middle East defence', 13 June 1951, FO371/92875.

17. *FR, 1951*, vol. 5, State Department–Joint COS meeting, 2 May 1951, p. 120.

18. *FR, 1951*, vol. 5, pp. 144–8, *FR, 1951*, vol. 6. part 2, pp. 2206 ff.

19. *FR, 1951*, vol. 5, pp. 144–5, 148.

20. CRO draft, 13 June 1951, FO371/92875.

21. Record of conversation between Gordon-Walker and Zafrullah Khan, 30 August 1951, FO371/92875.

22. CDC DO(51)22nd meeting, 10 September 1951, CAB131/40.

23. COS(51) 142nd meeting, 10 September 1951, DEFE4/46 and COSC to Arthur Bottomley, 13 September 1951, FO371/92875; Liesching to Strang, 24 September 1951, ibid. See also Liesching's note on his conversation with Ikramullah Khan, Permanent Secretary in the Pakistani Ministry of External Affairs, 18 and 20 September 1951, and Liesching to Attlee, 20 September 1951, ibid. Also see Frank Roberts to Stephen Holmes, 12 September 1951, and Joe Garner (New Delhi) to N. Pritchard (CRO), 29 September 1951, ibid. Garner thought Kashmir ruled out a Pakistani contribution to Middle East defence, since Indo–Pakistani antagonism could not be eradicated for a generation.

24. Washington to FO, tel. 3238, 8 October 1951, FO371/92876.

25. Ibid. and FO to Washington, tel. 5055, 13 October 1951, ibid., and COS(51) 160th meeting, 12 October 1951, ibid. and DEFE4/47.

26. Minute by H.H. Phillips, 21 December 1951, and FO to Washington, tel. 5194, 19 October 1951, FO371/92876.

27. Eden to Churchill, November 1951; G.W. Harrison's note on contributions by India and Pakistan to Middle East Defence, 20 November 1951; FO to Washington, tel. 6167, 12 December 1951; note by J.D. Murray on Pakistan and Middle East defence, 7 December 1951, FO371/92876. See also minutes by H.H. Phillips, S.J.L. Olver, E.M. Rose, 12, 14 and 17 November 1951 respectively; and note by Knox Helm on Pakistani approaches to Turkey, 17 December 1951, ibid.

28. Kashmir figured in the Truman–Churchill talks in Washington in January 1952. See State Department Negotiating Paper on Kashmir and the Middle

East, 3 January 1952 in file on Churchill–Truman meeting, box 116, PSF General files, Truman papers, TL. British views on Kashmir are summed up in C(51)47, 17 December 1951, 'Kashmir Dispute', by Ismay, CAB 129/48.

29. Ankara to State Department, tel. 464, 21 February 1952, box 1, file: Department of State Memos of Conversations January–June 1952, McGhee papers, TL. Jalal wrongly states that in 1954, 'Pakistan and Turkey announced their decision to consult and co-operate on matters of mutual interest in a spirit of Islamic brotherhood, albeit one injected by Washington.' 'Towards the Baghdad Pact', *International History Review*, vol. 11, 1989, p. 430. Between 1951 and 1954 American officials expended much effort in persuading Pakistan to tone down its enthusiasm for an 'Islamic' pact which would not be acceptable to Turkey.

30. Ankara to State Department, 14 March, 21 April and 7 October 1952 respectively, McGhee papers, TL. The Turks may also have played a part in persuading the Americans to distance themselves from the British. In July 1952 they told McGhee that they did not like secret Anglo–American discussions on MEDO which concerned Turkey. This led McGhee to wonder whether such confabulations with the British were worthwhile and to counsel the State Department that the US should not risk losing the confidence of the Turks but treat consultations with them on a par with consultations with the British and French. Sceptical of the extent of British and Commonwealth influence in the Middle East, the Turks wanted the US to take the lead in MEDO, because Britain and France, as former invaders, and even the Turks, as older invaders, were the "most hated people" in the Middle East. Ankara to DS, tels 99, 108, 255, 17 and 19 July, 23 August 1952 respectively, DS files 780.5/7–1752, 780.5/7–1952 and 780.5/8–2352 respectively.

31. Murray to Burrows, 8 January 1952, FO371/92876, Burrows to Murray, 28 January 1952; FO371/101198. For more British views against an initative to Pakistan, see FO to Ankara, 26 January 1952, FO371/101198; minute by H.H. Phillips, 4 February 1952; S.J.L. Olver to Burrows, 20 March 1952; G.P. Hampshire to Olver, 31 March 1952, ibid.

32. Note by J.N.O. Curle, 6 May 1952, FO371/101198; JP(52)14 Final, 13 May 1952, DEFE4/54; see also COS(52)91st meeting, 26 June 1952, and annex to the meeting, DEFE4/55; Washington to FO, tel. 143, 28 July 1952, and FO to Washington, tel. 3097, 30 July 1952, FO371/101217, C(52)202, 18 June 1952, CAB 129/53.

33. CRO draft note on proposed meeting of Muslim Prime Ministers in Karachi, 16 July 1952, enclosed in G.P. Hampshire to Gen. Scoones, 7 August 1952, DO35/6301 and FO371/101198; Karachi to CRO, tel. 23, 7 January 1953, FO371/106931, and minute by R.A. Burrows, 13 January 1953, ibid.

34. Minute by M.T. Flett (Treasury) to Sir James Crombie and Sir Leslie Rowan, 17 November 1952, T225/356; C(53)162, 27 May 1953, CAB129/61.

35. Minutes by R.J. Bowker, 16, 20, 26 January 1953; and minute by J.G. Tahourdin, 20 January 1953, FO371/106931.

36. UK–Karachi to CRO, tel. 23, 7 January 1953, and minute by Burrows, 13 January 1953; CRO to Karachi, tel. 23, 7 January 1953, and minute from Swinton to Eden, 8 January 1953, ibid.

37. UK–Karachi to CRO, tels 665, 679, 702, 17, 19, 21 April 1953 respectively, and tel. 86, 4 May 1953, PREM11/1519; minute by Churchill, 23 April 1953,

ibid.; see also Laithwaite to Swinton, 8 May 1953, ibid.

38. C(53)162, 23 May 1953, CAB129/61. See also note by W.J. Smith on Pakistan and anti-colonialism. 11 May 1953, DO35/6659A; Karachi to CRO, tel. 793, 6 May 1953, FO371/106923; J.D. Murray to R.R. Sedgwick, 8 July 1953, DO35/6654; note by R.W.D. Fowler, 14 May 1953, DO35/6654.

39. J.P. Bancroft (Treasury) to E. Gresswell (Defence), 11 February 1953, FO371/106935.

40. Ibid., and Washington to FO, tel. 77, 27 March 1953, FO371/106938; Laithwaite's despatch no. 49, 31 March 1953, FO371/106932; FO to Washington, tel. 1540, 7 April 1953, FO371/106938. In November 1952, American diplomats in Karachi reported that Pakistan was considering withdrawal from the Commonwealth if she was not offered membership of MEDO; and the Canadian High Commissioner in Karachi thought that the 'take it or leave it' attitude of the British was inspired by their belief that Pakistan got more out of the Commonwealth than she put in. US–Karachi to London, tel 3667, 26 November 1952, and US–Karachi to SS, tel. 832, 29 November 1952, DS files 780.5/11–2652 and 780.5/11–2952 respectively.

41. M.J.S. Ralston (Treasury) to R.C.C. Hunt (CRO), 27 June 1952; incorporated into FO to Washington, tel. 2734, 9 July 1952, FO371/10127.

42. Salisbury to De L'Isle and Dudley, and R.A. Butler, 16 and 17 June respectively, and reply from De L'Isle and Dudley, 19 June 1952, T225/355.

43. Washington to FO, tel. 693, 23 June 1952, T225/355; Ralston to Hunt, 27 June 1952, ibid.

44. Ralston to Hunt, 27 June 1952, and FO to Washington, tel. 3091, 30 July 1952, FO371/101217.

45. C(52)202, 18 June 1952, CAB129/53.

46. Byroade to J. Emerson (US–Karachi), 14 April 1953, DS file 780.5/4–1453.

47. *FR, 1952–1954*, vol. 9, part 1, pp. 379–86.

48. Ibid., p. 135.

49. SS to DS, tel. 802, 26 May 1953, ibid., p. 147; 147th NSC meeting, 1 June 1953, pp. 383, 384.

50. H.W. Brands, 'The Cairo Connection in Anglo-American Rivalry in the Middle East, 1951–1953', *International History Review*, vol. 11, 1989, pp. 434–56.

51. Memo of conversation between Beeley and Jernegan, 17 June 1953, *FR, 1952–1954*, vol. 9, part 1, pp. 389–90.

52. Dulles-Salisbury conversation, 11 July 1953, FO371/102732.

53. Memo from Stassen to Dulles, 22 June 1953, DS file 790D. 5MSP/6–2253.

54. Memo for Byroade from RLO'C, 22 June 1953, DS file: 790. 5-MSP/6–2253, and Dulles to Stassen, 25 June 1953, ibid.; Dulles to Charles Wilson, 26 June 1953, *FR, 1952–1954*, vol. 9, part 1, pp. 392–3.

55. NSC 155/1, 14 July 1953, *FR, 1952–1954*, vol. 9, part 1, pp. 402–3.

56. See chapter 3.

57. Memo of conversation between Dulles, Bowie and Byroade, 4 September 1953, DS file 780. 5-MSP/9–453.

58. Byroade to Dulles, 25 September 1953, DS file 790D. 4-MSP/9–2253. He referred to UK-US talks from 31 December 1952 to 7 January 1953, Joint COS to Secretary of Defence, 12 February 1953, enclosed in C. Wilson to Dulles, 16 February 1953, DS file 780. 5/2–1653. But this "evidence" ignored

the Eden-Dulles conversation on 6 March 1953. According to the DS record, Eden told Dulles that Pakistan's membership of MEDO would create problems with India, and he doubted whether Pakistan should be included in the original membership. *FR, 1952–1954* vol. 6, part 1, p. 915. See also the British record of the same meeting, FO800/839.

59. Minute by Scott on Anglo-American Cooperation: Comparison between Middle East and Far East (Brief for Bilateral Talks with Mr Acheson in Paris), 2 November 1951, FO371/92065.

60. Churchill to Mohamad Ali, 8 September 1953; Karachi to CRO, tel. 1309, 3 September and minute by Cable, 4 September 1953, FO371/106931. See also US-Karachi despatch no. 139, 26 August 1953, DS file 611. 90D/8–2653 and Evaluation of US-Pakistan relations in second half of 1953, no. A–5, 8 July 1953, DS file 611. 90D/7–853.

61. Helm to Salisbury, 29 September and Helm to G.W. Harrison, 5 October 1953, FO371/106924; Warren (Ankara) to DS, 28 September 1953, *FR 1952–1954*, vol. 9, part 1, p. 419.

62. US-Karachi despatch no. 290, 6 November 1953 (by C. Withers for ambassador), DS file 611. 90D/11–653 (refers to A-73, 17 October 1953).

63. PPS memo from Fraser Wilkins to Donald Kennedy, 23 September 1953, DS file 790D. 5-MSP/9–2253.

64. Memo, 'Political Considerations Bearing on United States Military Assistance Program to Middle East in Fiscal 1954', 24 September 1953, enclosed in Dulles to Wilson, 1 October 1953, DS file 780. 5-MSP/10–153; Byroade to Dulles, 25 September 1953, DS file 790D. 5-MSP/9–2253.

65. Byroade to Dulles, 25 September 1953, DS file 790D. 5-MSP/9–2523; memo of conversation between Dulles and Ayub on 30 September 1953, DS file 790D.5-MSP/9–3053; F.E. Nolting (Mutual Security) to F.C. Nash (Defence), 2 October 1953, DS file 790D. 5-MSP/10–253.

66. Memo from Dulles to Bedell Smith, 1 October 1953, Dulles papers, Chronological series, box 5, file October 1953 (3), EL.

67. Memorandum from Dulles to Byroade, 1 October 1953, ibid.

68. Dulles to Wilson, 1 October 1953, DS file 780. 5-MSP/10–153.

69. Meeting of Departments of State, Defence, FOA, and Bureau of Budget, enclosed in Daspit to Nolting, 8 October 1953, and Byroade to Dulles, 8 October 1953, DS files 780.5-MSP/10–653 and 790D. 5-MSP/10–853 respectively.

70. Memo, as in note 64, from Byroade to Bedell Smith, 24 September 1953, DS file 780. 5-MSP/10–153.

71. Washington to FO, tel. 2160, 9 October 1953, FO371/106935. One should distinguish between departmental decisions, or decisions in principle made by American officials, and the formal decision which was finally made by Eisenhower on 18 February 1954.

72. Acting UK–Karachi to CRO, tel. 1456, 12 October 1953, ibid.

73. Tahourdin (FO) to Lt-Col. E.V.M. Strickland (COS Sectt), 13 October 1953; and FO to Washington, tel. 4043, 13 October 1953, ibid.

74. Extract from COS(53) 116th meeting, 15 October 1953, ibid. Offshore aid from countries outside the US was one of three sources of supply of equipment in US military assistance programmes. Under the Mutual Defence Assistance Programme of 1949, it was intended that the US would supply

equipment to its allies, mainly from US stock. The Korean war upset these plans, since military equipment had to be diverted to meet US military requirements. From the US military viewpoint, it was therefore essential that American allies could arrange for maintenance, replacements and ammunition from their own sources, and that in case of hostilities, *matériel* could be obtained from sources as close as possible to the area of hostilities. These were the underlying reasons behind the introduction of the offshore procurement programme under a Defence Department directive on 17 August 1951. Contracts for production of military equipment could be placed abroad on the basis of favourable cost, availability, quality of items, and favourable location of the military production base on which the success of a joint defence effort depended. See Fairless Committee 1956–7, box 6, file: Department of Defence, and Commission on Foreign Economic Policy Report, January 1954, especially pp. 3–9, DDE papers, Administrative series, box 10, file: Commission on Foreign Economic Policy(1), EL.

75. CRO draft; 'Proposed US Military Aid to Pakistan', enclosed in Fowler (CRO) to Tahourdin, 14 October 1953, ibid. See also extract of COS(53) 116th meeting, 15 October 1953, ibid.

76. CRO draft, ibid.

77. Acting UK–Karachi to CRO, tel. 1471, 15 October 1953, ibid.

78. FO to Washington, tel. 4117, 16 October 1953, FO371/106935.

79. Memo from Byroade to Nash (Defence), 15 October 1953, *FR, 1952–1954*, vol. 9, part 1, p. 422. See also memo of conversation between Ayub and Byroade, 21 October 1953, DS file 790D. 5-MSP/10–2153.

80. On the views of the British High Commission in New Delhi see, among others, UK–New Delhi to CRO, tel. 1138, 13 October 1953, FO371/106935; G.H. Middleton to J. Garner, 16 October 1953, ibid., and UK–New Delhi to CRO, tel. 1266, 27 November 1953, FO371/106936.

81. Curson (CRO) to Gresswell (Defence), 20 October 1953, FO371/106935.

82. Memo of conversation between Beeley and Jernegan, 16 October 1953, DS file 79OD. 5MSP/10–1653; and FO to Washington, tel. 4117, 16 October 1953, FO371/106935. Interestingly, the US embassy in London informed the State Department that the CRO had instructed the British embassy in Washington that the UK would welcome the strengthening of Pakistan's armed forces, US–London to SS, tel. 1663, 16 October 1953, DS file 790D. 5–MSP/10–1653.

83. JWPC(AWP)/M(53) 25 meeting, 23 October 1953, and Curson to Gresswell, 26 October 1953, FO371/106935.

84. Ibid and FO comments on Laithwaite's memo of 21 October 1953, ibid.

85. JWPC (AWP)/P (53) 133, 23 October and JWPC (AWP)/P(53) 133, 29 October 1953, ibid.

86. Note by Laithwaite, 5 November 1953, ibid.

87. CDC meeting D(53)54, 9 November 1953, CAB131/13.

88. Jernegan to Henderson (Tehran), 9 November 1953, *FR, 1952–1954*, vol. 9, part 1, p. 426.

89. Ibid., pp. 426–7.

90. Memo from Dulles to Eisenhower, 10 November 1953, AWF, International series, box 36, file Pak(4), DDE papers, EL.

91. Eisenhower to Dulles, and Dulles to Eisenhower, both 16 November 1953,

AWF, Dulles–Herter series, box 1, file: Dulles (JF) November 1953, DDE papers, EL.

92. Fowler to Pritchard, 9 November 1953, and Fowler to Crawley, 11 November 1953, FO371/106935. CRO to Karachi, tel. 1180, 12 November 1953 and UK–Karachi to CRO, tels 1594 and 1595, 13 November 1953, FO371/106936. See also memo of Byroade–Haksar conversation, 5 November 1953, DS file 790D. 5-MSP/11–853.

93. Crawley to Fowler, 18 November 1953, FO371/106936.

94. Ibid and Crawley to Fowler, 23 November 1953, FO371/104944 and Washington to FO, tel. 2519, 16 November 1953, FO371/106936.

95. US–Ankara to SS, tel. 557, 30 November 1953, DS file 780. 5/11-3053 and Helm to Harrison, 30 November 1953, FO371/106924. One measure of British indifference to Pakistan – and their 'blissful ignorance' – is illustrated by Churchill's decision not to see Ghulam Muhammad, when the latter passed through London from 16 to 18 November, after his visit to Washington, because of very heavy engagements. See W. Crookshank to Churchill, 11 November 1953 and PM's personal minute to Crookshank, 12 November 1953, PREM 11/503. One can hardly blame the Pakistanis for not revealing all to the British.

96. Laithwaite to Pritchard, 30 December 1953, FO371/106924.

97. US–Karachi to DS, tel. 399, 2 December 1953, DS file 611. 90D/12–253

98. Ibid. At the FO, James Cable still entertained the notion that between them, India, the USSR and China had succeeded, by their vehement opposition, in overcoming Mohamad Ali's 'reluctance to seek United States military aid'. Minute by Cable, 10 December 1953, FO371/106936.

99. CRO brief for Eden before he left for Bermuda, 1 December 1953, enclosed in Fowler to Crawley, ibid. The Americans were fully prepared to counter British objections. See memo from Daspit to Byroade, 3 December 1953, DS file 790D. 5-MSP/12–353, and notes for Bermuda meeting, approved on 30 November 1953, DS file 611.41/11–3053.

100. Nehru, *Letters to Chief Ministers*, 1 December 1953, vol. 3, pp. 457–8.

101. Washington to FO, tel. 2531, 19 November 1953, and UK–New Delhi to CRO, tel. 1271, 30 November 1953, FO371/106936. See also memos from Byroade to Dulles, 14 November 1953, DS file 790D. 5-MSP/11–1453; memo of conversation between Dulles and G.L. Mehta, 16 November 1953, DS file 790D. 5-MSP/11–1653; US–New Delhi, tel. 784, 16 November 1953, ibid., and SS to US–New Delhi, tel. 527, 17 November 1953, ibid.

102. Minute by W.D. Allen, 3 December 1953, FO371/106936.

103. Minute by Eden, 4 December 1953, ibid.

104. Record of conversation between Eden and Dulles, 7 December 1953, FO371/106937. According to the State Department record, Dulles told Eden that 'a decision had not yet been reached by the President' on military assistance to Pakistan. *FR, 1952–1954*, vol. 5, part 2, pp. 1807–8.

105. Helm to Harrison, 7 December 1953, FO371/106924.

106. Scott to Murphy, 9 December 1953, DS file 790D. 5-MSP/12–953.

107. Byroade to Bedell Smith, 11 December 1953, DS file 790D. 5-MSP/12–1153.

108. Minute by Cable, 15 December 1953, FO371/106937.

109. Minutes by W.D. Allen and Reading, 6 and 7 January 1954 respectively, and minute by Cable, 17 December 1953, ibid.

110. 176th NSC meeting, 16 December 1953, AWF, NSC series, box 5, DDE papers, EL.
111. 177th NSC meeting, 23 December 1953, ibid.
112. SS to US–Ankara and US–Karachi, tels 686 and 475 respectively, 23 December 1953, DS file 780.5/11–3053.
113. Washington to FO, tel. 2793, 29 December 1953, FO371/106937.
114. Comment by Eden, dated 2 January 1954, on tel. 2793, FO371/106937.
115. Laithwaite to Pritchard, 30 December 1953, FO371/106924. See also Ankara to FO, tel. 1, 2 January 1954, FO371/112314, which makes clear how little Knox Helm had managed to uncover from the Turks.
116. Minutes by J.E. Cable, J.G. Tahourdin, W.J.M. Paterson and P.S. Falla, FO371/106924. Falla's minute formed the basis of a draft telegram from Eden to Makins which was not sent, and of C(54)4, 'US Project to Associate Military Aid to Pakistan with Middle East Defence', 5 January 1954, CAB 129/65. See also JP(54)13(FINAL), 13 January 1954, DEFE 4/68.
117. Eden's comment on minute by Tahourdin, 2 January 1954, FO371/112314.
118. *FR, 1952–1954*, vol. 9; part 1 pp. 444–6. The British record of the conversation is in Washington to FO, tel. 25, 6 January 1954, FO371/112314.
119. FO to Washington, tel. 97, 7 January 1954, ibid.
120. UK–Ankara to FO, tel. 13, 8 January 1954, ibid.
121. FO to UK–Ankara, tel. 25, 8 January 1954, ibid.
122. UK–Ankara to FO, tel. 14, 9 January 1954, and tel. 18, 11 January 1954, ibid.
123. Memo from Dulles to Eisenhower (no date), Dulles papers, White House memoranda series, box 1, file: meetings with President 1954(4).
124. Memo of Eisenhower–Dulles conversation, 5 January 1954, Dulles papers, Chronological series, box 6, file Jan 1954(4), EL.
125. DS to US–Ankara and US–Karachi, tels 721 amd 498 respectively, 6 January 1954, and memo of conversation between Eisenhower and Dulles, 14 January 1954, DS file 790D.5-MSP/1–1454.
126. Washington to FO, tel. 106, 15 January 1954, and minute by Cable, 18 January 1954, FO371/112315.
127. Record of conversation between Garner and Jernegan on 15 January 1954 (record dated 16 January), enclosed in Fowler to Cable, undated; and minutes by Cable and Paterson, 20 January 1954, ibid.
128. Swinton to Eden, 18 January 1954, FO371/112320.
129. Butterworth to Raynor, 12 January 1954, DS file 682.90D/11–1254 and Raynor to Merchant, 18 January 1954, DS file 682.90D/1–1254.
130. FO Brief for Eden, 15 January 1954, FO371/112315.
131. Memo of Dulles–Eisenhower conversation, 14 January 1954, DS file 790D.5-MSP/1454; Washington to FO, tel. no 29, 23 January 1954, and Berlin (Eden). to FO, tel. 7, 24 January 1954, FO371/112315.
132. Memo from Bonbright to Byroade, 23 January 1954, *FR, 1952–1954*, vol. 9, part 1, p. 461.
133. UK–Ankara to FO, tel. 48, 28 January 1954, and minute by Cable, 29 January 1954, FO371/112316. Emphasis mine.
134. UK–Ankara to FO, tels 76 and 77, 10 February 1954; Fowler to Tahourdin, 11 February 1954; FO to UK–Ankara, tel. 91, 15 February 1954, ibid, and minute by Tahourdin, 11 February 1954, FO 371/112317.

135. C(54)53, 15 February 1954, 'Middle East: Anglo–American Policy'; and C(54)53, 16 February 1954, 'United States Military Aid to Pakistan and Talks between Pakistan and Turkey', CAB129/66. Both papers were presented to the cabinet by Selwyn Lloyd.

136. UK–Karachi to CRO, tel. 200, 19 February 1954; minutes by Cable and Paterson, 22 February 1954, and by Tahourdin, 24 February 1954, FO371/112318.

137. Ibid.

138. Minute by Tahourdin, 19 February 1954, and *Hansard*, 1954, vol. 524, col. 14.

139. Minute by Joe Garner, on Pritchard to Garner, 20 February 1954, DO35/6659B.

140. Laithwaite to Liesching, 15 March 1954, FO371/112320.

141. US–Karachi despatch no. 649, 8 April 1954, and memo from Col. Ashworth, American Army Attaché to Hildreth, *c*. 10 April 1954, enclosure 3 to despatch no. 651, DS files 790D. 5-MSP/4–854 and 790D. 5-MSP/4–1054 respectively.

142. Ibid and memorandum from American Army Attaché to Hildreth, *c*. 10 April 1954, 790D. 5-MSP/4–1054. Emphasis in original.

143. Jernegan to Hildreth, 22 April 1954, *FR, 1952–1954*, vol. 9, part 1, pp. 500–1; Hildreth to DS, tel. 820, 9 April 1954, ibid., pp. 493–4.

144. DS to US–Karachi, tel. 883, 15 April 1954, DS file 790D. 5-MSP/4–954.

145. Record of conversation between Lord Alexander and Iskander Mirza on 12 March 1954, FO371/112320.

146. UK–Karachi to CRO, tel. 452, 3 April 1954, ibid.

147. Ibid.

148. UK–Karachi to CRO, tel. 460, 5 April 1954, ibid.

149. COS(54)39th meeting, 7 April 1954, DEFE4/69; Ministry of Defence note, 8 April 1954, FO371/112321; CDC D(54)5th meeting, 14 April 1954, CAB131/4.

150. Extract from JWPC(AWP)/m(54)9, 11 May 1954, FO371/112321.

151. Hildreth to DS, despatch no. 33, 16 July 1954, *FR, 1952–1954*, vol. 11, p. 1856, and Jernegan to Hildreth, 22 April 1954, *FR, 1952–1954*, vol. 9, pp. 500–2. See also note by Laithwaite on meeting with Hildreth, 9 July 1954, FO371/112321, and Washington to FO, tel. 2218, 16 October 1954, FO371/112322.

152. On 3 May 1954, a DS Intelligence Report opined that a tighter defence organisation, with planning and co-ordinating functions, would require a lessening of tensions between the West and Middle Eastern states, and that such an arrangement would gain force through 'an enlarged direct political and military assistance role of the US and continued US/UK cooperation'. But it was implied that British interests would create problems, since the UK, 'with its special treaty rights and positions, would be extremely vigilant in protecting its regional interests and would seek to reconcile the purposes of any regional arrangement with these interests'. *FR, 1952–1954*, vol. 9, part 1. p. 504.

153. Memo from F. Nolting Jr (special assistant to Stassen), 23 July 1954, DS file 790D. 5-MSP/7–2354.

154. US–Karachi to SS, tel. 225, 24 August 1954, DS file 790D. 5-MSP/8–2454.

155. JWPC(AWP)/M(54)14, 10 August 1954, FO371/112322.

156. UK–Karachi to CRO, tel. 1475, 8 October 1954, ibid
157. FO to Washington, tel. 5089, 12 October 1954, ibid.
158. Washington to FO, tel. 2217, 16 October 1954, and minutes by A.N. MacCleary and A. Leavett, 18 and 19 October 1954, respectively, ibid.
159. Washington to FO, tel. 2218, 16 October 1954, ibid.
160. Washington to FO, tel. 2265, 22 October 1954, ibid.
161. Minutes by MacCleary and Leavett, 26 and 28 October 1954 respectively, ibid.
162. Draft telegram from FO to Washington, enclosed in G. Wheeler (Defence) to W.A.W. Clarke (CRO), 29 October 1954, ibid.
163. Record of conversation between Ayub and J.P. Archer Shee, British Military Adviser in Pakistan, 27 October 1954, ibid.
164. Makins to Eden, 28 October 1954, FO371/112307.
165. J.D. Murray (CRO) to B.A.B. Burrows (Washington), 8 January 1952, provides one of the earliest clues to British incredulity at the idea of a Turco–Pakistani arrangement. On hearing that Ayub had approached the Turks in December 1951, Murray commented, 'This seems a most unlikely channel to have been adopted if the Pakistan Government were seriously interested in participating in the defence of the Middle East in the near future. We can only speculate whether it was a personal kite of General Ayub Khan's, or whether he was put up to it by the Pakistan Government in order to create a favourable impression without committing themselves.' FO371/92876. Given Zafrullah's talks with the Turks and McGhee in Ankara in 1952 – it was the kite that the Americans decided to fly. On the other hand, Montgomery bruited the idea in the summer of 1952 that Turkey and Pakistan would put some teeth into MEDO, and the FO was prepared to be guided by the Chiefs, even to the extent of an invitation going to Pakistan if invitations were sent to all the Arab states. But the balance of opinion was against including Pakistan as a founder member of MEDO, and nothing came of the idea at the British end.

Notes to Chapter 5

1. *Department of State Bulletin*, 13 February 1950, p. 244.
2. Record of FO meeting, 24 May 1949, FO371/76034; *Hansard*, 1950, vol. 475, col. 2089, and CP (50)200, 30 August 1950, CAB129/41. On Anglo–American differences over Indochina during the Second World War, see, C. Thorne, 'Indo–China and Anglo–American Relations, 1942–1945', in *Border Crossings: Studies in International History*, (Oxford 1988), pp. 86–106.
3. For a discussion of this point see I.W. Mabbett, 'The Indianization of Southeast Asia: Reflections on the Historical Sources', *Journal of Southeast Asian Studies*, vol. 8, 1977, pp. 143–61; and D.K. Emmerson, ' "Southeast Asia": What's in a Name?', ibid., vol. 15, 1984, pp. 1–21.
4. Ton That Tien, *India and South East Asia, 1947–1960* (Geneva 1963), p. 124; and G. Sardesai, *Indian Foreign Policy in Cambodia, Laos and Vietnam 1947–64*, (Berkeley, 1968), pp. 6–7.
5. UK–New Delhi to CRO, tels 322, 404, 444, 538, 845, dated 6 January, 5, 7, 14 February and 18 March 1950 respectively; F.E. Cuming-Bruce to M.R. Metcalf, 14 April 1950, FO371/83625. The quotation is from Maj.-Gen. W.H.A. Bishop to Tahourdin, 19 February 1953, FO371/106855.
6. Minute by R.C. Blackham, 9 August 1949, FO371/75996.
7. 'P' [N.R. Pillai], 'Middle Ground between America and Russia: an Indian View', *Foreign Affairs*, vol. 32, 1954, pp. 261–3, 266; and George Allen to DS, 25 April 1954, *FR, 1952–1954*, vol. 13, part 1, p. 1407.
8. C(53)330, 24 November 1953, CAB129/64, and C(54)134, 7 April 1954, CAB129/67.
9. CP(53)330, 24 November 1953, CAB129/64.
10. A. Eden, *Full Circle*, (London 1960), p. 87.
11. Minute by B.R. Pearn, 26 February 1954, FO371/112033.
12. Conversation between Eden and B.G. Kher, 10 March 1954; see also Eden to Nehru, sent in FO to UK–New Delhi, tel. 614, 16 April 1954, FO800/785.
13. 179th NSC meeting, 8 January 1954, AWF, NSC series, DDE papers, EL.
14. *FR, 1952–1954*, vol. 16, pp. 417ff; enclosure 1 to Defence Secretary to SS, 23 March 1954, ibid., pp. 472–5. See also memorandum by Bonsal, 8 March 1954, ibid., pp. 437ff, and 186th NSC meeting, 26 February 1954, AWF, NSC series, DDE papers, EL.
15. Eisenhower–Dulles telephone conversation, 5 April 1954, *FR, 1952–1954*, vol. 13. part 1, pp. 1241–2, and SS to Paris, 5 April 1954, ibid., p. 1242. See also G. Herring, 'Eisenhower, Dulles and Dienbienphu: The Day we Didn't Go to War', *Journal of American History*, vol. 71, 1984, pp. 349ff.; NSC

meeting, 6 April 1954 AWF, NSC series, DDE papers, EL; A. Short, *The Vietnam War* (London 1989), pp. 139–48.

16. *FR, 1952–1954*, vol. 13, part 1, p. 1281.

17. FO minute on British Policy Towards Indochina, 30 March 1954, FO371/112049; COS(54)36th meeting, 31 March 1954, enclosed in Secretary, COSC to Tahourdin, 1 April 1954, FO371/112050; record of Eden's conversation with US ambassador on 6 April 1954, ibid., confidential annex to COS(54)2nd meeting, 10 April 1954; annex to minute by W.D. Allen, on points for discussion with Dulles on 9 April 1954, FO371/112052. See also C(54)196, 14 June 1954, CAB129/68; Eisenhower to Churchill, 4 April 1954; FO to Washington, tel. 1458, 7 April 1954; record of interview at DS by Makins on 2 April 1954, FO371/112050, and minute by Tahourdin, 7 April 1954, FO371/112051.

18. Moran diary, cited in M. Gilbert, *Winston Churchill*, vol. 8, p. 974. Such petulance sat ill with Churchill's basically imperialist *mentalité*. In August 1952 he wrote Eden, 'Surely although we have cast away our own Empire we should not help to do in the French, who are fighting for theirs . . . America and Europe vs. Asiatic pretensions will steady the world movement to keep Negro Africa in its place!' To Eden, 4 August 1952, FO800/837. Eisenhower obviously found Churchillian imperialism a hard act to swallow; Eisenhower, *The White House Years: Mandate for Change* (London 1963), pp. 247–51.

19. Memo by SS, 19 and 25 April 1954, *FR, 1952–1954*, vol. 16, pp. 533 and 554–5 respectively, ibid., and SS to DS, 26 April 1954, ibid., p. 570.

20. Ibid., pp. 554–7 and C(54) 196, 14 June 1954, CAB 129/68 and annexes.

21. Minute, J.G. Tahourdin, 22 March 1954, 'The Commonwealth and Policy in South-east Asia', FO371/112213; minute by W.D. Allen, 8 April 1954, FO371/112051; and Eden's memorandum of 14 June 1954; annex C to minute by W.D. Allen, 8 April 1954, FO371/112052. Eden's views were broadly endorsed by the Chiefs, who thought that the choice of partition lines in Indochina should be dictated by the prospects of forming a reasonably strong Asian non-communist bloc. The most promising bloc would consist of Cambodia, Cochin-China and Laos, and it was possible that such a solution 'might have a particular appeal to India for ethnological reasons'. They perceived India as 'a major influence in the area', which would not, however, support any accord unless it was generally agreed upon at Geneva. Confidential annex to COS(54)55th meeting, 12 May 1954, DEFE4/70, and COS(54)68th meeting, 8 June 1954, ibid.

22. Nehru, *Letters to Chief Ministers*, 14 April 1954, vol. 3, p. 517; CRO to UK–New Delhi, tel. 584, 10 April 1954, FO371/112051.

23. E. Shuckburgh, *Descent to Suez*, p. 166.

24. Eden to Nehru, sent in FO to UK–New Delhi, tel. 614, 16 April 1954, FO371/112053; and C(54)134, 7 April 1954, CAB129/67.

25. UK–New Delhi to CRO, tels 374 and 376, 16 and 17 April 1954 respectively, FO371/112052.

26. George Allen to DS, tel. 1510, 5 April 1954, DS file 751G–00/4–554; and 6 April 1954, tel. 1515, *FR, 1952–1954*, vol. 13, part 1, p. 1267; memo from Jernergan to Byroade, 23 April 1954, DS file 751G–00/4–2354, and Donald Kennedy to Jernegan, 28 April 1954, DS file 751G.00/4–2854.

27. Nehru, *Letters to Chief Ministers*, 15 March, 14, 26 April, and 1 July 1954, vol.

3, pp. 504, 515–19, 528, 596–9. Nehru's fears of American intentions were echoed by Eden – though from a different perspective. According to Shuckburgh, Eden was convinced that 'all the Americans want to do is to replace the French and run Indo–China themselves. "They want to replace us in Egypt too. They want to run the world." ' Entry for 2 May 1954, Shuckburgh, *Descent to Suez*, p. 187.

28. Makins to K.L. Speaight, 18 March 1954, FO371/112212.

29. Minutes by Cable and Tahourdin, on above 1 April 1954, ibid.

30. Memo of conversation, 20 April 1954, *FR, 1952–1954*, vol. 16, p. 536.

31. Memo of conversation, 15 June 1954, *FR, 1952–1954*, vol. 12, part 1, p. 567.

32. C(54)134, 7 April 1954, CAB129/67. See also confidential annex to COS(54)2nd meeting, 10 April 1954, FO371/112052.

33. Memo of Dulles–Amjad Ali conversation, 9 April 1954, DS file 751G.00/4–954.

34. US–Karachi to SS, tel. 853, 20 April 1954, DS file 751G.00/4–2054.

35. UK–Karachi to CRO, tel. 503, 14 April 1954, FO371/112053, and CRO to UK–Karachi, tel. 492, 22 April 1954, FO371/112055.

36. UK–New Delhi to CRO, tel. 410, 24 April 1954, FO371/112055 and FO (Reading) to Geneva, tel. 20, 26 April 1954 and Geneva (Eden) to FO, tel. 24, 27 April 1954, FO371/112057. On American disapproval of Nehru's proposals, see *FR, 1952–1954*, vol. 16, pp. 636–8.

37. Memo of conversation by SS, 25 April 1954, *FR, 1952–1954*, vol. 16, pp. 556–7.

38. Entry for 27 April 1954, R.H. Ferrell (ed.), *The Eisenhower Diaries*, (New York 1981), pp. 279–80.

39. NSC meeting, 29 April 1954, AWF, NSC series, DDE papers, EL.

40. The phrase is that of Townsend Hoopes, *The Devil and John Foster Dulles*, (Boston 1973), p. 222.

41. Memo of conversation at the White House, 5 May 1954, *FR, 1952–1954*, vol. 13, part 2, pp. 1467–8.

42. UK–Colombo to CRO, tels 140 and 150, dated 28 April and 2 May 1954 respectively, PREM8/881; tels 153 and 154 both dated 3 May 1954, FO371/112059; see also Nehru to Eden, sent in UK–New Delhi to CRO, tel. 441, 5 May 1954, PREM11/649.

43. Nehru to Eden, sent in UK–New Delhi to CRO, tel. 441, 5 May 1954, PREM11/649.

44. UK–New Delhi to CRO, tel. 452, 8 May 1954, FO371/112062.

45. Geneva to FO, tel. 208, 10 May 1954, sent in CRO to UK–New Delhi, tel. 738, 10 May 1954, and FO to Geneva, tel. 362, 11 May 1954, ibid.

46. Geneva to FO, tel. 627, 8 June 1954, FO371/112070; tels 259 and 261, 12 May 1954, FO371/112064.

47. UK–New Delhi to CRO, tels 481 and 482, both dated 17 May 1954, FO371/112066 and FO371/112196 respectively, and Geneva to FO, tel. 332, 17 May 112066.

48. Memo of conversation by SS, 11 May 1954, *FR 1952–1954*, vol. 13, part 2, p. 1533. If this statement exaggerates the extent of Indian influence on the British, James Cable is overstating the case in saying that, 'There is no evidence that Nehru influenced him [Eden]'; *The Geneva Conference of 1954 on Indochina* (London 1986), p. 132. British officials took up Indian ideas

when expedient and turned them down when they ran contrary to British interests.

49. *FR, 1952–1954*, vol. 13, part 2, p. 1437.

50. FO to Geneva, tel. 443, 14 May 1954. PREM11/649.

51. Geneva to FO, incorporating personal message from Eden to R. G. Casey, tel. 414, 22 May 1954, PREM11/649.

52. *FR, 1952–1954*, vol. 6, part 1, p. 1090.

53. Geneva to FO, tels 414 and 415, 22 May 1954, PREM11/649.

54. Geneva to FO, tel. 415, 22 May 1954, ibid.

55. 198th NSC meeting, 20 May 1954, *FR, 1952–1954*, vol. 12, part 1, pp. 497–8; see also Geneva to FO, tel. 559, 2 June 1954, FO800/799.

56. Canadian delegation Geneva, to Government of Canada, 5 June 1954, enclosed in G.D. Anderson (FO) to G. Darvey (CRO), 11 June 1954, FO371/112073.

57. Makins to Eden, 29 May 1954, FO800/841.

58. US delegation Geneva to DS, Secto 463, 17 June 1954, *FR, 1952–1954*, vol 16, pp. 1170–1; SS to US delegation in Geneva, Tedul 215, 17 June 1954, ibid., p. 1175; DS memo on conversation with UK officials, 26 June 1954, *FR, 1952–1954*, vol. 12, part 1, p. 577; Washington to FO, tel. 298, 27 June 1954, FO 371/112075.

59. C(54)207, 22 June 1954, CAB129/64.

60. Eden to Nehru, sent in CRO to Acting UK–New Delhi, 23 June 1954, tel. 1073, FO371/112074.

61. Rangoon to FO, tel. 318, 29 June 1954, FO371/112075, Geneva to FO, tel. 910, 13 July 1954, FO371/112077 and W.D. Allen to W.J.M. Paterson, 18 July 1954, FO371/112080.

62. Geneva to FO, tel. 960, 18 July 1954, FO371/112079. Also Geneva to FO, tels 551 and 552, 2 June 1954; tel. 607, 5 June 1954, FO371/112069; tel. 627, 8 June and tel. 637, 9 June 1954, FO371/112070; Acting UK–New Delhi to CRO, tel. 562, 9 June, tel. 565, 10 June, tel. 573, 11 June 1954, ibid., Geneva to FO, tels 966 and 967, 18 July 1954, and Acting UK–New Delhi to CRO, tel. 717, 27 July 1954, FO 371/117079.

63. Menon to Eden, 15 and 17 July 1954, FO371/112081. See also Acting UK–New Delhi to CRO, tel. 717, 17 July 1954; Geneva to FO, tels 966 and 967, 18 July 1954; Geneva to FO, tels 969 and 1009, 18 and 19 July 1954 respectively, ibid.

64. For the terms of the Geneva accord on Indochina, see *Documents on International Affairs 1954*, pp. 138–40. See also *Documents Relating to the Decision on Indochina at the Geneva Conference*, Cmd 9239, (London 1954); *Documents Relating to the British Involvement in the Indochina Conflict 1945–1965*, Cmd 2834 (London 1965); Avon, *Towards Peace in Indochina* (London 1966), pp. 2–3; 20. See also the discussion in E. Colbert, *South East Asia in International Politics 1941–1956* (Ithaca and London 1977), pp. 292–301; R.H. Fifield, *The Diplomacy of Southeast Asia 1945–1958* (Archon Books, 1968), pp. 274–87; M. Leifer, *Cambodia: The Search for Security* (London 1967), pp. 60–1; R. Randle, *Geneva 1954: The Settlement of the Indochinese War* (Princeton 1969); R.B. Smith, *An International History of the Vietnam War* vol. 1, (London 1983), pp. 19–29; L.C. Gardner, *Approaching Vietnam*, pp. 281–314, and R.H. Immerman, 'The United States

and the Geneva Conference', *Diplomatic History*, vol. 14, 1990, pp. 43–66.

65. 206th NSC meeting, 15 July 1954, *FR, 1952–1954*, vol. 13, part 2, p. 1835.

66. Nutting to Reading, 23 May 1954, FO371/112068 and Churchill to Eisenhower, in FO to Washington, tel. 3256, 9 July 1954, FO800/762.

67. Acting UK–New Delhi to CRO, tel. 724, 28 July 1954, PREM11/651.

68. *FR, 1952–1954*, vol. 12, part 1, 21 July 1954, p. 649.

69. Ibid., pp. 667, 664.

70. Ibid., pp. 655, 668.

71. CRO to UK–New Delhi, tel. Y no. 334, 30 July 1954, PREM11/651.

72. Nehru to Eden, sent in Acting UK–New Delhi to CRO, tel. 739, 2 August 1954, PREM11/651.

73. Memo of conversation on 26 July 1954, *FR, 1952–1954*, vol. 12, part 1, 1954, p. 675. See also Dulles's memo of conversation with President, 17 August 1954, Dulles papers, White House Memoranda Series, EL. For a sympathetic account of Dulles and SEATO see R. Dingman, 'John Foster Dulles and the Creation of SEATO in 1954', *International History Review*, vol. 11, 1989, pp. 457–77.

74. Memo of conversation, 27 July 1954, *FR, 1952–1954*, vol. 12, part 1, pp. 676–7; DS to Karachi, tel. 246, 24 August 1954, DS file 790D. 5-MSP/8–1754; Hildreth to DS, 4 August 1954, *FR, 1952–1954*, vol. 12, part 1, pp. 704–5. See also memo by MacArthur to Acting SS, 28 August 1954, ibid., p. 807; memo of Dulles–Merchant telephone conversation, ibid., p. 821; Dulles to Byroade, 15 November 1954, Dulles papers, Chronological file, EL.

75. This paragraph is based on Ceylon fortnightly summary, 23 May–7 June 1954, PREM11/881; Gopal, *Nehru*, vol. 2, p. 232; note by Reading on conversation with Mrs Pandit, 17 January 1955, FO371/11729; G.H. Middleton to W.D. Allen, 22 January 1955, FO371/116976; New Delhi to CRO, tel. 359, 25 March 1955, ibid., New Delhi to CRO, tel. 393, 5 April 1955, FO371/11679; UK–New Delhi to CRO, tel. 437, 15 April 1955, FO371/116981. Two useful contemporary accounts of the Bandung conference are A. Appadorai, 'The Bandung Conference', *India Quarterly*, vol. 11, 1955, pp. 207–35, and G.M. Kahin, *The Asian–African Conference*, (Ithaca 1956). See also A.W. Stargardt, 'The Emergence of the Asian System of Powers', *Modern Asian Studies*, vol. 23, 1989, pp. 561–95.

76. Memo of Makins–Dulles conversation, 7 April 1955, *FR, 1955–1957*, vol. 2, p. 454.

77. Minute by W.J.M. Paterson, 24 November 1954, FO371/111922. The British generally expected Asian conferences to be anti-West. See FO Research Department paper on Asian conferences, 2 December 1955, FO371/116987.

78. Minute by Kirkpatrick, 24 November 1954, FO371/11192.

79. *FR, 1952–1954*, vol. 6, part 1, p. 1103, and CC(55)28th conclusions, 5 April 1955, CAB128/28.

80. A. Lennox-Boyd (Colonial Office) to Eden, 11 January 1955; minute by F.S. Tomlinson, 12 January 1955; W.A.C. Mathieson (Colonial Office) to Cable, 28 January 1955, FO371/116976.

81. Gopal, *Nehru*, vol. 2, p. 233.

82. G.H. Middleton to W.D. Allen, 22 January 1955, and Allen to Middleton, 12 February 1955, FO371/116976; undated note (probably early December) of conversation between Eden and Menon, FO800/798.

83. Minute by H. Smedley on talk between Swinton and Huggins, 2 February 1955. See also minute by Tomlinson, 4 February 1955. FO371/116977.
84. CC(55)3rd conclusions, 13 January 1955, CAB128/78. See also FO to Baghdad, tel. 212, and FO to Ankara, tel. 225, both dated 14 February 1955; FO371/116977.
85. Gopal, *Nehru*, vol. 2, pp. 232–3.
86. UK–Karachi to CRO, tel. 178, 28 January 1955, FO371/116976; N.H.C. Bruce to R.C. Hunt, 28 March 1955 and minute by Cable, 2 April 1955, FO371/116979.
87. Nehru, *Letters to Chief Ministers*, 28 April 1955, vol. 4, pp. 163–4.
88. Progress report on NSC 5409, 24 August 1955, Policy papers subseries, file NSC 5409: Policy towards South Asia (1) box 9, OSANSA, EL.
89. UK–Colombo to CRO, tel. 137, 26 March 1955, FO371/116979; Singapore to FO, tel. 384, 19 April 1955, FO371/116981, 'Communist Aims at Afro–Asian Conference', copy of *aide-memoire* given to Ceylon government by British High Commissioner in Colombo (undated but probably around mid-April 1955), and minute by Cable, 28 April 1955, FO371/116982. Kotelwala's enthusiasm probably owed something to the poor personal relations between himself and Nehru. See also Kotelwala's *An Asian Prime Minister's Story*, (London 1956), p. 187.
90. Kahin, op. cit., pp. 17–18.
91. Cabinet minutes, 29 April 1955, AWF, Cabinet series, box 5, DDE papers, EL.
92. FO brief for Reading in connection with his speeches in USA, dated 29 April 1955, FO371/116984; J.E. Marnham to E.R. Warner, 16 June 1955, FO371/117458.
93. I.A.G. Gdo Agung, *Twenty Years of Indonesian Foreign Policy 1945–65*, (The Hague 1973), p. 257.
94. Impressions of W.R. Crocker (Australian ambassador, Jakarta) FO371/116985; and O.C. Morland to Eden, 28 April 1955, FO371/116983; R. Stevens to Shuckburgh, 3 May 1955; FO371/116984; A. Chapman–Andrews to Kirkpatrick, 9 May 1955; P.E. Ramsbotham (New York) to SEA department, 14 May 1955, FO371/116985.
95. Cabinet minutes, 29 April 1955, AWF, Cabinet series, box 5. DDE papers, EL; and memo of conversation, 6 May 1955, *FR, 1955–1957*, vol. 2, p. 556.
96. Churchill to Nehru, 21 February 1955, and CC(55)15, 17 February 1955, CAB128/28, cited in M. Gilbert, *Winston S. Churchill, 1945–1965*, p. 1094.
97. CRO draft on Indian foreign policy, enclosed in J. Garner to Caccia, 11 December 1954, FO371/112197. After some revision, this became the FO review on Indian foreign policy, 22 March 1955, FO371/117283. From Washington, Makins emphasised that 'American–Indian relations are indeed one of the keys to progress in the Far East.' He wondered whether Japan could play a significant part because the economies of Japan and India were in some respects complementary. In India, Japan could find a market and a source of supply of much greater importance than Southeast Asia: 'Japan may perhaps prove to be the bridge between the United States and India.' Makins to Kirkpatrick, 3 November 1954, FO371/110189.
98. US–New Delhi to SS, tel. 246, 18 August 1954, DS file 611. 91/8–1854, and US–New Delhi despatch no. 387 to DS, 28 September 1954, DS file 611. 91/9–2854.

99. R.W. Heppel (Phnom Penh) to Eden, 6 November 1954, FO371/112042.
100. Nehru, *Letters to Chief Minsters*, 15 November 1954, vol. 4, p. 89. See also Nehru to Eden, 29 January 1955, FO371/115018.
101. Macdonald to Eden, 12 December 1954, PREM1/1310. See also Middleton to SSCR, 6 January 1955, FO371/117140.
102. Memo of conversation, 20 June 1954, *FR, 1952–1954*, vol. 16, p. 1206.
103. Heath to DS, tel. 113, 9 July 1954, *FR, 1952–1954* vol. 13, part 2, p. 1799.
104. 179th NSC meeting, 8 January 1954, AWF, NSC series, DDE papers, EL.
105. Dulles to Wilson, 18 August 1954, *FR, 1952–1954*, vol. 13, part 2, p. 1955.
106. 207th NSC meeting, 22 July 1954, ibid, p. 1869, See also pp. 1736; 1754–5, 2089–91, 2412, 2433–4, 2437.
107. *FR, 1952–1954*, vol. 13, part 2, pp. 2079, 2125–6. In FO to Washington, 25 July 1954, Eden instructed Makins that 'the whole understanding on which the agreements were reached was that none of the three Associated States, including Cambodia, should be members of any South East Asia defence organisation, though I agree that this need not preclude our covering them by the commitments assumed by the members of such an organisation.' FO371/112081. See also Tahourdin's minute dated 16 July 1954, FO371/112079, and his note 'Geneva Conference' for the Foreign Affairs Committee, 28 July 1954, FO371/112084; minute by Ford on meeting between Eden, Mendes–France and Chou Enlai on 19 July 1954, FO371/112082.
108. Eden–Dulles conversation in Paris, 16 December 1954, FO371/112042, and *FR, 1952–1954*, vol. 13, part 2, p. 2386. The draft message from Eden to Nehru was drawn up by the FO (the CRO concurred) and sent in CRO to UK–New Delhi, tel. Y.no. 547, 23 December 1954, FO371/112042.
109. FO draft on 'Indian Interest in Cambodia and Laos', 9 February 1955, FO371/117140.
110. FO memorandum on Manila treaty, 10 March 1955, FO371/117160; Eisenhower to Churchill, 29 March 1955, PREM11/1310.
111. Nehru to Eden, 29 April 1955, PREM11/1310.
112. ibid.
113. Eden to Nehru, 13 May 1955, ibid.
114. FO memo on Manila Treaty, 10 March 1955, FO371/117160.
115. McClintock to DS, 14 October 1954, *FR, 1952–54*, vol. 13, part 2, pp. 2140–1. But see Hanoi to FO, tel. 74, 14 March 1955 and minutes by Cable and Landymore, 15 March 1955, for a different view, FO 371/117169.
116. Cook to Macmillan, 23 May 1955; Millard to W.D. Allen, 20 June 1955; FO note on 'Military Aid to Cambodia', 5 June 1955, enclosed in Allen to Millard, 25 June 1955; CRO to Acting UK–New Delhi, tel. no 1325, 27 June 1955, PREM11/1310. See also UK–New Delhi to CRO, tel. 357, 25 March 1955, FO 371/117140.
117. Millard to Eden, 28 June 1955, ibid.
118. CP(55)64, 11 July 1955, PREM11/919. The phrase quoted was underlined by Eden in red ink.
119. Pnom Penh to SS, tel. 663, 29 November 1955, DS file 751.00/11-2955. In his embassy despatch no. 151, 18 November 1955, DS file 611.51H/11-1855, McClintock thought that India could make an important contribution to shore up Cambodian sovereignty, but this should be seen in the context of his overall dislike of the Indians and his call for the total replacement of the

French by the Americans in Cambodia. *FR, 1952–1954*, vol. 13, part 2, p. 2410.

120. Pnom Penh to SS, tel. 706, 8 December 1955, DS file 751H.00/12-855; Cook to Tomlinson, 21 July 1955, and Rumbold to Millard, 1 August 1955, PREM11/1310. See also R.W. Heppel to W.D. Allen, 18 November 1955 and Allen to Heppel, 28 November 1955, FO371/117140.

121. Memo of talks by Desmond Donnelly, 20 November 1954, FO371/112197. See also the telegrams in PREM11/1303, FO371/117169 and FO371/117175 – the evidence is voluminous.

122. UK–New Delhi to CRO, tel. 994, 10 September 1955, FO371/117169; FO brief for Commonwealth Prime Ministers' meeting, 11 June 1956, FO371/123392.

123. Ibid.

124. Pnom Penh embassy despatch no. 365 to DS, 3 May 1956, DS file 751H.00/5-356.

125. Memo from Walter McConaughy to Walter Robertson, 30 January 1956, DS file 611.41/1-3056.

Notes to Chapter 6

1. C(54)307, 11 October 1954, CAB129/71 and Appendix; C(55)43, 16 February 1955, CAB129/73.
2. Extract from Congressional Record of 28 January 1954, enclosed in D.J.C. Crawley (Washington) to SEA department, 1 February 1954, and minute by Cable, 6 February 1954, F0371/112212.
3. D.J.C Crawley to R. Fowler (CRO), 15 December 1953, F0371/106857; minute by Cable, 19 January 1954, F0371/112212; Macdonald to SSCR, 28 December, 1953, ibid.
4. Minutes by Tahourdin and Denis Allen, 11 and 12 November 1953, F0371/106855 and minute by Cable, 23 February 1954, F0371/112223.
5. Minute by Tahourdin, 24 October 1953, and Strang to Dening (Tokyo) and W.G.C. Graham (Seoul), 27 October 1953, F0371/106857.
6. Makins to Macmillan, 2 November 1955, F0371/114386 and CP(55)176, 17 November 1955, CAB129/78.
7. Note by B.R. Pearn on Britain's trade with South, Southeast, and East Asian countries, 23 September 1954, F0371/111917; David Eccles (Board of Trade) to Chancellor of Exchequer, 18 July 1958, F0371/135950.
8. The next two paragraphs are based on B.N. Ganguli, 'Indo–American Trade', *India Quarterly*, vol. 6, no. 1950, pp. 234–47, and 'India and the Commonwealth: Economic Relations' *India Quarterly*, vol. 10, 1954, pp. 125–43; see also chapter 1 of this book.
9. This paragraph is based on minute by Cable, 10 October 1953; P. Gaugrey to F. Doy, 22 October 1953, F0371/106861; G.J. MacMahon (Senior UK Trade Commissioner in New Delhi) to R.C. Bryant (Board of Trade), 4 December and Bryant to MacMahon, 17 December 1953; minutes by Cable, 10 October and 24 November 1953 and 7 January 1954; minute by Burrows, 23 December 1953; G. Wheeler (Defence) to N. Pritchard (CRO), 24 November 1953, ibid. See also Clutterbuck to Pritchard, 21 March 1953, and minute by D.F. Hubback (Treasury), 18 August 1953, T225/357.
10. National Intelligence Estimate, 5 January 1956, *FR, 1955–1957*, vol. 3, p. 239.
11. J. Thomson (CRO) to F.S. Tomlinson (FO), 5 Feb. 1955, F0371/117294; CRO note on Indian steel production, 25 May 1955, ibid. For one FO perspective on Indo–Soviet relations, see the note by the Soviet section of the FO research department, 15 April 1955, F0371/116667.
12. CA-9051, 21 June 1955, DS semi-annual review of US–India relations, DS file 611.91/6–2155; 248th and 267th NSC meetings, 12 May and 21 November 1955, AWF, NSC series, DDE papers. See also USCFEP papers of the

chairman, Intelligence Reports series, 'The Communist Economic Campaign in the Near East and South Asia', 30 November 1955, and 'Sino–Soviet Policy and Its Probable Effects in Underdeveloped Areas', 24 April 1956; USCFEP Policy Papers series, DS Intelligence report no. 81 on 'Communist Economic Diplomacy in Underdeveloped Areas', 2 April 1956, EL.

13. UK-New Delhi to SSCR, 17 December 1955, on 'India: Means of Countering Soviet Penetration and Improving Relations with the UK', PREM11/1303. On 'cultural containment', see UK–New Delhi to SSCR, 'India: Preservation of the British Link', 30 January 1956, F0371/123589.

14. UK–Moscow to FO, tel. 560, 10 June 1955; tel. 610, 23 June 1955; Hayter to Eden, 24 June 1955, F0371/117298, and CRO note on Nehru's East European tour, 8 July 1955, PREM11/919.

15. Macdonald to Home, 22 November 1955, PREM11/1606.

16. Nehru, *Letters to Chief Ministers*, 26 November 1955, vol. 4, p. 301, and Nehru to Eden, 2 December 1955, enclosure to CP(55) 199, 12 December 1955, CAB129/78.

17. Eden to Nehru, in CRO to New Delhi, tel. 2731, 9 December 1955, ibid.

18. Cited in Gopal, *Nehru*, vol. 2, p. 248.

19. Nehru, *Letters to Chief Ministers*, 26 November 1955, vol. 4, footnote 14, p. 305; 21 December 1955, ibid., pp. 316–17; and Macdonald to Laithwaite, 2 December 1955, PREM11/1606.

20. Nehru, *Letters to Chief Ministers*, 21 December 1955, vol. 4, footnote 16, p. 317; Hayter to Allen, 24 January 1956, FO371/123587. But US diplomats in New Delhi supported Dulles and lambasted '[t]he extent to which the Indians seemed to kowtow to Messrs. Bulganin and Khruschev, and their public acceptance of the Russian intervention in the Goa and Kashmir cases were, of course, deplorable.' The Indian reaction to Dulles's statement was condemned as 'intemperate behavior' and 'indefensible.' US–New Delhi to DS, despatch no. 1064, 31 March 1956, DS file 611. 91/3–3156.

21. Nehru to Vijayalakshmi Pandit, 2 December 1955, cited in Gopal, p. 252.

22. Nehru, *Letters to Chief Ministers*, 21 December 1955, vol. 4, p. 312.

23. K.P.S. Menon, *The Flying Troika*, (Bombay 1963), p. 119.

24. Middleton to Home, 17 January 1956, PREM11/1606.

25. Ibid. and Macdonald to Home, 17 December 1955, FO371/117291.

26. Minute by W.D. Allen, 12 January 1956, FO371/123587.

27. UK–New Delhi to CRO, tel. 1283, 16 November 1955, PREM11/1399.

28. CRO to UK–New Delhi, tel. 2620, 26 November 1955, ibid.

29. UK–New Delhi to CRO, tel. 1346, 28 November 1955, ibid.

30. Minute by Clark, 29 November 1955; minute from Home to Eden, 2 December 1955, ibid. See also minute from De L'Isle and Dudley to Eden, 15 December 1955, ibid.

31. Home to Eden, 2 December 1955, ibid.

32. UK–New Delhi to CRO, tel. 1401, 7 December and tels 1396, 1397, 6 December 1955, ibid.

33. FO to Washington, tels 5875, 5876, 5877, 10 December 1955, ibid. The drafts of the telegrams were checked by Eden.

34. Minutes from Home and Macmillan to Eden, 14 and 18 December 1955 respectively, and minute from De L'Isle and Dudley to Eden, 15 December 1955, ibid.

35. CRO to Acting UK–New Delhi, tel. 2888, 20 December 1955, ibid.
36. Memo, Allen (Assistant SS, NEA) to Under Secretary, 11 January 1956, DS file 791. 5622/1–1156.
37. John Sherman Cooper to Dulles, tel. 1410, 9 January 1956, DS file 791. 5622/1–956.
38. DS to US–New Delhi, tel. 1709, 17 January 1956, DS file 791. 5622/1–1756.
39. US–New Delhi to Secretary of State, tel. 1516, 19 January 1956, DS file 791. 5622/1. 1–956.
40. UK–New Delhi to CRO, tel. 120, 21 January 1956 and minute by Eden, 21 January 1956, PREM11/1399.
41. Memo from Allen (NEA) to SS, 24 January 1956, DS file 791. 561/1–2456.
42. CP(56)23, 27 January 1956; CP(56)24, 28 January 1956, CAB129/79; CM(56)8th conclusions, 31 January 1956, CAB128/30; minute by F.S. Tomlinson, 'Arms for India and Pakistan', 30 January 1956, FO371/123677.
43. CRO to UK–New Delhi, tel. 249, 30 January 1956; COS note, 31 January 1956, enclosed in note by J.R.A. Bottomley, 31 January 1956, PREM11/1399.
44. Eden to Eisenhower, 1 February 1956, ibid. This last line was added to the draft by Eden and incorporated in the letter sent to Eisenhower.
45. Memo for the record, 10 February 1956, DS file 791.5622/2–956.
46. UK–New Delhi to CRO, tel. 32, 14 February 1956, PREM11/1399.
47. F.A. Bishop (10 Downing Street) to H. Smedley (CRO), 21 February 1956, ibid.
48. Home to Eden and to De L'Isle and Dudley, both 20 February 1956, PREM11/1399.
49. Draft telegrams, CRO to UK–New Delhi, undated but probably 22 and 24 February 1956, ibid. They were seen by Eden, and the second one was sent as CRO to UK–New Delhi, tel. 471, 25 February 1956, ibid.
50. US–New Delhi to SS, Dulte 18, 10 March 1956, DS file 791.5622/3–1056.
51. Macdonald to Laithwaite, 16 March 1956, and UK–New Delhi to CRO, 16 March 1956, FO371/123677.
52. Draft, Eden to Nehru, around 3 March 1956; Home to Eden, 6 March; CRO-UK–New Delhi, tel. 646, 7 March; Mountbatten to Eden, 6 March; Eden to Mountbatten, 7 March; UK-New Delhi to CRO, tel. 420, 12 March; Nehru to Eden, 23 March 1956, forwarded by Mrs Pandit on 24 March, PREM11/1399. See also Macdonald's record of his conversation with Nehru and Pillai on 17 March, FO371/123587.
53. Minute from Home to Eden, 12 January 1956, and enclosures, FO371/123589.
54. Enclosure to above, ibid.
55. Eisenhower to Lewis Douglas, 20 January 1956, DDE papers, Administration series, ACW file, box 12, EL.
56. Memo on neutralism, 7 February 1956, AWF, International series, file: Eden visit, 30 January–1 February 1956 (4), DDE papers, EL.
57. Memos of conversations between Reading and J.S. Cooper and Cooper and Home, 28 and 29 February 1956 respectively, FO371/123588.
58. BBC television programme 'Panorama' on 9 April 1956; see Selwyn Lloyd's reaction in his letter to J. Risdale (MP), 9 May 1956, FO371/123673.
59. US–Karachi to DS, despatch no. 626, 1 March 1956, DS file 690D.00/3–2856.
60. Memo by Hildreth, 15 February 1956, DS file 611.90D/2–1756.
61. Memos of Dulles's conversations with Mohamad Ali and Mirza in Karachi on

5 March 1956, enclosure 1 to despatch no. 634, US–Karachi to DS, 6 March 1956, DS file 611.90D./3–656.

62. Memo of conversation on 16 March 1956 between Mirza and Hildreth, enclosure 1 to despatch no. 674, US–Karachi to DS, 21 March 1956, DS file 690D.91/3–2156.

63. Memo by Dulles of his conversation with Mohamad Ali, 6 March 1956, DS file 611.90D/3–656.

64. DS position paper on 'Problems in US–Indian–Pakistan Relations', prepared for Nehru visit to US, 11 December 1956, White House Central File, subject series, box 72, file: State Department 1956 Nehru material (1), DDE papers, EL.

65. A.W. Snelling to D.W. Haviland, 27 April 1956, FO371/123677 and Washington to FO, tel. 1086, 1 May 1956. See also minute by F. Tomlinson, 22 June 1956, ibid.

66. Washington to FO, tel. 1086, 1 May 1956, FO371/123677; *FR, 1955–1957*, vol. 8, pp. 74–5.

67. Washington to FO, tel. 1086, 1 May 1956, FO371/123677.

68. Paris (Jebb) to FO, tel. 117, 4 May 1956, ibid.

69. Symon to Laithwaite, 15 May 1956; UK–Karachi to CRO, tel. 1063, 26 June 1956; Symon to Laitwaite, 7 June 1956 and Laithwaite's reply, 21 June 1956; ibid.

70. Washington to FO, tel. 441, 7 June 1956, ibid.

71. Eden, *Full Circle*, p. 444; Lord Home, *The Way the Wind Blows* (London 1976), p. 140; H. Macmillan, *Riding the Storm 1956–1959* (London 1971), pp. 375, 200. See also CRO note on the effect of the Suez crisis on relations with India and Pakistan, undated but probably around mid-December 1956, DO35/6339, and D. Carlton, *Britain and the Suez Crisis*, (paperback, Oxford 1988), p. 72.

72. Nehru, *Letters to Chief Ministers*, 16 August 1956, vol. 4, pp. 417–18; Nehru to Vijayalakshmi Pandit, 27 July, note for Indian missions, 31 July and Nehru to Foreign Secretary, 29 July 1956, all cited in Gopal, pp. 277–8.

73. EC(56)1st meeting, 27 July 1956, CAB134/1217. The Egypt Committee comprised Eden, Lloyd, Macmillan, Salisbury, Home and Monckton. See also CM(56)54th conclusions, 27 July 1956, CAB128/30, and H.J. Dooley, 'Great Britain's "Last Battle" in the Middle East: Notes on Cabinet Planning during the Suez Crisis of 1956', *International History Review*, vol. 11, 1989, pp. 486–517.

74. K. Kyle, 'Britain and the Crisis 1955–6', in W.R. Louis and R. Owen (eds), *Suez 1956: the Crisis and its Consequences* (Oxford 1989), pp. 108–9: see also the essays by R. Bowie, S. Gopal and P. Lyon in the same book.

75. Eden to Eisenhower, 27 July 1956, *FR, 1955–1957*, vol. 16, p. 10.

76. AWF/DDE diary, 27 July 1956, box 8, file: July 1956, Staff memos, EL.

77. Supplementary note, conversation with President on 28 July 1956, ibid. See also Dulles's telephone conversations with Nixon and Senator Knowland, 30 and 31 July 1956 respectively, Dulles papers, Telephone calls series, box 5, EL.

78. Memo of conversation with President, 31 July 1956, AWF/DDE diary, file: Staff memos, July 1956, EL, and Eisenhower to Eden, 31 July 1956, *FR, 1955–1957*, vol. 16, pp. 69–70.

79. Eisenhower to Eden, 31 July 1956, *FR, 1955–1957*, vol. 16, pp. 69–70.
80. Memos of conversations with President on 28 and 30 July 1956, AWF/DDE Diary, box 16, file: Staff memos, July 1956, EL.
81. UK–Karachi to CRO, tel. 1242, 2 August 1956, DO35/6317, and UK–Karachi to CRO, tel. 1215, 30 July 1956, ibid.
82. Dulte 2, 2 August 1956, AWF, Dulles–Herter series, box 5, file: August 1956, DDE papers, EL.
83. UK–New Delhi to CRO, tel. 1004, 2 August 1956, DO35/6317.
84. UK–New Delhi to CRO, tels 1013 and 1014, 4 August 1956; and Nehru to Eden in CRO to UK–New Delhi, tel. 1801, 6 August 1956, ibid.
85. Eden to Nehru, in CRO to UK–New Delhi, tel. 1802, 6 August 1956, PREM11/1094.
86. Gopal, *Nehru*, pp. 278–9.
87. M. Heikal, *Cutting the Lion's Tail* (London 1986), pp. 134 ff.
88. Eden to Nehru, 7 August 1956, PREM11/1094.
89. UK–New Delhi to CRO, tel. 1037, 8 August 1956, PREM11/1094.
90. UK–New Delhi to CRO, tels 1039 and 1044, 8 and 10 August 1956 respectively, ibid.
91. Eden to Nehru, 11 August 1956, DO35/6319.
92. UK–New Delhi to CRO, tel. 1058, 13 August 1956, PREM11/1094, and record of Lloyd's conversation with Menon, 15 August 1956, ibid.
93. Note by Brook on conversation with Pillai on 14 August 1956, enclosed in Brook to Laithwaite, 16 August 1956, PREM11/1144.
94. D. Carlton, *Britain and the Suez Crisis*, p. 43.
95. CRO note on possible Commonwealth attitudes on use of force over Suez, 9 August 1956, PREM11/1094; and ME(0)SC(56)3 Revise, Official Committee on the Middle East, Suez Canal Sub-committee, 14 August 1956, CAB134/302.
96. UK–New Delhi to CRO, tel. 1080, 20 August 1956, DO35/6319. At the time of writing this chapter, the text of Dulles' letter has not been declassified.
97. DDE diary, Dulles–Eisenhower conversation, 8 August 1956, box 16, file: August 1956 Phone calls; see also draft letter from Eisenhower to Nehru, 24 August 1956, AWF, International series, box 26, file: India, PM Nehru 1956 (1), DDE papers, EL.
98. Nehru to Rajagopalachari, 10 August 1956, and Menon to Nehru, 15 August 1956, cited in Gopal, *Nehru*, p. 280; Nehru, *Letters to Chief Ministers*, 16 August 1956, vol. 4, p. 401; Heikal, *Cutting the Lion's Tail*, p. 135.
99. Memo of conference with President, 14 August 1956, White House Memoranda series, box 5, file: Meetings with President August–December 1956 (8), Dulles papers; and London to SS, Secto 6, 16 August 1956, AWF, Dulles–Herter series, box 5, file: August 1956 (2); and DDE Diary, memo for the record, 12 August 1956, box 17, file: August 1956 Diary Staff memos, DDE papers, EL.
100. London to SS, Dulte 7, 17 August 1956, ibid.
101. London to SS, Dulte 17, 20 August 1956, AWF, Dulles–Herter series, box 5 file: August 1956 (1), DDE papers, EL.
102. CRO to UK High Commissioners, Y-187, 21 August 1956, DO35/6319.
103. Eden to Nehru (drafted by Home), 21 August 1956, sent in CRO to UK–New Delhi, tel. 1901, 22 August 1956, ibid.

104. Nehru, *Letters to Chief Ministers*, 20 September 1956, vol. 4, p. 443; and UK–New Delhi to CRO, tel. 1095, 22 August 1956, PREM11/1094.
105. Menon's telegram from London to Indian ambassador in Cairo and tel. to Nehru, 21 August 1956, cited in Gopal, *Nehru*, p. 281; UK–New Delhi to CRO, tel. 1186, 13 September 1956, PREM11/1094.
106. London to SS, Dulte 19, 21 August 1956, AWF, Dulles–Herter series, box 5, file: Aug. 56 (1) DDE papers, EL.
107. For instance, see *FR, 1955–1957*, vol. 16, pp. 98, 285.
108. Eisenhower to Eden, 8 September 1956, PREM11/1100.
109. Memo of conversation with President by Dulles, 8 September 1956, White House memoranda series, box 4, file: Meetings with President, August–December 1956(5), Dulles papers, EL.
110. Gopal, *Nehru*, p. 283.
111. Minute from Home to Eden, 15 September 1956, and UK–New Delhi to CRO, tel. 1192, 13 September 1956, PREM11/1094.
112. Home to Eden, 15 September 1956, ibid.
113. Nehru to Eden, 15 September 1956, enclosed in Pandit to Eden, 15 September 1956, ibid.
114. Draft message from Eden to Nehru, prepared by Home and the redraft by Eden on 17 September 1956, enclosed in H. Smedley (CRO) to F.A. Bishop (Downing Street), DO35/6319; undated minute by Home, sent in CRO to UK–New Delhi, tel. 2077, 16 September 1956, ibid.
115. CRO to UK High Commissioners, Y. no. 253, 15 September 1956, DO35/6319.
116. UK–Karachi to CRO, tel. 1477, 15 September 1956; and Home's record of conversation with Australian, New Zealand and Pakistani leaders, 18 September 1956, PREM11/1094. See also *FR, 1955–1957*, vol. 16, pp. 530, 535.
117. CRO to UK–Karachi, tels. 1790 and 1791, 20 and 21 September 1956 respectively, PREM11/1095. See also *FR, 1955–1957*, vol. 16, p. 550.
118. Acting UK–Karachi to CRO, tel. 1518, 22 September 1956, J.J.S. Garner to Home, and minute by Eden, 21 September 1956, PREM11/1095.
119. UK–Karachi to CRO, tel. 1518, 22 September 1956, ibid.
120. Draft message from Eden to Suhrawardy, 23 September 1956; see also Washington to FO, tels 1990 and 1991, 24 September 1956, PREM11/1095.
121. *FR, 1955–1957*, vol. 8, pp. 470–1; UK–Karachi to CRO, tel. 1519, 22 September 1956, PREM11/1095.
122. Memo of conversation with President, 2 October 1956, Dulles papers, White House memoranda series, box 4, file: Meetings with President August-December 1956(5), EL.
123. Eisenhower to Hoover, 8 October 1956, AWF/DDE papers, Dulles–Herter series, box 6, file: Dulles October 1956(2), EL.
124. Memo from Hoover to President, 10 October 1956, ibid.
125. Cairo to FO, tel. 2209, 19 September 1956, sent as CRO to UK–New Delhi, tel. 2103, 20 September 1956, and Cairo to FO, tel. 2280, 22 September 1956, DO35/6319 and PREM11/1095 respectively.
126. Record of talks between Home and Menon and Eden and Menon, 25 and 28 September 1956 respectively, ibid. See also record of conversation between Menon and Lloyd on 28 September, and UK–New Delhi, tel. 1272, 1 October

1956, ibid.
127. CRO to UK–New Delhi, tel. 2185, 2 October 1956, PREM11/1095.
128. CRO to UK–New Delhi, tel. 2191, 3 October 1956, ibid.
129. New York to FO, tel. 772, 2 October 1956, ibid.
130. Nehru to Eden, sent in UK–New Delhi to CRO, tel. 1285, 4 October 1956, DO35/6320, and conversation between Home and Menon, 16 October 1956, PREM11/1095.
131. DS to London and Paris, tel. 1261, 4 October 1956, AWF/DDE papers, Dulles–Herter series, box 6, file: October 1956(2), EL.
132. Eisenhower to Hoover, 8 October 1956, ibid.
133. UK–New Delhi to CRO, tel. 1365, 24 October 1956, DO35/6320, and H. Trevelyan, *The Middle East in Revolution*, (London 1970), pp. 101–2.
134. Memo of conference with President, 29 October 1956, DDE diary, Staff memos, file: October 1956, EL.
135. Memo of conference (Dulles and others) with President, 30 October 1956, DDE diary, box 19, Staff memos, file: October 1956, EL.
136. Memo of conference (Colonel Goodpaster and A. Flemming) with President on 30 October 1956, ibid.
137. Minute by D.A.H. Wright, 19 November 1956 and enclosure, 'USA and the Middle East', 16 November 1956, FO371/120342.
138. 302nd NSC meeting, 1 November 1956, AWF/DDE papers, Dulles–Herter series, box 8, file: November 1956(1) Eisenhower–Dulles, EL.
139. 302nd NSC meeting, 1 November 1956, and Eisenhower to Dulles, 1 November 1956, ibid.
140. Ibid and New York to SS, tel. 472, 2 November 1956, AWF/DDE papers, Dulles–Herter series, box 6, file: Dulles November 1956(2). See also memo of conference between Eisenhower and other US officials on 2 November 1956, DDE diary, box 19, file: November 1956, Diary Staff memos, EL.
141. Memo of conference with President, 3 November 1956, ibid., and memo for Dulles from Hoover, 2 November 1956, Dulles papers, White House Memoranda series, box 4, file: Meetings with President, August–December (3), EL.
142. Eisenhower to Nehru, 6 November 1956, AWF/DDE papers, International series, box 26, file: India PM Nehru 1956(2), EL.
143. Memo of conversation with President, 5 November 1956, AWF/DDE diary, box 19, file: November 1956 Diary Staff memos, EL.
144. Acting UK–Karachi to CRO, tel. 1745, 31 October 1956, PREM11/1096; tels 1760 and 1766, 2 November 1956, DO35/6340; R. Stevens (Tehran), tel. 856, 2 November 1956, ibid; Suhrawardy to Eden, 4 November 1956, PREM11/1096.
145. CRO notes of telephone conversation with James in Karachi, 3 November 1956; UK–Karachi to CRO, tels 1777, 1778, 3 November 1956; tel. 1789, 4 November 1956, PREM11/1096.
146. *FR, 1955–1957*, vol. 8, p. 472.
147. UK–Karachi to CRO, tel. 1842, 9 November 1956, PREM11/1097.
148. Symon to Home, 27 December 1956, DO35/6340.
149. DTC (56) 20th meeting, 5 November 1956, CAB134/815; and undated CRO note of mid-December (?) 1956, on Suez, India and Pakistan, DO35/6339.
150. Gopal, *Nehru*, vol. 2, p. 288.

151. CRO note, as in note 149 above.
152. Record of conversation between Mrs Pandit and Home, 14 November 1956, and UK–New Delhi to CRO, tel. 1556, 17 November 1956, FO371/123589.
153. Canada to CRO, tel. 1417, 24 November 1956, PREM11/1094.
154. Nehru visit, DS Position Papers, December 1956, White House Central file, Subject series, EL.
155. Minutes by Gore-Booth and Hankey, 13 and 15 November 1956 respectively FO371/120342.
156. Caccia to D.P. Reilly, in Washington to FO, cypher 2359, 28 November 1956; Caccia to Reilly, 29 November 1956, and extract from the same, FO371/120342.
157. New York to FO, tel. 1457, 28 November 1956, ibid.
158. Caccia to D.P. Reilly, 29 November 1956, ibid.
159. UK–New Delhi to CRO, tel. 1556, 17 November 1956, FO371/123589.

Notes to Conclusion

1. G. Crowther, 'Reconstruction of an Alliance', *Foreign Affairs*, vol. 35, 1957, p. 177.
2. Minute from Noel-Baker to Attlee, 20 April 1949, CAB21/1824.
3. Brief for Carrington on Soviet Policy in Europe, Asia and Africa, draft seen by W.D. Allen and sent in Allen to H. Godfrey (Defence), 30 November 1955, as 'Communist Policy Following the Geneva Conference', FO371/116914.
4. Oral History interview with A.J. Goodpaster on 8 September 1967, EL, p. 106; Eisenhower to Edgar Eisenhower, 27 February 1956, AWF, DDE Diary, DDE papers, cited in Gaddis, *Strategies of Containment*, p. 154; diary entry by Eisenhower's press secretary, 24 February 1955, *FR, 1955–1957*, vol. 2, pp. 306–7.
5. DS paper on Nehru's visit to US, 12 December 1956, White House Central File, Subject series, box 72, file: State Department 1956, Nehru material (1), EL.
6. Mohammad Ayub Khan, *Friends Not Masters*, (New York 1967), p. 130.
7. Steel, *Walter Lippmann and the American Century*, p. 504.

Select Bibliography

(I have included in this bibliography only those works which I have found especially useful or stimulating.)

UNPUBLISHED SOURCES

Bodleian Library, Oxford
Attlee papers
Churchill College, Cambridge
Attlee papers
Bevin papers
Gordon Walker papers
Noel-Baker papers
India Office Library and Records, London
L/P&J/10 Papers on the transfer of power
L/WS/1 War Staff files
R/3/1 Government of India records transferred to London
Middle East Centre, St Antony's College, Oxford
Grafftey-Smith papers
National Archives of India, New Delhi
Home Establishments Files, 1946–7
Reform Office Files, 1942.
Public Record Office, Kew, London
CAB128 Cabinet conclusions
CAB129 Cabinet memoranda
CAB131 Cabinet Defence Committee
CAB134 Far Eastern (Official) Committee; China and South-East Asia Committee.
DEFE4 Chiefs of Staff Committee minutes
DEFE5 Chiefs of Staff memoranda
DEFE6 Chiefs of Staff Committee, Joint Planning Staff
DO35 Dominions Office
FO371 Foreign Office
FO800 Bevin papers
PREM8–11 Prime Minister's Office
T225 Treasury

WO War Office
Dwight D. Eisenhower Library, Abilene, Kansas
John Foster Dulles papers
Dwight D. Eisenhower papers
Joseph Rand papers
US President's Committee to Study the Military Assistance Programme records
White House Office records
US Council on Foreign Economic Policy records
US Council on Foreign Economic Policy, Office of the Chairman records
US President's Citizen Advisers on the Mutual Security Programme records
National Archives, Washington
Records of the Department of State, RG 59
Harry S. Truman Library, Independence, Missouri
Dean Acheson papers
Henry Grady papers
George McGhee papers
Harry S. Truman papers
Korean War, records
National Security Committee, records
Naval Aide to the President, files
White House Office

Oral histories

Dwight D. Eisenhower Library, Abilene, Kansas
Winthrop Aldrich
George V. Allen
Eugene Black
Robert Bowie
William Draper
Dwight D. Eisenhower
Andrew J. Goodpaster
Raymond Hare
Loy Henderson
Robert Lovett
Livingston Merchant
Robert Murphy
Walter Robertson
Harry S. Truman Library, Independence, Missouri
Dean Acheson
J. Wesley Adams
John M. Cabot
John F. Cady
Henry L. Deimel
Lord Franks
Loy Henderson
Paul Hoffman
Robert Lovett

George McGhee
Roger Makins
Livingston Merchant
Joseph Satterthwaite
Nehru Memorial Museum and Library, New Delhi
Chester Bowles
C.D. Deshmukh
T.T.K. Krishnamachari
K.M. Munshi

PUBLISHED SOURCES

Great Britain
Documents on British Policy Overseas, series 1, vol. 3, (London 1985).
Korea: The Indian Proposal Cmd 8716, (London 1952).
Korea: A Summary of Further Developments in the Military Situation, Armistice Negotiations and Prisoner of War Camps up to January 1953, Cmd 8793, (London 1953).
Documents Relating to the Decision on Indochina at the Geneva Conference, Cmd 9239, (London 1954).
Documents Relating to the British Involvement in the Indochina Conflict 1945–1965 Cmd 2834 (London 1965).
Hansard
N. Mansergh *et al.*, *The Transfer of Power*, 1942–7, vols. 1 to 12, (London 1970–83).
India
Constituent Asembly Debates
Lok Sabha Debates
Ministry of Information and Broadcasting, *Jawarharlal Nehru's Speeches*, 4 vols. (New Delhi 1958–65).
S. Gopal (ed), *Selected Works of Jawaharlal Nehru*, vol. 15, (New Delhi 1982).
S. Gopal (ed), *Selected Works of Jawaharlal Nehru*, second series, vols. 1 to 8 (New Delhi, 1984 ff).
G. Parthasarthy (ed), Nehru's *Letters to Chief Ministers*, 1947–64, vols. 1 to 5, (New Delhi 1985–88).
United States
Congressional Record, 1951, 1954; (Washington DC).
Department of State Bulletin
US Congress. Senate. *Executive Sessions of the Senate Foreign Relations Committee*, vol. 3, part 1, 82nd Congress, first session, 1951, Historical series, (Washington DC, 1976).
——— , *Executive Sessions of the Senate Foreign Relations Committee*, vol. 4, part 1, 82nd Congress, second session, 1952, (Washington DC, 1976).
US Department of State, *Foreign Relations of the United States*,
1947, vol. 3, *The British Commonwealth and Europe*, (Washington DC, 1972).
1948, vol. 1, *General: The United Nations*, (Washington DC, 1976).
1948, vol. 5, *The Near East, South Asia and Africa*, (Washington DC, 1975).

1949, vol. 1, *National Security Affairs: Foreign Economic Policy*, (Washington DC, 1976).

1949, vol. 6, *The Near East, South Asia and Africa*, (Washington DC, 1977).

1949, vol. 7, *The Far East and Australasia*, (Washington DC, 1976).

1949, vol. 9, *The Far East: China*, (Washington DC, 1974).

1950, vol. 1, *National Security Affairs: Foreign Economic Policy*, (Washington DC, 1977).

1950, vol. 5, *The Near East, South Asia and Africa*, (Washington DC, 1978).

1950, vol. 6, *East Asia and the Pacific*, (Washington DC, 1976)

1950, vol. 7, *Korea*, (Washington DC, 1976).

1951, vol. 1, *National Security Affairs*, (Washington DC, 1979).

1951, vol. 4, *Europe: Political and Economic Developments* (Washington DC, 1985).

1951, vol. 5, *The Near East and Africa*, (Washington DC, 1982).

1951, vol. 6, *Asia and the Pacific*, (Washington DC, 1977).

1951, vol. 7, *Korea and China*, (Washington DC, 1983).

1952–4, vol. 1, *General: Economic and Political Matters*, (Washington DC, 1983).

1952–4, vol. 2, *National Security*, (Washington DC, 1983)

1952–4, vol. 5, *Western European Security*, (Washington DC, 1983).

1952–4, vol. 6, *Western Europe and Canada*, (Washington DC, 1986).

1952–4, vol. 9, *The Near and Middle East*, (Washington DC, 1986).

1952–4, vol. 11, *Africa and South Asia*, (Washington DC, 1982).

1952–4, vol. 12, *East Asia and the Pacific* (Washington DC, 1984).

1952–4, vol. 13, *Indochina*, (Washington DC, 1982).

1952–4, vol. 15, *Korea*, (Washington DC, 1984).

1952–4, vol. 16, *The Geneva Conference*, (Washington DC, 1981).

1955–7, vols 2 and 3, *China*, (Washington DC, 1986).

1955–7, vol. 8, *South Asia*, (Washington DC, 1987).

1955–7, vol. 16, *Suez Crisis*, (Washington DC, 1990).

Public Papers of the Presidents of the United States: Dwight D. Eisenhower (Washington DC, 1961–63)

Public Papers of the Presidents of the United States: Harry S. Truman (Washington DC, 1961–66)

Books

Acheson, D., *Present at the Creation: My Years in the State Department* (New York 1969).

Allen, H.C., *Great Britain and the United States 1783–1952* (London 1954).

Ambrose, S., *Rise to Globalism: American Foreign Policy Since 1938* (Penguin books, 3rd edition 1983).

—— , *Eisenhower the President* (London 1984).

Amery, L.S. and others, *Six Oxford Lectures* (Conservative Political Centre 1952).

Anderson, T.H., *The United States, Britain and the Cold War, 1944–1947* (New York 1981).

Attlee, Earl, *Empire into Commonwealth* (London 1961).

Avon, Lord, *Towards Peace in Indochina* (London 1966).

Barker, E., *The British Between the Superpowers* (London 1983).

Barnds, W.J., *India, Pakistan and the Great Powers* (New York 1972).

Barnett, C., *Britain and Her Army* (London 1970).

Baylis, J., *Anglo–American Defence Relations 1939–1980: The Special Relationship* (London 1981).

Bell, C., *The Debatable Alliance: An Essay in Anglo–American Relations* (London 1964).

Best, Jr, R.A., *'Cooperation With Like-Minded Peoples'. British Influences on American Security Policy 1945–1949* (New York/Westport 1986).

Blum. R., *Drawing the Line: The Origin of American Containment Policy in East Asia* (New York 1982).

Bond, B., *British Military Policy Between the Two World Wars* (Oxford 1980).

Bowie, R., *Suez 1956* (paperback, Oxford 1974).

Brecher, M., *India and World Politics* (London 1968).

Bullock, A., *Ernest Bevin: Foreign Secretary 1945–1951* (paperback, Oxford 1985).

Burke, S.M., *Pakistan's Foreign Policy: An Historical Analysis* (Oxford 1973).

Cable, J., *The Geneva Conference of 1954 on Indochina* (London 1986).

Carlton, D., *Anthony Eden: A Biography* (London 1981).

—— , *Britain and the Suez Crisis* (Oxford 1988).

Chandra, B. (ed.), *India's Struggle for Independence* (New Delhi 1987).

Chang, G., *Friends and Enemies* (Ithaca 1986).

Choudhury, G.W., *Pakistan's Relations With India 1947–1966* (London 1968).

Colbert, E., *South East Asia in International Politics, 1941–1956* (Ithaca and London 1977)

Connell, J., *Auchinleck* (London 1959).

Craig, F.W.S., *British General Election Manifestos 1918–1966* (Chichester 1970).

Dalton, H., *High Tide and After* (London 1962).

Darby, P., *British Defence Policy East of Suez 1947–68* (Oxford 1973).

—— , *Three Faces of Imperialism: British and American Approaches to Asia and Africa 1870–1970* (New Haven and London 1987).

Darwin, J., *Britain and Decolonisation: The Retreat from Empire in the Post-War World* (London 1988).

Dayal, S., *India's Role in the Korean Question* (Delhi 1959).

Deighton, A. (ed.), *Britain and the First Cold War* (London 1990).

Dimbleby, D. and Reynolds, D., *An Ocean Apart* (London 1988).

Dockrill, M., and Young, J. (eds), *British Foreign Policy 1945–56* (London 1989).

Dutt, S., *With Nehru in the Foreign Office* (Calcutta 1977).

Eden, A., *Full Circle* (London 1960).

Edmonds, R., *Setting the Mould: The United States and Britain 1945–50* (Oxford 1986).

Eisenhower, D.D., *The White House Years: Mandate for Change 1953–56* (Garden City 1963).

Eldrige, P.J., *The Politics of Foreign Aid in India* (London 1969).

Farrar-Hockley, A., *The British Part in the Korean War*, vol.1, (London 1990).

Ferrell, R.H., (ed.) *The Eisenhower Diaries* (New York 1981).

Fifield, R.H., *The Diplomacy of Southeast Asia 1945–1958* (Archon Books 1968).

Foot, R., *The Wrong War* (Ithaca 1985).

—— , *A Substitute for Victory: The Politics of Peacemaking at the Korean Armistice Talks* (Ithaca 1990).

Frankel, J., *British Foreign Policy 1945–1973* (London 1975).

Gaddis, J.L., *Strategies of Containment: A Critical Appraisal of Postwar American National Security Policy* (paperback, New York 1982).
— , *The Long Peace: Inquiries into the History of the Cold War* (New York 1987).
Gallichio, M., *The Cold War Begins in Asia* (New York 1988).
Gardner, L.C., *Approaching Vietnam* (New York 1988).
Gdo Agung, I.A.G., *Twenty Years of Indonesian Foreign Policy 1945–1965* (The Hague 1973).
Gilbert, M., *Winston S. Churchill, 1945–1965*, (London 1988).
Gopal, S., *Jawaharlal Nehru: A Biography vol. 2, 1947–1956* (London 1979).
Gordon Walker, P., *The Commonwealth* (London 1962).
Gupta, P.S., *Imperialism and the British Labour Movement 1914–1964* (London 1975).
Gupta, S., *Kashmir: A Study in India–Pakistan Relations* (New Delhi 1966).
Hall, D., *Commonwealth: A History of the British Commonwealth of Nations* (London 1971).
Harbutt, F.J., *The Iron Curtain: Churchill, America and the Cold War* (New York 1986).
Harding, H. and Ming, Y. (eds), *Sino–American Relations 1945–1955: A Joint Reassessment of a Critical Decade* (Wilmington 1989).
Harris, K., *Attlee* (London 1982).
Hathaway, R.M., *Ambiguous Partnership: Britain and America, 1944–1947* (New York 1981).
Heikal, M.H., *Cutting the Lion's Tail: Suez Through Egyptian Eyes* (London 1986).
Heimsath, C.H., and Mansingh, S., *A Diplomatic History of Modern India* (New Delhi 1971).
Herring, G.C. *America's Longest War: The United States and Vietnam, 1950–1975* (New York 1979).
Hess, G. *The United States' Emergence as a Southeast Asian Power 1940–1950* (New York 1987).
Home, Earl of, and others, *World Perspectives* (London 1955).
Hoopes, T., *The Devil and John Foster Dulles* (Boston 1973).
Howard, M., *The Continental Commitment* (London 1972).
Hunt, M., *Ideology and US Foreign Policy* (New Haven 1987).
Immerman, R.H., (ed.) *John Foster Dulles and the Diplomacy of the Cold War* (Princeton 1990).
Inder Singh, A., *The Origins of the Partition of India 1936–1947* (New Delhi 1987, 1989, paperback 1990, 1992).
Isaacs, H., *Scratches on Our Minds: American Images of China and India* (New York 1958).
Jain, R.K. (ed.), *Soviet–South Asian Relations 1947–1978*, 2 vols, (New Delhi 1978).
James, R.R., *Anthony Eden* (London 1986).
Kahin, G.M. *The Asian–African Conference: Bandung, Indonesia, April 1955* (Ithaca 1956).
Kaufman, B., *The Korean War: Challenges in Crisis, Credibility and Command* (Philadelphia 1986).
— , *Trade and Aid: Eisenhower's Foreign Economic Policy, 1953–1961* (Baltimore 1982).
Kaul, T.N., *Diplomacy in Peace and War* (New Delhi 1979).

Kennan, G., *Memoirs, 1950–1963* (paperback, New York 1972).

Kidron, M., *Private Investment in India* (London 1968).

Kolko, J. and Kolko, G., *The Limits of Power: The World and the United States Foreign Policy 1945–1954* (London 1972).

Kotelwala, J., *An Asian Prime Minister's Story* (London 1956).

Kyle, K., *Suez* (London 1991).

La Feber, W., *America, Russia and the Cold War 1945–1980* (New York 1980).

Leifer, M., *Cambodia: The Search for Security* (London 1967).

—— , *Foreign Relations of the New States* (Melbourne 1974).

Lewis, J., *Changing Direction: British Military Planning for Post-War Strategic Defence 1942–47* (London 1988).

Lipton, M., and Firn, J., *The Erosion of a Relationship: India and Britain since 1960* (London 1975).

Lloyd, S., *Suez 1956: A Personal Account* (London 1978).

Louis, W.R., *The British Empire in the Middle East, 1945–1951: Arab Nationalism, the United States, and Postwar Imperialism* (Oxford 1984).

—— , and Bull, H. (eds), *The Special Relationship: Anglo–American Relations since 1945* (Oxford 1986).

—— , and Owen, R. (eds), *Suez 1956: The Crisis and its Consequences* (Oxford 1989).

Low, D.A., *The Contraction of England* (Cambridge 1985).

Lowe, P., *The Origins of the Korean War* (London 1986).

Lucas, W.S., *Divided We Stand: Britain, the US and the Suez Crisis* (London 1991).

Lundestad, G., *The American Empire* (Oslo and Oxford 1990).

Lyon, P., *Neutralism* (Leicester 1963).

Macdonald, C.A., *Korea: The War Before Vietnam* (New York 1986).

Macmillan, H., *Tides of Fortune: 1945–1955* (London 1969).

—— , *Riding the Storm: 1956–1959* (London 1971).

Mansergh, N., *The Name and Nature of the British Commonwealth* (Cambridge 1954, reprinted 1955).

—— , *Commonwealth Perspectives* (Durham 1958).

—— , *The Commonwealth Experience* (London 1969).

Martin, E.M., *Divided Counsel: The Anglo–American Response to the Communist Victory in China* (Lexington 1986).

Mayers, D.A., *Cracking the Monolith: US Policy Against the Sino–Soviet Alliance, 1949–1955* (Baton Rouge 1986).

McGhee, G., *Envoy to the Middle World* (New York 1983).

McIntyre, W.D., *Colonies into Commonwealth* (London 1966).

McMahon, R.J., *Colonialism and the Cold War: The United States and the Struggle for Indonesian Independence, 1945–49* (Ithaca 1981).

Menon, K.P.S., *The Flying Troika* (London 1963).

Merrill, D., *Bread and the Ballot: The United States and India's Economic Development 1947–1963* (Chapel Hill and London 1990).

Millar, T.B. (ed.), *Australian Foreign Minister, the Diaries of R.G. Casey 1951–60* (London 1972).

Moore, R.J., *Escape from Empire* (Oxford 1983).

—— , *Making the New Commonwealth* (Oxford 1987).

Nagai, Y., and Iriye, A. (eds), *The Origins of the Cold War in Asia* (New York and Tokyo 1977).

Nutting, A., *No End of a Lesson* (London 1967).

O'Neill, R., *Australia in the Korean War 1950–53, vol. 1: Strategy and Diplomacy* (Canberra 1981).

Osgood, R.E. *Alliances and American Foreign Policy* (Baltimore 1968).

Ovendale, R., *The Foreign Policy of the British Labour Governments 1945–1951* (Leicester 1984).

—— , *The English-Speaking Alliance: Britain, the United States, the Dominions and the Cold War 1945–51* (London 1985).

Pandit, V. *The Scope of Happiness* (London 1979).

Panikkar, K.M., *In Two Chinas: Memoirs of a Diplomat* (London 1955).

Pearson, L., *Memoirs: 1948–1957, vol. 2* (London 1974).

Porter, B., *Britain and the Rise of Communist China: A Study of British Attitudes, 1945–1954* (London 1967).

Ram, R., *Soviet Policy Towards Pakistan* (New Delhi 1983).

Randle, R., *Geneva 1954: The Settlement of the Indochinese War* (Princeton 1969).

Reid, E. *Envoy to Nehru* (Oxford 1987).

—— , *Hungary and Suez* (Indian edition, New Delhi 1987).

Reynolds, D., *Britannia Overruled: British Policy and World Power in the Twentieth Century* (London 1991).

Rothwell, V., *Britain and the Cold War 1941–1947* (London 1982).

Rotter, A., *The Path to Vietnam: Origins of the American Commitment to Southeast Asia* (Ithaca 1987).

Sardesai, G., *Indian Foreign Policy in Cambodia, Laos and Vietnam 1947–64* (Berkeley 1968).

Schaller, M., *The American Occupation of Japan: The Origins of the Cold War in Asia* (New York 1985).

Scott, R., *Major Theatre of Conflict: British Policy in East Asia* (London 1968).

Short, A., *The Origins of the Vietnam War* (London 1989).

Shuckburgh, E., *Descent to Suez: Diaries, 1951–56* (London 1986).

Sked, A., and Cook, C., *Post-War Britain* (Penguin books 1979).

Sked, A., *Britain's Decline: Problems and Perspectives* (Oxford 1987).

Smith, R.B., *An International History of the Vietnam War, vol. 1: Revolution vs Containment 1955–61* (London 1983).

Steel, R., *Walter Lippmann and the American Century* (London 1981).

Stein, A., *India and the Soviet Union: The Nehru Era* (Chicago 1969).

Stueck, Jr, W.W., *The Road to Confrontation: American Policy toward China and Korea* (Chapel Hill 1981).

Thorne, C., *Allies of a Kind* (London 1978).

—— , *American Political Culture and the Asian Frontier 1943–1973* (London 1988).

Tien, T.T., *India and South East Asia 1947–1960* (Geneva 1963).

Tucker, N., *Patterns in the Dust: Chinese–American Relations and the Recognition Controversy, 1949–50* (New York 1983).

Venkataramani, M.S., Shrivastava, B.K., *Quit India: The American Response to the 1942 Struggle* (New Delhi 1979).

—— , *Roosevelt, Gandhi, Churchill: America and the Last Phase of India's Freedom Struggle* (New Delhi 1983).

—— , *The American Role in Pakistan* (New Delhi 1984).

Watt, D.C., *Succeeding John Bull: America in Britain's Place* (Cambridge 1984).

Wolfers, A., *Alliance Policy and the Cold War* (Baltimore 1959).

Young, J. (ed.), *The Foreign Policy of Churchill's Peacetime Administration, 1951–1955* (Leicester 1988).
Ziegler, P., *Mountbatten* (Fontana paperback 1986).

ARTICLES

Adamthwaite, A., 'Britain and the World, 1945–9: the View from the Foreign Office', *International Affairs*, vol. 61, 1985, pp. 223–36.
—— , 'Overstretched and Overstrung: Eden, the Foreign Office and the Making of Policy, 1951–5', *International Affairs*, vol. 64, 1988, pp. 241–59.
Altrincham, Lord, 'The British Commonwealth and the Western Union', *Foreign Affairs*, vol. 27, 1949, pp. 601–17.
Appadorai, A., 'The Bandung Conference', *India Quarterly*, vol. 11, 1955, pp. 207–35.
Arya, H.C., 'The Korean War and US-Pakistani Relations, *International Studies* (New Delhi), vol. 9, 1968, pp. 332–9.
Attlee, C.R., 'Britain and America: Common Aims, Different Opinions', *Foreign Affairs*, vol. 32, 1954, pp. 190–202.
Beloff, M., 'The Special Relationship: An Anglo–American Myth', in Gilbert, M., (ed.), *A Century of Conflict, 1850–1950: Essays for A.J.P. Taylor* (London 1966), pp. 151–71.
Bernstein, B.J., 'New Light on the Korean War', *International History Review*, vol. 3, 1981, pp. 256–77.
—— , 'The Struggle over the Korean Armistice: Prisoners of Repatriation?', in Cumings, B. (ed.), *Child of Conflict: The Korean–American Relationship, 1943–1953* (Seattle 1983), pp. 261–307.
Brands, H.W., 'India and Pakistan in American Strategic Planning 1947–54: the Commonwealth as Collaborator', *Journal of Imperial and Commonwealth History*, vol. 25, 1986, pp. 41–55.
—— , 'The Cairo Connection in Anglo–American History in the Middle East 1951–1953', *International History Review*, vol. 11, no. 3, 1989, pp.434–56.
Brecher, M., 'India's Decision to Remain in the Commonwealth' *Journal of Commonwealth and Comparative Politics*, vol. 12, 1974, pp. 62–90.
Bull, H., 'What is the Commonwealth', *World Politics*, vol. 11, 1959, pp. 577–87.
Bullen, R., 'Great Britain, the United States and the Indian Armistice Resolution on the Korean War: November 1952', *International Studies*, 1984/1, pp. 27–44.
Clymer, K.J., 'Franklin D. Roosevelt, Louis Johnson, India and Anticolonialism: Another Look', *Pacific Historical Review*, vol. 57, 1988, pp. 261–84.
—— , 'Jawaharlal Nehru and the United States', *Diplomatic History*, vol. 14, 1990, pp. 143–62.
Cohen, W., 'Acheson, His Advisers and China 1949–50', in Borg, D., and Heinrichs, W., (eds), *Uncertain Years: Chinese-American Relations, 1947–1950*, (New York 1980), pp. 15–52.
Crowther, G., 'Reconstruction of an Alliance', *Foreign Affairs*, vol. 35, 1957, pp. 173–83.
Cutler, R., 'The Development of the National Security Council', *Foreign Affairs*, vol. 34, 1956, pp. 441–58.

Darwin, J., 'The Fear of Falling: British Politics and Imperial Decline since 1990,' *Transactions of the Royal Historical Society*, (London 1986), pp. 27–43.

Devereux, D., 'Britain, the Commonwealth and the Defence of the Middle East, 1948–1956', *Journal of Contemporary History*, vol. 24, 1989, pp. 327–45.

Dingman, R., 'Truman, Attlee, and the Korean War Crisis', *International Studies*, 1982/1, pp. 1–42.

——, 'Atomic Diplomacy During the Korean War', *International Security*, vol. 13, 1988/9, pp. 50–91.

——, 'John Foster Dulles and the Creation of SEATO in 1954', *International History Review*, vol. 11, 1989, pp. 457–77.

Dockrill, M.L., 'The Foreign Office, Anglo–American Relations and the Korean War, June 1950–June 1951', *International Affairs*, vol. 62, 1986, pp. 459–76.

Dooley, H.J., 'Great Britain's "Last Battle" in the Middle East: Notes on Cabinet Planning during the Suez Crisis of 1956', *International History Review*, vol. 11, 1990, pp. 486–517.

Dulles, J.F., 'Policy for Security and Peace', *Foreign Affairs*, vol. 32, 1954, pp. 353–64.

Eden, A., 'Britain in World Strategy', *Foreign Affairs*, vol. 29, 1951, pp. 341–50.

Emmerson, D.K., ' "Southeast Asia": What's in a Name?', *Journal of Southeast Asian Studies*, vol. 15, 1984, pp. 1–21.

Farrar, P.N., 'Britain's Proposal for a Buffer Zone South of the Yalu in November 1950', *Journal of Contemporary History*, vol. 18, 1983, pp. 327–51.

Foot, 'Anglo–American Relations in the Korean Crisis: the British Effort to Avert an Expanded War, December 1950–January 1951', *Diplomatic History*, vol. 10, 1986, pp. 43–57.

——, 'Nuclear Coercion and the Ending of the Korean Conflict', *International Security*, vol. 13, 1988/9, pp. 92–112.

——, 'Making known the Unknown War: Policy Analysis of the Korean Conflict in the Last Decade', *Diplomatic History*, vol. 15, 1991, pp. 411–31.

Ganguli, B.N., 'Indo–American Trade', *India Quarterly*, vol. 6, 1950, pp. 234–47.

——, 'India and the Commonwealth: Economic Relations', *India Quarterly*, vol. 10, 1954, pp. 125–43.

Goldstein, S.M., 'Sino–American Relations, 1948–50: Lost Chance or No Chance', Harding, H. and Ming, Y. (eds), *Sino–American Relations, 1945–1955: A Joint Reassessment of a Critical Decade* (Wilmington 1989), pp. 119–42.

Goldsworthy, D., 'Britain and the International Critics of British Colonialism, 1951–56' *Journal of Commonwealth and Comparative Politics*, vol. 29, 1991, pp. 1–24.

Good, R.C., 'The United States and the Colonial Debate', in Wolfers, A.C., (ed.), *Alliance Policy in the Cold War*, (Baltimore 1959), pp. 224–70.

Gowing, M.M., 'Britain, America and the Bomb', in Dilks, D., (ed.), *Retreat from Power*, vol. 2, (London 1981), pp. 120–37.

Gupta, S.K., 'Stalin and India, 1946–47: From Cooperation to Hostility', *Australian Journal of Politics and History*, vol. 33, 1987, pp. 78–92.

Hahn, P.L., 'Containment and Egyptian Nationalism: the Unsuccessful Effort to Establish the Middle East Command, 1950–53', *Diplomatic History*, vol. 11, 1987, pp. 23–40.

Hall, D.G.E., 'The Integrity of Southeast Asian History', *Journal of Southeast Asian Studies*, vol. 4, 1973, pp. 159–68.

Harrison, S., 'India, Pakistan and the US – I', *New Republic*, 10 August 1959, pp. 10–17.

Herring, G., 'Eisenhower, Dulles and Dienbienphu: "The Day We Didn't Go to War" ', *Journal of American History*, vol. 71, 1984, pp. 343–63.

Hess, G., 'Global Expansion and Regional Balances: The Emerging Scholarship on United States Relations with India and Pakistan', *Pacific Historical Review*. vol. 56, 1987, pp. 259–95.

Hudson, G.F., 'Will Britain and America Split in Asia', *Foreign Affairs*, vol. 31, 1953 pp. 536–47.

—— , 'How Unified is the Commonwealth?', *Foreign Affairs*, vol. 33, 1955, pp. 679–88.

Immerman, R.H., 'In Search of History – and Relevancy: Breaking Through the "Encrustations of Interpretation" ', *Diplomatic History*, vol. 12, 1988, pp. 341–56.

—— , 'The United States and the Geneva Conference', *Diplomatic History*, vol. 14, 1990, pp. 43–66.

Inder Singh, A., 'Imperial Defence and the Transfer of Power in India, 1946–7', *International History Review*, vol. 4, 1982, pp. 568–88.

—— , 'Decolonization in India: the Statement of 20 February 1947', *International History Review*, vol. 6, 1984, pp. 191–209.

—— , 'Keeping India in the Commonwealth: British Political and Military Aims, 1947–49', *Journal of Contemporary History*, vol. 20, pp. 469–81.

—— , 'Post-Imperial British Attitudes to India: The Military Aspect, 1947–51', *The Round Table*, no. 296, October 1985, pp. 360–75.

—— , 'Containment Through Diplomacy: Britain, India and the Cold War in Indochina, 1954–56', *International Studies*, 1987/III, pp. 1–17.

—— , 'Britain, India and the Asian Cold War, 1949–54', in Deighton, A. (ed.), *Britain and the First Cold War* (Macmillan 1990), pp. 220–36.

—— , 'The Limits of "Superpower": The United States and South Asia', *International History Review*, vol. 14, 1992, pp. 98–108.

—— , 'Divergent World Views, Divergent Strategies: How America Took Britain's Place in Pakistan, 1947–54', *Contemporary Record*, vol. 6, 1992, pp. 474–96.

Jacob, Maj. Gen. Sir Ian, 'Principles of British Military Thought', *Foreign Affairs*, vol. 29, 1951, pp. 219–28.

Jisi, W., 'The Origins of America's "Two China" Policy', in Harding, H. and Ming, Y. (eds), *Sino–American Relations 1945–1955: A Joint Reassessment of a Critical Decade* (Wilmington 1989), pp. 198–212.

Kahler, M., 'The United States and the Third World: Decolonization and After', in Brown, L.C. (ed.), *Centerstage* (New York 1990), pp. 104–20.

Keefer, E.C., 'President Dwight D. Eisenhower and the End of the Korean War', *Diplomatic History*, vol. 10, 1986, pp. 267–89.

Kennan, G. "(X)" 'The Sources of Soviet Conduct', *Foreign Affairs*, vol. 25, 1947, pp. 566–82.

Kent, J., 'Bevin's Imperialism and the Idea of Euro-Africa, 1945–9', in Dockrill, M., and Young, J. (eds), *British Foreign Policy 1945–56* (London 1989), pp. 47–76.

—— , 'The British Empire and the Origins of the Cold War, 1944–49', in Deighton, A. (ed.), *Britain and the First Cold War* (London 1990), pp. 165–83.

Leffler, M., 'The American Conception of National Security and the Beginnings of the Cold War, 1945–1948', *American Historical Review*, vol. 89, 1984, pp. 346–81.

Lowe, P., 'Great Britain, the United Nations and the Korean War, 1950–3', *International Studies*, 1987/1, pp. 1–22.

Lundestad, G., 'Empire by Invitation? the United States and Western Europe 1945–1952', *Journal of Peace Research*, vol. 23, 1986, pp. 263–77.

—— , 'Moralism, Presentism, Exceptionalism, Provincialism, and Other Extravagances in American Writings on the Early Cold War Years', *Diplomatic History*, vol. 13, 1989, pp. 527–46, and in his *The American "Empire"*, (Oslo and Oxford 1990), pp. 11–29.

Mabbett, I.W., 'The Indianization of Southeast Asia: Reflections on the Historical Sources', *Journal of Southeast Asian Studies*, vol. 8, 1977, pp. 143–61.

Mabon, D.W., 'Elusive Agreements: The Pacific Pact Proposals of 1949–1951', *Pacific Historical Review*, vol. 57, 1988, pp. 147–77.

Makins, R., 'The World Since the War: the Third Phase', *Foreign Affairs*, vol. 33, pp. 1–16.

Mansergh, N., 'Postwar Strains on the British Commonwealth', *Foreign Affairs*, vol. 27, 1948, pp. 129–42.

McLean, D., 'American Nationalism, the China Myth, and the Truman Doctrine: the Question of Accommodation with Peking, 1949–50', *Diplomatic History*, vol. 10, 1986, pp. 25–42.

McMahon, R.J., 'Eisenhower and Third World Nationalism: A Critique of the Revisionists', *Political Science Quarterly*, vol. 101, 1986, pp. 453–73.

—— , 'Food as a Diplomatic Weapon: the India Wheat Loan of 1951', *Pacific Historical Review*, vol. 56, 1987, pp. 349–77.

—— , 'The Cold War in Asia: Towards a New Synthesis?', *Diplomatic History*, vol. 12, 1988, pp. 307–28.

—— , 'US Cold War Strategy in South Asia: Making a Military Commitment to Pakistan 1947–54', *Journal of American History*, vol. 75, 1988, pp. 812–40.

Merrill, D., 'Indo–American Relations, 1947–50: A Missed Opportunity in Asia', *Diplomatic History*, vol. 11, 1987, pp. 203–26.

Mookerjee, G., 'Peace Settlements in the Far East Since 1945', *India Quarterly*, vol. 6, 1950, pp. 262–76.

Morgenthau, H., 'Another "Great Debate": The National Interest of the United States', *American Political Science Review*, vol. 46, 1952, pp. 961–88.

Nachmani, A., ' "It is a Matter of Getting the Mixture Right": Britain's Post-War Relations with America in the Middle East', *Journal of Contemporary History*, vol. 18, 1983, pp. 117–40.

P. (Pillai, N.R.), 'Middle Ground Between American and Russia: An Indian View', *Foreign Affairs*, vol. 32, 1954, pp. 259–69.

Pandit, V.L., 'India's Foreign Policy', *Foreign Affairs*, vol. 34, 1956, pp. 432–40.

Panikkar, K.M., 'The Twentieth Century in Asian and World History', *India Quarterly*, vol. 12, 1956, pp. 217–49.

Pemberton, G.J., 'Australia, the United States and the Indochina Crisis of 1954', *Diplomatic History*, vol. 13, 1989, pp. 45–66.

Pollack, J.D., 'The Korean War and Sino–American Relations', in Harding, H. and Ming, Y. (eds), *Sino–American Relations, 1945–1955: A Joint Reassessment of a Critical Decade*, (Wilmington 1989), pp. 213–37.

Potter, D., 'Manpower Shortage and the End of Colonialism', *Modern Asian*

Studies, vol. 7, 1973, pp. 47–53.

Rajan, M.S., 'India and the Commonwealth, 1954–56', *India Quarterly*, vol. 16, 1960, pp. 31–50.

—— , 'Indian Foreign Policy in Action, 1954–56', *India Quarterly*, vol. 16, 1960, pp. 203–36.

Ramasubbu, C.G., 'India and the Sterling Area', *India Quarterly*, vol. 5, 1949, pp. 244–53.

Rao, B.S., and Kondapi, C., 'India and the Korean Crisis', *India Quarterly*, vol. 7, 1951, pp. 295–315.

Rao, V.K.R.V., 'The New Commonwealth – Will It Endure', *India Quarterly*, vol. 6, 1950, pp. 3–17.

Reid., B.H., 'The Northern Tier and the Baghdad Pact', in Young, J.W. (ed.), *The Foreign Policy of Churchill's Peacetime Administration 1951–55*, (Leicester 1988), pp. 159–80.

Reynolds, D., 'The Origins of the Cold War: the European Dimension', *Historical Journal*, vol. 28, 1985, pp. 497–515.

—— , 'A "special relationship"? America, Britain and the International Order since the Second World War', *International Affairs*, vol. 62, 1985/86, pp. 1–20.

—— , 'Rethinking Anglo–American Relations', *International Affairs*, vol. 65, 1988/89, pp. 89–111.

—— , 'Eden the Diplomatist, 1931–56: Suezide of a Statesman?', *History*, vol. 74, 1989, pp. 64–84.

Rothwell, V., 'Britain and the First Cold War, in Crockatt, R., and Smith, S., (eds), *The Cold War Past and Present*, (London 1987), pp. 58–76.

Salmon, J., 'Dean Acheson, the Cold War, and the Limits of Politics', *Comparative Strategy*, vol. 7, 1988, pp. 51–74.

Sbrega, J., 'The Anticolonial Policies of Franklin D. Roosevelt: a Reappraisal', *Political Science Quarterly*, vol. 101, 1986, pp. 65–84.

Stargardt, A.W., 'The Emergence of the Asian System of Powers', *Modern Asian Studies*, vol. 23, 1989, pp. 561–95.

Steel, R., 'Birth of an Empire', *Reviews in American History*, vol. 16, 1988, pp. 151–7.

Stockwell, A.J., 'Insurgency and Decolonisation during the Malayan Emergency', *Journal of Commonwealth and Comparative Politics*, vol. 25, 1987, pp. 71–81.

Stueck, Jr., W.W., 'The Korean War as International History', *Diplomatic History*, vol. 10, 1986, pp. 291–309.

—— , 'The Marshall and Wedemeyer Missions: A Quadrilateral Perspective', in Harding, H. and Ming, Y. (eds), *Sino–American Relations 1945–1955: A Joint Reassessment of a Critical Decade* (Wilmington 1989), pp. 96–118.

Tarling, N., 'The United Kingdom and the Origins of the Colombo Plan', *Journal of Commonwealth and Comparative Politics*, vol. 24, 1986, pp. 3–34.

Thorne, C., 'Indo-China and Anglo–American Relations 1942–1945', in his *Border Crossings: Studies in International History*, (Oxford 1988), pp. 86–106.

—— , 'After the Europeans: American Designs for the Remaking of Southeast Asia', *Diplomatic History*, vol. 12, 1988, pp. 201–8.

Tomlinson, B.R., 'Indo–British Relations in the Post-Colonial Era: The Sterling Balances Negotiations, 1947–49', *Journal of Imperial and Commonwealth History*, vol. 13, 1985, pp. 142–62.

Trachtenberg, M., 'A "Wasting Asset": American Strategy and the Shifting

Nuclear Balance 1949–1954', *International Security*, vol. 13, 1988/89, pp. 5–49.

Venkataramani, M.S., and Arya, H.C., 'America's Military Alliance With Pakistan: The Evolution and Course of an Uneasy Partnership', *International Studies* (New Delhi), vol. 8, 1966, pp. 73–125.

Venkatasubbiah, H. 'Prospects for an Asian Union', *India Quarterly*, vol. 5, 1949, pp. 212–28.

—— , 'Political Alignments of Asian Countries', *India Quarterly* vol. 7, 1951, pp. 195–206.

Warner, G., 'The Anglo–American Special Relationship', *Diplomatic History*, vol. 13, 1989, pp. 479–500.

Watt, D.C., 'Perceptions of the United States in Europe, 1945–83', in Freedman, L. (ed.), *The Troubled Alliance: Atlantic Relations in the 1980s* (London 1983).

—— , 'Britain and the Historiography of the Yalta Conference and the Cold War', *Diplomatic History*, vol. 13, 1989, pp. 67–98.

White, D.H., 'History and American Internationalism: The Formulation from the Past After World War II', *Pacific Historical Review*, vol. 48, 1989, pp. 145–72.

Williams, J., 'ANZUS: A Blow to Britain's Self-Esteem', *Review of International Studies*, vol. 13, 1987, pp. 243–63.

Wolf, D.C., 'To Secure a Convenience: Britain Recognises China 1950', *Journal of Contemporary History*, vol. 18, 1983, pp. 299–326.

Wolfers, A.C., 'Collective Defense Versus Collective Security', in his *Alliance Policy and the Cold War*, (Baltimore 1959), pp. 49–74.

Yufan, H. and Zhizhai, Z., 'China's Decision to Enter the Korean War: History Revisited', *China Quarterly*, no. 121, 1990, pp. 94–115.

Index

Acheson, Dean, 60, 61, 64, 77, 83, 84, 86, 92, 101, 102–4, 105, 233
Administrative breakdown in India, 14–15
Ali, Muhammad, 138, 139
Allen, Denis, 139, 140
American Chiefs of Staff, 2, 56, 137, 188
Amery, Leo, 17–18
Anglo-American relationship, ix–xi
  nature of, 1 ff, 44, 108 ff, 127, 130, 226
  and Asian cold war, 7–8, 9, 10, 229 ff
  and Middle East, 8–9, 10, 111 ff, 128 ff, 130, 133, 151, 153 ff
  and recognition of China, 66 ff
  Korean war and, 90 ff, 94 ff, 98 ff, 106 ff
  Indochina and, 171 ff
  SEATO and 179
  Cambodia and 187 ff
  Suez crisis and, 209 ff
Asian cold war
  British conceive India's role in, 46 ff, 229, 301
Asian nationalisms
  British attitude to, 48, 159, 229–30
Attlee, Clement, 13, 31, 32, 43, 77, 78, 79, 80, 83, 88, 121, 233
Auchinleck, Field Marshal Sir Claude, 15
Austin, Warren, 104

Baghdad Pact, 113
Bajpai, Girija Shankar, 59, 62, 70
Bandung Conference, 1955
  Western attitudes to, 182 ff
  anti-Indian sentiment at, 183–5
  Western differences with India, 180 ff

Chou En-lai and 184–5
Afro-Asian consensus at, 185
Bao Dai, 158, 159, 160
Beeley, Harold, 129
Bevin, Ernest, 3, 12, 18, 26, 27, 29, 52, 61, 67, 69, 76, 77, 78, 79, 80, 83, 87, 88–9, 114
Bowker, R.J., 119
Bowles, Chester, 92
Britain
  and Asian cold war, x, 6, 47 ff, 74 ff, 157 ff, 229–30
  debate over her decline, xi–xii
  aims of post-1945 foreign policy, 1 ff
  possibility of leading a Third Force, 3
  decolonisation in South Asia, x, 4, 9 ff, 16 ff, 21, 25–7
  and India, 5–7, 35 ff, 46 ff, 96–7, 125 ff, 185–6, 195 ff, 202 ff, 224–5, 229 ff
  decides on withdrawal from India, 22–5
  and Indo-US friction, 64–5, 76, 79, 82, 97–8, 106 ff, 168–9, 186, 190, 191
  and recognition of China, 66 ff
  and Korean war, 74 ff
  controversy over POWs 97 ff
  against Western approaches to Pakistan, 122–3
  and Pakistan, 57 ff, 123 ff
  ignorance of US intentions, 133 ff, 137 ff, 142 ff, 237–8
  against US military aid to Pakistan, 133 ff, 151, 155
  and Turco-Pakistani pact, 143, 144 ff, 234–5
  and Indochina, 157 ff, 162 ff, 170 ff, 188 ff